D0099831

JOHN HAY

FROM POETRY TO POLITICS

Portrait of John Hay in 1903 by John Singer Sargent. Owned by
Clarence L. Hay.

JOHN HAY

From Poetry to Politics

By

TYLER DENNETT

PROFESSOR OF INTERNATIONAL RELATIONS, PRINCETON
UNIVERSITY; FORMERLY HISTORICAL ADVISER OF
THE DEPARTMENT OF STATE

KENNIKAT PRESS, INC./PORT WASHINGTON, N. Y.

8599

CONTENTS

CONTENTS

ILLUSTRATIONS

ACKNOWLEDGMENTS

For many manuscripts and most of the illustrations, to Mrs. Alice Hay Wadsworth, Mrs. Helen Hay Whitney, and to Mr. Clarence L. Hay; but most of all for their fine tolerance which left the author under no obligation except to discover and interpret as best he could. This is in no sense a "family biography," but it is a pleasure to know that the publication will not make unhappy those who best knew and most loved the subject.

To certain princes in the house of scholarship, for gifts of counsel, erudition, and criticism: J. Franklin Jameson, Charles A. Beard, M. A. DeWolfe Howe, and Allan Nevins.

To former colleagues in the Department of State whose pleasure it would have been to do as much for any other student, but whose assistance in this book is but one other of many happy memories: Hunter Miller, Edward Cyril Wynne, and Mrs. Natalia Summers.

To the blessed librarians: Miss L. A. Eastman, Miss Ruth Savord, H. L. Koopman, William A. Slade, Curtis W. Garrison, and Miss Martha L. Gericke; and especially to that great democratic institution of letters, the Library of Congress.

For permission to use other material, chiefly manuscripts, privately owned or controlled: to Harry A. and James R. Garfield, Mrs. Archibald Hopkins, Robert A. Taft, Elihu Root, Worthington C. Ford, Mrs. Theodore Roosevelt, Charles S. Hamlin, William E. Louttit, Jr., and to Miss Helen Nicolay who, in letters from John Hay to her distinguished father, first appeared as "the Blessed Babe" and then as "Miss Butterfly."

For help so varied as only biographers know: to Paul M. Angle, Poultney Bigelow, James P. Baxter, 3rd., Christopher B. Coleman, Dixon Ryan Fox, David Gray, Joseph C. Green, Frederick A. Gutheim, Logan Hay, Philip C. Jessup, John Bassett Moore, Henry F. Pringle, Roger L. Rice, Mrs. Jackson H. Ralston, Mrs. Ward Thoron, Charles Franklin Thwing, Alfred Vagts, A. T. Volwiler, James W. Wadsworth, Jr., and B. S. Warner.

To Raymond Dennett, who has thus been deprived of other interesting diversions to assist in proof-reading and checking.

The list of the published writings of John Hay, perhaps not definitive but sufficiently complete to exhibit the development of his literary genius, published as Appendix I, is the contribution of William E. Louttit, Jr.

It is due the reader to make one further acknowledgment. The following pages are not all biography; a little history crowded in. No one will be offended if the less historically minded reader skips the history. After all, man is more interesting, and instructive, than men.

TYLER DENNETT

June 13, 1933

JOHN HAY

FROM POETRY TO
POLITICS

NOTE

In the following pages there are frequent references to "Letters and Diaries." Although Mr. Hay destroyed a large mass of his letters, he preserved copies of many in letter press copy-books, and in rough drafts. He also kept journals or diaries, intermittently, between 1861 and 1869, and, again, from January 1, 1904 to the end of his life. In 1908, Mrs. Hay privately printed and distributed to friends a small edition of three volumes which carry the title-page: "Letters of John Hay and Extracts from Diary." While the compilation was in process, Mrs. Hay asked for the return of many letters of her husband's. In some instances the originals were returned and are still in the Hay Papers. Other correspondents supplied only copies of originals, and, in one notable instance, important letters were entirely withheld. "Letters and Diaries" comprises a selection drawn only from manuscripts now in the Hay Papers. The three volumes were prepared with an excess of caution; many letters were badly mutilated; and, as was reasonable so soon after the death of John Hay, many of the letters and diary entries most valuable as historical sources, were omitted entirely. The proof-reading was inadequate. The result is that these three privately printed volumes must be used with caution. In the following pages the writer has referred to "Letters and Diaries" only where he has been able to check back to original sources, or has reason to believe that the reference is trustworthy. He is now preparing for publication a new selection of the letters and diaries of John Hay, but the work has not yet progressed to the point where it is possible to make foot-note citations. However, references to "Letters and Diaries" are usually accompanied by names and dates, so that it will be possible, when the new edition appears, to locate in it all, or nearly all, of the references which now appear to "Letters and Diaries."

"I HAVE always wished to found a family," wrote John Hay's father, Dr. Charles Hay, on his seventy-fifth birthday. All his life he had been conscious, he stated, of only that one ambition, but he hastened to add: "I mean, of course, not in any aristocratic, still less in any plutocratic sense; but I have hoped to leave behind me children, and children's children—and the greater the number, the better I would be pleased—with whom intelligence, honor, and thrift would be matters of instinct and tradition." [1]

The conditions had been favorable for the establishment of just such a family, one which would display many of the characteristics of American life.

The term "Western expansion," as applied to the development of the United States, was only partially descriptive. A Western area was appropriated and settled, but it is by no means true that even the main current of the population movement in southern Indiana and southern Illinois was from east to west. From all points of the compass the settlers straggled in as though to fill a vacuum. This swirling migration was especially notable in the regions where the Hay family lived. A few moved west by way of Pittsburg and drifted down the Ohio, but the vast majority, on foot, in the saddle, or by cart, went almost directly north to occupy this land, creating peculiar economic, social, and political conditions not elsewhere uniformly characteristic of the frontier.

John Hay was born on the authentic frontier. His father came from near Lexington, Ky.; his mother was from the region east of Narragansett Bay; and the village of Salem, Ind., was described by his father, because of the origin of the largest portion of the inhabitants, as a "North Carolina town."

There was no old homestead in the Hay family. His father moved twice, each time to the edge of cultivation. His grandfather Hay also moved twice, once from the lower Shenandoah Valley over into Kentucky, and thence to Springfield, Illinois. The great-grandfather had

[1] *Biographical Review of Hancock County,* Illinois, p. 160.

moved to Virginia from Pennsylvania, and prior to that the Hay fore-
bears had come to the new world from Scotland by way of the Rhenish
Palatinate, where a Hay had served as a mercenary soldier, and had
married a daughter of the people. In John Hay, himself, the pioneer
spirit had been nearly bred out, but it left its marks. He was never
willingly a pioneer but he became the most migratory Hay in America.

John Hay, the grandfather, parted with his father, Adam Hay, in
Deikeley County, Virginia, about 1792, at the age of eighteen. It was
an escape from stern discipline, but the parting seems to have been
friendly, for in Kentucky the young man was supplied with at least
enough capital to take up land at Walnut Hill, just outside of Lexington, where he became a neighbor of Henry Clay. His grandson described him as a "man of Herculean build, and altogether quiet and
peaceable in disposition, of great strength of will and force of character." [1] He married Jemima Coulter, who is believed to have come from
Pennsylvania. With that prodigality of the race which was common
where land was cheap and progeny had the value of capital, they
had fourteen children, of whom Charles, born in 1801, was the oldest
to survive.

John Hay was never a farmer's boy. His traditions were not of the
wilderness and the prairie, but of the village. The Hays, grandfather
as well as father, had little desire for isolation and they lodged their
families always in communities. The economic traditions were of Hamilton rather than of Jefferson. The family bought and sold farms, but
they did not cultivate them. John Hay, as a man, had never been accustomed to work with his hands, a fact which was probably important in
determining his point of view. The grandfather, in a small way, was
even a manufacturer and a merchant. At Walnut Hill he operated a little
cotton-mill, not so large that he could not carry it with him to Illinois,
and at Springfield he started a brick-kiln, thus utilizing, as was the
custom of the country, the labor of his growing sons until they were
twenty-one, while the daughters, all unmarried, were employed within
the home.[2] It was a simple, almost primitive, economic unit, which in

---

[1] *Dr. Charles Hay.* [By John Hay. New York. 1885.] Privately printed at the DeVinne
Press. See also *Historical Encyclopedia of Illinois and History of Sangamon County,* II,
pt. 2, 1294–95.

[2] The brick-kiln appears to have been adopted after the failure of the cotton-mill.
The Sangamon *Journal* of Springfield, July 6, 1833, carried the following notice over
John Hay's signature:

"The subscriber has commenced the cotton spinning business in Springfield, south west

the grandson's mind was being contrasted with more modern forms of economic organization when he wrote *The Bread-Winners*.

In an affectionate memoir of his father, prepared in 1885 for private distribution, John Hay stated that the elder John Hay had been prompted by dislike of slavery to move in 1831 to the free soil of Illinois. From a package of old family letters, which may not have been accessible when the memoir was written, it would appear that this statement should be qualified. Central Kentucky did not prosper for several decades following the close of the War of 1812. Slavery was but one of several retarding factors. The Hays prospered only moderately, acquired a chattel mortgage, and removed to improve their economic condition. Their attitude toward the slavery question developed as Lincoln's, not Lovejoy's, did.

The important aspect of the life in Fayette County was that it was lived under the shadow of Transylvania University, a cultural center west of the Alleghenies which was unique and comparable with the best which the Atlantic seaboard could offer in the period 1810–1830. Supported by a popular conviction of the desirability of both general and higher education, the brilliant Dr. Horace Holley, president of Transylvania until he was driven out by sectarians, led a remarkable intellectual movement in the blue grass region. The elder John Hay was not a part of this awakening, but he allowed his children to share its benefits. Charles profited from life in Lexington. Of him his son wrote:

From a very early age he had been a devoted student, although in the West, at the beginning of this century, the opportunities for instruction and even for extensive reading were rare. The ease and rapidity with which he mastered his elementary text-books surprised his teachers, who could hardly be convinced that he was not playing a practical joke upon them, when they saw a child learning his alphabet one day and reading with facility a fortnight

of the court house; where he expects to keep a supply of yarn by wholesale or retail. He flatters himself, from his long experience in the business, together with the good quality of his machinery, that his yarn will be equal to any manufactured in the United States. He hopes a generous public will patronize him should he merit it.

"Spun cotton will be exchanged for raw cotton; picked or ginned cotton would be preferred, but will not be refused in the seed. Cash will be accepted.

"He wishes to employ a few hands. Boys 10 or 12 years of age would be preferred. He also wishes to purchase a few blind horses."

In the same issue of the paper the editor commented as follows: "We bespeak the favorable notice of our merchants and citizens for Mr. Hay's Cotton Manufactory in this town. It is now in successful operation, and if we may be permitted to judge, the Yarn manufactured is of the first quality. The money sent from Sangamon County every year for Cotton Yarn would support an extensive manufactory in this town. . . . The hands employed in this establishment, five in number, are his [Hay's] own sons."

later. He went rapidly through the classes of the common schools, and then
entered a classical school at Lexington, where he made the same easy progress
in Latin and Greek. His knowledge of these languages was remarkable for the
time and place, and he never lost it during his life. In later years it was one
of his greatest pleasures to teach his own children, in such a manner that their
reading of Homer and Virgil, which was a simple drudgery at school, became
an intellectual enjoyment at home.[1]

The graduation of Charles Hay from the Medical School of Tran
sylvania at the age of twenty-eight, after he had "served his time" with
his father at Walnut Hill, marked the turning-point in the Hay family.
Three other sons subsequently entered the professions, two becoming
physicians and one a lawyer. A professional tradition was thus established. It was strengthened when Dr. Charles Hay married the daughter
of a Baptist minister. John Hay, thirty years later, barely qualified for
a profession by passing the bar examinations at Springfield, but it is
understandable that his inclinations and associations through life were
professional.

One could hardly imagine in that Western country a family tradition
more in contrast with that of the Lincoln family, the shadow of which
was contemporaneously thrown across these same regions of Virginia,
Kentucky, Indiana, and Illinois.

Early in June, 1829, two years before his father migrated, the young
physician saddled his mare and rode north from Lexington. He carried
letters of introduction, and broke the journey to enjoy the rude hospitality of the Kentucky road. On the evening of the 5th he arrived
at Salem, Ind., thirty-three miles from Louisville, on the road to Vincennes. He put up at the tavern, pastured his mare on the edge of the
village, and rented a "shop." Salem was one of those numberless boom
towns of the pioneers which made little sound in the world. It had been
laid out as a land speculation by General John De Pauw, with a grape-
vine, so it is alleged, as a measuring-rod. Fifteen years had been required to gather the 800 inhabitants who were there when Dr. Hay
arrived; the village never prospered. Although it took more than ten
years to convince Dr. Hay of the fact, he had made a poor choice.
Unlike his son, he lacked the instinct to associate himself with greatness.

"There are several circumstances to prevent my getting into busi-

---

[1] *Dr. Charles Hay*, pp. 6–7.

David Augustus Leonard and Mary Peirce, John Hay's maternal grandparents, both were from the region east of Narragansett Bay. The grandfather was poet of his class at Brown in 1792 and then, successively, Baptist minister, teacher, editor, business man, and pioneer settler on the banks of the Ohio River.

Dr. Charles Hay and Mrs. Helen Leonard Hay in their later years. The portrait of John Hay's mother is owned by Mrs. Payne Whitney.

ness immediately," wrote Dr. Hay shortly after his arrival. "In the first place, it has been generally healthy owing to our dry and cool summer; in the next place I find it a pretty general custom in the town to engage the practice of families by the year. Of course they are generally engaged for the present year; in the third place the mania for steam doctors has not yet ceased and owing to their great numbers they have shared a good deal of the practice among them although there is as great a proportion of the community that treat them with merited contempt as there is in Kentucky. In the third place I am a stranger in the country and must wait till the people become acquainted with me."

The qualities of John Hay's father emerge so vividly from this old package of letters from which quotations have been made that one cannot do better than permit Dr. Hay himself to record the building of his career in Salem.

"There are two physicians here," he wrote to his brother Nathaniel in September, 1829, "Dr. Bradley from Connecticut and Doct Newland from North Carolina. They are both respectable in professional acquirements and character, but Doct Bradley gets not much more practice than I do although he has been here for ten years, and the only reason why he does not get more is because he is yankee and is stiff-necked, that is, does not bow often enough. Sectional prejudices I find run very high here and as the yankees and North Carolinians have their favorite I will have to be the favorite of the Kentuckians who are quite numerous although perhaps not so numerous as the North Carolinians. . . . There is to be a meeting of the citizens held here on the first Saturday in October to endeavor to bring about measures to cause the expulsion of the free negroes from the state." In the same letter he added that he had access to two or three good libraries while he was waiting for his practice to grow.

It was an uphill professional climb, but Dr. Hay's intelligence, general education, and lively interest in affairs, almost immediately gave him an important place in the community. That he was from south of the Ohio appears to have been a distinct advantage. The following year he was the Fourth of July orator at the courthouse before "a very crowded audience of gentlemen and ladies" and was happy to find his sentiments cordially cheered by the company. The only objection made known to him was that the oration contained nothing about "Washington, Jefferson and the 'hero of two wars' (alias Jackson)." These criticisms did not annoy the doctor, for he had expressly designed not to mention these men. Only a few "ultra Jacksonians" complained. He had been requested to furnish a corrected copy of the speech to the paper in Charleston but hesitated. "I am not in favor of too much puffing," he explained. John Hay, also, was like that.

"The tide of emigration has set in," Dr. Hay wrote his sister, Elizabeth, in September, 1830, in response to a letter which may have announced that the father and brothers were also thinking of emigrating, "and families are passing through Salem every day. There is as much talk of moving here as there is in your state. The people talk about moving out here as if they were not already out. I am sometimes afraid that the Western part of this state and Illinois is settled with a great deal of the sweepings of Indiana itself. But I presume that there will be some leven [sic] of a better character. The unsettled character of the emigrants to this country is injurious to its improvement in every respect. It is injurious to beginners in every kind of business as mechanic or merchant or a physician sets up in a town in any part of the state. He stays a few months and thinking he can do better somewhere else, he takes a notion to go and gives his accounts up to an officer for collection and there is nobody so much dreaded as the constables and the sheriffs. This makes people very cautious about encouraging a man until they see he has become 'settled' as they say." In the midst of a restless people Charles Hay, always the conservative, tried valiantly to remain fixed. He was not a wholly willing pioneer.

"The word 'moving' is almost as odious to me as the term revolution is said to be in France," he remarked in another letter. . . . "The census of Salem as just taken is 853, increase since last year 53. The census of the whole state is expected to be about 400,000; in ten years more it will exceed that of Kentucky in all probability. So much for slavery! I would pay some regard to the source of emigrants when I went to look for a home for, although Kentuckians are no better than other people, yet birds of a feather will flock together pretty much everywhere."

Dr. Hay prospered slowly and had ample time to exhibit a lively community interest which characterized him through life. In the meeting of the medical society representing three counties held at Salem in the autumn of 1830 he took an active part. He recognized many members of the society as men of ability, and was pleased to report that several measures were introduced with a view to raising the character of the profession in the state. He himself introduced a resolution proposing a law to prevent the transfer of patients from one state to another without the consent of at least two consulting physicians. The motive was not so much to spare the patient the discomforts of travel as to place an embargo on the export of patients to Cincinnati and Louisville for operations which, in the judgment of Dr. Hay, the physicians at home were quite competent to perform.

Early in 1835 Dr. Hay became part owner of the printing office from which the *Western Annotator* was issued. This did not mean, he hastened to inform his family, that he had turned from the profession for which he had been trained to the business of printer and editor. It happened that there had appeared in town a competent young printer who needed an editor to join in issuing a paper. Salem needed one and Dr. Hay thought he saw a way to supplement an inadequate income, finding also satisfaction in the new opportunity for literary self-expression. The name of the paper was changed to *Salem Monitor*. In another letter Dr. Hay mentioned farming cares, from which one infers that he was allowing business still further to trespass upon his attention.

Dr. Hay found a congenial friend in John Hay Farnham, a capable young lawyer of refinement and scholarly tastes. Farnham was well connected in the East. He was born in Newburyport, and was a distant cousin of Ralph Waldo Emerson. In 1821 he had married Evelyne Leonard. He was a Clay Whig, as was also Dr. Hay. The Farnham home offered just the kind of circle which this young bachelor, fresh from the intellectual society of Transylvania, would enjoy. Evelyne Leonard Farnham must have been to Dr. Hay a new type of woman, for Kentucky, with all its enthusiasm for education, still clung to the southern ideas about the education of women. Mrs. Farnham, like her husband, was a woman of cultivation. Since the Leonard family was soon to be joined to the Hay family, we now turn to a narrative of the other stream of influences which, combined with those from Kentucky, made up the immediate social as well as physical heredity of John Hay.

David Augustus Leonard, the other grandfather of John Hay, had to a marked degree the mercurial qualities of which we have observed traces in Dr. Hay. Although he died nineteen years before the grandson was born, it is evident that John Hay owed much both to him and to his wife, Polly Peirce Leonard. From his maternal grandfather John Hay received a strain of liberalism which was always at war with the sober conservatism of the Hay family.[1]

Grandfather Leonard was graduated from Brown University in 1792, the poet of his class, as was the grandson sixty-six years later. One infers that he was a man of strong and instant convictions; he was, during his college days, baptized by immersion through the ice in the Seekonk River and he was ordained, two years after graduation, to the Baptist ministry at Bridgewater, Mass. There he married Mary, or, as she was commonly called, Polly Peirce, who was remembered in her family as a woman of exceptional ability, which subsequently she had abundant opportunity to demonstrate.

For some years Mr. Leonard was pastor of one of the principal Baptist churches in New York City,[2] but liberalism was not long in asserting itself. His active mind offered hospitality to the Unitarianism of the day, to such an extent that he retired from the ministry and began a new translation of the New Testament. Politically, he turned to Thomas Jefferson and by the latter was appointed postmaster in 1806 at Bristol, R. I. where he also conducted the affairs of a commercial house, managed an insurance company, and edited the Bristol *Republican*. At length David Leonard's native restlessness overpowered him and, having met with some business reverses, he gathered his large family together and set out for the West. His intention was to establish himself at Vincennes, the most flourishing town in Indiana. He never reached his destination.

"His health, already gravely impaired," wrote the grandson,[3] "failed on the journey. Arriving in December at the little town of Laconia, near the Ohio River, in Harrison County, he concluded to go no further.

---

[1] *Memorial: Genealogical, Historical, and Biographical of Solomon Leonard, 1637 of Duxbury and Bridgewater, Massachusetts, and some of his Descendants.* By Manning Leonard. The sketch of David Augustus Leonard was prepared by John Hay.

[2] This upon the authority of the grandson, in the Leonard Genealogy. From an inscription on the back of a portrait owned by Mrs. Payne Whitney, probably a more trustworthy source of information and not available when the above was written, it would appear that John Hay somewhat magnified the achievements of his grandfather. Mr. Leonard occupied pulpits in Nantucket and Templeton, Massachusetts, but, for the two years he was in New York, he taught school. The most significant quality of the grandfather was that, like the grandson, he never continued long in any one occupation. He died of tuberculosis, thus bequeathing an heredity which John Hay may have regarded with some concern, since he, also, all his life was very much subject to infections of the respiratory organs.

[3] *Ibid.*, p. 222.

He bought a considerable estate in land, but was unable to continue the active habit of life to which he was accustomed. He died the 22d of July, 1819. After his death his widow had occasion to display her remarkable powers of intelligence and character. She was forty-two years of age, with eleven children; separated from home and friends by a distance hardly conceivable in these days of railroads and tele-graph, with a property consisting almost entirely of unproductive land. It was not only without dismay or repining, but probably with no idea that her conduct was especially meritorious, that she betook herself to the care of her large family and the management of her affairs. She had the success which was due to her merit. The matron of the Prov-erbs was not better spoken of at the city gates than was this notable widow, on both sides of the Ohio River."

Mrs. Leonard appears to have been quite unwilling that her eleven children, eight of whom were girls, should be surrendered to the wilder-ness and denied the advantages from which their removal to the West had threatened to separate them. We do not know just what happened to the lands on the Ohio but soon the girls were in Louisville and other larger centers. One of them is rumored to have opened the ball with Lafayette at Indianapolis in 1825, and it is evident that Polly Peirce knew the importance, and the trick, of giving her girls position in life. The plow was in the furrow; there was no turning back to the East, but the children married "well."

Helen, the fourth child and daughter, came to Salem, Ind., in the autumn of 1830, to live with the Farnhams and teach school. To a sister in Walnut Hill Dr. Hay wrote on November 2: "I spoke in my last of Miss Helen Leonard, Mrs. Farnham's sister, having been ex-pected here; she has come and as I expected the young ladies became splenetic as soon as she arrived. The causes of this are she is far better educated than any of them; besides, she is witty and a little sarcastic withal, these two latter qualities never made any lady popular with her own sex." It would not have soothed the feelings of many dis-tinguished men three quarters of a century later to have learned that John Hay's mother also had a sharp tongue, but this testimony from her future husband helps to explain many a sharp word we shall en-counter in the following pages.

Dr. Hay and Miss Leonard were married between seven and eight in the morning, October 12, 1831, at the home of a younger married sister, in Albany, Ind., by a Presbyterian clergyman, and late that day set up in Salem what promised from the outset to be a very interesting home.

Mrs. Hay was remembered as "a strong-minded woman in the best sense of the term. Her mental endowments were equalled only by her modesty and domestic qualities." [1] Her domestic qualities had ample opportunities for exercise. Within three years of her marriage, four years before John was born, her husband wrote to a brother: "We now have six children in our family besides Edward," the latter being the first born. Two of the children were the Farnham orphans whose parents had been carried off by cholera. There were in addition a young brother of Mrs. Hay, "two little Yankee boys of 11 and 9 years," left by their father to board and go to school, and "the little black girl." Fourteen years later the situation had not improved. There were then five regular boarders and also two children of a sister of Mrs. Hay, as well as John, his two sisters and two brothers. All this for "one lady to superintend in the character of Mrs. of the drawing-room, superintendent of the wardrobe, and kitchen girl to boot," as Dr. Hay put it. It is evident that Mrs. Hay was sharing the lot of pioneer women. They were a heroic race. There were in all six children, and John, born October 12, 1838, was the third.

Dr. Hay was a lovable man. Although lacking the "Herculean build" of his father, and the spirit of adventure which prompted the latter at the age of fifty-seven, to pull up stakes, find a new home, and make a success of the venture, he had individuality and character. "With talents which might have gained him distinction," wrote his son,[2] "he was destitute of that interior spur of restlessness which goads men into the race of competition." He was, in fact, ill-fitted to live in a competitive society, but this very willingness, even determination, to be an obscure country doctor gave character to the home. Too little a visionary to have been attracted by Robert Owen to New Harmony, not far away, he was, nevertheless, the kind of a man whom Owen would have liked to claim. The doctor hung on stubbornly in Salem for a dozen years, but there came a time when conditions were no longer tolerable. He yielded to the common temptation to speculate in land, buying on the edge of the village with a view to subdividing acres into

---

[1] Quoted from letter of Dr. A. W. King in *John Hay: Author and Statesman*. By Lorenzo Sears, p. 5.

[2] *Dr. Charles Hay*, p. 13.

house-lots, and the speculation failed. The newspaper was not a financial success. At the age of forty, with four children, he was forced to admit defeat and seek a new home. It was characteristic of him that he selected, not Springfield, where his father was already an important citizen, where his brothers, Nathaniel and Milton, were doing well; not any large center of population like Cincinnati or Louisville, but a new village less than half the size of Salem, on the eastern bluffs of the Mississippi, just below the mouth of the Des Moines River—Warsaw. The village was already larger than Keokuk, across the river, and hoped to rival St. Louis, but the hope was not to be realized. With some financial assistance from his brother Nathaniel, he settled there in 1841, and, until his death in 1885, rarely left the village, except to ride across the country caring for his patients. The year of his arrival marked the founding of the village library association, and during the greater part of his life he remained its president. Such men were the salt of the frontier. At his funeral the preacher could not claim him as a member of his flock, but he remembered that Dr. Hay had no enemy in all the world.

Warsaw was not a wholly unfavorable station for a growing boy to view the life of the nation in the forties. There were all kinds of people in the village; more, perhaps, from Kentucky than from any other one place, but a cousin of Theodore Roosevelt's grandfather was a neighbor, and there was a sprinkling of the new Irish, British, and German immigrants. Nauvoo, the Mormon settlement, lay less than twenty miles to the north. All Hancock County was up in arms about the growth of this strange city, jealous of its growth as well as suspicious of its character. Warsaw was on a main thoroughfare to the West. Many settlers bound for Iowa, and later for "bleeding Kansas," crossed the Mississippi at that point. The up and down traffic on the river also kept the horizon wide. Almost every kind of people came to Warsaw, or passed by it. It was an obscure village, but from it an alert boy could draw a fairly correct inference as to what the American people were like in the fifth decade of the last century.

"The years of my boyhood were passed on the banks of the Mississippi, and the great river was the scene of my early dreams," Hay recalled sixty years later.[1] "The boys of my day led an amphibian life

[1] Address at the opening of the Press Parliament of the World at the Louisiana Purchase Exposition, St. Louis, May 19, 1904.

in and near its waters in the summertime, and in the winter its dazzling ice bridge, of incomparable beauty and purity, was our favorite playground; while our imaginations were busy with the glamour and charm of the distant cities of the South, with their alluring French names and their legends of stirring adventure and pictures of perpetual summer. It was a land of faery, alien to us in all but a sense of common ownership and patriotic pride. We built our forts and called them the Alamo; we sang rude songs of the canebrake and cornfield; and the happiest days of the year to us who dwelt on the northern bluff of the river were those that brought us, in the loud puffing and whistling steamers of the olden time, to the mecca of our rural fancies, the bright and busy metropolis of St. Louis."

One line of the Underground Railroad passed up the west bank of the river to a point farther north and then crossed in the direction of Galesburg, but occasionally a black man came through Warsaw on his flight to freedom. One doubts whether the Hay family, with its Kentucky connections, had any definite part in the Underground Railroad, but it is inconceivable that Dr. Hay could ever have been one of those to send a man back to slavery. His was a home of gentleness and light.

In later years Dr. Hay became the owner of some farms near Warsaw, which he rented to tenants. It is remembered affectionately of him, however, that he was a tender landlord. He was inclined to look upon his tenants as children, or wards, whose interest he preferred to any financial profit which might accrue to him from their labor.[1]

In John Hay not two, but many, natures were at war. Sometimes spoke the restless, radical, poet grandfather; again, it was the cool, industrious, calculating mother; but most often, perhaps, it was the voice of the father, somewhat indolent and content with relatively small accomplishments, but knowing how to live and be loved. But for a series of circumstances which John Hay looked upon as accidents, the son would probably have been the kind of man his father was.

[1] *Biographical Review of Hancock County,* p. 15.

Too EARLY for the public school system, John Hay submitted to the ministrations of one of the old-time schoolmasters, and exhausted the educational resources of Warsaw before he was twelve. At home, with his father, he acquired a fondness for the classics, marks of which remained through life; Hay's literary style revealed a preference for a vocabulary of Latin derivation, and his allusions to classical mythology were frequent. The translation of Latin and Greek became a discipline of his ready imagination. It is stated that he had read six books of Virgil and some Greek by the time he was twelve.[1] He had also picked up a speaking knowledge of German from an itinerant teacher. A visiting relative remembered that about that time he was committing to memory pages of *Paradise Lost*. A quick mind appears to have relieved him of the necessity of arduous mental application; he was, perhaps, more bookish than studious. In 1849 his uncle, Milton Hay, invited him to his home in Pittsfield, in the neighboring county of Pike, to take advantage of a better village school, a private academy, kept by Mr. John D. Thompson and his wife. For two years he attended this school, which, according to tradition, was an exceptionally good one.

The village of Pittsfield offered to the boy something new and very different from Warsaw. Settled chiefly from western Massachusetts, and named for the famous town of the Berkshires, it had a "Square," with a Congregational Church and a courthouse on it, and a general atmosphere unmistakably of New England. Even though there were in the region such characters as afterwards appeared in "Pike County Ballads," Pittsfield was relatively a center of light and learning, particularly when the circuit court came to the town. It is asserted that an old court record reveals a case, involving only about fifty dollars, in which were engaged no fewer than eight lawyers, six of whom subsequently became United States Senators.[2] Pittsfield was a favorable

---

[1] A. S. Chapman, *Century Magazine,* July, 1909, p. 446.
[2] Clark E. Carr, *The Illini: A Story of the Prairie,* p. 137. The lawyers were: Stephen A. Douglas, O. H. Browning, Richard Yates, E. D. Baker, James A. McDougall. William Richardson, D. D. Bush, and William R. Archer.

place for the education of a statesman.

Between Milton, the uncle, and John Milton,[1] the nephew, there was a difference in age of only twenty-one years. They became very different kinds of men, but the uncle was an important influence on the life of the growing boy. Milton had been fifteen years old when his father moved from Kentucky to Springfield. Deprived of the educational opportunities which meant so much to John's father, he was, nevertheless, not content to accept the handicap and somewhere in his new home found a compensation. He served his time, or part of it, in his father's brick-kiln, but he learned how to write so well that Simeon Francis, editor of the famous *Sangamon Journal*, and loyal friend of Abraham Lincoln, employed Milton to report for the paper the early sessions of the State legislature after the capital was removed from Vandalia. The since famous law-firm of Stuart and Lincoln accepted him in its office to read law. He was admitted to the bar almost as soon as he came of age. In a village of 1600 people everybody knew and liked "Milt" Hay.

In Pittsfield, where Milton began the practice of law, he maintained a professional correspondence with E. D. Baker, afterwards distinguished in the Mexican War, a United States Senator from Oregon, and destined to be one of the early and gallant victims of the Civil War, in which he was killed at Ball's Bluff. Hay carried on the current work of the law office and, in the earlier stages of his practice, prepared the cases to be tried by Baker, who travelled the noted circuit with Douglas, Lincoln, and the other famous ones, and twice a year came to the courthouse in Pittsfield. The young lawyer married in the village and there were two children, both of whom died. The uncle appears to have all but adopted John, and for several years he was to the boy all that an elder and successfully established brother could have been.

The contrasts between John, the best dressed boy in the village, with a head full of *Paradise Lost* and Virgil, and his uncle, with whom carelessness of dress was almost an affectation, who was hail-fellow-well-met to every one, are too obvious to require elaboration. One settled down in Illinois and forced his way to recognition as, perhaps, outside of Chicago the best lawyer in the State; the other always,

[1] John Hay carried the middle name, Milton, until he was in college, dropping it, so it is alleged, because it seemed to him pretentious and inappropriate that he, who aspired to be a poet, should claim such a distinguished name.

even during those years in Pittsfield, gave the impression of belonging to another, a more delicate and fragile, world, and appeared to be not even at home in the home of his own kin. It was many years before the influence of the uncle began to show through in the nephew, but thirty years later, although the intimate relationship had long since lapsed, John began to display a business conservatism and a party regularity which made him in those respects much like his uncle. To Milton Hay, John owed a great deal for it was the uncle who gave the boy the lift which took him out of Warsaw, and, as will appear later, it was the same hand which guided John into the Lincoln circle in Springfield.[1]

With his removal to Pittsfield, still another important influence came into the life of John Hay, for there he met John George Nicolay. The latter was a half-orphan, an immigrant with his family from Bavaria. Nicolay was representative of the German immigration which was then filtering into Illinois by way of Cincinnati and St. Louis. Too young to have brought with him from the old world the culture and refinement with which such brilliant figures as Carl Schurz enriched American life, he seems to have had a love of letters not common in the land of his adoption. Ill-favored at home, deprived of the educational opportunities which he would have so eagerly grasped, he was still the child of a civilization older and richer than that of America. Nicolay had been picked up from the prairie and brought to Pittsfield to serve as printer's devil in the shop of the Pike County *Free Press*. The printing shop became his school and year by year he advanced himself until, before he was twenty-one, he was not only editor of the paper but also an important cog in county politics.

The office of the *Free Press* was the center of the political and literary interest of the village. There, around the fire on a dull winter day, were discussed the great themes in the life of the nation, and there Hay and Nicolay, six years apart in age, one a boy and the other not yet a man, met and formed what was for Hay altogether his most important friendship. It was, in fact, the only friendship which he carried through from youth to age and it became one of the few continuities of his life.

In 1851 or '52, having finished the school in Pittsfield, John was passed on with his elder brother, Leonard, to the grandfather, uncles,

[1] In 1857 Milton Hay's wife died and he returned to Springfield, where he became the junior partner of Stephen T. Logan, and married the daughter of his partner.

and aunts in Springfield, where he attended a school which opened in April, 1852, as the Illinois State University. It was the predecessor of the present Concordia College, a Lutheran institution. The so-called university had a preparatory department and while no records remain to indicate the nature of the studies which the young man entered upon, it may be inferred that his work was well advanced, for in 1855 he was supposed to be prepared to enter the junior year at Brown University.

Of Hay's school life little is known, but one catches a glimpse of it from a reminiscence of his brother, Leonard, thirty years later: [1]

I wonder if Lincoln ever studied by a "tallow dip" as you and I did at Springfield when Phelps and See argufied on metaphysics, and when they were done Uncle Nat came up with an apple in each pocket, and bit his thumbs and spoke to each of us words of wisdom, while Herodotus, in the original greek, lay waiting and neglected in the corner to reassert himself, and floor us next morning before the faculty of I. S. U. How painful to the eyes was that tallow dip with its everlasting flicker! How wearisome to the brain the obfuscations of Phelps and See trying to show off the great unseen unknown! And the lesson next morning appalled me more with its infinite weight of responsibility than the problems in after years of my soul's salvation. Did we ever imagine in those days that we would be gray headed and wear spectacles? That we would ever grow obese and obtuse and absurd? Of course we could fall in love—but that, the mere precipitation into the fathomless abyss, was the be-all and end-all of it.

In these years two other important influences should be noted: life in Springfield as compared with Warsaw and Pittsfield; and the grandfather's home.

Hay's impressions of Springfield are probably recorded in some of the chapters of the first volume of *Abraham Lincoln: A History*. Between the time when Lincoln came to Springfield and when Hay came there, the city had more than trebled in population, claiming in 1852 more/than 5000, but probably its outward appearance had not greatly changed in fifteen years. "The richness of the soil," wrote Hay,[2] "was seen in the mud of the streets, black as ink, and of an unfathomable depth in time of thaw. There were, of course, no pavements or sidewalks; any attempt at crossings was made by laying down large chunks of wood. The houses were almost all wooden, and were disposed in rectangular blocks. A large square had been left in the middle of the

---

[1] From Leonard Hay, Nov. 14, 1886.
[2] John G. Nicolay and John Hay, *Abraham Lincoln: A History*, I, pp. 156, 153.

town, in anticipation of future greatness. . . ." "It would have seemed a dreary village," remarked Hay, "to any one accustomed to the world," but it was the largest and most important collection of people whom he had seen until he was nearly seventeen years old.

Perhaps because poverty and ignorance seemed to Hay in later years to rob the world of beauty, he was always a little inclined to overstate the prosperity and culture of his family. This inclination appears in the sketches of his grandfathers and of his father, to which references have already been made, and it also appears in his description of Springfield life. "There had been very little of what might be called pioneer life in Springfield," he wrote.[1] "Civilization came in with a reasonably full equipment at the beginning. The Edwardses, in fair-top boots and ruffled shirts; the Ridgelys brought their banking business from Maryland; the Logans and Conklings were good lawyers before they arrived; another family came from Kentucky, with a cotton manufactory which proved its aristocratic character by never doing any work." It was doubtless true, as the writer intended to convey, that the town was from the beginning of a more settled and orderly type than was common in the South and West, but it could hardly be claimed that there was about his grandfather's home anything, even an abandoned cotton manufactory, aristocratic in origin or character.

The grandfather, now a widower, lived with his bachelor son, Nathaniel, and the four unmarried daughters. Nathaniel managed the brickkiln, and the sisters managed the household. The elder John Hay was, as to religion, a Missionary Baptist, the straitest of the Baptist sects. It was a very religious home in a narrow way, the first environment of that sort to which young John had been subjected. Dr. Hay, having passed through Transylvania in the days of the Unitarian Dr. Holley, and having had a scientific training, seems never to have found a place in the churches of Warsaw. His wife, although the daughter of a Baptist minister, remembered her father most clearly from the days when he became a religious liberal, and resigned from the ministry. John Hay's home was clearly one of conscience and of high principle, but it does not appear to have been a home of dogma. It was placed in the Peter Cartwright country where the periodic revival meeting was an important religious festival, but no such influence seems ever to

[1] *Ibid.*, p. 154.

have touched John Hay. His parents may have been liberals in religion but they were in other matters conservatives, and they were by nature conformists. In Springfield, however, the boy was immersed in an atmosphere of pioneer religion. It made upon him little or no permanent impression. He became a man of independent, though conventional, religious faith, but the dogmas of religion did not greatly interest him, while his esthetic sense provided what was for him an adequate emotional expression. No record remains of the boy's reaction to the religious life of the grandfather's home, unless we may assume that in the first two lines of one of his poems, "Sister St. Luke," he was thinking of one of his aunts, when he wrote:

> "She lived shut in by flowers and trees
> And shade of gentle bigotries." [1]

In a letter to his sister, March 5, 1854, the boy revealed himself as a stilted, self-conscious youth who was already seeking the company of those elect souls who would be poets:

The receipt and perusal of your last conferred great pleasure upon me. I am glad to learn that our little village is assuming the habits and appearance of a city: for in my opinon, all the sentimental talk we hear from the poet and the novelist, about the simplicity and quiet ease of village life, is all humbug. The city is the only place to gain a knowledge of the world, which will fit a man for entering upon the duties of life. I also wish you and your coadjutors the best success in your praiseworthy enterprise. The graveyard at Warsaw is a beautiful place in the summer, when the trees are covered with their rich foliage, affording a pleasant shade to anyone who may wish to wander in the cool paths, or to sit at the foot of some spreading oak, to read or meditate. But I object to the propriety of allowing the same privileges, to the cows and hogs who may be passing by.

In your opinions in regard to poetry, I fully agree. I think, with you, that it is one of the noblest faculties of our nature, and should be cultivated to the fullest extent. The true poet *will* cultivate this gift. One who is highly gifted, can no more keep silent and withhold from pouring out a flood of song, than can the songsters of the grove refrain from warbling their notes of praise, or the rivulet refuse to flow. His thoughts and meditations are not common with other men; his studies are not the everyday concerns of life. His imagination soars above the dark and gloomy real, to mingle with the bright and ever glorious ideal creations of his own fancy, and converses with kindred spirits of the past. His book is not the counting house ledger, or even the page of

---

[1] *The Complete Poetical Works of John Hay,* with an introduction by Clarence L. Hay, p. 74.

philosophic lore; but the great book of Nature is ever open before him and from this he draws the most priceless stories of Wisdom. To him there is exquisite happiness in contemplating the grandeur of the hoary mountains, the calm solitude of the forest, the roar of the boundless ocean, the headlong career of the torrent, and the merry laugh of the dancing rill. There are few to whom this great and glorious gift is granted and the names of both Milton, Byron, Moore and Burns are familiar to every admirer of the beautiful. These I almost worship. There is nothing I so much *love* as good poetry. But if real, sterling, heart-moving poetry is good, I think there is nothing worse than bad rhymes, (such as the one enclosed).

The Legislature adjourned yesterday. During the session I went several times to the Hall, but heard nothing of interest, except on one day where there was quite an animated debate on the Nebraska Bill.

We are studying Latin, Greek, Rhetoric and Algebra. We are now reading the odes of Horace which are beautiful. Tomorrow we commence the Iliad of Homer. We are busy every night with our studies, except Sunday and Friday nights. On Friday our Society meets for the purpose of debating, reading original essays, and criticising. I manage to come in as often as possible for speaking, which takes up no time in the week. . . .

To Ella,

Yours fraternally,

J. M. Hay.

In the selection of Brown University as the college where John was to continue his education, there was more significance than in the mere fact of its being a Baptist institution. The Hay family, collectively, had discovered that it possessed an unusual boy. There was common consent that this boy must have, not only good educational opportunities, but the very best. Uncle Milton and other members of the family, themselves deprived of such opportunities, were willing to pay the bills which were quite beyond the resources of Doctor Charles. There were many Baptist colleges nearer than Providence, but Brown University was the best that any one in Warsaw, or Springfield, could think of for John Hay. We are witnessing just that kind of transformation of family traditions which Dr. Hay so earnestly and modestly wished for, the kind of alteration which was going on in the middle decades of the century all along the frontier. The free, migrant life stifled provincialism and the keen competition bred ambition. The best was none too good. And so, in the fall of 1855, John was started off to Providence, R. I., to his Grandfather Leonard's college.

The transition from home to college, always an ordeal, was for Hay especially difficult because of his shyness. He passed also from the village to the city, and from the frontier to one of the best established communities of the East. A little undersized, and much less mature than the usual boy of his age, he entered with advanced standing, and was thus denied the relief that one new boy in the class gives to another. It was always difficult to call Hay by his first name; the boys dubbed him "Thaddeus of Warsaw." He had a natural reserve which did not encourage intimacies. The older and better established fraternities passed him by, but Theta Delta Chi invited him to join, and he became the twenty-fifth initiate in the most recently installed secret society on the campus. In the fraternity he appears to have taken an active interest while in college, contributing some songs which are still in vogue, but he formed in the society no intimate friendship which endured through the years, and his subsequent relations with his fraternity brothers, while cordial, were not close.

Hay quickly discovered that he would be undertaking too much to attempt to finish in two years, and dropped back into the sophomore class. His curriculum studies for the three years comprised: one half year, each, of Latin, Greek, chemistry, mathematics, physics, political economy, intellectual philosophy, and declamation; and, one year, each, of rhetoric, history, French, German, and moral philosophy. Taken all in all, it must have been a rather thin diet for a three-year college course. He immediately assumed and always maintained a relatively high standing as a student, his grades, transposed into modern terms, having been above ninety, many of them above ninety-five. He was admitted to Phi Beta Kappa, but seems never in after life to have dangled its key from a watch-chain. As might be expected from his inclinations, as they appeared in later years, he did least well in mathematics and moral philosophy. His best work was in history, political economy, and in German and French. "I used to say that he was the best translator I ever had in my classes," said James B. Angell, afterwards president of the University of Michigan.[1] "He not only apprehended with precision the meaning of the original, but he excelled all others in the felicity of finding the exact English equivalent of the original." Thus early he displayed what became, probably, the greatest of his accomplishments—the ability to grasp the thought of another and give to it instant and accurate expression.

Hay appeared at Brown at a time of academic depression. When

[1] Dedication of the John Hay Library, Brown University. Providence. [1911]. p. 31.

Francis Weyland retired as president in 1852, he bequeathed to his successor, Barnas Sears, what was known as the "New System," which had for its praiseworthy motive the bringing of the college closer to the people.[1] The system, however, was not a success. Its effect had been to lower both the standards of admission and the quality of the work. The new president frankly described it as a system of "under-bidding other colleges" and soon proposed reforms. For the class of 1858, to which Hay belonged, the new system, unfortunately, remained in force, and while ostensibly the college offered the master's degree, which Hay took, for five years' work, the conditions were hardly complied with. President Sears asserted that no more work was actually being required than for a bachelor's degree. It is, perhaps, unfair to charge the college with what subsequently appeared to be Hay's deficiencies of education, for, doubtless, the boy took what he desired and left the remainder, but it does not appear that any teacher there, with the exception of Angell, greatly impressed him. Hay, in fact, did not in college get the intellectual awakening which colleges have in their power to offer. He matured far more slowly than most boys, and the best part of his student days were the years he spent in Paris, Vienna and Madrid between 1865 and 1870. When in later years Hay's mind came in contact with Henry Adams's it was evident that there was a difference not only in the quality of the two intellects, but also in the quality of the training they had received. Notwithstanding the fact that Hay became in later years the joint author of *Abraham Lincoln: A History,* it could hardly be claimed that he was ever a scholar. His logic was, perhaps, less trustworthy than his perceptions.

The only college association of which Hay appears to have made any use in later life was with Richard Olney of the class of 1856, who appeared in Washington thirty-five years later as President Cleveland's Attorney-General and, subsequently, Secretary of State. Scattered official records at Brown [2] help to fill out the not very distinct picture of John Hay in college. His scholastic success was evidently in spite of considerable poor health: more than thirty days of illness the first year, forty-two days the next, but only six the last year. The term bills, including tuition, rent, and such a strange item as his share

[1] Walter C. Bronson, *The History of Brown University, 1764–1914,* p. 321.
[2] Gleaned for the writer by William Easton Louttit, Jr.

of the registrar's salary, ranged from $33.50 to $64.25; not much luxury, evidently. The library records show that he was reading the British quarterly reviews regularly, and a great deal of literature: Beowulf, Spencer, Beaumont and Fletcher, Percy's Reliques, Wordsworth, Goethe, and Béranger. In the Philermenian Society, of which he was vice-president in his senior year, he was once on the negative side of: "Resolved: That Mormonism is a sufficient cause for not admitting Utah as one of the United States." Early in his course, with some fellow students, he was inspired by De Quincey to make an experiment with hashish. James B. Angell, after Hay's death, still remembered how he had been routed out of bed very late one night to minister to the very sick boys who had participated in the adventure. The Providence *Journal*, July 11, 1856, carried the notice, over the name of "B. Sears, President": "In Rhetoric, the first premium to J. M. Hay."

The officer of Theta Delta Chi who presided when Hay was initiated, wrote after the latter's death: "Of course I did not appreciate his abilities—he was very young, very innocent and affectionate in his manners." [1]

Hay's most notable achievement at Brown was the class poem. Although he never chose to include it in any collection of his published verse, possibly because of its uneven quality, it must stand as a very real accomplishment for a young man not yet twenty years old. Its theme was praise of poesy. The following lines reflect not only the prevailing mood of his college days, but also give a clue to his attitude toward life for many subsequent years:

> Oft let the poet leave his toil and care
> To greet the spirits of the sky and air;
> Let him go forth to learn of love and truth,
> From Nature smiling in eternal youth;
> To ponder long on infinite wealth and power,
> Squandered to deck with gold one wayside flower;
> And share the peaceful majesty that fills
> The emerald circuit of the sunny hills.
> Earth grows not old, nor niggard of her joys
> But spells as genial on our souls employs
> As when Greek sunsets poured their purple dyes
> In wasteful splendor on blind Homer's eyes.

[1] F. Burge to Wm. L. Stone; original in the Louttit collection.

Class photograph, Brown University, 1858. The three Hay brothers about 1860; Augustus Leonard, the eldest, became a Captain in the U. S. Army. Charles Edward, the youngest, established himself in Springfield, Illinois, where he became a prominent citizen.

President Lincoln and his two secretaries, John George Nicolay and John Hay, Nov. 8, 1863. Later Hay became the equivalent of Military Aide with the brevet rank of Lieutenant Colonel. The original of this photograph, which is usually reproduced without the background, is owned by Miss Nicolay, whose father had the details painted in, thus making an interesting contemporary record.

The closing stanza, although it has often been quoted, cannot be omitted for it is a summary of what John Hay had learned of life in his first twenty years.

> Our words may not float down the surging ages,
>   As Hindoo lamps adown the sacred stream;
> We may not stand sublime on history's pages,
>   The bright ideals of the future's dream;
> Yet we may all strive for the goal assigned us,
>   Glad if we win and happy if we fail;
> Work calmly on, nor care to leave behind us,
>   The lurid glaring of the meteor's trail.
> As we go forth, the smiling world before us
>   Shouts to our youth the old inspiring tune;
> The same blue sky is bending o'er us
>   The green earth sparkles in the joy of June,
> Where'er afar the beck of fate shall call us,
>   Mid winter's boreal chill or summer's blaze,
> Fond memory's chain of flowers shall still enthrall us,
>   Wreathed by the spirits of these vanished days.
> Our hearts shall bear them safe through life's commotion,
>   Their fading gleam shall light us to our graves;
> As in the shell the memories of the ocean
>   Murmur forever of the sounding waves.[1]

[1] *The Brown Alumni Monthly*, VI, July, 1905, p. 29.

THE home-coming of the college youth in the last century is a worthy theme for the painter. One could find in it humor and pathos, but also the very genius of American life, where the college was the principal gateway to the only kind of peerage native to the soil. The first line of advance across the frontier had mustered its full strength to build the shelters, break the sod, and throw up barricades against starvation and physical discomfort. The demand of the day was for leadership by the acknowledged strongest, the nature's noblemen, in whom disciplined and cultured minds were luxuries rather than necessities. The prairie yielded to them, its masters. Then, as the older generation spent itself, up came the replacements, the products of the schools and colleges. For another quarter century it was still the fashion, especially at election time, to glorify the "self-made" man, but it is noticeable that most of the men thus put forward were self-made, not in the Lincoln sense, but with the help of a society which had already set high value on formal education.

For a generation before John Hay came home from college in 1858, Illinois had been furnishing a field of opportunity for the young college graduates of the east. Even greater possibilities lay in front of Hay for he was not so much going out to Illinois as returning home to a place already made. He was not an outlander; he was a son of the people. And yet he went reluctantly, unwillingly, and because he had no other place to go. He was out of place, having already hurdled a generation of prairie life. His grandfathers had belonged to the first line of advance, his father and his uncles to the replacement troops, and he, so far as concerned life in Illinois, had been born before his time.

"My father, with more ambition and higher ideals than I," wrote Hay one dull day in January, 1859,[1] "has dwelt and labored here a lifetime, and even this winter does not despair of creating an interest in things intellectual among the great unshorn of the prairies. I am not suited for a reformer. I do not like to meddle with moral ills. I

---

[1] *A Poet in Exile: Early Letters of John Hay,* edited by Caroline Ticknor; pp. 23–24.

love comfortable people. I prefer, for my friends, men who can read."

Here emerges the first dependable portraiture of John Hay which has come down to us. While engaged on the life of Lincoln twenty years later, he determined, somewhat facetiously, that his own biography would have to be written only from official documents, and he destroyed all early letters which he could reclaim. Only a few, like the one from which quotation has been made, have survived and these, unhappily, disclose him in a mood considerably below his best. The superficial characteristics of Warsaw repelled him, as they would any boy back from three years in Providence, but his discomfort was more profound. He was unlike his father in that the latter could go about the county as healer, confessor and friend, and then come home with pity and sympathy in his heart to organize a public library or a lyceum to ventilate the village. The son shrank from personal contact with moral maladies as one turns from a street accident. John liked to be comfortable among comfortable people who did not require to be made over. It is not so remarkable that he should have felt that way at the age of twenty-one, as that he should have had command of the words to state his feelings with so much force. The discomfort from which he suffered was deeper even than disappointment at finding no ready handle by which he could take hold of life. It is quite clear, when one comes to understand the degree of emotional conflict which marked his later life, that he was already suffering from the multiplicity of his disjoined gifts. He did not know what to do with his life. His talents fought with one another. Unable to satisfy the conflicting claims of his nature, he took refuge in an appearance of high disdain.

The village preacher, seeing in him the moralist which his good friend, William Dean Howells, afterwards rediscovered, urged him to study for the ministry. He dismissed the idea in an amusing letter to his uncle Milton: "I would not do for a Methodist preacher, for I am a poor horseman. I would not suit the Baptists for I dislike water. I would fail as an Episcopalian, for I am no ladies' man." As for his masculine charms, he was too modest. The girls were already giving his distracted father much to worry about. He was correct, however, about the church. In subsequent years he was rebuked by a literary critic for "mounting the pulpit," and he is numbered among the hymn-writers, but he had no love of people adequate for the cure of souls. The advice to prepare for the ministry may have been prompted by the success of a lecture given that winter in one of the local churches on the "History of the Jesuits."

The spread of the Jesuit influence through camp and court to the ends of the earth kindled the imagination of the young orator. "The black-robed fathers," he pointed out, had even "left their memories in the hearts of the red men who dwelt by the rushing rapids of the Mississippi and an enduring memorial of their presence in the names they stamped on hill and river, Marquette, Joliet, Des Moines, and Illinois. The very ground we walk on has felt the tread of their unresting feet."

A few adjectives in the lecture betrayed the Baptist instruction under which Hay had received his glimpses of the old world, but the general tone of the address was surprisingly tolerant for Warsaw, where still smouldered the embers of the Know-Nothing movement. The lecture closed, however, by contrasting the intolerant political conditions of Europe with the "young republic standing on the shores of the new Atlantis":

> In the grave dignity of our institutions you may seek in vain for a trace of either bigotry or licentiousness. The vigor of the Anglo-Saxon mind enlightened by the large results of the Reformation laid its foundations deep enough to stand the utmost shocks of fate or time. No considerations of interest or faith were allowed to warp its plan, or stifle the immutable truth that speaks to all centuries that are to come in the immortal manifesto of its independence. There was nothing exclusive in the Revolution. Side by side, under the sacred shadow of its banner, walked Jefferson the free-thinker, Paine the Deist & Washington the Christian. The temple of liberty is wide enough to admit every creed & every nation. We can admire and imitate the faith & fervor of the Jesuits & yet not tremble when we hear afar the thunder of coming reforms. Thus, scorning neither the examples of the past nor the lessons of the present, we may in the light of both, pray with the fondest love, at the altar of our common country

> > That her fair form may stand and shine,
> >   Make bright our days and light our dreams,
> > Turning to scorn with lips divine
> >   The falsehood of extremes.

This unexpected emphasis on the "falsehood of extremes" is of some significance in Hay's intellectual and spiritual development. Immature as he appeared to be in many ways, it is evident that his habits of thought were beginning to take permanent form. Throughout life he detested the extremists and the fanatics.

In his theme the lecturer had found something else of even greater significance. The most vivid paragraphs were those describing Ignatius Loyola, the courtier, and Francis Xavier, the scholar and traveler. It was a select little group of gentlemen who formed the original Society of Jesus. They were at home among kings and princes. "Their preachers filled the most richly endowed pulpits; their writers flooded the continent with works of faith and controversy; their priests listened to penitents in the most fashionable confessionals and taught the children of the rich in the most popular schools. In courts and camps their power was felt though unseen. They ruled the masses by love and the potentates by fear." Although Hay lacked the zeal of Loyola, the latter was born in a station of society such as Hay loved to let his imagination dwell upon. And Xavier also had Hay's admiration. The nearest approaches to the type in the United States in 1859, however, were Wendell Phillips and William Lloyd Garrison whom John Hay felt no urge to follow.

It is understandable that the young man was not stirred by the abolition movement, even though he was just returned from Brown, for abolition was an odious word in Southern Illinois. On the other hand, it is a little difficult to explain why Hay displayed so little interest in the moral aspects of slavery. It is even harder to understand why he, destined for a great political rôle forty years later, was so little moved by the political debates which were then convulsing Illinois. Lincoln and Douglas had already electrified the atmosphere and filled it with emotion. Hay was an emotional man, but there remains no evidence that he was stirred.

His three years in Providence appear to have broken all but the most intimate ties with his home. In Illinois John Hay was, in effect, a foreigner. He had decided to be a poet, and, as an applicant now for citizenship in the world of letters, he seems to have foresworn allegiance to the land of his people. His mood was revealed in a series of letters to Mrs. Sarah Helen Power Whitman and Miss Nora Perry, two Providence ladies whom he had met shortly before his graduation.[1]

---

[1] The letters to Mrs. Whitman have been published in *Poe's Helen,* by Caroline Ticknor. *A Poet in Exile* contains the letters to Miss Perry. The originals are in the John Hay Memorial Library at Brown University.

Mrs. Whitman had represented something wholly new in the experience of the young man. The women he had known were of the frontier. Many of them were household drudges and even in those cases where they possessed intellectual and esthetic interests, there was little or no provision in the household economy for their exercise. Pioneer life was conspicuously ugly in its superficial aspects, and particularly hard on women. The society which Hay had known in Illinois was impoverished, if not rude. So often lacking in feminine grace, it lacked also the refinements of life. At Providence, in the spring of 1858, Hay was invited to the home of Mrs. Whitman. Passing through her door, he entered an undreamed-of world, the glimpse of which ravished his starving soul.

In her home not far from the campus, Mrs. Whitman knew how to create an atmosphere. She was frail and delicate. Miss Ticknor states that in clothes she was entirely unconventional, dressing in a style all her own. She loved silken draperies, lace scarfs, and floating veils, and was always shod in dainty slippers. She invariably carried a fan to shield her eyes from any glare, and her pleasant rooms were pervaded only by a subdued light. It was a carefully organized household, unmarred by the painful thrift and economy to which the young man had been accustomed. Here dwelt comfort, refinement, genuine culture.

Mrs. Whitman was a woman of literary importance in her day. She had a fine classical education, a sound literary sense, and critical ability of superior quality. George William Curtis, fresh from Brook Farm, often invited her judgment on his work; she was accepted in the literary circle at Concord. To both the Providence *Journal* and the New York *Tribune* she was a valued contributor, and in 1853 she published a volume of verse, some of which had previously appeared in the *Atlantic*. Her most famous literary association, however, was with Edgar Allan Poe, to whom, after a whirlwind courtship, she was engaged for a few brief weeks in 1848. That she deeply loved Poe there is ample evidence, for she discussed the affair with singular yet delicate frankness in many letters which have been published by Miss Ticknor. A painting of Poe, who died shortly after the engagement was broken, hung in the parlor where she received her guests. John Hay had never seen a woman like this before.

Hay came from a home of bourgeois respectability and he was

cast in the mold of conventionality. Mrs. Whitman, in contrast, had a modest amount of the spirit of adventure. She understood such people as Margaret Fuller; she was a spiritualist and one of the best known writers on the subject in the early fifties. She took up the cause of Shelley in a day when it cost her the displeasure of an influential Providence family, which felt that, as an atheist, Shelley was not entitled to defense. Always living in secure respectability with her mother and sister, she expressed heterodox opinions which shocked staid, believing Providence. Underlying her literary gifts was a vein of good sense and judgment. Her parting with Poe revealed qualities which would lead a modern to call her a "good sport." Best of all, from the standpoint of Hay's education, she was fifty-five years old when he met her, a year older than his own mother.

The other-worldliness of the Whitman home and circle, which included Nora Perry and William Douglas O'Connor, editor of the *Saturday Evening Post,* author in 1866 of the phrase, and the defense, "The Good Gray Poet," swept Hay off his feet. Viewing the group with bated breath, he was awed in the presence of a greatness which he overestimated. The literary accomplishments of his hostess and her friends he seems to have regarded more as a divine visitation than as the reward of long years of arduous toil and painful experience. They spoke pleasantly of his verses and urged him to go on with his literary work; they did not have him long enough to teach literary self-criticism and discipline. The introduction to the Whitman circle turned Hay's head, sent him back to Warsaw rebellious at his poor fate, and in a mood which blinded him to much in Illinois life which he might have appreciated with great credit to himself and profit to his future.

To these two semi-Victorian ladies, Mrs. Whitman and Miss Perry, John Hay poured out his soul. He wrote that in Warsaw he was in a "Bœotian atmosphere" and expressed concern lest he be cut off from "Providence and civilization." In the little circle at Providence he had found the objects for which his mind had always longed, "true appreciation and sympathy."

"In spite of the praise which you continually lavish upon the West," he wrote to Miss Perry six weeks after his return to Warsaw,[1] "I must respectfully assert that I find only a dreary waste of heartless ma-

[1] *A Poet in Exile,* pp. 18–24.

terialism, where great and heroic qualities may indeed bully their
way into the glare, but the flowers of existence inevitably droop and
wither." And again, "there is, as yet, no room in the West for a genius."

The letters are obviously over-written and reveal a boy in need of
hard work and of good healthy diversion. In a single phrase in one of
them, Hay excepted his own family from the uncomplimentary generalizations as to his cultural environment, but one looks in vain for
a sense of obligation that he, who had been picked out of the family
to receive opportunities superior by far to those enjoyed by his
brothers and sisters, ought now to be lightening the very heavy
financial burdens of the household in which he was living. A few years
later, however, the young man assumed important family financial responsibilities.

"He is restless," wrote Dr. Hay to Milton, "and wishes to know his
destiny, although he expects me to decide for him entirely." His older
brother and his mother had protested that John must not be con-
signed to the fate of serving as a mere village schoolmaster in Warsaw.
His father agreed that the boy was earmarked for peculiar fame but
felt, soberly, that he should be outfitted with some sort of professional
training upon which he might rely until he arrived at his higher
destiny. The family looked with favor upon having him turn his attention wholly to literature, and plans for a return to the East appear to
have been discussed and discarded for financial reasons. Certainly in
his own home there had been no lack of that "true appreciation and
sympathy" which he had craved from the ladies. His older brother,
Leonard, was willing to make the necessary sacrifices and, if he had
been able, would have been glad to finance postgraduate work at
Brown where John might "read extensively, and write for Eastern
periodicals until a time and opening offered for taking a high position
somewhere."

While these earnest family discussions were going on Hay himself
was reduced to black despair. In May, 1859, he wrote to Miss Perry: [1]

I have wandered this winter in the valley of the shadow of death. All the
universe, God, earth and heaven, have been to me but vague and gloomy
phantasms. I have conversed with wild imaginings in the gloom of the forests.
I have sat long hours by the sandy marge of my magnificent river, and felt
the awful mystery of its unending flow, and heard an infinite lament breathed

---

[1] *Ibid.*, pp. 41–42.

in the unquiet murmur of its whispering ripples. Never before have I been so much in society. Yet into every parlor my Daemon has pursued me. When the air has been fainting with prisoned perfumes, when every spirit thrilled to the delicate touch of airy harmonies, when perfect forms moved in unison with perfect music, and mocked with their voluptuous grace the tortured aspirations of poetry, I have felt, coming over my soul colder than a northern wind, a conviction of the hideous unreality of all that moved and swayed and throbbed before me.

Such a paragraph is, obviously, a little piece of fine writing performed for the ladies, but it is more than that, for the depression was genuine while it lasted.

In explaining these moods, of which Hay was a victim all his life, his family remembered what was known as the "Leonard melancholy," a trait of character which seemed to have been common among the Leonards. Hay himself, in his chapter on Lincoln's marriage,[1] expressed the opinion that the "taint of constitutional sadness" was "endemic among the early settlers of the West." He ascribed its origin to the "severe and dismal loneliness" of their lives, and also to malaria. "In many instances," he wrote, "this miasmatic poison did not destroy the strength or materially shorten the lives of those who absorbed it in their youth; but the effects remained in periodical attacks of gloom and depression of spirits which would seem incomprehensible to thoroughly healthy organizations, and which gradually lessened in middle life, often to disappear entirely in old age." It is probable that in this passage Hay was as much explaining his own melancholies as those of Lincoln. While he ascribed the cause to the "miasmatic poison" of malaria, the modern diagnostician might be searching the nose and throat for some sign of a focus of infection, but the latter would probably agree that the cause of the melancholy of which Hay, as well as Lincoln, was a victim, was largely pathological.

Those nine months in Warsaw were an unpromising beginning. After making all the allowances which ought to be made it is apparent that the boy lacked self-reliance. His only ambition was to be a poet, and such an ambition, at such an age, and under such circumstances, is admissible only to those of high courage. If the drama had closed in the winter of 1858–59 one must have pronounced it another tragedy in American life: a boy had been educated above his place. Hay was

[1] N. and H., I, pp. 187–90.

unfitted to cope, as his parents and grandparents had done, with the unshorn prairies, unfitted by the gifts and tastes which subsequently made his success elsewhere. The year at home was critical. Again we may pay our respects to the patient and sympathetic family, which, even if it did not wholly understand the boy, nevertheless, carried him through. Some would have said that they were spoiling him, but they might have done so many unwise things which they did not do.

In the spring Milton Hay, now removed to Springfield and in partnership with Stephen T. Logan, the "exact and methodical Logan," as Beveridge called him, came again to the rescue by inviting his nephew to begin the study of law in his office. It was an office in which Lincoln had been the junior partner for a few years in the early forties, and the firm of Lincoln and Herndon now occupied an adjoining room. The young man returned again to the home of his grandfather and the old-maid aunts. He also resumed his association with John G. Nicolay, who, while Hay was in college, had made some strides in politics, and was now in Springfield as clerk in the office of the Secretary of State, and in charge of the Library in the State House. Nicolay was already a devoted follower of Lincoln. Thus, while Dr. Hay in Warsaw breathed a sigh of relief to have his son moved out of the little river-town, and separated from its flirtatious temptations, John passed into the Lincoln circle with which he was ever afterward to be associated.

"For several weeks I have been wandering through the dark places of Missouri," he wrote to William L. Stone, a college friend, May 20, 1859, "getting up extempore romances in the villages, & dreaming away the hours in the excitement of the cities. I am stranded at last, like a weather-beaten hulk, on the dreary wastes of Springfield—a city combining the meanness of the North with the barbarism of the South. Let the cry of your mourning go up continually for your brother of old time, for he hath fallen upon evil days. There is no land so sad as this. The sky is forever leaden with gloomy clouds, or glowing with torrid fervors. But the Aborigines are contented & happy. If the air is a furnace, they say 'Powerful nice weather for the wheat.' If the day weeps in sad-coloured showers they shake the rain from their hats & grin, 'This is given to send the corn up amazin'.' Yet these barbarians are men of large substance, & 'marvellous witty fellows.' Dogberry ought to have been an Illinoisan. Yet such as it is, for the present Springfield is my home. I am settled here—a student of Law, an't please you,—& here I shall abide for many days to come."

The next two years in Springfield must have been very distracting ones for a law student. The little city was already beginning to divide with Washington the political attention of the nation. Long before the Chicago Convention, which opened May 16, 1860, the New York papers were sending reporters out to Illinois to trail Lincoln and record his thrusts at Douglas. John Hay, as it were, sat on the hub of a great political chariot. It would have required rare concentration on the part of even an ambitious law student to have done much work in those dizzy days. Not much legal learning was required then of candidates for the bar in Illinois, or, for that matter, anywhere in the United States, and it is presumed that still less was required of a young man in Hay's circumstances. He was admitted to the bar February 4, 1860, exactly one week before his departure for Washington with the Lincoln entourage.

Only vague records remain of John Hay during those two years in Springfield. Perhaps he, on rereading his letters for the period, was chagrined to discover to what an extent the great events of the time had passed over his young head. The correspondence with Mrs. Whitman and Miss Perry continued, but the mood of his winter in Warsaw was passing. With Miss Perry the letters swung from the formal "My dear Miss Perry" to the familiar "Nora" and then, upon his arrival in Springfield, back to the initial formality. He flits through the pages of Anna Ridgely's diary,[1] "a very pleasant young fellow and very intelligent." With some one of the Ridgely girls or their friends he was attending the monthly concerts, going to hear Abraham Lincoln lecture on "Discoveries and Inventions," waiting on the steps after prayer-meeting to escort the girls home, accompanying them to church, and returning to the honeysuckle-embowered summer-house to finish out the evening. If any significance at all attaches to this village social life, aside from the fact that Hay was obviously having a very good time, it lies in the fact that the Ridgelys were Democrats and that their establishment was the best in town. Whatever partisanship Hay may have claimed, at that time, was not allowed to restrict his enjoyment of the best social life which the town afforded, while

[1] *A Girl in the Sixties: Excerpts from the Journal of Anna Ridgely. Journal of the Illinois State Historical Society,* October, 1929, p. 404.

black "Becky," the remnant of slavery which remained to the Ridgely household on the free soil of Illinois, did not present the issues of slavery in a form which excited lively sympathy.

Following the nomination, or following the election of Lincoln, Hay found some diversion from reading law in helping his friend Nicolay, now Lincoln's secretary, with the constantly swelling correspondence. It appears to have been an entirely voluntary service, acceptably performed. Accounts differ as to whether Hay owed his definite selection for the Lincoln service to his uncle Milton, who may have recommended him to the President-elect, or to the importunities of Nicolay who required immediate help. The latter is the more dependable tradition. Three years in Providence, a few calls in Mrs. Whitman's parlor, and two years as young-man-about-town in Springfield had given to John Hay a sophistication of which the Lincoln party, as it set out for the capital of the nation, was in conspicuous need. The young man also introduced a touch of gaiety to lighten the more prevailing and somber moods of the President-elect, moods which Hay was so well able to understand because they were like his own.

TECHNICALLY, John Hay was never a secretary to President Lincoln. For nearly three years he was a clerk of the Pension Office, and after that he was an officer in the army, out of which he was not actually mustered until April 8, 1867. "As the existing laws do not provide for an assistant for me," wrote Nicolay, March 10, 1861, "I have had John Hay appointed to a clerkship in the Department of the Interior and detailed to special service here at the White House, so that he gives me the benefit of his whole time." The salary was $1600 a year, increased a year later to $1800.[1]

Hay was dropped from the roll of the Pension Office January 12, 1864, and the same day commissioned by the War Department Major and Assistant Adjutant General of Volunteers, and assigned to the Executive Mansion. The position was thus transformed into the equivalent of military aide, although the latter term was not used. Fifteen months later the rank was increased to that of lieutenant colonel. On May 31, 1865, Hay became colonel, and on the same day he was granted leave of absence without pay.[2] In contrast, however, to this somewhat remote official status, Hay, as well as Nicolay, was actually all but a member of the Lincoln household.

The office arrangements of the White House in Lincoln's time would not please a modern office manager. The secretaries slept in the northeast corner room on the second floor. Directly across the broad corridor, on the southeast corner, was their office. Adjoining the latter, on the west, was the President's office, while beyond it was the reception room. The secretaries, therefore, were placed, not in the line of the callers' advances, but in the rear, where they could cover only the President's retreat. The physical factors in the relationship did, in fact, somewhat resemble the psychological factors. There was a bell-cord at the President's desk to summon the secretaries from the adjacent room, but the President was quite as likely to go in to them, where he found a ready refuge.

[1] Information kindly supplied by Helen Nicolay, and by W. Bertrand Acker, Chief Clerk of the Interior Department.
[2] Official statement furnished by authority of the Secretary of War.

The private rooms of the Lincoln family were in the west wing of
the second floor, along the same transverse corridor which, in the
opposite direction, led to the offices. While the relations with the
President were as informal as, and much more intimate than, they
had been in Springfield, where the office of Lincoln and Herndon was
on the same floor with the office of Logan and Hay, the secretaries
found Mrs. Lincoln more difficult. In Hay's letters to Nicolay, and
in the diary, the President was affectionately known as the "Tycoon,"
but Mrs. Lincoln, sometimes "Madame," was, on occasion, the "Hell-
cat," who became more "Hell-cattical day by day." The senior secretary, and Hay in his absence, appears to have been the disbursing
officer of the appropriations for the up-keep of the establishment,
about $20,000 a year. There were sharp differences of opinion with
Mrs. Lincoln, as to whether the wages for an unfilled position in the
household might be turned over to her directly; there was also trouble
over the payment for the grain consumed by the secretaries' horses in
the neighboring stables. In all these disputes it would appear that the
secretaries were not at fault, and eventually they found it more comfortable to take up their lodgings at Willard's. These difficulties, however, in no way disturbed their relations with the "Ancient," which
was another of Hay's affectionate titles for his chief. With Robert
Lincoln, who was much of the time away at school or in the army,
Hay's relations were particularly close, there having been a difference
of only eight years in their ages. On the night of the assassination Hay
and Robert Lincoln were together in a room on the second floor, engaged, so it has been said, in the study of Spanish.

In the handling of callers in the east wing there was little or no
system. Those around the President "strove from the beginning to
erect barriers to defend him against constant interruption, but he was
always the first to break them down," wrote Hay thirty years later.[1]
The correspondence could be more easily handled. Gone was the day
when the President could carry his important papers in his hat. Now
he could not even answer personally more than one in a hundred of the
letters which were addressed to him. The secretaries disposed of the
remainder. Many of the answers, no doubt, followed forms which
tended to repeat themselves, just as the inquiries did. Hay first signed

[1] *Century,* November, 1890.

letters as "Assistant Secretary to the President," but subsequently he was "one of the Secretaries to the President," and he exercised the franking privilege, writing his name in the upper right-hand corner of the envelope on official correspondence.

From the time when the great democrat, Thomas Jefferson, served as Secretary of State, the Department of State has always been the repository of precedent and the guardian of tradition for the White House. From Mr. Seward the secretaries lost no time in securing such advice and suggestions as seemed necessary to safeguard the dignity of the President in his formal social relations. There were lists of the social functions which would be expected, and even hints as to suitable dress and the use of visiting cards. The department also furnished a list of the cases of disputed precedence, indicating what people should not be invited to sit together. There was little gaiety, but there were the usual formal receptions, and the traditional state dinners, for which one or the other of the secretaries made out the seating diagrams, placing the President and Mrs. Lincoln opposite each other in the middle of the long table, and sometimes placing themselves opposite each other at the far ends.

The young men tried loyally to save the President's wife from her own rashness and lack of tact but in this effort they were not wholly successful. The character of the exchanges is well illustrated by Mrs. Lincoln's pencilled reply to a very courteous note from John Hay, stating that the Secretary of the Navy had called to inquire whether she had any objection to having the Marine Band to play on the lawn the following day. The Secretary was waiting in the office for her answer. This was on May 23, 1862. The reply was queenly if nothing more: "It is our *especial* desire that the Band does not play in these grounds this Summer. We expect our wishes to be complied with."

The most cherished tradition of the Department of State, handed down unbroken until very recent years when it has been somewhat badly battered, was a style of correspondence which billows and rolls with suspended sentences, rounded periods, much dignity, and, at the hand of the unskillful, considerable affectation. It amused Hay and seems to have amused also the President. Only two months after his arrival in Washington, Hay, always an apt literary imitator, tried his hand at the style with so much success that the resulting letter was included, with slight variation, in the edition of Lincoln's complete works which was edited by Nicolay and Hay, and published in 1894.[1] A State senator in Kentucky had addressed to the President a truculent protest at the occupation of Cairo, Illinois, by Federal troops. To this Hay, with the President's permission, replied as follows:

.Executive Mansion,
May 6, 1861.

Hon. John M. Johnson,
My Dear Sir:

The President has the honor to acknowledge the receipt of your communication of the 26th ult. protesting against the stationing of U. S. troops at Cairo.

The President directs me to say that the views so ably stated by you shall have due consideration; and to assure you that he would certainly never have ordered the movement of troops complained of, had he known that Cairo was in your Senatorial district.

Allow me, sir, to subscribe myself, with sentiments of high regard,

Your humble Servant,
John M. Hay
Assistant Sec. to the President

To Hon. John M. Johnson, State Senator
Paducah, Ky.

"I wanted to add," wrote Hay in his diary, "that the President respectfully requested that on all future occasions he would spell 'solemly' with an 'n.' But this hypercritical orthography the Chief disapproved. So the missive went. It will take the quiet satire of the note about half an hour to get through the thick skull of this Kentucky Senator, and then he will think it a damned poor joke." [2]

Hay also could dip his pen in acid and, on behalf of his chief, write such letters as later in life he was so prone to write on his own account. A Mr. Gibson, having accepted an appointment from Lincoln, subsequently tendered his resignation during the campaign of 1864, with the statement that he wished to be free to take a position in opposition to the President. In acknowledging the receipt of the resignation, Hay replied: "He [the President] says that he was not aware that he was so much indebted to Mr. Gibson for having accepted the office at first, not remembering that he ever pressed him to do so, or that he gave it otherwise than as was usual, upon request made on behalf of Mr. Gibson. He thanks Mr. Gibson for his acknowledgement that he has

[1] John G. Nicolay and John Hay, *Abraham Lincoln: Complete Works*, I, p. 43.
[2] *Diary*, May 6, 1861.

been treated with personal kindness and consideration, and he says he
knows of but two small drawbacks upon Mr. Gibson's right to still
receive such treatment, one of which is that he never could learn of
his giving much attention to the duties of his office, and the other is
this studied attempt of Mr. Gibson's to stab him." [1]

It is apparent that while Hay performed his duties faithfully, he
was also the court jester. Forney once congratulated him on the attitude he was taking toward his work, and remarked that he had
"laughed through his term." One who encountered him at Willard's
just after the arrival of the Lincoln party from Illinois in February,
1861, remembered a youth leaning back against the cigar stand, his
arms stretched out languidly on either side. When one of the boys
ventured to congratulate him on his distinguished position, he replied
in mock seriousness: "Yes, I'm the keeper of the President's conscience." [2] The entries in the diary, and the letters to "Dear Nico,"
suggest the common attitude of a young man who delights in under-
statements of dignity, yet with no lack of appreciation of the underlying seriousness of the subject.

The personal relations of Lincoln and Hay came closely to resemble
those of father and son. They told each other stories of Illinois, and
had their laughs. With Lincoln Hay went to the theatre where, according to the Secretary, they carried on a "hefty flirtation" with the girls
in the wings. They rode back and forth to the Soldiers' Home in the
summer. To Hay the President came at night, his long legs protruding
from a night-shirt that curled up behind, "like the tail-feathers of an
enormous ostrich," to read from Tom Hood, not realizing that in the
eyes of the secretary he, himself, was far funnier than the lines he read
to ease the torture of his soul.[3]

The humorous episodes and the pretty girls did not pass unnoticed,
but Hay's personal attitude toward the war is elusive. He did not
have a reflective type of mind, nor was he inclined to generalizations
or philosophy. The significance of the struggle in constitutional government and in the long march of human freedom did not seem to
lodge in his thought.

The movement and color of the early mobilization of troops in

---

[1] *Complete Works*, II. p. 554.
[2] From F. A. Mitchell, East Orange, N. J., to Hay, Feb. 12, 1905.
[3] *Letters and Diaries*, I, p. 191.

Washington appealed primarily to his esthetic and literary sense.
"The Seventh Regiment Band played gloriously on the shaven lawn
at the South front of the Executive Mansion," he wrote in his diary,
April 27, 1861. "The scene was very beautiful. Through the luxuriant
grounds the gaily dressed crowd idly strolled, soldiers loafed in the
promenades, the martial music filled the sweet air with vague suggestions of heroism, and Carl Schurz and the President talked war."
This is the comment of an onlooker, rather than of a participant in
the war. A few days earlier an entry in the diary reveals how another
aspect of the conflict offended his fastidious sense and moved him to
ridicule. He wrote, April 24, 1861:

On account of the stoppage of trains, on the Northern Railroads, we have
nothing this morning but a Southern mail. I have been reading it with new
surprise and astonishment at the depth of degradation of which the human
mind, in unfavorable conditions of existence, is capable. Nothing but the vilest
folly & feculence, that might have simmered glimmeringly in the narrow brain
of a chimpanzee, flow from the pens of our epistolary Southern brethern. . . .
There is style in cussing as in other things, and elegant oaths, as the Scotch
baroness said are "a great sett-off to conversation." But only a gentleman can
swear with grace, and blasphemy rolls as awkward and malformed from a
seceding pen, as patriotism or purity from the lips of James Gordon Bennett.

The grim earnestness of the events was first recorded in the diary
on April 30, 1861. He was still an onlooker, but stirred, and stirred
in a characteristic way, for Hay greatly respected aristocracy. He
wrote:

I went up to the Interior Department to see the Rhodian heroes. I saw
Goddard, Hoppin, DeWolf, Sackett, Pearce and others of the whilom loungers
of Westminster, all dressed in the coarse blue flannel and all doing duty, the
severest duty, without a murmur, and without any apparent consciousness
that there was anything at all remarkable about it. Scattered through the rub-
bish and camp-litter of Company C's quarters there was enough of breeding
and honor to retone the society of the Gulf and wealth enough to purchase the
entire state of Florida, and take the poor beggarly Montgomery loan. When
men like these leave their horses, their women and their wine, harden their
hands, eat crackers for dinner, wear a shirt for a week and never black their
shoes,—all for a principle—it is hard to set any bounds to the possibilities
of such an army. The good blood of the North must now be mingled with that
of the South in battle and the first fight will determine which is the redder.

But Hay recorded no desire to join them.
The shooting of Col. E. E. Ellsworth in Alexandria, May 24, 1861,

seems to have brought the conflict home to Hay to a degree which he had not felt before. In Springfield Hay had known Ellsworth, who had been reading law in the office of Lincoln and Herndon. He was a romantic and very gallant figure, restless, in the opening weeks of the war, at the cumbersome methods of the War Department. Having been commissioned as lieutenant, somewhat abruptly he went to New York and organized a company of Zouave Cadets which he drilled effectively and dressed so picturesquely that they attracted wide attention. He led his company into Alexandria early one morning and, spying a Confederate flag above the Marshall House, where it had been fixed to wave defiance across the Potomac toward the White House windows, climbed the pole to tear it down. He was shot by the hotel-keeper, and the death lighted fires of indignation throughout the North. The funeral service was conducted in the East Room of the White House, the President mourning as for a son. Hay was moved to write an account of Ellsworth, which was published in the *Atlantic* for July, 1861.[1] The sketch closed with a contrast between Ellsworth and "the poor wretch who murdered him," which, seventy years later, seems to reveal how superficially, rather than how deeply, the war was affecting John Hay. He wrote:

"The two stand in the light of that event—clearly revealed types of the two systems in conflict today: the one brave, refined, courtly, generous, tender, and true; the other, not lacking in frail courage, reckless, besotted, ignorant, and cruel. Let the two systems, Freedom and Slavery, stand thus typified forever, in the red light of that dawn, as on a Mount of Transfiguration."

Hay was never either physically or temperamentally a military man. He was, however, of military age and in the white light. It was not to be expected that he would escape comment and even criticism for being in a relatively comfortable post far removed from the smoke of battle. Gurowski wrote: "The streets of Washington, the bureaus in the Departments, and I am certain that the country at large is also, so to speak, filled with young men who dodge or escape the military service. It is a shame if those in power patronize or yield to such unmanly practice and keep as clerks individuals who could well go to the field." [2]

---

[1] Personal Reminiscences of Colonel E. E. Ellsworth. This article was rewritten by Hay and published in *McClure's*, March, 1896, under the title, "A Young Hero."
[2] Gurowski, Adam, *Diary 1863–'64–'65*. III, p. 306.

The foregoing was written August 2, 1863, when the draft law was
beginning to make itself felt. Although a secretary to the President,
Hay did not escape the draft. Five days later he wrote jocularly to
Nicolay:

Your advice relative to John H. coming the fine old previous enrollment
dodge was very good but it came too late. He had drawn a prize in the great
lottery here and the P. M. Gen'l had decided that this was his domicile & that
he must do or die or substitute or pay. He intends to pass his physical examination—has a vague hope that he may be found saddled with consump-
tion, gout, tic-dolorem, aneurism of several aortas and hereditary insanity.
He is . . . [at this point the bottom of the page is torn off]. He thinks even
if he passes the surgeons he can get a substitute for less than $300. They are
selling rather cheap here now. I have taken considerable time to the matter &
made careful inquiries, but I can't see how he can get out of paying, if the
surgeons pass him. Fry [1] says there is no way.

The draft fell pretty heavily in our end of town. William Johnson (cullud)
was taken while polishing the Executive boots and rasping the Imperial Abolition whisker. . . .

The reference to previous enlistment probably is to a brief period
of service a few months earlier as a volunteer aide to Gen. David
Hunter, at Stone River, South Carolina, to which place Hay had been
sent as a bearer of dispatches from the Navy Department. Hay appreciated the distinction. To Nicolay, under date of April 8, he wrote:
"I am glad of it, as the thing stands. If I had not been published as
having accepted, hesitated and rejected such an appointment I would
not now have it. But I want my abolition record clearly defined and
that will do it better than anything else, in my own mind and the
minds of the few dozen people who know me." Three days later, however, he wrote to Nicolay in great disgust, and with characteristic
modesty, that they had "made a d—d burlesque of the thing" by
giving him so much rank. The title was Colonel and Volunteer Aide-
de-Camp. It was a purely courtesy designation, representing only the
action of the commanding officer. The trip to Stone River, an inac-
tive station, was, in fact, a vacation from secretarial cares, and provided an opportunity for Hay to spend some time with his brother
Charles, who was attached to Gen. Hunter's staff, and was then
convalescing from pneumonia at Stone River.

As the months passed Hay appears to have become less and less

[1] Probably Asst. Adj. Gen. James B. Fry.

at ease at the White House. At length, either at his own request, or at the suggestion of the Secretary of War, he was regularly commissioned Major and Assistant Adjutant General. He was assigned to the Executive Mansion, but immediately ordered to Hilton Head, South Carolina, where he undertook for the President the most difficult task to which, up to that time, he had been assigned. Had it been successful, probably it would have changed his entire career.

In the winter of 1863–64 Gen. Quincy A. Gillmore, commanding the Department of the South, obtained authorization to make an advance into Florida. He hoped to secure an outlet for trade through the St. John's River; to cut off the commissary supplies of the enemy; and, to obtain recruits both white and black. Subsequently it was decided to take advantage of the military advance to try out a project which had appealed to the President and which he had incorporated into his proclamation of December 8, 1863. This proclamation offered amnesty to citizens of the Southern states on condition of taking an oath of loyalty to the Constitution and the Union. It also promised recognition to any state government which might be re-established by those who had taken the oath, provided they equalled not less than ten per cent of the total number of voters in the state at the presidential election of 1860. To Hay, at his own request, was entrusted the duty of inaugurating the campaign of oath-taking. He prepared himself carefully for this work, even writing out an appeal which he intended to use as an address to the people of Florida. The effort was premature, perhaps ill-advised, and came to nothing. Hay dismissed it in a single modest sentence in *Abraham Lincoln: A History:* [1] "The special duties assigned to him occupied little time; there were few loyal citizens to enroll."

The Florida project did not escape the critical eye of James Gordon Bennett. In the New York *Herald* of February 23, 1864, Bennett charged that the sole purpose of the Gillmore expedition into Florida had been to trump up a State organization to send Lincoln delegates to the approaching Republican national convention, and to send John Hay to Congress. The *Herald* estimated the cost of the military operation at one million dollars. It is quite probable that, if the conditions in Florida had turned out to be as the President had expected, there would have been Florida delegates at Baltimore, and that they would

[1] N. and H., VIII, p. 283.

have been instructed for Lincoln. There is also some plausibility to the inference that under such conditions Hay, who, while in Florida, invested $500 in land, might have been the first carpet-bagger Congressman.

Hay may have smarted under the Bennett charge, but he kept his poise. "The Tycoon never minded it in the least," he wrote to C. G. Halpine, April 13, 1864, "and, as for me, at my age the more abuse I get in the newspapers, the better for me. I shall run for constable some day on the strength of my gory exploits in Florida." [1]

The carpet-bagger story followed Hay for many years and, if he had chosen to run for Congress in Ohio in 1880, as he at one time considered doing, doubtless Hay's Florida expedition would have received attention in the canvass for election.

That the President was satisfied is proved by the fact that a few weeks after Hay's return from the South, he directed the young man, June 10, 1864, to proceed to St. Louis on a confidential mission to General W. S. Rosecrans. [2] The general had reported to the President that he was in possession of evidence of a general conspiracy to promote revolution and secession in some of the western states. Rosecrans wished to send an officer to Washington to elaborate on the matter, but there was involved in his recommendation an ill-concealed desire to have countermanded an order of the Secretary of War. The President was already well informed about the conspiracy, which he did not regard very seriously, and he had no desire to sustain Rosecrans against Stanton. Major Hay went to St. Louis, made an investigation and report which sustained the President's previous opinion, and Lincoln took no action. Hay's duties called for tact, careful observation, and accurate reporting.

On the way back from St. Louis, Hay dropped off for a brief visit in Springfield. On the Ridgely family, at least, he seems not to have made an impression equal to the earlier one. "Mary," who the next year married his brother Charles, "was disgusted with him," wrote Anna. [3] "He had a major's uniform on and he talked in the most affected manner possible. . . ."

While, in later years, Hay was always known by his military title,

---

[1] *Letters and Diaries*, I, p. 182; Lieut. Col. and Asst. Adj. Gen. Charles G. Halpine, whose war letters under the name of Miles O'Reilly appeared in the *Tribune*.
[2] N. and H., VIII, pp. 10–13.
[3] *A Girl in the Sixties*, p. 437.

he made no claims based on military service. Speaking in 1879 at a soldiers' reunion in Cleveland, he said: ". . . I declined making a speech, for I knew, of course, there would be plenty here who were better worth hearing than myself, and many more whose service in the field was more conspicuous and efficient than mine, which was certainly obscure and insignificant enough. . . . Like thousands of others, I went where I was sent, and did what I was ordered, without gaining any glory or establishing any claim upon the consideration of my fellow-citizens, and when I was mustered out of the army, I regarded the Nation as acquitted of any debt toward me thenceforth and forever." [1]

Almost immediately after his return from St. Louis, Hay was assigned to the most delicate task which the President ever asked him to perform, the Greeley peace mission to Niagara Falls.

Any weakening of the President in the summer of 1864 would have been fraught with portentous consequences to the Union cause. Yet this was the very time which Horace Greeley, whether naïvely or malevolently it is difficult to say, selected to place the President in a position where he appeared to be willing to make peace at any price. Early in July Greeley informed the President that he had reason to believe that there was at Niagara Falls, on the Canadian side, a representative of the Confederacy, supplied with full powers to negotiate a peace. Greeley urged the President to invite this man and his associates to Washington to "exhibit their credentials and submit their ultimatum." [2]

Lincoln, having serious doubts as to the accuracy of Greeley's representations, and yet wary of a trap, determined to take up the editor's challenge and appointed Greeley himself to proceed to Niagara Falls and to escort to Washington any representatives of the Confederacy who might be able to show that they had authority to treat for peace. Greeley was reluctant to proceed, whereupon Lincoln sent Hay to New York to deliver to Greeley a somewhat curt and peremptory message to the effect that the President not only intended to make a sincere effort toward peace but also intended that Greeley himself should be a personal witness to the offer. Greeley, thus caught, found himself in a position where he himself had to take up, with its accompanying liabili-

[1] Cleveland *Herald*, Friday, October 31, 1879.
[2] N. and H., IX, Chap. 8.

ties, the project which he had thought to put upon Lincoln.

At Niagara Falls Greeley discovered that the alleged envoys were without credentials. Instead of returning to New York, the editor asked for fresh instructions. He would have favored having the President open the negotiations by proposing terms to these strangers. The situation thus presented to the President was the more delicate because he knew, from past experience, that Greeley was quite capable of misrepresenting the facts and setting forth in the *Tribune* that the President was suing for peace. The political as well as the military effect of such a report would have been disastrous. At this juncture Lincoln decided to send Hay, as his personal representative, to Niagara Falls.

Hay carried with him a paper reaffirming the safe conduct to Washington for the envoys, provided they could show that they represented the authority which could control the armies then at war against the Executive Government of the United States. As soon as this message was presented to the so-called commissioners Greeley slipped away to New York while Hay remained at Niagara to receive any communications the professed agents might make. At length they replied, though not to Hay, charging the President with bad faith in having changed the conditions of the negotiation. Hay never felt certain whether they were guilty of the bad faith or whether Greeley had failed to make clear to them that the safe conduct was only for those who could show the proper credentials.

Again Hay carried himself well. The episode turned out to be of little importance, and is interesting most of all because only six years later Hay went to work on the *Tribune* from which Greeley had not yet been separated, and won the approval of the great editor, though equally poor politician. In 1890 Col. Hay presided at the unveiling of the Greeley statue in front of the *Tribune* Building in New York, but he skillfully evaded any comment on Greeley's relation to Lincoln.[1]

On the morning of April 15, 1865, in the little hall bed-room at 453 Tenth Street, when the Surgeon General pronounced the death of the

---

[1] New York *Daily Tribune*, Sept. 21, 1890. "What do you think? I relapsed from my good resolutions a while ago, and presided over a crowd of ten thousand people in New York to inaugurate a statue to Horace Greeley. I had built a monument to him myself—but *l'un n'empêche pas l'autre*. His daughter was there, on the whole the prettiest woman in America, (outside of your breakfast table), and she smiled at me so good-naturedly that I am more than ever convinced no human being has read a word of my calumnies." Hay to Henry Adams. Oct. 9, 1890. *Letters and Diaries*, II, p. 200.

This portrayal, by E. H. Miller, of the death of Abraham Lincoln is of interest less for the historical accuracy of the grouping than for the fact that even in 1866 John Hay was assigned the most prominent position in the group.

Milton Hay of Springfield, Illinois, an uncle, must be reckoned as among the strong influences of John Hay's early years. Others to be mentioned in this connection, aside from his parents and Abraham Lincoln, are James B. Angell, then professor of modern languages at Brown, John G. Nicolay, William H. Seward, and John Bigelow.

President, there were twenty witnesses—too many, one would think, to be in such a small room at such a time. It was characteristic of Hay that he stood, not in the front but in the outer circle, in fact, in the corner of the room behind the head of the bed. He was reluctant to witness human suffering, but he was even more reluctant to shoulder himself forward in any crowd. It was proper that he, at least, should have been there. Among those present his name alone is now remembered, except by the erudite, aside from that of Stanton who made the singularly fitting, if somewhat oratorical remark: "Now he belongs to the ages." [1]

The evidence is convincing that, although John Hay lingered longer than most young men on the threshold over which one passes from youth to maturity, he won the confidence of Abraham Lincoln to a marked degree. The President chose Hay as a companion not merely to laugh with, but as one before whom he could think out loud and whose attentive ear helped him to clear his thoughts. Hay's diaries and letters were thoroughly combed for information to be used in the preparation of *Abraham Lincoln: A History,* and they do not now yield new and startling information to form footnotes to history, but they are in no way out of line with the composite portraiture of Lincoln in the war period which has emerged from the most varied and detailed searches. The ability to interpret, which Professor Angell had discovered at Brown, appears in the random notes about Lincoln which Hay jotted down in the diary. Hay knew his man. Even early in 1861 Lincoln was phrasing to Hay thoughts as deep and as comprehensive as he was placing before his cabinet. Hay recorded that on May 7, of that year, he was recounting to the President the grandiose project of Congressman O. H. Browning, Lincoln's very good friend, to subjugate the South, establish a black republic, and then place a protectorate over it. Lincoln's comment was:

Some of our Northerners seem bewildered and dazzled by the excitement of the hour. Doolittle [2] seems inclined to think that this war is to result in the entire abolition of Slavery. Old Col. Hamilton,[3] a venerable and most respectable gentleman, impressed upon me most earnestly the propriety of enlisting the slaves in our army.

For my own part, I consider the central idea pervading this struggle is the

[1] N. and H., X, p. 300.
[2] Probably Senator James R. Doolittle of Wisconsin.
[3] Possibly Congressman Andrew J. Hamilton of Texas.

necessity that is upon us of proving that popular government is not an absurdity. We must settle this question now, whether in a free government, the minority have the right to break up the government whenever they choose. If we fail it will go far to prove the incapability of the people to govern themselves. . . .

In the summer of 1863 Nicolay was absent for several weeks, leaving Hay as the acting secretary. The young man and his chief were much together, and it was during this period that Hay began to record the admiration which he had come to feel.

"The Tycoon is in fine whack," he wrote to Nicolay, August 7, 1863. "I have rarely seen him more serene & busy. He is managing the war, the draft, foreign relations, and planning a reconstruction of the Union, all at once. I never knew with what tyrannous authority he rules the Cabinet, until now. The most important things he decides, & there is no cavil. I am growing more and more firmly convinced that the good of the country absolutely demands that he should be kept where he is till this thing is over. There is no man in the country so wise, so gentle and so firm. I believe the hand of God placed him where he is."

"The old man sits here," Hay wrote September 11, 1863, "and wields like a backwoods Jupiter the bolts of war and the machinery of government with a hand equally steady and equally firm." But he added, in another letter, November 25, 1863: "Don't, in a sudden spasm of good-nature, send any more people with letters to me requesting favors from L———. I would rather make the tour of a smallpox hospital."

"He will not be bullied," in another letter, "even by his friends. He tries to reason with these infuriated people. The world will hear him, if they do not."

If even Hay, with his literary sense, did not entirely grasp the Gettysburg Address, it should be remembered that others failed with him, and it should be recorded that Hay did not, in fact, completely lose it. "Mr. Everett spoke as he always does, perfectly; and the President, in a firm, free way, with more grace than is his wont, said his half dozen lines of consecration,—and the music wailed, and we went home through crowded and cheering streets, and all the particulars are in the daily papers." [1]

---

[1] *Letters and Diaries,* I, p. 125; Nov. 18, 1863.

The differences between Lincoln and Hay are so marked that it is especially creditable to the latter that he did both appreciate and understand the President. Hay had to overlook many standards upon which he himself set great store. Never after Lincoln's death did he choose to associate with any man who remotely resembled the President either in externals, or in the more subtle qualities of his character. In later years Hay was more inclined to spend his time with men like Seward, or like his old college teacher, James B. Angell. In coming to view Lincoln with affection, and profound respect, Hay did not in any way compromise his own set of values. Imitative though he was, he never tried to be Lincolnesque, and there are only a few lines of his published writings which reveal the mark of his association with Lincoln. Hay, young as he was, was his own man. Lincoln was less an influence than an episode in a life which also was exceptional. Ultimately, on his own account, John Hay achieved greater distinction than any other man who ever served as a secretary to a President of the United States, with the exception of the Adamses.

To attempt a final determination of what the Lincoln association meant in John Hay's life is impossible. It is clear that from the fame of his service under Lincoln, Hay derived a large part of his capital for successful living in America; this was most often his card of introduction. But Hay added to and enriched that capital with a variety of personal contributions. It is impossible to show what, beyond the fame of being Lincoln's secretary, he obtained, because one can never know what kind of man Hay would have been had he never known Lincoln. He missed Lincoln's tolerance, so that McClellan, for example, fared harder at the hand of Hay, the biographer, than he did at the hand of Lincoln, the Commander-in-Chief. He failed to learn Lincoln's political sagacity. On the other hand, it may be that this association for four years with American democracy incarnate held Hay from being led off into what would have been in the United States an unreal and alien world of aristocracy, toward which he had already displayed inclinations, but in which his own gifts would have been entirely frittered away. It may well be that, while Hay never became like Lincoln, he did, in the end, become less like the John Hay he otherwise would have been.

JOHN HAY was never to escape from situations which tended to tear life asunder rather than to unify it. The forces of the Kentucky pioneers, represented by his Herculean grandfather in Springfield, claimed him for their own, but the traditions of the poet-preacher grandfather from Rhode Island also made their demands. He belonged to both, as well as to his simple-living, elevated-thinking father, and his ambitious, energetic mother. In Washington two other conflicting influences entered his life: association with Abraham Lincoln, and residence in the nation's capital. The young man was required to choose which pattern he would follow, as well as which master he would serve. His loyalty to his chief never wavered, but he chose to follow the other pattern, a choice which must have contributed no little confusion to his life.

"It has been said that a residence in Washington leaves no man precisely as it found him," wrote the biographers of Lincoln in the chapter on the conclusion of the latter's service as Congressman in 1849.[1] The saying was less true of Lincoln than it was of Hay, and yet we must not forget that it was no unshorn youth of the prairies who came to Washington with Lincoln. With all his youth, and his even greater immaturity, Hay had a standard of discriminating judgment which held his feet firmly to the ground.

As the young secretary looked out of the window of the bedroom to which Nicolay and Hay had been assigned, on the second-floor corner of the Executive Mansion, the physical aspects of the "miserable, sprawling village" of Washington, as he called it, did not impress him.[2] Between him and the unfinished rear of the Greek temple which housed the Treasury were the presidential stables where he and Nicolay were permitted to lodge their horses. The two streets which now separate the White House from the Treasury and the State, War, and Navy Building had not been cut. The north lawn of the President's house was flanked, at the corner of Fifteenth Street and Pennsylvania Avenue, by the three-storied, red-brick Department of State, later

---

[1] N. and H., I, p. 294.
[2] William Roscoe Thayer, *The Life and Letters of John Hay*, I, p. 85.

removed to make way for the completed Treasury. On the corresponding corner of Seventeenth was the War Department. The south lawn
fell away to the uncompleted Washington Monument, and to the
Potomac, half a mile away, where John Quincy Adams used to go for
his morning swim. The north lawn ran out into Pennsylvania Avenue,
which marked the boundary between it and the "President's Park"
across the street, as Lafayette Square was still often called. Both
names were too dignified; during the War it was used for stabling
cavalry horses.

Washington claimed a population in excess of 60,000, but from a
White House window such a figure would have seemed very excessive.
Around Lafayette Square, very untidy, and about the size of the village green in Pittsfield, was a little ganglion of life, spreading out a
few blocks east and west, but quickly losing itself in pastures on the
north, where no one at night went unlighted or unarmed. A mile
farther east on Pennsylvania Avenue there was another ganglion
around the Capitol, also unfinished. The Avenue, like an artery, connected the two centers, and fed a fringe of life which bordered its
north side, and spread up the hill a few blocks to what is now the main
business street of the city. The settlement straggled on from the White
House along the Avenue in the direction of Georgetown, but from
1861 to 1865 the latter was a Southern village to which Lincoln people did not commonly resort. Aside from the crowds which all through
the four years thronged the Executive Mansion, most of the people
whom John Hay came to know lived within four or five blocks of
Lafayette Square. The unfinished, ill-furnished, and unkept character
of the city gave the White House the appearance of a manor-house,
out of place and being encroached upon by a very ragged city.

With the moral aspects of the town he was still less impressed. "It
imagines it is a city because it is wicked," he wrote to one of the girls
in Warsaw.[1] The wickedness of Washington was conceded even by its
permanent residents. A guide-book, published in 1861, described the
city as the "abode of a legion of foul vices." [2] The blame was laid on
Congress, the "camp-followers" of which elected a bachelor mode of
living and devised too few elegant ways of spending their leisure time.
The morals of Washington are important to this narrative because

[1] *Ibid.*, p. 85.
[2] *Phillip's Washington Described*, edited by William D. Haley, p. 204.

Hay viewed them with such scorn. In the midst of the kind of temptations which ruined many young men, he had good taste in conduct. An eligible young bachelor, and always an agreeable companion, he ranged freely over the town, dining, flirting, making friends, but with people whose company did him credit.

Among the statesmen, William H. Seward, Secretary of State, seems to have made upon him the first and the most lasting impression. Seward was Hay's kind of man, carefully tailored, a man of the world. Indeed, one suspects that Hay came to appreciate Seward, in spite of his strong brandy and cigars, which he did not like, more quickly and more easily than he came to appreciate the President, who was in all superficial respects the kind of man that Hay never desired to be. In December, 1861, probably at Christmas, Hay inscribed to the Secretary of State a sonnet which concluded:

> And so, a generous people, at the last,
> Will hail the power they did not comprehend.
> Thy fame will broaden through the centuries;
> As, storm and billowy tumult overpast,
> The moon rules calmly o'er the conquered seas.[1]

Seward's fame has, in fact, broadened through seven decades; Hay's enthusiastic estimate was more than a mere holiday compliment. Several months elapsed before the young man appears to have recorded any estimate of Abraham Lincoln in comparable terms, and, strangely enough, the Emancipator never supplied him with a theme for verse.

A letter to Nicolay under date of April 9, 1862, after mentioning that Hay had undertaken the study of French, gives one a further glimpse into his leisure hours. "I have taken a devil of a notion to the Gerolts.[2] I went to see them the other day. The children were less scared than usual and they and Madame La Baronne talked long and earnestly of the state of your hygiene and said, 'it was good intentions you for to go to the West for small time.'

"The latest rumor in 'our set' is that Mr. Hay and Miss Hooper are *engagèd*, as Count Gurowski calls it. I wish I had that old nuisance's neck in a slip noose. I'm afraid the Hoopers will hear it and then my good times there will be up." Miss Hooper was the daughter

---

[1] Frederick W. Seward, *Seward in Washington as Senator and Secretary of State*, p. 35.
[2] Baron Gerolt was the Prussian Minister. He was, unlike many of his colleagues, outspoken for the North.

of Samuel Hooper, Congressman from Marblehead, Mass. The Count Gurowski complained of was one of the most picturesque as well as exasperating characters in Washington. He was believed to have been a Polish nobleman, a fugitive from Russia. For a time he was employed in the Department of State "to read the German newspapers and keep Sec. Seward from making a fool of himself." He claimed that he found the latter difficult. Seward and Gurowski parted company abruptly. Hay suspected that Gurowski supplied the New York *Tribune,* on which he had once been employed, with information which was used to embarrass the Administration.[1]

What Mrs. Helen Whitman had been to Hay toward the close of his life in Providence, Mrs. Charles Eames came to be in Washington. The Eameses were already old residents, having come from Massachusetts in 1845 with Bancroft when the latter became Secretary of the Navy under Polk. Eames at Harvard had been a classmate of Motley and Wendell Phillips. First engaging in editorial work on the Washington *Union,* he later held two diplomatic appointments, to the Sandwich Islands and to Venezuela, and in 1861 was described as an admiralty lawyer engaged in private practice. Without great wealth or ostentation Mrs. Eames became as a social leader, a successor to Mrs. Dolly Madison. She had, in fact, what was described as the first salon in Washington. Her Sunday evenings were notable. If one may believe her sister, "there was no house in Washington, except perhaps the President's, where one was sure of meeting throughout the year so many people of distinction." [2]

Of the Eameses Mr. Nicolay wrote, after attending one of their evening parties:

Both he and his wife are very intelligent, amiable, and hospitable, and by reason of their position and long residence here as well as abroad, know almost everybody, and constantly draw around them the most interesting people who visit Washington. Although they have but a small house, and live in very moderate style, their parlor is really a sort of focal point in Washington society, where one meets the best people who come here. By the "best" I do not mean mere fashionable "society people," but rather the brains of society —politicians, diplomats, authors and artists, and occasionally too, persons whose social and political positions merely, and not their brains, entitle them

[1] Marian Gouverneur, *As I Remember,* pp. 246–47; also notes supplied by Miss Helen Nicolay.
[2] *Ibid.,* p. 178. See also, Watterson, *Marse Henry,* II, pp. 15–17.

to consideration, such as titled foreigners, pretty women, &c. Politically it is a sort of neutral ground, where men of all shades of opinion—Republicans, Democrats, Fossil Whigs, with even an occasional spice of a Secessonist, come together quietly and socially. Usually we go there on Sunday evenings—say from 8 to 11—without any formality whatever; merely "drop in," coming and going entirely at pleasure, and talking to whom and about what every one pleases. A variety of people, of course, bring with them a variety of languages; and so, while the key note is almost always English, the conversation runs into variations of French, German and Spanish. Mr. and Mrs. Eames speak all of them but the German.

On one evening Nicolay found there Lady Georgiana Fane, daughter of the Earl of Westminster, two cabinet members, a senator, N. P. Willis, Leutze, the painter, "and other celebrities." The following week Charlotte Cushman was there, "getting old and ugly." [1]

On another evening Hay might be at the home of Henry A. Wise, where he found Edward Everett supplying knees for his grandchildren to climb over, or at the Sewards', where he took a hand at whist. He did not limit his circle to those who gave undivided allegiance to his chief, for his diary shows that although he dined with Stanton, he also dined with "Sunset" Cox, discussing the prospective nomination of McClellan in 1864. He attended the theatre with the President, but also with parties of his own selecting, and he spent no little time with such typical newspaper men as J. W. Forney and John Russell Young, sharing their conviviality, however, with caution.

All through his life people either liked John Hay very much or they disliked him in equal degree. This was true in the early years in Washington as well as in the later ones. When his literary work had made him famous at the end of the next decade, people began to recall their impressions of the young man as he had appeared in the White House during the war.

"In those days he didn't impress us overwhelmingly," wrote one man in the St. Louis *Dispatch*, May 30, 1871. "We saw a young, good-looking fellow, well, almost foppishly dressed, with by no means a low opinion of himself, either physically or mentally, with plenty of self-confidence for anybody's use, a brain active and intellectual, with a full budget of small talk for the ladies or anybody else, and both eyes keeping a steady lookout for the interests of 'number one.' "

Another newspaper man, who had known Hay more intimately, had

[1] Helen Nicolay, *Our Capital on the Potomac*, p. 362.

come away with a more favorable impression which was published in the *Sedalia* [Mo.] *Times* on May 11, 1871. He remembered a smooth-faced, ruddy-cheeked, vivacious, witty, polished, urbane, and intellectual youth. "Though he constantly pursued his *belles lettres* studies and went much into society, he was a hard worker also, as his twelve or fourteen hours a day of hard work in the White House . . . sufficiently attested. . . . We saw much of Hay during those years, most of the time boarding at the same club house and dining in the same mess. He was always the same witty, genial, agreeable, effervescent and insinuating fellow. No one could be with him and not discover that he had decided genius and unusual literary culture."

Commenting in 1868 upon Hay's appointment as editor of the Springfield *State Journal,* an editor remarked, slyly: "If he makes as much impression upon Western readers as he did upon Washington ladies, he will make himself felt as a journalist."

America could have furnished at that time no more ideal education for a young man who desired to be a man of the world. It was, however, the kind of an education which might easily have been ruinous. Hay, steadied by the elder Nicolay, and never forgetting the dignity of his association with the President, kept his head. The breeding of thrifty, earnest, abstemious pioneers, back through the Leonards to Polly Peirce, and through the Hays to old Adam of Berkeley County, Virginia, was beginning to show.

"Wise and Fox and Leutze and Aulick and I have dined together hundreds of pleasant evenings," wrote Hay five years later, one lonely evening in Madrid. "I can see them and hear them all tonight,—Wise's fantastic fun, Fox's lambent humor, Leutze's crabbed wit, and Aulick's gentle culture." He remembered also "Mrs. Eames and pretty Fanny," and Mrs. Wise and her "clever daughter." "I knew so many clever people in Washington that there will be a sort of insipidity about society the rest of my life, I suppose." [1]

There was that danger.

On the other hand, he did not forget the family in Warsaw, visiting there at least once each year. Out of his modest salary he saved money. More significant even than his thrift is the fact that, after

---

[1] Madrid Letterpress Copybook, June 30, 1870. It was in this letter to Miss Harriet Loring that Hay expressed the hope that those who participated in the outrage of changing the name of his boyhood home from Spunky Point to Warsaw would be called Smith in heaven.

making a canvass of various girls' schools, with the approval of his parents, he selected the Convent of the Visitation in St. Louis for his sister Helen, and arranged for her to continue her education there. So far had John Hay, and his family, travelled from the Scotch ancestry and the Baptist minister grandfather.

MORE than two weeks prior to the surrender of Lee at Appomattox, perhaps a full month before the assassination of the President, John Hay had determined to sever permanently his intimate association with Abraham Lincoln. On March 22, 1865, he accepted an appointment as Secretary of Legation at Paris.

"You have probably seen from the papers," he wrote his brother Charles,[1] "that I am to go to Paris as Secretary of Legation. It is a pleasant and honorable way of leaving my present post which I should have left in any event very soon. I am thoroughly sick of certain aspects of life here, which you will understand without my putting them on paper, and I was almost ready, after taking a few months' active service in the field, to go back to Warsaw and try to give the Vineyard experiment a fair trial, when the Secretary of State sent for me and offered me this position abroad. It was entirely unsolicited and unexpected. I had no more idea of it than you have. But I took a day or two to think it over, the matter being a little pressing,—as the Secretary wanted to let Mr. Bigelow know what he was to expect—and at last concluded that I would accept. The President requested me to stay with him a month or so longer, to get him started with the reorganized office, which I shall do, and shall sail probably in June. . . .

"I very much fear that all my friends will disapprove this step of mine, but if they knew all that induced me to it they would coincide."

In attempting to portray John Hay, it is impossible to overlook this extraordinary decision. When he made it he could not foresee the end of the war, although it may have seemed not far off. Sherman reached the sea and received the surrender of Savannah December 20, 1864; in the middle of March he was well on his way through North Carolina to make a junction with Grant. The latter began the siege of Richmond and Petersburg in the summer of 1864, but the prospects, when Hay made his decision, seem hardly to have warranted the conclusion that the President's great responsibilities were over, and that he could easily spare from his personal staff an assistant who had served with him from

[1] *Letters and Diaries,* I, p. 253; March 31, 1865.

the beginning. In no other letters now extant does Hay advert to the mysterious reasons which led him to the decision. One is left, therefore, with no alternative but to suggest an explanation which is in accord with other known traits of his disposition.

Hay was the victim, as already mentioned, of periods of depression and indecision, quite similar to those which visited Abraham Lincoln in his earlier years and which caused the postponement of the latter's marriage to Mary Todd. Furthermore, Hay disliked routine; disliked, as will appear later, to give his constant attention over a long period to anything. He liked change; the varied character of his activities in the next thirty years was their most outstanding characteristic. Three years after the decision to leave the White House, in a letter to Nicolay, June 30, 1868, Hay supplied a faint clue to his reason for leaving the White House. He wrote:

"It gives me a shudder to think that there have been two or three times in my life when I stood on the brink of a red-tape career. It may have been accident that saved me. It may have been an underlying protest of my own Illinois nature—but that danger any how is passed. I may be a poor shoat all my days, but I shall never wear a livery, or do other men's work, if I know myself."

It is not easy to view the varied nature of Hay's duties in 1864 as belonging to a "red-tape career," but, when one remembers Hay's melancholy, it is entirely possible to understand why he may have come to regard his work as an intolerable grind. He made several similar decisions in later years.

The determination to leave the President did not cost him the friendship of the latter, nor did it involve the loss of Seward's confidence, for it was the Secretary who, doubtless with the approval of the President, offered the way of escape. With Robert Lincoln he remained a warm friend and, upon his return from Paris, Mrs. Lincoln was more than cordial. The change in no way interrupted his relations with Nicolay who, to the end of his days, remained Hay's oldest friend.

Forty years later Hay referred to the appointment to Paris as an accident. In response to the inquiry of a young man about diplomatic service as a career, he wrote in 1904: "It is true, as you say, that I have held a good many diplomatic positions, but they were all the result of accident, and no one had any relation to the other."

If it was variety that Hay required, the five years from 1865 to 1870 did not fail to supply it; altogether, he served a little less than forty-eight months in Paris, Vienna, and Madrid. In the intellectual development of the young man these four years were more important than the entire period of his formal education, and perhaps more important also than service in the White House. When he went to Europe he was in many ways still a boy; he returned at the age of thirty-two, a man.

Before he proceeded to his post his military rank, as already noted, was twice raised; he could appear in the court of Napoleon III in a colonel's uniform. He was not a tall man and his photographs of the day reveal a singularly boyish face. The combination seems to have given him the appearance of being somewhat overdressed. The psychological effect was to develop in Hay a trace of pompousness, which remained for many years. Perhaps it was this quality which led the Cleveland *Plain Dealer*, in the heat of a political campaign fifteen years later, to refer to him mischievously as "Little Breeches" Hay, after he had delivered in that city an important political speech.[1] When he was presented to the Emperor, the latter exclaimed, according to Hay's diary, September 30, 1866: "But you are very young to be a Col-o-nel. Did you make the war in America?," and a few moments later the Empress betrayed a similar astonishment.[2]

"Hay is a bright, gifted young man, with agreeable manners and refined tastes," wrote Thurlow Weed to Bigelow.[3] "I don't believe that he has been spoiled, though he has been exposed. If he remains the modest young man he was, I am *sure* you will like him."

John Hay, almost uniformly fortunate in his friends, was never more so than in Paris. John Bigelow, graduate of Union College and close friend of William H. Seward, also a Union graduate, after twenty-five years in newspaper work, was his chief. Bigelow had been made consul general in Paris in 1861 because of his journalistic experience, for Seward wished to employ him in France as propagandist for the Union cause. Upon the death of William L. Dayton, December 1, 1864, Bigelow succeeded him as Chargé d'Affaires, and later as Minister. He was just the sort of man to understand and appreciate Hay, and Mrs. Bigelow also took him in. He became as one of the family, and the Bigelow children, like Robert Lincoln, came to regard him in the light

---

[1] *Plain Dealer*, August 2, 1880.
[2] *Letters and Diaries*, I, 267–69.
[3] Bigelow's *Retrospections*, II, p. 521.

of an elder brother. Bigelow could teach the young man the technique of diplomacy, but more important, he could guide him toward the literary work which he followed subsequently with so much success. Quite likely Seward had this in mind when he sent Hay to Paris.

In the latter part of 1866 John A. Dix of New York replaced Bigelow, and although the former expressed a wish that Hay remain as secretary of the legation, the young man was already restless again, and decided to return to America, where he arrived in January, after a service of about eighteen months. His duties had not been onerous, far less important than his previous assignments at the White House. There had been ample time to revel in the experiences of life abroad. Stimulated by the contact with new scenes, and encouraged by Bigelow, he had commenced in earnest his literary work, and, when he began to publish four years later, it was found that some of his best verse had been written in Paris.

The resignation of Bigelow brought Hay up with a sharp turn; he began to think seriously of a vocation for life. To his uncle Milton, now just established in a new partnership for the practice of law, he drafted a letter, September 30, 1866, clearly stating his case.

I believe I have got as much out of this place as there is to be got by me. I have lived within my means and have learned French and the machinery and mechanism of the Diplomatic service. I have still on hand a few hundred dollars that I think I can profitably use by going to Germany and setting down quietly somewhere to study German for a few months.

I write now to ask you whether you want me, and how much you think my work would be worth, to begin with. I can of course make more money for the next few years by staying in the east and picking up odd jobs. The magazines and newspapers began to pay me decent prices before I stopped writing. But I am getting too old to be drifting about much longer. I want some steady employment. I could get anything reasonable I asked for in Washington but I would rather not hold any more offices if I can help it.

I am not conceited about my value to you. I know very well I should be worth very little. I have forgotten most of the law I read with you and would have to learn it all over again. I am not even a good clerk as I know very little about money or business. It is nearly an even chance whether I would ever get to be worth my salt at the bar, but I feel like trying it on.[1]

[1] This letter is quoted from a draft in pencil, found in John Hay's papers. It is given without change as an interesting study of Hay's literary composition at that time. No doubt the letter was corrected both as to style and punctuation before it was sent. When compared with others, addressed to such friends as Bigelow and Seward, and published in Bigelow's *Retrospections*, it is apparent that Hay's gift of literary expression, far from being perfectly spontaneous, was the result of careful rewriting and polishing. His early

A fine letter, from a modest young man whose head had not been turned by life under very favorable conditions in two capitals of the world. An underlying vein of common sense comes out clearly. But Uncle Milton could offer no encouragement. The new law firm of Hay and Palmer was just getting under way, and there was in it no place for a third lawyer who knew so little law. John Hay arrived in New York in a period of financial depression, and without prospects of employment any more definite than when he had started home from college nine years earlier.

Viewed in retrospect, the decade following the Civil War offered young men extraordinary opportunities to make their starts in life. New chapters were being opened in every phase of national development. Industry, under the impetus of the war and the Morrell tariff, was adopting new methods and expanding in an unparalleled manner. The homestead law of 1862, administered by an indulgent and not always honest government, was opening up in the West enormous areas which are now studded with rich cities. The demand for metals promoted the development of mines. Transportation, also encouraged by an indulgent government, was extending itself in new ways and into vast new fields. The tides of a mighty European immigration were beginning to flow in. The swelling population called for the improvising of a multitude of new forms of human organization which beckoned young men to such opportunities for wealth and fame as the world had never known before.

Many of Hay's contemporaries saw the opportunities and seized them. Iron and steel offered their rewards to Carnegie and his associates; transportation called the younger Charles Francis Adams, Chauncey M. Depew, Pullman, and a host of men with whom Hay was subsequently thrown; journalism provided careers for Reid and Watterson; publishing, for Holt and Putnam; the opportunities in law and finance were without number. As one views it now, it was a glorious time to be alive.

Government service also was alluring, but the prospects were in fact more specious. In the next generation a good war record was the best possible introduction to public office, but the bright rewards were usu-

---

discipline in rhetoric and composition had been obviously sketchy. To the end of his days he had trouble with "will" and "shall," with relative pronouns, and even with forms of the double negative involving "only."

ally for those who sought election rather than appointment. The difficulties in appointive office lay not merely in the "spoils system," which in the unbroken succession of Republican administrations came to be a struggle for office by warring factions within the party, but also in the unwillingness to recognize the need for expert service in government. The age of specialization had not come and it was assumed that there was nothing so peculiar to government work that it could not be learned by a new appointee in a few days. As the armies were disbanded there was a rush on Washington for government jobs and in the following three decades there were no greater tragedies than those of the men who had slipped out of the army into civilian positions, only to find their livelihood always precarious and threatened, while their minds were hardening to dull routine and losing the spirit for adventure.

John Hay was not the kind of a man to go out and wrestle with political life as McKinley, Cannon, Cullom, Foraker, and Hanna did. It is doubtful whether in all his years he ever slapped a man on the back. Hay was not a politician and, in spite of his origins, not a pioneer. Perhaps it would have been the making of him had he been forced out into the world for a few years to toughen himself with tasks which he would not have liked, but one doubts.

John Hay played for a few weeks with the idea of seeking outside the government a permanent position, a career. His friends in New York had made millions while he had been away, but now they had lost them, and there was no encouragement to be had in the metropolis.

In Washington the situation was a little better, for the claims-agent business had been thriving as the loose ends of the war were being gathered up. Lamon was getting rich, Cox had made a fortune, Eames had built a "palatial residence" at the corner of H and Fourteenth Streets. Hay was offered a partnership in a law firm which specialized in claims, and took the offer under advisement but five months later rejected the idea. "I have great distaste to the life of a claims agent in the Federal City," he wrote in his diary, June 3, 1867, "where my associations have been so different." Put it down also to his great credit that he did not allow himself to fall a victim to some unscrupulous adventurer who might have been willing to pay Hay well for the mantle of his respectability as a disguise for the crooked ways which made such a stench in the nation's capital in the next ten years. A less wary, less careful young man might easily have ruined his life at this time.

Hay gravitated back to the Department of State. The government was, after all, a sure paymaster and while it might never pay richly, it was likely to offer the young man a better position, and more remuneration to begin with, than private business could afford. Furthermore, in Seward, Hay still had a friend at court. The Secretary, however, sized up the situation and improved the opportunity to give Hay some very fatherly advice. As the latter described it in a letter to Nicolay: "He went into a long and very clever disquisition on the dangers of a man holding office—the desiccating and fossilizing process—illustrating it by Mr. Hunter [1] and saying that he feared Nicolay was getting into the same way. I assured him that Nicolay was not; that he was single-heartedly pursuing 10,000 dollars, and that when he got it he would come home and go to his ranch."

Hay did not miss the point of the admonition. He knew that Seward was right, but money was running low and the young man needed a job. The Secretary displayed no lack of good will and even somewhat jocularly suggested the position of minister to Sweden as a suitable opening. This was promptly claimed for some one else, but there remained the possibility that the Senate would fail to confirm the appointment of Dix to Paris, thus creating a vacancy which Hay might fill as Chargé d'Affaires. It must have chagrined Hay to discover that he had now joined the "horde of office-seekers" which he, as Lincoln's secretary, had formerly viewed with so much disgust. One by one the prospects faded.

"I start West today," he wrote March 5, 1867. "Dix is confirmed and I bid farewell to diplomacy. I have received three fair offers in business. I shall not decide for a month." He was already drawing on his scant savings.

"Poverty everywhere," he wrote from Warsaw, March 18. "In the East it is still tempered by the fever of speculation. But in the West everything and everybody is flat as a buckwheat cake, *de la veille.* There is no money and no business. One endless Sunday seems to gloom over all the little towns you pass. A man can live for *almost* nothing here. But he just misses that, and he makes nothing." He tried to sell his Florida land, but there were no purchasers. With Munroe

[1] William Hunter entered the Department of State in 1829 as a clerk. In 1855, for a few weeks, he was made Assistant Secretary of State, and then resumed his position as Chief Clerk, where he remained until 1866 when he was appointed Second Assistant Secretary of State. He died in office in 1886. Alvey A. Adee became his worthy successor.

and Company, New York bankers with an office in Paris, he had had some previous conversation about employment, but now that offer was withdrawn.

"I am settling so quietly into my aimless life here," he wrote Mrs. John Bigelow on April 21, 1867, "that I think I shall remain a good while. It is so easy to do nothing—to ride through the green plains and over the magnificent hills—to sleep soundly and dream little—to eat and drink, to watch my apple trees and my grape vines growing, and to make the most serious part of my day's work the reading of the Chicago paper of the day before! Everybody is so poor and so idle—in vague anticipation of a great crash coming—that I feel quite at home among them. I have no money—but I could not spend any if I had it. I never so fully appreciated the folly of the bees, who make more honey than they can eat, wasting in that useless way the pleasant summer."

"No, I have not written any verses," he added a month later to Mrs. Bigelow. "I go to work early in the morning, and go to sleep early in the evening. So, though the whole day is my own, I have no time. I have received invitations from several colleges in the East to make their annual poems. I have declined them all. I am not quite sure in my own mind whether it was because I was too poor to pay my railway fare, or too lazy to write. It is a curious question." [1]

Then, unexpectedly, came the indignant resignation of John Lothrop Motley as minister at Vienna. Seward would have patched up the situation, but the President insisted upon making of Motley a "high-priced martyr," as Hay described him. That left at Seward's disposal a vacancy of the grade for which Hay's previous experience fitted him. He was immediately offered an appointment as Secretary of Legation, which was no better than the position from which he had resigned at Paris. However, in the absence of a minister, Hay was to act as Chargé d'Affaires *ad interim,* and as such was entitled to $6,000, half the salary of a minister. Hay had the persistent luck to land on his feet. He sailed for his post June 29, 1867.

At Vienna he found practically nothing to do. Indeed, Seward appears to have intimated to him before his departure that frequent despatches were neither expected nor desired. Nominally, Hay was in the Austrian capital just a year, but he found time to tour from Warsaw to Constantinople, and he spent two months in the Alps. He devoted

---

[1] Copies of these letters were supplied by the late Miss Grace Bigelow.

himself assiduously to perfecting his German, while neglecting neither the galleries nor the music. So successfully did he learn to take his duties lightly that upon his return he concluded his mission with an expense account which claimed forty-eight days in transit, a fact which troubled the Fifth Auditor of the Treasury, but which Hay had no difficulty in explaining to Seward's complete satisfaction. The Vienna assignment was little less than one long holiday, of which Hay did not waste an hour. Office-holding was becoming more and more sweet.

On his return from Vienna he could not refrain from going again to Washington, but with diminishing success. To Nicolay he wrote, December 8, 1869: "I . . . came to Washington in the peaceful pursuit of a fat office. But there is nothing now available. I go back to the West tonight a broken-down politician. The Secretary says he will keep his weather eye open for me, and 'wrastle' with Andy for anything that turns up." Nothing is likely to turn up in the closing days of an Administration, but no sooner had Grant been inaugurated than Hay, now an earnest suppliant for office, began again. Seward was gone and Hay was reduced to the procedure of writing to Senators. One of these pleas was addressed to Sumner, at whom in other days he had been inclined to poke fun. He wrote: [1]

"I am an applicant for the mission to Portugal.

"I admit that I have no political *claims* to urge. I think my studies and experience have given me some qualifications. Mr. Seward twice presented my name to Mr. Johnson for a mission—but the President preferred some one who made personal court to him."

The appeal was in vain. In May he made a hurried visit to New York and Washington, but with no better immediate results. "You will find Washington intolerable," he informed Nicolay, May 14, 1869. "I have been here one day. I am sure that by hanging around and eating dirt, I could get some office. But my stomach revolts. It is almost too great a strain of a man's self-respect to *ask* for an office; still worse to beg for it.

"I thank God today that I am independent in my poverty and capacity of content with little."

Meanwhile the *Illinois State Journal* in Springfield offered him the editorship. "I will make a stagger at it this summer and see what I can make of it. I assume the scissors on Monday morning next."

[1] March 13, 1869; Sumner Papers

Within a month after entering the *Journal* office the new editor was made Secretary of Legation at Madrid. There was a difference between $6,000 in Austria the year before and $1,800 in Spain, but the newspaper salary was probably still more meagre. He lost no time in debate over whether it was better to stay and fight it out with himself in Illinois: on July 29 he took up his duties in Madrid.

"I have determined, *malgré* my better judgment," he wrote to Bigelow,[1] "to go to Spain for a little while. I have read and thought a good deal about revolutions, and I cannot resist an opportunity so favorable of lifting the very pot lid and seeing the 'hellbroth seethe and bubble.' I submit to all your reproaches—agree in advance that I am an idiot for going—but go. The ease with which I slip my newspaper cable, answers several of your questions. . . .

"(This in confidence), I shall not be gone more than a year at the utmost. I must get settled some time. I have some debts also, and cannot postpone seeking some gainful employment more than a year longer."

The threatened revolution, like most such disturbances in Spain, petered out, but it was a lost cause which had Hay's lively sympathy. Following the mutiny at Cadiz in 1868, and the flight of Queen Isabella, a constituent Cortes was assembled in February, 1869, but the Republicans under Castelar were hopelessly in the minority. Although sporadic revolts continued for more than a year, Hay was not to witness any triumph of republican principles. With thinly veiled eagerness, he hailed each new disturbance and in *Castilian Days*, written while there and published in 1871, he was reluctant to admit that his faith had been misplaced.

General Daniel E. Sickles, under whom he served, is a somewhat tarnished figure in American history, but Hay accepted his leadership, admired his ability, and shared his views on the only question of major importance touching American interests which the Legation was required to handle, the contemporaneous revolution in Cuba.

The Spanish Government, embarrassed and disorganized, made poor headway in quieting the disturbances in Cuba. The situation, in its relation to the United States, had many parallels with that in 1898. There was some damage to American interests, some filibustering, a vigorous propaganda in New York in favor of Cuban independence, and a wide-

[1] Bigelow, *Retrospections*, IV, pp. 294–95.

spread desire that the American government recognize the belligerency of the insurgents. A large number of Congressmen favored such a course and the President was known to be sympathetic. Some would have gone much further. The purchase of Alaska, just consummated, suggested that Cuba, also, might be purchased, or, if not purchased, then acquired by other means: the spirit of the Ostend Manifesto was still lively. This undercurrent of popular feeling presented the utmost difficulty to Grant's able Secretary of State, Hamilton Fish. The American government had already agreed to arbitrate with England the claims arising out of the Civil War, and was resting its case, in part, on the assertion that Great Britain should not have recognized the belligerency of the Southern Confederacy. The United States would have been in an awkward position at Geneva, if it had appeared there just after granting recognition to the Cuban insurgents. Sickles and Hay were plainly in sympathy with the radicals at home and felt encouraged, at first, to believe that the sale of the island to the United States might be effected with Spanish approval. They could not have been very helpful to the harassed Fish.

"Our State Department is a failure, *selon moi*," wrote Hay to Nicolay, October 7, 1869. "Vacillation and fuzziness seem to trail over everything it does." Hay failed to grasp that the Secretary of State was quietly laying the foundation for a structure of understanding between the English-speaking nations, which, a generation later, Hay took such pleasure, as Ambassador and as Secretary of State, in completing. Happily Fish held steady the ship of state, in spite of Congress, in spite, even, of the President himself. The revolution in Cuba continued. Hay came home in September, 1870, but in London in 1897–98, he must have seen some telegrams which were strangely reminiscent of the despatches he had helped to draft in Madrid twenty-nine years before.

Obviously, John Hay was still too young for great responsibilities. His service abroad was important not for its contributions to American history, but as a part of the training of a future Secretary of State. Its immediate significance in his personal development was that it culminated in an intellectual awakening which he had missed in college, and which he had also failed to receive in the White House.

"For the first time since I can remember," he wrote to Miss Harriet B. Loring, from Madrid, June 10, 1870, "I have been busy this year, and it does not suit my complexion. There is a great deal to do in the

Legation, and I have imposed a good deal of work upon myself besides having gotten interested in Spanish History. I have a veritable worship for the fellows who know things. I cannot conceive how a man like Mr. Motley should have preferred England with its pitiful annoyances, to Austria with its quiet and its archives. I should like to read about twenty years. The first ten would be necessary to reach the proper point of humility, and then, at last one might hope to gain something substantial."

Another letter of this period, reclaimed from his letterpress copybook, but with no certain clue as to the lady addressed, discloses another phase of his development. The writer never wholly lost the contempt here expressed for "New York society," even after he had been given so many opportunities to know it better. If a New York society belle of the eighteen seventies required a spanking, behold at least one way in which it was actually done. To the lady, now unknown, Hay wrote: [1]

I believe on second thought I will write to you and not to ——. You say he is out of danger. You are not.

I do not pretend that I understand you. You are too clever to wear your heart on your sleeve. Of your set of fashionable New York girls you are the cleverest—easily the cleverest, I have ever seen. You have beauty enough to be a first rate belle, if you had less wit. Perhaps you are; I know so little of New York. If so, there is no hope for you. But it seems to me that you are too young and in too perfect health to be a belle just yet. There may be time for repentance, before you reach that dreadful eminence.

I had a very different idea of you. —— talked incessantly about you but he gave me no impression of your cleverness. You were the nicest, brightest, prettiest, jolliest, and various high colored superlatives like that. Is it possible that he never knew you, or have you changed so wonderfully in a year?

Do you ever think of measuring yourself in comparison with others? Do you know you have something of the goddess about you? A Venus, not the gay goddess of fable, but the severe and magnificent Lady of Milo. The ancients called her the Laughter-loving—that is all they knew about it. You are witty, but you are not hearty and cordial. Your wit is as cold as an icicle.

When one thinks of what you should be—are there words strong enough to condemn New York society? With your natural gifts and advantages, every hour of your life ought to be a delight to yourself and to those around you. And you are bored from the rising of the sun to the going down of the same. You are restless as a young eagle. You carry a critical mind and a vacant heart

[1] To F. S., April 13, 1870; Madrid Letters, p. 149.

Secretary Marcy, by his famous order, had sought to enforce upon American diplomats abroad the simple garb of commoners, but very many of the appointments went to men of military rank, thus permitting military dress on ceremonial occasions. John Hay as Chargé d'Affaires *ad interim* in Vienna, in 1867, wore a colonel's uniform.

Before John Hay was thirty-five years of age he had achieved sufficient distinction as a public lecturer to be included in this group of notable Lyceum speakers. The names, corresponding to the numbers, are: 1. T. DeWitt Talmage; 2. E. Yates; 3. "Eli Perkins"; 4. "Josh Billings"; 5. W. H. H. Murray; 6. James T. Fields; 7. Theodore Tilton; 8. John Hay; 9. Bret Harte; 10. Mrs. Scott Siddons; 11. "Mark Twain"; 12. "Petroleum V. Nasby"; 13. Carl Schurz; 14. J. M. Bellew; 15. Rev. Henry B. Chapin; 16. Miss Charlotte Cushman; 17. Miss Edgarton; 18. Harriet Beecher Stowe.

through what should be a keen and lively joy to a woman of sixty. Mrs. ——,
who might be your grandmother, enjoys life more than you do. I believed you
when you said you did not care for conquests. The exhibition of your own
power has ceased to interest you much.

And this is success. Nobody speaks of you without some expression of admiration. I heard of you all over Europe and the nicest people spoke best of
you.

I wish you were as thoroughly happy as you ought to be. You could be
very easily. A little sympathy with nature and with your race is all you need,
your youth and health would do the rest. Most people say contentment is happiness but that is simply begging the question. How are we to be contented?
It is not religion that will accomplish it. "He prayeth best, who loveth best, all
things both great and small."

I know you are clever enough to see that this letter is not impertinent:
That it is the expression of sincere—I will not say friendship, but admiration.
I have confidence in your honor. I know how ridiculous this letter would seem
if read by any one but you. I ask—as one man of honor might ask of another—
that you will put it in an envelope and send it back to me as soon as you have
read it. Do this—and I will have a better opinion of the world in general.

I have written because I had this to say, and did not have the audacity to
say it. I was afraid either of being crushed by your superb anger or ex-
tinguished by your sourire moquer half sarcasm and half ennui.

Upon which, as we Spaniards say, I kiss your feet, and may your Grace
go with God.

Possessed of a purpose more serious than the mere urge to earn a
living, Hay came home with the desire to become a writer. Upon arrival in New York, he did not, as before, hurry to Washington, where
now ruled those who knew not Joseph. At the age of thirty-two, he was
not, and was never likely to be, one of those stalwart souls who can
seize the nearest weapon and rough-hew a destiny. In one of his poems,
soon to be published, there were the lines

> "for soon unhorsed I lay
> At the feet of the strong god Circumstance." [1]

While Hay was well equipt to take advantage of such fortune as circumstance might bring, he was not the master of his mount. He was
easily unhorsed and inclined to see events as a series of accidents. But
life was closing in on him and demanding inexorably that he, like other
mortals, find a niche and fit himself into it, even at the cost of some

[1] "Una." *Complete Poetical Works*, p. 173.

discomfort. The credit drawn from having once been Lincoln's secretary being now temporarily exhausted, John Hay was, for the first time in his life, on his own resources. It was to become a productive experience.

MILTON HAY, his uncle, had not needed him in his law office; Munroe and Company had not wanted him in the bank; the *Illinois State Journal* at Springfield had not been seriously incommoded when he left so suddenly for Madrid in 1869; there had even been an element of uncertainty about the initial employment on the *Tribune* which began in 1870.[1] Then, suddenly, in 1871, fame and prosperity.

In that one year, Hay appeared five times in the *Atlantic*, once in *Harper's Monthly*, and six times in *Harper's Weekly*. "Little Breeches" was published in the *Daily Tribune*, November 19, 1870; "Jim Bludso" appeared first on January 6, 1871, in the semi-weekly *Tribune*. They ran like wild-fire over the country, copied and recopied from coast to coast. A pamphlet of these ballads, selling at twenty-five cents, was rushed through the press to meet an insistent demand. The pamphlet was followed closely by *Pike County Ballads and Other Pieces*, one hundred and sixty-seven pages of verse, and this, in turn, carried the publisher's announcement that *Castilian Days*, by the same author, was soon to be published. Before the end of the year many of his poems had appeared in an English edition. Within ten months Hay's literary fame, rising from complete obscurity, reached its zenith. By the end of 1871 his name was probably known to as many people in the United States and abroad as in 1897 when he was appointed Ambassador to the Court of St. James's. A brilliant young man.

To his friends the success was not unexpected. This literary talent, evident in college days, had been finding occasional expression for a decade. Hay had won his first recognition by the *Atlantic* with the Ellsworth sketch in 1861.[2] The article had been accepted hurriedly and bore witness to the desire of the *Atlantic* to "do its bit" more than to the literary excellence of the essay; yet for Hay it was recognition. Three years later *Harper's Magazine*, June, 1864, published "Northward," one of his few war poems, and in October, 1865, the same magazine carried "The Monks of Basle." This poem revealed a line of thought which frequently recurred in both his verse and his prose:

[1] See Chapter VIII, "New York and Journalism."
[2] p. 41.

So goes the tale of the monkish books,
The moral who runs may read,—
He has no ears for Nature's voice
Whose soul is the slave of creed.

Not all in vain with beauty and love
Has God the world adorned;
And who Nature scorns and mocks,
By Nature is mocked and scorned.

During the long months of waiting after his return from Vienna and before the appointment to Spain, Hay had been busy with his pen. One result was "The Foster Brothers," a short story laid in Warsaw (called Moscow in the story), with a slavery background. It appeared in *Harper's Monthly,* September, 1869. "Down the Danube," a travelogue with some slight political comment, was published in *Putnam's,* June, 1870, as the leading article. His second appearance in the *Atlantic* had been in December, 1869, with "The Mormon Prophet's Tragedy," his best prose up to that time. It was an account of the so-called Mormon War of 1844, which was limited largely to Hancock County, Illinois. A hastily recruited regiment, Hay's father acting as surgeon, had marched on Nauvoo, and, although officially disbanded by Governor Ford, had assassinated Joseph Smith in the jail at Carthage. Smith's "robust profligacy" was reviled and "his fellow blackguards" were not neglected, while the ensuing jury trial in Warsaw, resulting in a verdict of "not guilty" for the leaders of the mob, was related in vivid detail. William Dean Howells, in a review of Hay's literary work after the latter's death, found in the Mormon article an intimation of the coming Pike County Ballads. It was a vivid portrayal of the Western frontiersmen and the grotesque situations in which they were prone to place themselves.[1]

A mind, fertilized for many years, now brought into contact with other minds in the atmosphere of a metropolis, gathering confidence from each new success, had come into fruition. It seemed as though, in 1871, John Hay had found his place. Although it was hardly equal to Mark Twain's, no other writer who passed through the *Tribune* office in those days could claim any single literary year such as had come to this young man who a few months earlier, out of a job and in debt, began to peddle his wares.

[1] "John Hay in Literature," *North American Review,* September, 1905, pp. 343 ff.

Hay's poetry, as well as his prose, of this period divides itself easily into two classes. On one side are the subjects and passages which are characterized primarily by esthetic appreciation; on the other side are those in which the author appears as a social or political moralist.

Whether on the bank of his beloved river or standing in the galleries of Madrid, John Hay had the sentiments of a poet. He had a rare feeling for color, but what is at least as uncommon, for light and shade. He could catch the sparkle of the sunlight, as for example, in the almost forgotten "On the Bluff," where mood and scene are perfectly blended:

> O grandly flowing River!
> O silver gliding River!
> Thy springing willows shiver
>   In the sunset as of old;
> They shiver in the silence
> Of the willow-whitened islands,
> While the sun-bars and the sand-bars
>   Fill air and wave with gold.
>
> O gay, oblivious River!
> O sunset-kindled River!
> Do you remember ever
>   The eyes and skies so blue
> On a summer day that shone here,
> When we were all alone here,
> And the blue eyes were too wise
>   To speak the love they knew?
>
> O stern impassive River!
> O still unanswering River!
> The shivering willows quiver
>   As the night-winds moan and rave.
> From the past a voice is calling,
> From heaven a star is falling,
> And dew swells in the bluebells
>   Above her hillside grave.[1]

By way of introduction to the Royal Museum in Madrid, he wrote in "An Hour with the Painters": [2]

"If one knew he was to be blind in a year, like the young musician in Auerbach's exquisite romance, I know of no place in the world where

[1] This was set to music and published by William A. Pond & Co. Copyrighted in 1874.
[2] *Castilian Days*, p. 129.

he could garner up so precious a store of memories for the days of darkness, memories that would haunt the soul with so divine a light of consolation, as in that graceful Palace of the Prado." Before Murillo's "Holy Family" and his "Virgin," hanging side by side, he could burst into colorful prose:

The Word was made Flesh, and not a phosphorescent apparition; and Murillo knew what he was about when he painted this view of the interior of St. Joseph's shop. What absurd presumption to accuse this great thinker of a deficiency of ideality, in the face of these two glorious Marys of the Conception that fill the room with light and majesty! They hang side by side, so alike and yet so distinct in character. One is a woman in knowledge and a goddess of purity; the other, absolute innocence, startled by the stupendous revelation and exalted by the vaguely comprehended glory of the future. It is before this picture that the visitor always lingers longest. The face is the purest expression of girlish loveliness possible to art. The Virgin floats upborne by rosy clouds, flocks of pink cherubs flutter at her feet waving palm-branches. The golden air is thick with suggestions of dim celestial faces, but nothing mars the imposing solitude of the Queen of Heaven, shrined alone, throned in the luminous azure. Surely no man ever understood or interpreted like this grand Andalusian the power that the worship of woman exerts on the religions of the world. All the passionate love that has been poured out in all the ages at the feet of Ashtaroth and Artemis and Aphrodite and Freya found visible form and color at last on that immortal canvas where, with his fervor of religion and the full strength of his virile devotion to beauty, he created, for the adoration of those who should follow him, this type of the perfect Feminine,—

"Thee! standing loveliest in the open heaven!
Ave Maria! only heaven and Thee!"

While Hay's poems having woman for a theme are quite conventional, they have sincere feeling. The reviewer of his verses, in the *Tribune,* May 31, 1871, obviously a friend, reprinted "Una" and remarked: "A more touching picture of exquisite womanhood, and of the tragic element in human love, has rarely been presented by poetic art than is found in the sadly sweet flow of these verses." They begin:

In the whole wide world there was but one,
Others for others, but she was mine,
The one fair woman beneath the sun.

The poet's subsequent choice to be novelist, historian and statesman does not permit us to dwell exclusively, or even primarily, upon his esthetic sense, although one might argue that it was the truest side of his many-sided nature.[1]

If we may judge from his verse, and his letters confirm the impression, all of Hay's earlier years were filled with emotional tumult. A Puritan sense of ought disturbed his fantasies. It demanded that he conform, that he do the conventional thing, that he go out and measure his strength against his fellows, that he "amount to something." Conscience was at war with feeling. In time he made peace with himself by making concessions to what the wholly consecrated artist regards as worldly standards. Otherwise he might have been a poet; as it was, he became a minister of foreign affairs. What the struggle cost him no one knew, but that it nearly tore him to pieces in his earlier years there can be no doubt. "God send me tears!" he wrote in "Lagrimas,"

> Loose the fierce band that binds my tired brain,
> Give me the melting heart of other years,
>   And let me weep again!
>
>   .   .   .
>
> In life's high noon
> Aimless I stand, my promised task undone,
> And raise my hot eyes to the angry sun
>   That will go down too soon.

Another aspect of this conflict was the desire to set the world right, to preach. Scornfully in 1858 he had rejected the idea of preaching, yet preacher he was, in spite of himself. While the issues of the Civil War do not appear to have stirred him very deeply, and while his distinctly war poems never reached high, and many of them dropped to the level of doggerel, with other themes, such as "God's Vengeance," Hay became a veritable Peter the Hermit. This poem is alleged to have been inspired by Lincoln's assassination. He cried, angrily:

> Sleep not in imbecile trust
>   Waiting for God to begin,
> While growing strong in the dust,
>   Rests the bruised serpent of sin.

The same mood finds even more vigorous expression in "Thy Will Be Done," which first appeared in *Harper's Magazine*, October, 1891. The poem was later picked up for inclusion in many church hymnals.[2]

---

[1] "He is an example," wrote William Rose Benét (*Poems of Youth: An American Anthology*, p. 151), "of the mind that found government service and emoluments worth more than the exercise of his true literary gift which he always seems to have distrusted."

[2] For example, *Hymns for the Living Age*, ed. by H. Augustine Smith, p. 285. This poem

When Tyrant feet are trampling
   Upon the common weal,
Thou dost not bid us bend and writhe
   Beneath the iron heel.
In Thy name we assert our right
   By sword or tongue or pen,
And even the headsman's axe may flash
   Thy message unto men.

Such incitement was too stern even for the Church to accept unmodified and in the hymn, as it now appears, the next to the last line, a metrically defective one, has been changed to read: "And oft a people's wrath may flash." When Hay was in such moods he was lighted by the indignation of the reformer, whom at all other times he abhorred.[1]

"In all his literary work," wrote Howells,[2] "Hay was prevalently a moralist." This is a startling generalization, especially when one recalls Hay's own protest that he did not like to meddle with moral ills. The statement is, however, profoundly true, and, once pointed out, jumps at one from page after page of both his verse and his prose.

This hortatory quality appears in such verse as "The Sphinx of the Tuileries," where Hay paid his respect to Napoleon III as "charlatan," "beast," "craven cur," "bastard sphinx," and closed with the lines:

The people will come to their own at last,—
   God is not mocked forever.

In more gently flowing measures, touched by a finer imagination, the same faith in the people appears in "The Prayer of the Romans."

Let the People come to their birthright,
   And crosier and crown pass away
Like phantasms that flit o'er the marshes
   At the glance of the clean, white day.
And then from the lava of Aetna
   To the ice of the Alps let there be
One freedom, one faith without fetters,
   One republic in Italy free!

was not included in the 1899 edition of the author's *Poems,* nor does it seem to have been reprinted exactly as he wrote it until 1916 when Clarence L. Hay included it in *The Complete Poetical Works of John Hay.*

[1] "I have never met a reformer who had not the heart of a tyrant," he wrote to Edmund Clarence Stedman, August 13, 1881. "Boundless conceit and moral selfishness seem the necessary baggage of the professional lover of liberty."

[2] *Op. cit.*

Hay preferred to derive his poetical fame from such poems as have been cited above, rather than from the Pike County Ballads, which have always been, and always will be, his best known verse. The latter were his only lapse into anything approaching the vulgarity of the river-town where his parents lived. Perhaps he was frightened to realize the degree to which that life had laid hold on him, for the authenticity of these ballads is their outstanding quality. Here was a voice raised from southern Illinois, the home of the Clary Grove boys and of many a purple story, the home also of Lincoln. Hay himself liked to remember the "grandly flowing river," and the rolling prairie, the waving woodlands, where nature had been lavish with color and light, when, suddenly, there leapt to his lips these ballads of human life on the frontier. The life shocked him but the truth of it was irresistible. He found there also a sincerity and a hatred of sham in marked contrast to monarchical Europe from which his soul had turned with loathing. By the side of his portrait of Napoleon III he placed Jim Bludso. Still the poet was the preacher. Jim may have had "one wife in Natches-under-the-hill, and another one here, in Pike," but

> Christ ain't a going to be too hard
> On a man that died for men.

As for the angels and "Little Breeches,"

> I think that saving a little child,
> And fetching him to his own,
> Is a derned sight better business
> Than loafing around the Throne.

An old-fashioned scrap-book, in the possession of his son, still preserves not only the reviews but also the editorials from periodicals, secular and religious, and from some hundreds of newspapers. The ballads were something upon which every one was expected to take sides and argue. No author in America was ever more reviled by a conventionally minded public. Compared with "A Psalm of Life" and Watts' Hymns, "Jim Bludso" and "Little Breeches" were almost too shocking to be noticed and therefore every one was talking about them. They were the "Main Street" of their day. The creatures of John Hay's imagination were called dissolute and vulgar, and their language had been preserved in all its pristine coarseness. "This," cried an outraged culture, "is not literature."

In vain did Hay's old friend, Henry Watterson, come to his defense in the Louisville *Courier-Journal*. Hay would have preferred to have the ballads forgotten, but Watterson met the issue squarely.[1] He found a dash of Browning in the poems and ranked Hay with Whittier. " 'Jim Bludso' is in every way equal to 'Skipper Ireson's Ride,' and 'Little Breeches' is hardly inferior to 'Maud Muller.' In each the commonplace is made intensely dramatic." A few emancipated souls grasped the significance of the new themes and the new treatment, but the prevailing tone was that of the Hartford *Post:* "It is poor poetry, foolish argument, wretched logic, and shameful theology."

The religious press, detecting a spiritual descendant of Tom Paine and an affinity of Robert Ingersoll, brought up its big guns. The *Congregationalist* declared that the ballads were "*not* humorous, and they are coarse. What is more, they are profane, or bordering on the profane, and aim to teach religious doctrine which many will be loath to receive." This paper, however, was candid enough to add: "We fear they are true." The Rev. Marvin R. Vincent, D.D., an eminent theologian of the day, discussed the theology of the ballads. He found it contrary to Scripture, and insinuated that John Hay should be regarded as a corrupter of youth.

"Mr. Hay's hero," deplored Vincent, "such is the plain inference, goes from his engine straight to Heaven. No true man can be insensible to an act of self-devotion, by whomsoever it may be wrought: but when admiration grows to such proportions as to obscure the simplest principles of Divine Justice; when it leads one to regard a single act, no matter how generous, as an offset to an unrepented life of debauchery —it goes beyond the bounds not only of Scripture, but of common-sense. . . . His single grand deed will no more insure him immortality of bliss than 'Little Breeches' will give Mr. Hay a place among the immortal masters of theology." The reviewer, however, neglected to add his own opinion as to just where Bludso's spirit did go.

The "blasphemy" of the last quatrain of "Little Breeches" was particularly offensive to popular taste: "loafing around the Throne." The act of worship thus described, denounced the Syracuse *Journal*, November 25, 1870, is a "prostitution of the mission of poetry. It is vulgar doggerel. Its inception was a low attempt at plagiarism; and though it may, for the moment, catch the popular ear, it will speedily meet the

[1] *Courier-Journal,* May 9, 1871.

fate of plagiarism. Had it first appeared in some of the sensation papers, now published to gratify depraved tastes, we very much doubt whether a respectable newspaper could have been found ready to lift it up before the eyes of their readers; and yet the *Tribune* gave it a prominence which it in no wise deserved. But every friend of true literature, and every lover of true poetry will protest against this degradation of poetical composition." The last lines of "Little Breeches" were pronounced "presumptuous blasphemy." [1]

A critic in *Scribner's*, August, 1871, warned Hay against "mounting the pulpit." If the moral to be pointed was that in every sinner there is something good, all very well, but "for the doctrine that one virtue can compensate for the absence of another—that bigamy can be condoned by bravery, or infidelity to one's wife by fidelity to one's business—we have only horror and disgust. . . . If that is the doctrine of the last stanza of Jim Bludso (as perhaps the popular reader may easily enough have imagined) then it is simply mischievous and odious."

James Redpath expressed the prevailing mood in a rhyme which he called "The New Evangel," making Harte equally the target of his sarcasm.

> This is the day of Skimpton and Bludso,
>   This is the day of the gambler unstained;
> Roughs are like Christ (St. John Hay has said so),
>   Pardon is now by stage thunder acts gained;
> You may murder or steal, keep a house of ill-fame,
>   And still go to Heaven—*if you only die game.*

Thus John Hay was again involved in the contradictions of his own nature. He was a conventional man, punctilious in dress, careful to observe even the trivial rules of society. He shunned extremes and devoted himself to respectability. He was sensitive to criticism and abhorred being made conspicuous. Now he was being publicly flayed, along with

---

[1] The reference to plagiarism is to a lively dispute as to whether Hay had not merely imitated Bret Harte, who was also developing the Pike theme. The debate persisted for more than thirty years. Mark Twain, among others of his friends, was eager to claim that Hay's verses were written first and that Harte drew his inspiration from Hay. See "John Hay and the Ballads," a letter to *Harper's Weekly*, October 21, 1905. The evidence is clear, nevertheless, that Harte, not Hay, was the first to publish a Pike theme, nor is there anything to show that Hay's verses were written long before they were printed. "Biglow Papers" had already revealed what could be done in such a style. Harte made some experiments as early as 1869, and quite possibly started Hay. The products, however, were fundamentally different, Hay's being far more veracious. "Jim Bludso" sprang straight from the soil where its author spent his boyhood.

Bret Harte, for his alleged coarseness and just escaping brackets with
Walt Whitman. Hay had no very firm conviction that he was right
when conventionality and respectability were leagued against him. The
criticism was therefore crushing. His perceptions were better than his
logic. Without much thought he had sensed a nascent popular rebellion
against conventional religious dogma and had blundered into the pulpit
with a few rhymes to which the theologians could not reply without
being ridiculous. He had also left the polite literary critics in confusion.
It was quite unintentional; probably he would have left the ballads unpublished if he had foreseen the immediate consequences. They were
not like the man he had decided to be, but "Little Breeches" has already appeared in at least twelve anthologies and Jim Bludso in
twenty-six.[1]

John Hay, at thirty-three, had within his grasp the leadership of the
new school of radicals in literature and thought. The iconoclastic note
of the ballads was in harmony with scorn of monarchical and ecclesiastical sham which ran through *Castilian Days*. Howells called it a "morality severe almost to austerity." The essays were a tract in favor of
republican government.[2]

"There is nothing we like better in his book," said the *Atlantic* reviewer, "than the very hearty tone of his democracy or—if Americanism is yet to mean something better than democracy—his Americanism. No fair-minded man can now look at any part of Europe, and not
be glad of America, in spite of New York; and Mr. Hay is above all
fair-minded."

Of invective John Hay was a master, and the twin despotism of
church and crown in Spanish history provided themes which made him
quiver with indignation. "Through all the vicissitudes of Spanish history," he wrote in the essay on the influence of tradition in Spanish life,
"the force of these married superstitions—reverence for the Church as
distinguished from the fear of God, and reverence for the King as distinguished from respect for law—have been the ruling characteristics
of the Spanish mind." In Philip II, Hay found a target equal to his
wrath. Of him he wrote:

---

[1] Compilation of Sister Saint Ignatius Ward, *The Poetry of John Hay*. A dissertation
submitted to the Catholic University of America, and published by that institution.
[2] *Harper's Magazine*, from June, 1872, intermittently until October, 1875, carried Emilio
Castelar's *The Republican Movement in Europe*. Hay was the translator who put these
articles into English.

Yet this horrible monster, who is blackened with every crime at which humanity shudders, who had no grace of manhood, no touch of humanity, no gleam of sympathy which could redeem the gloomy picture of his ravening life, was beloved and worshipped as few men have been since the world stood. The common people mourned him at his death with genuine unpaid sobs and tears. They will weep even yet at the story of his edifying death,—this monkish vampire breathing his last with his eyes fixed on the cross of the mild Nazarene, and tormented with impish doubts as to whether he had drunk blood enough to fit him for the company of the just!

The most illogical chapter in *Castilian Days* is the last, in which the author argued for the necessity of a republic. He reached his conclusion by a process of elimination, showing how neither an absolute nor a constitutional monarchy was likely to succeed. Predicating these failures, he took a mystical leap to the conclusion that the only alternative would be a republic. As to what might constitute successful government on Spain he was vague, but in one interesting paragraph he unfolded his unthinking faith in republicanism, as follows:

Comparisons drawn from the republics that have flourished and fallen are not altogether just. The condition of the world has greatly changed. We are nearing the close of the nineteenth century. The whole world, bound together in the solidarity of aspiration and interests by a vast publicity, by telegraphs and railways, is moving forward along all the line of nations to larger and ampler liberty. No junta of prominent gentlemen can come together and arrange a programme for a nation, in opposition to this universal tendency. It is too much for one to prophesy what will be the final result of this great movement. But it cannot well be checked. The people have a right to govern themselves, even if they will do it ill. If the republics of the present and future are to be transient, it is sure that monarchies can make no claim to permanence; and the republics of the past have always been marked by prodigious developments of genius and activity.

While never attaining a vogue equal to that of "Pike County Ballads," the essays were an immediate success and added to the author's increasing fame. The demand for the book persisted and nineteen years later it was reprinted. To this edition Hay added a note: "I have nothing to add to this little book. Reading it again after the lapse of many years, I find much that might be advantageously modified or omitted." Nevertheless the faults appeared to the author "immanent and structural"; they were those of youth. He begged for an "indulgent smile" for the "rapid judgments," the "hot prejudices," the "pitiless condemnations," and the "lyric eulogies." He pled that the essays were "born of an honest enthusiasm," unchecked by the reserve which comes with age and experience. While Hay was Secretary of State there was a new edition, illustrated by Joseph Pennell. It now seems amazing that Hay should have consented to the republication of a volume of comment on another country, the very authorship of which would today be sufficient to disqualify a man for appointment to the high office of foreign minister. The 1903 edition, however, contained a publisher's note stating that it had been thought desirable to omit a few chapters which were "less descriptive than the rest of the book, and not so rich in the picturesque material which the illustrator demands." The omissions included the political chapters: "A Field Night in the Cortes," "The Moral of Spanish Politics," "The Bourbon Duel," and "The Necessity for a Republic."

Even with the omission of the most objectionable chapters, the author did not entirely escape. On the eve of the Presidential election of 1904 a Roman Catholic editor in New York petitioned the Lenox Library to remove John Hay's poems and essays from its shelves, on the ground that the books were blasphemous and insulting to adherents of the Roman Catholic faith.[1] A pamphlet containing extracts from both prose and verse was distributed outside some of the Catholic churches the Sunday morning before election. A copy was sent to President Roosevelt, who turned it over to Hay. In returning it the Secretary wrote, November 3, 1904: "I certainly was a very stout and irresponsible Protestant and Republican in those days." He made no other comment. It is apparent, however, that if Hay had ever become a candidate for elective office he would have had to answer publicly some politically embarrassing questions.

Hay's literary success in 1871 created a lively demand for his appearance on the lyceum circuits where he won a success comparable with that in literature. An old lecture bureau advertising card is still preserved which shows his immature face in a galaxy with such popular idols as Wendell Phillips, Harriet Beecher Stowe, Horace Greeley, John B. Gough, Josh Billings, Petroleum V. Nasby, and Mark Twain. Hay had two popular lectures. One was "Phases of Washington Life, or The Heroic Age in America," which gathered about President Lincoln and the war years in the Capital. The other was "The Progress of Democracy in Europe." The former, according to the Chicago *Tribune*,

---

[1] Pamphlet of clippings in Rare Book Room of the New York Public Library.

revealed "something of the inner life of the great Lincoln, unspoken before in public, with such persuasiveness of oratory and finish of speech" that the audience was thrilled. The latter lecture was in the political vein of *Castilian Days*. It was a sympathetic review of the republican movement in Europe from the days of the French Revolution; "strongly in the interests of the struggling peoples of the old world," a Rochester paper stated. "Several portions of his lecture were relieved by vivid and earnest descriptions full of eloquence and power. This was especially the case in the powerful passage, in which he described the communists' leaders, who suffered death at the hands of the Versaillists, or subsequently by the decrees of the Thiers government." The lecturer on the platform was as severe on Napoleon III, "The Sphinx of the Tuileries," as he had been in verse and betrayed an almost equal distrust of Bismarck. "Mr. Hay has a good voice, a fine elocution, spirit and earnestness," commented another paper; "he can place his audience in sympathy with himself, and is altogether a good speaker."

Almost a radical for his day; but not quite. He had fractured literary conventions but he could not endure the pelting criticism. He had been deeply touched by the struggles of the oppressed masses in Europe, but he had thought about their problem only casually. He had no philosophy of life adequate to include the Ballads, and no political theory which embraced a remedy for Europe. He had been expressing moods rather than settled conclusions. He spoke as a poet, but not as a prophet, least of all as a reformer.

Hay had another mood which, in the end, proved to be more characteristic of the man. It was perfectly expressed in one of his conventional poems, "How It Happened":

"I believe we were meant to be gay."

This was his native impulse; "gay" was his favorite adjective. Gaiety and austerity; conventionality and radicalism: impossible combinations. He believed that men were meant to be gay, but in repeating the text he had sometimes to clench his teeth. He spoke the line grimly. If one could have stripped off the protective coloration which in society he cast about his soul, by which he made himself to appear gay when he was not, it would have been found that the gaiety had often been frustrated into melancholy. John Hay's successes were obvious; his failures were more subtle. He was unable to integrate the conflicting qualities of his mind and heart. He lacked the courage of a Loyola or a Xavier.

The underlying truth in the Ballads is that creeds fetter the spirit, that sham is stultifying, that love is the best part of life. It is often claimed that the Ballads were not like their author; at least not like what he desired to be. In so far as this is true it does not require much imagination to trace them to their source. They were fundamental characteristics of Abraham Lincoln, and so was the melancholy. How far the two men drew from a common well deep in the soil of Illinois, or how far the younger man, in his most plastic years, was shaped by intimate association with the more mature, and more courageous personality, one would not dare to say. Hay's native gaiety was the core; the other quality was laid on and the two were never perfectly fused. "Jim Bludso," in the facile words of John Hay, is the voice of Abraham Lincoln, the kind of story he would have liked to tell, the kind of a moral he would have liked to point. So likewise, is the next to the last line in "The Sphinx of the Tulieries,"

"The people will come to their own at last."

The same may be said for the last two sentences of the preface to the first edition of *Castilian Days:* "There are those who think the Spaniards are not fit for freedom. I believe that no people are fit for anything else."

One of the most thoughtful as well as sympathetic reviews of Hay's verse was by John G. Saxe, in the Albany *Evening Journal*. He wrote: "Of these poems it is but just to say that they are informed with the finest poetic feeling; that they are abundant in fresh and striking thought; that they are written with an ease which is not carelessness, and finished with an elegance which could only be imparted by a fine natural genius, improved by the grace of good scholarship." Saxe there added, hopefully: "Strong and hearty as are these words of praise, we cannot avoid the feeling that Mr. Hay has yet to write far better things than are to be found in this delightful book."

The promise was not fulfilled. Hay never wrote better verse than at the age of thirty-three. The personal quality which made Jim Bludso's name a household word throughout two nations escaped, for a time, the grasp of its creator. But not forever: after twenty-five years of aimless wandering in which there had been more anguish of heart than

Hay liked to confess, he at length caught up with the man who "seen his duty a dead sure thing, and went for it thar and then." At last John Hay found himself and wrote in life the better words which had so long eluded his pen.

A LODGE in the wilderness, in Florida, or, better still, a little place on
the bluff of his beloved river, a shelter where, living simply, he could be
quiet and write. John Hay in the tumult of the White House, and,
again amidst the sophistication of Vienna and Madrid, cherished this
Omaresque dream. In such a place he believed that he could be happy,
and, to realize his modest ambition, he had been exercising a thrift
which is not usually associated with the other qualities he displayed.
In Washington he saved a sum relatively large as compared with his
salary, and in 1864 he purchased an orange-grove in Florida.[1] The
same year he considered an investment in Kansas, but at length
decided on his boyhood home. "Land is getting up near the stars in
price," he wrote to Nicolay, August 25, 1864. "It will take all I am
worth to buy a tater-patch. I am after one or two small pieces in
Hancock for reasonable prices; 20 to 30 dollars an acre. . . . Everybody who has green-backs is forcing them off like waste paper for
land."

The purchase was effected and became a vineyard. No doubt it
satisfied his sense of the fitness of things that as a verse-maker he
should become a vineyard-keeper: ease, quiet, the beauty of the
sunlight, and freedom to write, or not to write, as the spirit might
impel. John Hay was a born free-lance.

"After I have accumulated a revenue of six hundred dollars a year
(a point I am rapidly approaching)," he wrote soon after his arrival in
Vienna,[2] "I shall do no more work but what I like. I tried it once
five months, and the results were satisfactory."

This, however, was but one of his moods; the other was to look
upon the economic future with apprehension. It was part of the conflict within him to sigh one day for the care-free bucolic joys, and
the next day to cast up his accounts and worry about his debts, which
he, unlike Bret Harte and so many more of his comrades of the pen,
never quite dared to let grow. In the latter mood, one day in Spain,

---

[1] Royal Cortissoz, *The Life of Whitelaw Reid,* I, pp. 122–23.
[2] Bigelow's *Retrospections,* IV, p. 195; July 14, 1868.

he seems to have written to Bigelow in such a vein as to bring an immediate and apprehensive response. The reply found him in a happier mood, and he explained: [1]

"My affairs are not so desperate as my letter may have caused you to think. I have a sure income of two or three hundred dollars in ordinary times, and that is opulence in Warsaw—where living costs nothing and where I have all the comforts of a home, within five minutes walk of the station. If I go away from that bower of innocent repose, I shall spend more and make more." [2]

Newspaper work represented for Hay a compromise with desire; it was imposed upon him by his inbred thrift. With reservations he entered upon its routine in 1870, at the age of thirty-two. He bore for five years the discomfort of the inexorable demands of its daily deadline, which, on a morning paper, came at a time of night when he often preferred to be elsewhere. Then he claimed his freedom. He never entirely gave up his dream of the lodge in the wilderness; in later years, both in Colorado, where he had a camp, and at Lake Sunapee, N. H., where he could lose himself in his own twelve hundred acres of woodland, he often sought a refuge to cultivate his kinship with Omar, from whose spirit he was most of all separated by his own providence.

In 1865 a group of Illinois capitalists started the Chicago *Republican,* and invited Charles A. Dana, formerly of the New York *Tribune,* but most recently Assistant Secretary of War, to become editor. In the group of stock-holders were Jesse K. DuBois and Jacob Bunn, of Springfield. The following year Dana resigned on the grounds that insufficient funds were being provided, and returned to New York, where, with the help of friends, he took over the *Sun.* Jacob Bunn became the principal owner of the *Republican.* Two editors followed in quick succession, and then John G. Nicolay, for five years American consul in Paris after his service with Lincoln, became the editor. Hay applied for a subordinate position on the *Republican,* and Nicolay offered him a place. Although Hay remembered his experience of the

---

[1] *Ibid.,* p. 359; July 9, 1870.

[2] In later years John Hay was a great admirer of FitzGerald's Omar Khayyam and his speech at the dinner of the Omar Khayyam Club, in London, December 8, 1897, was one of the most popular of the addresses made by him as Ambassador. (*Addresses of John Hay,* pp. 45–50). There is in the address, however, nothing to indicate when Hay first came to read Omar. The second edition of FitzGerald's translation was published in London in 1869. The poem was not well known in the United States until some years later.

year before on the *Illinois State Journal,* chiefly for its drudgery, he hastened home, prepared to accept the offer. By the time he reached Chicago the *Republican,* never adequately launched, was hopelessly water-logged. The paper offered no prospect for Hay, who immediately turned south to Warsaw, where he expected to indulge his dream of simple living until the following spring. However, he took the precaution to notify his friends in the East of his address, and intimated that he was in a receptive mood.

John Hay was already friendly with William Dean Howells, assistant editor of the *Atlantic,* which had just accepted the Spanish essays. He was also known to several New York editors who had published his contributions. In Washington he had met Whitelaw Reid, who, during the greater part of the war, had been the Washington correspondent of the Cincinnati *Gazette.* Reid was now second in command of the *Tribune,* and, at the moment, actually in charge of the paper while Horace Greeley was touring the West. When Hay was passing through New York on his way to Chicago, Reid had talked to him about the position of Paris correspondent of the *Tribune.* There is a tradition, unverified, that Hay at that time wrote a leader for the *Tribune* on some topic of European news. It is a matter of record, however, that from Chicago he sent Reid a dispatch which was promptly published.

"I am inclined to think now that I will not accept Paris this fall if it is offered me by Reid," he wrote from Warsaw,[1] reluctant to give up his dream of a "cabbage-patch." "I will try to skin around and keep afloat until spring and then act *en connaissance de cause.* If I can make a raise, I shall be strongly tempted to follow you to Florida."

On learning that he was available, Reid wrote promptly intimating that Hay would be considered before all others if it should be decided to send a correspondent to Paris, but suggesting that it might not be the best arrangement for Hay. "I would rather indeed have you come to New York," he wrote,[2] "and if you were not a fellow of such diplomatically extravagant habits as to be beyond the reach of our modest salaries I should try to tempt you . . . I should quite like to have you there [Paris] on many accounts, though if you will permit me the freedom of saying so, I doubt whether it would be really so good for you, in case you have definitely determined on journalism,

[1] To Nicolay, October 13, 1870.
[2] Cortissoz, I, p. 162.

as steady work here or in some large city on a leading newspaper and on the magazines."

Late in October Hay went East to "talk *au serieux* with Reid and Howells," expecting, however, to return to Warsaw for the winter and to postpone a permanent engagement until the following spring. Reid made a very attractive offer, a position as editorial writer at $50 a week, an extraordinary salary for the day, as much as Greeley had drawn as late as 1851,[1] and probably more than Dana ever had from the *Tribune*. In a few weeks this sum was increased to $65.[2] The erstwhile keeper of vineyards took up residence at the Astor House, close to the *Tribune* office, and launched upon a metropolitan career, which, nevertheless, he regarded as tentative. This was a critical moment in Hay's life. The week following the increase of salary he wrote to Nicolay: "My Florida dream is fading into thin air. I cannot afford it. If I stay here, I can keep even and have a dollar or two to begin the summer on."

If Hay had any misgivings about joining Greeley's staff after witnessing the latter's abortive negotiations at Niagara Falls six years before, he did not betray them. Probably he had none, for he must have known that Lincoln himself had so far overlooked the affair as to promise Greeley the position of Postmaster-General in his new cabinet after the second inauguration.[3] Greeley, however, upon his return was wroth, and it must have been some relief to Reid, who had presumed so much in Greeley's absence, to have the veteran editor at length forget his prejudice and hand down the verdict that Hay was the most brilliant man who had ever entered the *Tribune* office.[4]

The year 1870 was a good one in which to join the *Tribune*. Under Greeley, who was then relaxing his hold, the paper had become as prosperous as it was influential. Within two years the great editor was to retire from his battered desk to run for the Presidency, and then in a few weeks to die. As though foreseeing the end, he was bringing in new blood; there was about the old building a spirit of change. The paper was one of the richest newspaper properties in the United States, which meant that there was ample money with which to do things, and Reid was a man of affairs.

[1] Edward P. Mitchell, *Memoirs of an Editor*, p. 229.
[2] Cortissoz, p. 165.
[3] Don C. Seitz, *Horace Greeley*, p. 268.
[4] Joseph Bucklin Bishop, *Notes and Anecdotes*, p. 45.

Whitelaw Reid, also a son of the West, almost exactly a year older than Hay, was a masterful person; he knew the newspaper business from every angle, having owned and edited the Xenia *News* in Ohio before he was twenty-one. What was more important for a young man who had just entered the New York arena, he knew exactly what he wanted from life. His father, like Hay's, had been born near Lexington, Ky., but beyond that there had been few parallels in the two lives. Hay belonged to a village culture; Reid to the farm. While one had gone East to college at the expense of his uncle, and lived in somewhat easy circumstances, the other entered Miami, and helped to support himself by news-gathering. After graduation, while the younger man had gone back home and waited for his father to show him his destiny, the other plunged directly into the rough and tumble of newspaper work. While Hay had been killing time at law, which he did not like, Reid had branched out and become the correspondent at the State capital of a string of papers. Reid went to the front in 1861 for the Cincinnati *Gazette*. When in 1865 Hay chose to continue on the government pay-roll, Reid thought to seize his opportunity in the new day by investing in a plantation in Louisiana, for which he gave up journalism for three years. In 1870 one would have said, comparing the two men, that Reid had the edge on Hay, that he had more of the elements essential to success in life. One quality Whitelaw Reid lacked which Hay possessed: modesty, a coin which is almost always redeemable in love and sympathy.

Life in the old *Tribune* office was keyed to a high pitch. There were not enough desks and chairs, but there was gathered there the ablest set of writers that any paper of the day could boast. Godkin remarked that the names on the staff read like the index to some manual of American letters. It may have been a painful experience for Hay, but it was the best possible place for him to be. Thus far in life he had escaped discipline; never before had he been thrown into daily competition with his peers and been required to deliver a product which could easily and accurately be appraised. Such surroundings put him on his mettle. One can understand why he was unable to endure the ordeal very long, but it is equally understandable that these years were his most productive ones.

Hay would have preferred, so he thought, the Warsaw vineyard, but what he needed was a task-master. Probably this was why Reid

Others in the group of Lyceum lecturers with whom John Hay was appearing were: 19. John G. Saxe; 20. De Cordova; 21. George William Curtis; 22. Gen. Kilpatrick; 23. Bishop Matthew Simpson; 24. Elizabeth Cady Stanton; 25. Susan B. Anthony; 26. E. Faithful; 27. John B. Gough; 28. Kate Field; 29. A. Livingston; 30. Wilkie Collins; 31. Bayard Taylor; 32. "Fat Contributor"; 33. Edward Everett Hale; 34. Charles Sumner; 35. James Anthony Froude; 36. Ralph Waldo Emerson; 37. A. Emily Dickinson; 38. Elihu Burritt; 39. Sidney Woollett; 40. Wendell Phillips; 41. Robert Collyer; 42. Henry Ward Beecher; 43. Prof. John Tyndall; 44. George MacDonald; 45. James Parton.

Clara Louise Stone of Cleveland, Ohio, whom John Hay married February 4, 1874. "She is a very estimable young person, large, handsome and good. I never found life worth while before." Hay to Nicolay, August 27, 1873.

desired to have him in New York rather than in Paris. The latter talked of sending him to Washington "as a sort of heavy-swell correspondent" but Hay objected. "I do not like to blame and I mortally hate to praise," he wrote,[1] "which somewhat narrows a letter-writer's field." Reporting would, in fact, have been something like the rôle of a claims agent, which he had already rejected. He was too fastidious to be a reporter, and he lacked the drive for successful news-hunting. Reid sent him to Chicago to report the famous fire in October, 1871. The Syracuse *Standard* commented that Hay's dispatches from Chicago were like DeFoe's accounts of the great London fire, but one infers from Hay's own report to Reid that he had been far less useful than his Irish assistant, who knew how to gather the spot news and, better still, how to get the telegraph wire and hold it. Hay needed office routine to teach him how to master his mount. The presses cannot wait for "inspirations." "I do not feel at all firm in the saddle for the career of journalism," he wrote modestly to Bigelow.[2] "I waste two-thirds of my time trying to think of something to write about. Hassard [3] writes his column while I sit staring at the City Hall in blank imbecility. Reid writes very little, but when it is necessary, he beats me two to one. This is not encouraging, but on the other hand, I get large pay and many good words. I satisfy myself less than any one else."

Hay was, in fact, an amateur among professionals. It was in no small degree this spirit of the amateur which won him the devotion of men like Joseph Bucklin Bishop. Hay was never quite willing to professionalize his gifts; he preferred to play a lyre on Mount Olympus. Always generous in his praise of the work of others, always depreciatory of his own work, he trampled none under his feet in a mad scramble for credit. His writing, which lay chiefly in the field of foreign topics, political, social, and literary, made him no one's competitor; he wanted no man's place.

"It was a liberal education in the delights of the intellectual life," wrote Bishop, who came to the *Tribune* soon after Hay,[4] "the highest gift that Heaven has bestowed upon mortals, to sit in intimate companionship with John Hay and watch the play of that well-stored and

---

[1] To Nicolay, December 12, 1870.
[2] Bigelow's *Retrospections*, IV, p. 478; March 12, 1871.
[3] John R. G. Hassard, a brilliant writer whose sparkle might easily be mistaken for that of Hay.
[4] *Notes and Anecdotes*, p. 67.

brilliant mind. No one who had enjoyed that supreme privilege could ever forget it—forget the musical voice, which in every tone and fibre was the voice of the intellectual man; the clear-cut enunciation; the unerring use of the right word and the only right word in every instance; the wide knowledge of men and nations, of peoples and governments; the familiar and ever-ready knowledge of all that is best in literature, and over it all the play of a humor which was next-door neighbor to melancholy and all the finer for that close association." Such a tribute, so full of superlatives, is given here as an illustration of the kind of admiration that Hay evoked among his fellows. Outside the office he was equally successful.

Augmented by his magazine contributions, his book royalties, and not infrequent lectures, Hay's fortunes rose and he moved up-town to lodgings at 111 East 25th Street, a suitable neighborhood from which to join in the social life of the city. A letter to his father, under date of December 11, 1872, presents a vivid picture of the close of his second year in New York:

I arrived here without accident on Monday after a pleasant visit in Cleveland. I found stacks of letters waiting for me but nothing of any great importance which had been neglected. There were two lecture invitations, one from Poughkeepsie which I was rather sorry to lose. But the most were invitations to dinner which I am as well pleased to be free from.

Last night I went to an amusing supper party. It was at S. L. M. Barlow's and consisted of Manton Marble and Hurlburt of the *World*, Sam Ward, son-in-law of Astor, a witty old scape-grace, General (Rebel) Dick Taylor, son of the President and, ostensibly, Father Burke, the great Dominican orator. We were especially invited to meet Father Tom, but we waited an hour and he did not come. We sat down and were very merry without him. When supper was about half over there was a loud ring at the bell and we thought it must be his Reverence; but when the door opened, a woman, half crazy with excitement shouted "Save yourselves! the Fifth Avenue Hotel is on fire." This was true, but Madison Square was between us and the fire and not a man budged from the table, and when we went home at midnight, the fire was subdued, and the hotel not much hurt.

We have not quite settled down after the events of last month, and I am not yet perfectly sure about Mr. Reid's permanence but of this I can tell you more definitely after a week or two. My diamond shares, of course, turn out worthless, but I lose nothing as Mr. Barlow gives me back the money I gave him for them.[1] My other affairs look a little better than they did, though

---

[1] It was Clarence King who exposed the great swindle in the "salted" diamond fields of Wyoming, late in 1872. *Clarence King Memoirs*, pp. 396–400. Had the fraud remained

I do not quite yet see daylight through them. I am about embarking, with powerful friends, in another enterprise, where the loss, if any, will be small, and the profit, if it comes, will be large.

My lecture before the Christian Association has been postponed a week— Gough taking my place and I taking his. I shall speak the 20th. The Steinway Hall lecture (The Heroic Age) will be towards the end of January.

I anticipate rather a pleasant winter. I am arranging so as to work more in the daytime, to get up and go to bed earlier. I have cheerful lodgings and good attendance.

Reid watched with a little apprehension the increase of the social demands upon Hay's time and strength, but was able to report to Bigelow, at the end of the first year:[1] "Hay is doing admirably and even growing corpulent. Society has many rumors of his engagement to this and that beauty, among the rest to Christine Nilsson, but if he has left any fair friend behind him in Paris, she may set her heart at rest, as to any serious danger yet."

In contrast to Boston, literary New York in the seventies had a larger number of young men; there was rather more of the spirit of youth. Henry Holt, in his octogenarian days, used to recall a Saturday night at the Century, where Hay was admitted in 1871, from which he, Bayard Taylor, Whitelaw Reid, Quincy Ward, and Hay adjourned at 2 A. M. the following morning, and as they departed played leap-frog over the ash-cans. He recalled also a dinner given by himself at which Hay, at one end, and Clarence King at the other end of the table, fired conversation back and forth all the evening and left to the others no necessity to share except in the laughter.[2] "I don't think it's merely because I am a very old man and therefore a *laudator temporis acti*," Holt wrote wistfully, "that I think the talk was better then than now; for there was better stuff to talk about."

To Edmund Clarence Stedman, Hay had written in 1869, when on his way through New York to Madrid: "How you can keep your spirit so green and fresh in Wall Street is a marvel to me. I think a month or so in this town would drive me melancholy mad." And yet, once there, in his varied circles of friends, his melancholy disappeared. He was never again so contented until he settled in Washington fifteen years later. In the five years in New York he completed his circle of

undisclosed till the following spring, large sums of money would have been wasted in the costly purchase of worthless property. Many well-known capitalists were imposed upon.
[1] Bigelow's *Retrospections*, IV, pp. 489, 572.
[2] Henry Holt, *Garrulities of an Octogenarian Editor*.

literary friendships, Mark Twain, Bayard Taylor, Gilder, Clarence King, St. Gaudens, La Farge, Stoddard; there remained only to add Henry Adams. Hay was never the play-boy that some of the group were; not one of these men, except Adams, and King rarely, ever called Hay by his first name, but the pleasure they had in his company was a mark of distinction worthy of any young man's effort. If conversation may be admitted on equal terms with literary production as a form of artistic expression, John Hay, before he left New York, had won still another triumph.

The importance of the *Tribune* experience is too obvious to require elaboration. Hay's early, grandly flowing paragraphs were full of Macaulayisms. They cried for such prunings as are required by the inexorable demands of newspaper space. Hay needed an editor. He needed also the contact with affairs to enforce precision of thought and statement which had been lacking in *Castilian Days*. Most of all he was enriched by the experience of sitting in an office, day after day, and learning to gauge public opinion. Thus his perceptive faculties, always good, were sharpened. Perhaps there has never been a Secretary of State who could so quickly and clearly as Hay feel the world's pulse from his desk. Nor was any other Secretary ever so apt in coining phrases to make headlines. Hay knew how to make news. The *Tribune* years were brief, but, as a part of the education of a statesman, they were invaluable. On the other hand, there were offsets. Hay's term of service as an editor coincided with that period in life when enthusiasms begin to fail and youth's idealism is in peril. The experience was valuable, but it made it less likely that John Hay would ever follow up the literary promises of 1871 and break another lance at conventionality.

In New York men have a way of burning bright, and then burning out. Commonplace souls, hardy souls, and those with no souls at all can survive, but for others the great city offers a destructive environment. Only those who knew John Hay as intimately as he revealed himself in his letters could have realized that these early meteoric successes offered no certainty that he would ever be known in history as more than the passing author of some Spanish essays and of some very popular rhymes. He had talent, but geniuses are not so well poised as John Hay was. He was, for example, quite incapable of the spectacular adventures of Mark Twain in this period although, in lesser degrees, he had many of Twain's other qualities.

About every third year was a critical one in Hay's adult life; he seemed to lack the dogged persistence to follow through. His genuine modesty, which made people love him, left him with too little courage to solve the personal equation, complicated as it was by so many values. His confessions of indolence, often reiterated, were more than mere self-depreciation. One reason why he preferred to remain an amateur was that to play by ear required less effort.

"In sober sadness I am convinced that I am not up to that mark," he had written to Bigelow in 1868.[1] "I am growing more indolent and scatterbrained day by day. It is a torture to work now, and if I continue in my present way, I will be fully qualified to live in the realization of my old dream of a cabbage-garden in the west, where I can forget I ever had any brains. My indolence is not physical but mental. . . . I know myself better than anybody. If I could deceive myself or be deceived by my friends, I might blunder along and be a jollier man. But I can't do it."

In New York John Hay was able to increase his standard of living to a point which was fatal to his dream of a cabbage-garden in the west. After he had moved up to East Twenty-fifth Street it was unlikely that he would ever be willing to follow his bucolic ambition to indulge a poetic fancy. For a time, even the moods which induced the

[1] Bigelow's *Retrospections*, IV, p. 195. July 14, 1868.

fancy seemed to disappear. Underlying these moods, however, was a pathology which the doctors could not cure. They could find little or nothing wrong with him, but the terrifying headaches continued. There were moments of partial blindness, "half-vision," which were more than the results of eye-strain in the badly lighted office of a morning paper. In time his heart became affected, his pulse reduced and irregular, and before he had reached middle age, under the direction of his physician, he was resorting to digitalis. Never a sturdy boy, he was never a completely healthy man, and yet so obscure to the diagnosticians of his day was the cause, that in the end he had almost to die to prove that he was unwell. John Hay was poorly equipped to survive in New York, and nothing was more certain than that he would not be able to stick it out on the *Tribune* very long.

In the gay winter following his literary successes of 1871, in New York, at the temporary home of her uncle, Mr. A. B. Stone, John Hay met Miss Clara Louise Stone of Cleveland, Ohio. Possibly they had met before, for in 1866 her uncle and his family carried to Europe a letter of introduction to Hay, and two years later when Hay was in Vienna Miss Stone, her parents, and her sister, spent the year abroad. In any event he saw her often that winter, and there followed visits to Cleveland, where Hay gave a lecture in December, 1872. At the end of March, 1873, although the announcement was delayed another five months, John Hay became engaged to Clara Stone. On August 24 Hay wrote to an old friend of his bachelor days, Albert Rhodes:[1]

"I have become *tout ce qu'il y a de plus rangé,* since you left. The example of T—— was too much for me. I have been brought down. Mourn for me. *La Femme* has ceased to exist for me. There is only one—and one is enough. I am sorry for you and P——, for I know that in your gentle hearts my untimely fate will be tenderly regretted. *Que voulez-vous?* I was mortal and you knew it.

---

[1] Albert Rhodes for a brief period assisted Mr. Bigelow in Paris in 1865 until the arrival of Hay. Subsequently he served many years in the consular service and published at least two volumes of essays. The *Letters and Diaries of John Hay* contain many letters to Rhodes, with whom Hay maintained an active correspondence for many years. In March, 1902, a collection of Hay's letters to Rhodes were placed on sale by a dealer in New York and purchased by Oscar S. Straus, who immediately notified Hay. The latter replied, March 25, 1902: "I have your letter of the 23rd, and was somewhat disturbed to learn that my old friend Rhodes had taken such good care of my young and careless communications to him. I would like very much to see them and shall doubtless be compelled to take advantage of your kind offer and withdraw some of them from circulation. I wish I had seen them on sale before you did."

"I part from the old life without regret save for the dear old reprobates whom I shall hereafter love in secret, and remorselessly cut in public. If you should hereafter meet me with Madame, I should say 'I know thee not, old man, fall to thy prayers. Believe me, I am not the thing I was.' It will grieve me bitterly, but I hope strength will be given me to make the sacrifice." [1]

Three days later Hay wrote to Nicolay: "I ought not to leave you to learn from strangers that I am engaged to be married to Miss Clara Stone of Cleveland, O. I do not know when it will be. There will be an internecine war before Mrs. Stone consents to give up her daughter—wherein I sympathize with her. But before many centuries I shall win. She is a very estimable young person, large, handsome, and good. I never found life worth while before."

They were married in Cleveland, February 4, 1874, and established their new home, far from the cabbage-patch, at 11 East Forty-second Street, New York City.

It would seem that there were already enough crosscurrents in John Hay's life, but with his marriage he assumed new relationships which brought many more; currents, however, which were not of Clara Stone's making. She, twenty-four years old at the time of her marriage, was all that her husband claimed for her, "large, handsome, and good." Larger than her husband, a queen in her strong beauty, she was, above all else, "good" in her eager desire to serve John Hay's welfare. In thirty years she seems never to have interposed a personal preference which could thwart his well-being, and, at times, she could, with unruffled temper, exclaim "John!" in just the tone required to reclaim him from a petulant outburst. Her part was to follow her husband, make a perfect home, manage a household as her father had managed railroads, keep the shutters from banging, buy the railway tickets, rear quietly the children whom he loved pathetically but never disciplined, take him to the church which he never joined, and protect him from excursions which would have dissipated his strength and, quite likely, would have ruined him. The richness of the new life and love, far from smothering him, released his strength and gave, if not a perfectly constant purpose, at least greater constancy than he had shown before. Henceforth he was able to direct his energies straight

[1] This text is from a typewritten copy found in the Hay papers, and presumably made for inclusion, with other letters to Rhodes, but not included in the *Letters and Diaries*.

to the task in hand, undistracted by the cares which so often rob literary and public life of their finest accomplishments.

It is conceivable that without such assistance as marriage brought to John Hay he might measurably have solved his problems, but the prospect in 1874 was not promising. Clarence King was somewhat similarly gifted, although, as Henry Adams pointed out, much better educated to face the world of his day, yet he made only a limited success and his end was disastrous.[1]

Hay had more character than King, but, lacking the economic security and the domestic stability which came to him in 1874, it is doubtful whether he could have achieved very much. Marriage set his hands free. Mrs. Hay was not what is called an intellectual woman and did not share in his literary work, but without her, it is unlikely that he would have finished his part of *Abraham Lincoln: A History*. She was not a woman to put her husband forward, and shared in his political life only as it became necessary to do her part, but, without her, it is almost inconceivable that John Hay ever would have been Secretary of State for almost seven years.

However, while Mrs. Hay gave to her husband's life a unity of interest which he had never been able to attain for himself, marriage involved him in another diversification of interests. Fifteen months later he resigned from the *Tribune,* forsook journalism, and moved to a wholly new and strange environment in Cleveland where, for the following eleven years, he had his legal residence. By the middle of the summer of 1875, in the office of Amasa Stone, his father-in-law, he was established as a business man, "ready to skin the pensive Buckeye with neatness and despatch." [2] For this new vocation he was not wholly unprepared. He had been thrifty and was by no means a penniless person when he married. He was, nevertheless, proposing to do something quite unlike anything he had ever done before. Changing vocations, changing friends, and, at the age of thirty-seven, coming under the tutelage of Amasa Stone, involved readjustments of a pro-

---

[1] "In 1871 he had thought King's education ideal, and his personal fitness unrivalled. No other young American approached him for the combination of chances—physical energy, social standing, mental scope and training, wit, geniality, and science, that seemed superlatively American and irresistibly strong. . . . The result of twenty years effort proved that the theory of scientific education failed where most theory fails—for want of money . . . John Hay, Whitelaw Reid, and William C. Whitney; all of whom owed their free hand to marriage, education serving only as an ornament . . ." *Education of Henry Adams,* pp. 346–47.

[2] From a letter to Reid, July 19, 1875.

found character.

For four years, at a plastic age, John Hay had worked in the
room next to Abraham Lincoln, but having a desk ten years later
when he had already made his own reputation, next to that of Amasa
Stone, was a very different kind of discipline, so different that it becomes important to the narrative to know more of John Hay's father-in-
law.

About the time that John Hay was born, while his father was
struggling vainly with the economic problems of an over-crowded
household in Salem, Ind., a tall, lank youth, Amasa Stone, came down
from the farm where he was born in Charlton, Mass., to Worcester
to practice his trade as carpenter. He was a skillful craftsman and
soon was prepared to undertake the finer forms of cabinet-making.
From cabinet-work he passed rapidly to bridge-building, purchasing
from his brother-in-law, an inventor with whom he became associated
in 1839, the patent rights for New England of a truss design for wooden
bridges.[1] The young bridge-builder in 1842 married Julia Gleason
of Springfield, a seamstress in the days when American girls lost nothing
by supporting themselves with their hands, when Lucy Larcom worked
in the mills at Lowell and read her poems to Whittier. It was a simple,
frugal New England home which they established, similar in most
respects to the newly established Hay home in Warsaw, save that
while the head of one family mended broken bridges, the other mended
broken bones and read the Greek and Latin classics. At twenty-six,
young Stone, still a contractor, entered upon a career as railway operator
by becoming superintendent of the New Haven, Hartford & Springfield Railroad.

From New England Amasa Stone transferred his operations to the
Western Reserve just in time to take advantage of a rising tide.
Everywhere railways were supplanting the canals and other unde-
pendable waterways upon which the State had lavished so much effort
in the preceding twenty years. While others were hurrying across the
Isthmus, or the still more deadly plains, lured by the gold of California,
Stone found wealth by tapping the less elusive resources of Ohio.
With two partners he undertook the contract to construct the railroad

---

[1] *Amasa Stone. Born April 27, 1818. Died May 11, 1883.* This was a memorial sketch prepared by Hay shortly after the death of his father-in-law, and beautifully printed by the
DeVinne Press. It was similar in style to the volume prepared two years later as a memorial of Dr. Charles Hay, to which references were made in Chapters I and II.

from Cleveland to Columbus, and after its completion became its superintendent, establishing his home in Cleveland. A few years later he quietly gathered sufficient votes to go into a directors' meeting and vote himself in as president of the road in place of the man who had raised the capital and brought him to Ohio to build it. Amasa Stone was remembered in Cleveland for more than one coup like that.

With confidence born of one success after another, Stone marched forward through three decades of Ohio history until he became a national figure, forgotten now except where he lived, but recognized then as one of the great builders in the empire of the West. The range of his activities, and their variety, increased and included mines, iron and steel, banking, and communications. Buying stock in the feeble Western Union Telegraph Company when it was supposed to be nearly worthless, he saw the company emerge from the Civil War potentially rich and powerful. With John D. Rockefeller, Stephen V. Harkness, and H. M. Flagler, majority stockholders, he petitioned that the capital stock of the new Standard Oil Company be increased from one to two million dollars in 1872. He was also the officer of the Lake Shore Railroad who entered in the little book, without further comment, the names of the oil refining companies in Cleveland which had come to terms with the South Improvement Company, and were entitled to the rebates on the shipment of their oil. The arrangement saved the oil refining industry to Cleveland, but it made bitter enemies among the producers.[1]

Amasa Stone's principal interest always remained the construction of railroads. With his partner, he built the Chicago & Milwaukee, of which he became a director; he built the old Union Passenger Station in Cleveland; but his great monument was the Lake Shore Railroad, formed out of several links, some of which he built, of which he became an officer, and which passed in 1870 into the control of Commodore Vanderbilt to be welded into the famous line from New York to Chicago.[2] For two years, 1873–75, at the request of the Vanderbilts, Stone became managing director of the line from Buffalo to Chicago, but it irked him to see the control of the road which he knew so much better than others concentrated in the New York office, and he resigned.

[1] Documents Number 3 (Affidavit of James H. Devereux) and 6, in Vol. I of *The History of the Standard Oil Company*, Ida M. Tarbell.
[2] Stone was president of the Cleveland, Painesville & Ashtabula for thirteen years before it was merged in the Lake Shore & Michigan Southern.

A dominant, even a domineering, man, he could not endure a subordinate position.

The Lake Shore was his monument, but it was also his sorrow. Most of all Amasa Stone had prided himself on being a bridge-builder. When it came to re-building the long bridge at Ashtabula in 1863, he, although president of the road and not concerning himself with other similar details of the construction, reserved the right, or the pleasure, to design the bridge. He used the famous Howe truss principle with which he was so familiar, but specified iron rather than wooden timbers. His engineer warned him that his truss was not adapted to iron with its greatly increased weights; that a bridge such as he had designed would not be safe. Stone, so often in the past right when others were wrong, made confident by a quarter century of unbroken success, burst into anger and ordered the engineer from the room. The bridge was built as planned, and stood for eleven years. Then, one bitter night, December 29, 1876, the Ashtabula Bridge went down into the gorge, carrying a train-load of people to destruction in a twisted, burning wreck. The verdict went against him; "at a fearful cost of human life and suffering," the coroner said, Mr. Stone had persisted in an experiment "which ought never to have been tried." [1]

With too few friends to begin with, Amasa Stone walked the streets of Cleveland, the target of charges which were doubtless both unjust and malicious; at night he walked the floor of his sleepless chamber, tormented by his thoughts, a man who had lived over into a technological age which he did not understand, and for which a carpenter's rule-o'-thumb was not sufficient. Within a month after the disaster, Charlie Collins, his division superintendent, ended his own life, and five and a half years later, broken in health, if not humbled in spirit, Amasa Stone, as exacting of himself as he had been of many others, did likewise.

In his home Mr. Stone was both autocratic and indulgent. Adelbert, his only son, wanted to go to war, but the father had marked him for his own and sternly ordered him to Yale. Just after the surrender at Appomattox the boy was drowned while swimming in the river. The grief must have been doubly hard to a man accustomed to strangle

---

[1] Report of the Joint Committee concerning the Ashtabula Bridge Disaster, under Joint Resolution of the General Assembly. Columbus, 1877; also, *The Ashtabula Disaster*, by the Rev. Stephen D. Peet, which gives the text of the verdict of the coroner's jury.

his emotions. He would have liked to have John Hay take the place of the lost son. The two men were too near of an age and too far apart in temperament; the older man represented the qualities in American life without which it would not now be possible to go from New York to Chicago by rail in twenty hours; the younger was the son of a man without whose qualities America would have become too brutal to live in. For the Hays, Amasa Stone built on Euclid Avenue, next to his own, a luxurious house, and lavished upon it the finest woodcarving and cabinet-work that he could buy, a vicarious exercise of his own creative skill in wood-working. He did not demand of the new couple the frugality which had been required in his own first household.

John Hay, in turn, did his filial duty. He applied himself to the lesson, set by his father-in-law, for "skinning the pensive Buckeye." He utilized his connections with the *Tribune* to set Amasa Stone before the public in the best possible light. To Reid he telegraphed the news, July 14, 1880, of Stone's offer of half a million dollars to Western Reserve University, conditioned upon the removal of the institution from Hudson to Cleveland, and he became one of the newly appointed trustees, remaining on its board to the end of his life. He prepared the affectionate memoir of Amasa Stone, to which reference has been made, and saw it through the DeVinne press. He was, no doubt, responsible for the editorial in the *Tribune,* March 28, 1880, designed to release his father-in-law from the odium which had attached from the bridge disaster. When Amasa Stone's will was opened it was found that he had provided generously for John Hay directly, and had made an even more generous display of his confidence by naming him, and Samuel Mather, the other son-in-law, the executors. In the residuary estate the sons-in-law together with the daughters were to share and share alike.

John Hay had also an earnest desire to like his adopted city. Cleveland welcomed him not only as a member of the family of one of its richest citizens but also as a celebrity in his own right. To the provinces he had come, a man of the world; he had fine manners; he could preside gracefully at public meetings; and he could make a forceful, witty speech. For example:

A great many Americans, I know, trace their undoubted ancestry from well-known families in the Old World. I do not refer to those pitiable beings who invent or appropriate the arms of others; but at best this is a child's amusement, unworthy a full-grown man. We have no distinction of classes in this country. I believe and hope we never shall have. But descended as you are from a race of men pre-eminent in virtue and capacity, you have the obligation laid upon you never to forget your origin, and never to fall below the standard which they unconsciously set up. As the result of their fruitful labors, our lives have become more complex than theirs, our wants greater, our duties not so simply defined. But one or two ideas come out clearly enough from the study of their character. They believed in order, decency, sobriety; in reverence for all things reverend, for religion and for law. They were always more ready to fight in a public than in a private quarrel. They were honest, and severe in their honesty; they claimed their own, while they allowed each man his own. The enemy of the public welfare was their enemy, but they did not rashly conclude that their enemy was necessarily the enemy of the public good. They were loyal to the last drop of their blood, to their consciences, to their families, to their country.

We can hardly hope to emulate a character so unique, so simply complete and heroic. . . .[1]

Most mysterious of all in Cleveland, Amasa Stone's son-in-law wrote books.

With the western reserve as a state of mind Hay had some kinship, but, in general, his idea of the good life and the prevailing ideals of the territorial Western Reserve—which had no theory or place for a leisure class—impinged on one another acutely. He was a spiritual outlander. He organized the "Vampire Club" [2] which met once a month at the Union Club, but not in a whole year was there so much good conversation as there was likely to be any night in the old *Tribune* office while they were putting the paper to bed, on a Friday evening at the Gilders', or at the Century on Saturday night. That he did not like Cleveland, and why he did not like it, is recorded, between the lines, in *The Bread-Winners*, the novel which began serial publication in the *Century* in August, 1883. That was the real reason, one suspects, why the novel was published anonymously. There was not in *The Bread-Winners* a single character, with the exception of Alice Belding, whom Hay would ever have brought on social terms a few years later to his home in Washington.

Other aspects of *The Bread-Winners* obscured the fact that it was

[1] "The Pioneers of Ohio," an address delivered before the Pioneers' Association of the Western Reserve, at Burgess' Grove, Cuyahoga County, Ohio, August 27, 1879. This was published in pamphlet form at the time, and was reprinted in the *Magazine of Western History*, Extra Numbers 101–108; Cleveland.

[2] *James Ford Rhodes, American Historian*, by M. A. DeWolfe Howe, pp. 26, 45, 184; Rhodes, *The McKinley and Roosevelt Administrations, 1897–1909*, pp. 120–21.

as much as anything a critique of Cleveland society. As such, the novel may be logically referred to here without borrowing from the following chapter. It completes the picture of Colonel Hay in Cleveland. There is, for example, a drawing-room scene, written with some restraint, which shows quite clearly how the social life of the city impressed him, and why he moved to Washington, as soon as he was free to do so:

It was the usual drawing-room of provincial cities. The sofas and chairs were mostly occupied by married women, who drew a scanty entertainment from gossip with each other, from watching the proceedings of the spinsters, and chiefly, perhaps, from a consciousness of good clothes. The married men stood grouped in corners and talked of their every-day affairs. The young people clustered together in little knots, governed more or less by natural selection—only the veterans of several seasons pairing off into the discreet retirement of stairs and hall angles. At the farther end of the long drawing-room, Farnham's eyes at last lighted upon the object of his quest. Alice sat in the midst of a group of young girls who had intrenched themselves in a corner of the room, and defied all the efforts of skirmishing youths, intent upon flirtation, to dislodge them. They seemed to be amusing themselves very well together, and the correct young men in white cravats and pointed shoes came, chatted, and drifted away. They were the brightest and gayest young girls of the place; and it would have been hard to detect any local color in them. Young as they were, they had all had seasons in Paris and in Washington; some of them knew the life of that most foreign of all capitals, New York. They nearly all spoke French and German better than they did English, for their accent in those languages was very sweet and winning in its incorrectness, while their English was high-pitched and nasal, and a little too loud in company. They were as pretty as girls are anywhere, and they wore dresses designed by Mr. Worth, or his New York rivals, Loque and Chiffon; but they occasionally looked across the room with candid and intelligent envy at maidens of less pretensions, who were better dressed by the local artists.[1]

The opening chapter of *The Bread-Winners* introduces the reader to Arthur Farnham in his library. It was Hay's library, with windows looking out on a pretty garden of five or six acres behind the house, or on a carefully kept lawn, extending a hundred or more feet from the front door to the gates of hammered iron which opened upon wide, paved Euclid Avenue. "The whole expression of the room was of warmth and good manners. The furniture was of oak and stamped leather. The low bookcases were covered with bronzes, casts, and figurines, of a quality so uniformly good that none seemed to feel the

---

[1] *The Bread-Winners*, p. 173.

temptation either to snub or to cringe to its neighbor. The Owari pots felt no false shame beside the royal Satsuma; and Barbédiénne's bronzes, the vases of Limoges and Lambeth, and the bowls from Nankin and Corea dwelt together in the harmony of a varied perfection." [1]

Buffland, made up, perhaps, by combining the first and last syllables, respectively, of Buffalo and Cleveland, was a big city. "Its air was filled with the smoke and odors of vast and successful trade, and its sky was reddened by night with the glare of its furnaces, rising like the hot breath of some prostrate Titan, conquered and bowed down by the pitiless cunning of men. Its people were, as a rule, rich and honest, especially in this avenue of which I have spoken. If you have ever met a Bufflander, you have heard of Algonquin Avenue. He will stand in the Champs Élysées, when all the vice and fashion of Europe are pouring down from the Place of the Star in the refluent tide that flows from Boulogne Wood to Paris, and calmly tell you that 'Algonquin Avenue in the sleighing season can discount this out of sight.' Something is to be pardoned to the spirit of liberty; and the avenue is certainly a fine one. It is three miles long and has hardly a shabby house in it, while for a mile or two the houses upon one side, locally called 'the Ridge,' are unusually fine, large, and costly. They are all surrounded with well-kept gardens and separated from the street by velvet lawns which need scarcely fear comparison with the emerald wonders which centuries of care have wrought from the turf of England."

The Bread-Winners was, among other things, a patronizing description of pretentious wealth. Hay supplemented this picture with another designed to reveal the political and economic background:

A week had passed by; the great strike was already almost forgotten. A few poor workmen had lost their places. A few agitators had been dismissed for excellent reasons, having no relation with the strike. The mayor had recovered, from his panic, and was beginning to work for renomination, on the strength of his masterly dealing with the labor difficulties, in which, as he handsomely said in a circular composed by himself and signed by his friends, he "nobly accomplished the duty allotted him of preserving the rights of property while respecting the rights of the people, of keeping the peace according to his oath, and keeping faith with the masses, to which be belonged, in their struggle against monopoly."

The rich and prosperous people, as their manner is, congratulated them-

[1] *Ibid.*, p. 6.

selves on their escape, and gave no thought to the questions which had come so near to an issue of fire and blood. In this city of two hundred thousand people, two or three dozen politicians continued as before to govern it, to assess and to spend its taxes, to use it as their property and their chattel. The rich and intelligent kept on making money, building fine houses, and bringing up children to hate politics as they did, and in fine to fatten themselves as sheep which should be mutton whenever the butcher was ready. There was hardly a millionaire on Algonquin Avenue who knew where the ward meetings of his party were held. There was not an Irish laborer in the city but knew his way to his ward club as well as to mass.[1]

Marriage and Cleveland left with John Hay, however, one permanent deposit, aside from the felicity of his married life, of great importance in view of his subsequent career as Secretary of State. It made of him, to a degree rarely to be found in a man of letters, a man of affairs. He replaced his father-in-law on the board of directors of the Western Union Telegraph Company in 1883 and served until his duties as Secretary of State made it invidious that he should remain as director any longer. He was accustomed to go into the market to buy and sell. Always having a firm grip on realities, he brought to his investing not only the experience gained from a desk in the office of Amasa Stone, but also a perception which was apparent in his other relationships. He had a sense of business which did not often lead him wrong. "The moral is, buy real estate and don't speckylate," he wrote to Reid in the midst of the panic of 1873, when for a few days, he supposed that Amasa Stone had lost everything, and when he was not wholly unhappy about the prospect, since it might hasten his marriage. Known best as a verse-maker, John Hay became actually a better business-man.

[1] *Ibid.*, p. 246.

THE writing of *The Bread-Winners* was an interlude to the preparation of *Abraham Lincoln: A History,* upon which Nicolay had already been engaged for some years, and to which Hay had expected to give his earnest attention when he went to Cleveland. It is impossible to be sure of the dates within which the novel was thrown off, but it seems most probable that it was done while Hay was abroad in 1882–83.[1] The author had a gift for extraordinarily rapid composition. Images flashed upon his mind and he wrote them out hurriedly, with little subsequent revision. The language and tone of the novel suggest that it may have been done in England, where there is a vocabulary to apply to the "working-classes" which, to American ears, is both alien and irritating. Or perhaps the book was finished in France, where stalked the spectre of a rising proletariat. That it represented as much as four months of labor is doubtful.

The full title, *The Bread-Winners, a Social Study,* was bad. It was sarcastic; the book was less a social study than a study of society in the higher altitudes. The plot ran away from the title. Hay knew very little about social organization, but he knew Euclid Avenue. It was inevitable that the life he knew should be drawn with crystal clearness while the more remote pictures should be suffused with fuzziness.

On this canvas of ostentatious wealth, thin culture, and civic indifference—a money-mad world—Hay drew the outlines of a plot which involved the family of a workman, content with his wages, and an unscrupulous agitator, sarcastically called a reformer, the leader of the Brotherhood of Bread-Winners.

Matchin "was a carpenter, of a rare sort. He was a good workman, sober, industrious, and unambitious. He was contented with his daily work and wage, and would have thanked Heaven if he could have been assured that his children would fare as well as he. . . . When he got on well enough to build a shop for himself, he burdened himself with debt, building it firmly and well, so as to last out his boys' time as

---

[1] Henry Adams knew of the title as early as January, 1883. Howells saw some of the chapters in London in the summer of 1882. The Hays returned to New York in May, 1883, just after the death of Mr. Stone.

well as his own." Matchin's children, unlike their father, possessed "the restless haste and hunger to rise which is the source of much that is good and most that is evil in American life." In contrast to Matchin, who belonged essentially to the older economic age of household industries, was the reformer, a type which in later years was commonly assigned to the Industrial Workers of the World. He was somewhat angrily portrayed in language which described also the cheap politician of the day, as Hay had seen him about the streets of Cleveland.[1]

"He was, in fact, possessed of very considerable natural aptitude for political life. He had a quick smile and a ready tongue; he liked to talk and shake hands; he never had an opinion he was not willing to sell; he was always prepared to sacrifice a friend, if required, and to ask favors from his worst enemies. He called himself Andrew Jackson Offitt—a name which, in the West, is an unconscious brand. It generally shows that the person bearing it is the son of illiterate parents, with no family pride or affections, but filled with a bitter and savage partisanship which found its expression in a servile worship of the most injurious personality in American History." Twice in the book Hay pointed out that Offitt was outside the trade-union movement and wholly unconnected with it, but he neglected to set forth a trade-union and it was not apparent that he regarded such an association as very different from the Brotherhood of Bread-Winners.

The author intended to make Maud, the daughter of the carpenter, the heroine of his tale. She was, in fact, the outstanding literary invention of the book, as Howells pointed out. But the author, Henry Adams remarked, "showed too much prejudice against his own characters." [2] Maud failed to play the rôle. In Hay's judgment she should have entered domestic service, "this easiest and best paid of occupations," which American girls were even then leaving to "more sensible foreigners." Hay thought Maud should never have gone to the high school which, it must be conceded, had done her little good, unless it is a good to become discontented with one's station in life. She read dime-novels and the society columns, and aspired to some such elegant vocation as library work. She was, in an innocent, blundering way, the prototype of the modern "gold digger." In Hay's judgment she should have been content to marry Sam Sleeney, a stupid lout, more ignorant

---

[1] *The Bread-Winners*, p. 89.
[2] Worthington Chauncey Ford, Editor, *Letters of Henry Adams (1858–1891)*, p. 354.

The requirements of successful amateur photography in 1883 did not permit the fun of this portraiture to show through. John Hay is shown conspicuously holding the French edition of "Democracy," the novel which Henry Adams had published anonymously, and the authorship of which Hay was suspected, wrongly, of having shared. The negative was made by Mrs. Henry Adams and is now in the Massachusetts Historical Society.

This sketch of Col. Hay by J. W. Alexander, engraved by J. H. E. Whitney, in 1886, shows the subject in his forty-eighth year, about six months before the beginning of the serial publication of "Abraham Lincoln: A History." By permission of the Century Company.

than herself. Instead, she sought to snare Arthur Farnham in the big house on Algonquin Avenue. There she engaged in unequal combat with Mrs. Belding, a rich and rather common widow, who had marked Farnham for her daughter Alice. The latter was the perfect Victorian young lady, the finished product of Madame Veaudrey's very select finishing school, the sort of girl who could not read "As pants the hart for cooling streams" without feeling that perhaps she ought to blush.

The stage for the characters was the commercial and industrial situation to which Hay had been introduced when he came to Cleveland in 1875. The recovery from the panic of 1873 had been long delayed, bringing large losses to capital and to labor great distress. It was estimated that Amasa Stone alone had lost about a million and a half.[1] As for the deplorable condition of labor in Ohio, the annual reports of the State Bureau of Labor Statistics, are eloquent. The average annual net earnings of coal miners for 1879 was a "fraction over $1.00 a day." [2] In Cleveland unskilled labor was receiving a little over $7 a week while work was fitful and irregular. Skilled mechanics earned about $2 a day. There were great abuses in "company stores"; industrial accidents were common. Hours of labor were what would now be considered excessive. It could not fairly be claimed that the losses of capital on the one hand, and of labor on the other, were comparable. To offset the distress of capital was the fact that since the beginning of the Civil War there had been great expansion, and in many instances gross over-capitalization, from which those who were able had drawn great wealth, while the workers had vainly to struggle against inflated prices and depreciated currency. The industrial distress of the late seventies greatly promoted the labor union movement and developed radical and irresponsible leadership. The famous strikes of 1877 at Pittsburgh, St. Louis, Louisville, and elsewhere, together with the reign of the Molly Maguires in Pennsylvania, raised the spectre of the Paris commune. Revolution it was; not, however, that of Europe, but the delayed arrival in the United States of the British industrial revolution.

The only industrial problems with which Hay had any previous contact were those of an age which, in Cleveland, was already past. He

[1] New York *Tribune,* May 12, 1883; see also Cincinnati *Commercial Gazette* of the same date.
[2] *Annual Report,* Bureau of Labor Statistics, Ohio, 1879, p. 85.

remembered how his grandfather had the little horse-motored cotton-mill on his farm at Walnut Hill, and later the brick-kiln in Springfield, where his sons served their time, as was the custom, until they were twenty-one. He had vivid memories of the economic struggles of the little village of Warsaw, but he had forgotten that in this forlorn settlement, lured into being by the expectation that it would be on a main line of transcontinental travel, economic distress was greatly mitigated by the farm, to which the workman could always turn. *Progress and Poverty,* published in 1877, was not the kind of book that Hay would be likely to read. As he had once written to Nicolay, at a time when his own highest economic ambition was for $600 a year, one required practically no money to live in Warsaw. Since he left Illinois in 1861 a new industrial age had come, and with it Hay, having lived fifteen years in the capitals of the world, was wholly unfamiliar. Furthermore, as much by temperament as by his heritage of pioneer village life, Hay was an individualist. The idea of a labor union violated his sense of liberty. Even in politics he was finding party regularity very difficult. As for strikes, they incensed him. Rogues and strikers he placed together.

The Bread-Winners continued serially in the *Century* through January, 1884. It was the outstanding literary success of the season. While there was general agreement among the critics that it must be a first novel, for the plot creaked a bit in places, it was hailed as a notable literary accomplishment. The author had seized upon a new theme and treated it with cleverness. In London the *Saturday Review,* Feb. 2, 1884, described the novel as "one of the strongest and most striking stories of the last ten years." It compared it with *Democracy,* which Henry Adams had published anonymously four years earlier, and greatly to the disadvantage of the latter. "There can be no doubt as to the relative merits of the two books. In England *Democracy* was ludicrously overrated, was indeed accepted as a revelation; in America it was seen to be quite as superficial as it was clever—even its title was dishonest. . . . *The Bread-Winners* is a story of another sort; it is quite as clever as *Democracy,* and it is much more than merely clever; while the merits of *Democracy* were fully summed up in the one word cleverness, *The Bread-Winners* is the work of a very clever man; it is told with many lively strokes of humor; it sparkles with epigram; it is brilliant with wit; but it has what *Democracy* has not—it has depth."

Immediately following the serial publication Harpers brought out the book in the United States. Warne and Company took an English edition and distributed it to Canada and Australia. There was a French translation under the title *Bien d'autrui,* published first as a serial in *Revue Britannique* (January–March, 1885) and later as a book by Hachette. There were also Swedish and German translations.[1]

While *The Bread-Winners* was everywhere winning plaudits for its literary cleverness it was also provoking a storm of criticism, some superficial, and some more serious.

As a novel of manners *The Bread-Winners* put forward Arthur Farnham and Alice Belding, with Maud Matchin by way of contrast. The absorbing question in the society journals was whether Farnham and Alice were, respectively, veracious portrayals of a "perfect gentleman" and a "perfect lady." In the case of Farnham the disputed point was as to the extent he had abdicated his claim by accommodating Maud Matchin in the greenhouse with not merely a rose but also with a kiss. And how should Alice Belding have acted toward Farnham when her mother, accidentally a witness to the greenhouse scene, informed her of the facts? Alice moved through the story a beautiful French doll and gave to *The Bread-Winners,* as read today, a "pervasive effect of unreality," to borrow a phrase from Mr. DeWolfe Howe.[2] Such discussion greatly promoted the vogue of the serial which, one ventures to observe, was being admirably handled by the Century Company.

The more serious criticism was that the book misrepresented the laboring classes generally and the trade-union movement in particular. "As a 'social study,' as it purports on its title page to be," stated the *Dial,* "it is worse than a failure; it is deliberately insulting to workingmen and women, and to all who sympathize with them."

This aspect of the novel had already been picked up by a correspondent in an open letter published in the *Century.* "The story is well

[1] So great was the popularity of *The Bread-Winners,* that a former reporter on the *Tribune,* Henry F. Keenan, the next year wrote *The Money Makers, A Social Parable.* It was advertised as a reply to *The Bread-Winners* and took the labor side of the controversy. As a novel it was trash, but it attained some circulation by reason of the fact that Hay, Whitelaw Reid, and Amasa Stone were portrayed with thin disguises. Hay made every possible effort to have the book suppressed because of the almost libellous treatment of Amasa Stone under the name of Aaron Grimstone.

[2] M. A. DeWolfe Howe, *James Ford Rhodes,* p. 46.

written, and I all the more regret the assumption in its second number that trade-unions are composed either of ignorant and lazy dupes or of such wretches as Offitt. It is a bit of snobbishness imported from England where even it has been an impossible position to be taken by good writers since *Put Yourself in His Place* was written." The substance of the criticism was that the author evidently belonged to the school of economic thought which regarded labor as a commodity. "Thackeray and Dickens were powerful because they supported justice against prejudice not less than by reason of their great genius; and the author of *The Bread-Winners* will never turn out permanently valuable work, so long as he misrepresents a legitimate force in the interest of a false political economy and an antiquated spirit of caste."

Hay appears to have been nothing less than astonished at this kind of criticism. He had come back from Europe in 1870 a declared republican and his reiterated sympathies with political democracy had at length drawn more than one rebuke from the critics. He believed that all men ought to be free, that they would "come to their own at last." There is nothing to indicate that he was aware that he had in any way altered his fundamental convictions. Hay smarted so much under the criticisms that he was betrayed into making two anonymous replies in the *Century*, November, 1883, and March, 1884:

Mr. Shriver makes the familiar claim of the harmless and rational processes of trades-unions; yet he knows that no important strike has ever been carried through without violence, and that no long strike has ever been ended without murder. He insists on the right of the workingman to sell his labor at the best price; yet he knows that trade-unionism is the very negation of that right. The inner circle of petty tyrants who govern the trade-unions expressly forbid the working-man to make his own bargain with his employer; his boys may become thieves and vagabonds, his girls may take to the streets, but they shall not learn his trade, or any other honest trade, without the consent of the union. It is only a few years since we saw the streets of Pittsburgh devastated by murder, arson and rapine, through a rising which agitators could originate but could not control; it is only a few weeks since we saw some thousands of telegraph operators foolishly give up their means of livelihood at the dictation of a few conspirators, whose vanity and arrogance had blinded them to the plainest considerations of common sense.[1]

[1] The Brotherhood of Telegraphers, July 16, 1883, presented to the Western Union Telegraph Company, of which Amasa Stone had been a director, and in which Hay subsequently assumed a similar position, the following bill of grievances:

"Sec. 1. Believing that a man's physical and mental welfare requires that at least one day in seven be accorded him for rest and recreation, we ask for the total abolition of

Evidently the *Century* began to feel the onus of carrying a novel which was regarded by many as a tract against collective bargaining. Among the editorials in the February, 1884, number we find a note, presumably by Gilder, on this subject. It expressed sympathy with the strike of the telegraphers and stated: "There are no respectable writers on political economy of the present day who do not distinctly say that such associations of workingmen are, under the present system, not only permissible, but indispensable."

Hay smarted under criticism always and it was one of his weaknesses that in such conditions he could not restrain his ready pen. Unwisely, still behind the shelter of anonymity, Hay again took up the defense of his novel in a letter to the *Century* which occupied four columns in March. This letter was even more intemperate in tone than the preceding one. It unfolded his own social philosophy and was in many ways more self-revealing than anything else he ever published. He wrote:

For several months I have listened in silence to a chorus of vituperation which seems to me unjust and unfounded, until my original purpose of replying to no form of misrepresentation has been so far shaken that I beg for a little space to correct some errors and justify at least my intentions.

The charges of my critics may be divided into three heads: 1. *The Bread-Winners* is conceived from an aristocratic point of view. 2. It is not well written. The incidents are extravagant and untrue to nature. 3. It is a base and craven thing to publish a book anonymously.

The first charge seems to me too absurd to be considered seriously. I hardly know what is meant by an aristocratic point of view. I am myself a working man, with a lineage of decent working men; I have been accustomed to earning my own living all my life with rare and brief holidays. I have always been in intimate personal relations with artisans and with men engaged in trade. I do not see how it is possible for an American to be an aristocrat; if such a thing exists, I have never met one. But because, in my little book, more attention is bestowed upon certain dangerous and vicious tendencies among the poor than upon the faults incident to wealth, I am called an aristocrat, or a snob,—a name equally vague and senseless, which, so far as I can discover, merely

---

Sunday work as a compulsory duty, unless compensated as extra service.

"Sec. 2. That eight hours shall constitute a regular day's work, and seven hours a regular night's work, and that both sexes shall receive equal pay for equal work.

"Sec. 3. That a universal increase of fifteen per cent on all salaries paid shall be petitioned for now."

Three days later the executive committee of the Western Union sustained the officers in refusing to deal with the Union. July 19 a strike was declared. On August 17, 1883, the strike was by the officials of the Brotherhood officially declared a failure, and the members were advised to seek to return to their jobs. Seventh *Annual Report* of the Bureau of Labor Statistics, Ohio, 1884, p. 213.

denotes that the man using it does not like the man to whom it is applied. The question may be asked, Why do I talk more about the failings of the poor than about those of the rich? Simply because I know more about them.

The germ of *The Bread-Winners* was a remark made to me by a friend of mine, a carpenter of Detroit. He said one day, when we were walking past the High School and talking of social matters: "There is hardly a carpenter's daughter in this town who will marry a carpenter." The image of Miss Maud Matchin then formed itself in my mind. A few days later I met Mr. Offitt in a railway train, and afterwards, I came to know him well in a boarding house we both frequented. Almost without my consciousness the story took shape as it was written. The hero of the tale is Offitt, not Farnham; the heroine is Maud, and not Alice. I care little about Farnham. It is true I gave him a fine house and a lot of money,—which cost me nothing,—but that was only because Miss Matchin would never have looked at him otherwise. He is a commonplace soldier, with a large property; he pretends to be nothing else. Some of my critics, to my amazement, have said, as if they were making a great discovery, that there is nothing remarkable about him. I never intended there should be. I probably could not have made him wise or learned or witty if I had tried,—but I certainly never tried. I wanted him to be a gentleman, and I think he is; but that I cannot discuss, for I have never known two people to agree upon a definition of a gentleman.

The only other rich people at all kindly treated in the book are Mrs. Belding and her daughter. And here another astonishing criticism has been made. This comes from the Boston *Transcript*. The writer rebukes me for my aristocratic leanings, and then goes on to discover a glaring inconsistency in the fact that Miss Belding is a nice sort of person, while her mother is not especially refined, and her father was a successful mechanic. My gentle, though wabbling critic, was it not I who decided that this nice young person should be a daughter of the people as well as Miss Matchin? and is it not possible that I knew what I was about as well as you? . . .

Hay defended the incidents and traits as true to life on the ground that he had gathered them largely from the daily newspapers of Cleveland, Louisville, and elsewhere, at the time of the strikes of 1877. He even quoted from a recent report in a Cleveland paper in which the mayor of the city was reported to have said: "If I was hungry and had no money with which to buy bread, I would beg for it; and if nobody would give me anything, I would knock down some fellow who was smaller than I, and get some money. An empty stomach knows no law."

"I contend," wrote Hay, "that the book is true, and was written with an honest purpose."

The author concluded with a defense of his anonymity. "I am engaged in business," he wrote, "in which my standing would be seriously compromised if it were known that I had written a novel. I am sure that my practical efficiency is not lessened by this act; but I am equally sure that I could never recover from the injury it would occasion me if known among my own colleagues. For that positive reason, and for the negative one that I do not care for publicity, I resolved to keep the kowledge of my little venture in authorship restricted to as small a circle as possible. Only two persons besides myself know who wrote *The Bread-Winners*." [1]

On one statement, at least, of this amazing letter, all can agree. The disclosure of the authorship of the book, and of the two published letters, would have done him great injury; so much, in fact, that it is quite unlikely that McKinley ever could have been able to secure his confirmation as Ambassador to the Court of St. James's, and as Secretary of State, if the facts had been known. It is doubtful, however, whether Hay himself ever realized how damaging to his career the novel, or at least the letters, could have been. At any rate, a "biographical edition" of *The Bread-Winners*, brought out in 1899, contained the parts of the letter last quoted, beginning with the words "The germ of *The Bread-Winners*," as a "prefatory sketch."

"The discussion evolved an interesting fact," wrote a correspondent (most probably William Dean Howells), in the *Century* for May, 1884, "which we recommend to all intending novelists, that among us at least the novelist is hereafter to be held to account as a public teacher."

In *The Bread-Winners* Hay had again mounted the pulpit and put himself forth as a moralist, a rôle which it is not legitimate to play anonymously. As a preacher he showed himself a better master of invective than of the facts on which he rested his case. He sincerely thought that he was a believer in democracy, but he meant political democracy only. Industrial democracy was to him incomprehensible.

In recent years there has been a revival of interest in *The Bread-Winners*. The late Professor Parrington has dwelt upon the novel as

[1] The authorship of *The Bread-Winners* was first officially disclosed in 1907, when Mrs. Hay permitted the editors of *A Manual of American Literature* for the Tauchnitz Edition to credit Hay with the novel. (*Nation*, August 10, 1916). However, at the time of publication, many critics guessed correctly, although other names as widely separated as James G. Blaine and Grover Cleveland were also suggested. As early as November, 1883, it was pointed out that the style resembled that of *Castilian Days*, that one character was born in Salem, Indiana, that the library described in the novel exactly described Hay's, that the author was familiar with the habits of office seekers in Washington, that he knew Cleveland intimately, and, most significant of all, that the sarcasm of the book was characteristic of Col. Hay. N. Y. *Tribune*, November 29, 1883.

"the first recognition on the part of literature that a class struggle impended in America—a first girding of the loins of polite letters to put down the menace that looked out from the underworld of the proletariat; and as such it assumes importance as an historical document quite beyond its significance as a work of art." [1] The Beards have called it "perhaps the best vindication of raw capitalism" of the period. [2]

"That *The Bread-Winners*," wrote Parrington, was conceived in a spirit of benevolent paternalism towards the proletariat, the present day reader will have no difficulty in discovering. It is too frank in defense of vested interests, it looks with too stern a disfavor upon all labor leaders who refuse to accept the finality of the present industrial order, it exudes too strong an odor of property-morality to deceive the intelligent reader. Read today it is clearly a partisan defense of economic individualism, an attack upon the rising labor movement, a grotesque satire smeared with an unctuous morality—and because of this, a perfect expression of the spirit of upper-class America in those uneasy eighties with their strikes and lockouts and Haymarket riots." [3]

John Hay, it may be observed, although never at loss for words to describe what he did not like, never exceeded Parrington's unctuous assurance. The former, according to the latter, bore the marks of a "skillful climber." "He was temperamentally one of John Adams's 'natural aristocrats,' and having gained entrée into aristocratic circles he took the coloring of his new environment. A son of the frontier, he became a man of the world. Prosperity was necessary to him." A more recent writer has described *The Bread-Winners* as marking "the conversion of John Hay" to the defense of capitalistic society. [4]

In both of these criticisms there is the inference that in writing the novel Hay abandoned convictions previously held, and that his motive was not a worthy one. Parrington definitely charges lack of sincerity. "That *The Bread-Winners* was a dishonest book Hay certainly could not have been brought to believe; nevertheless a Tory purpose with a mantle of democracy can hardly be reckoned intellectually sincere." [5]

[1] Vernon Louis Parrington, *The Beginnings of Critical Realism in America, 1860–1920*, p. 173.
[2] Charles A. Beard and Mary R. Beard, *The Rise of American Civilization*, 1927, II, p. 440.
[3] *Op. cit.*, p. 174.
[4] Granville Hicks, "The Conversion of John Hay," *The New Republic*, June 10, 1931.
[5] *Op. cit.*, p. 178.

It is not apparent in what respect Hay had undergone a conversion. The opinions he expressed of the industrial ferment were not more those of Euclid Avenue and the Union Club of Cleveland than they were of Warsaw, Ill., and the other rural villages of America. Trade-unionism made its way very slowly outside of industrial communities. Hay was reared in a home where the daily income probably did not exceed the wages of carpenters in Cleveland in 1879. To assert that the author had singled out the deluded working-men of Ohio for caricature and had suffused the capitalists with an unctuous morality, is to ignore the description of the vapid evening party, already quoted, and the sneering denunciation of the wealthy for their indifference to civic duty. To portray the Mrs. Beldings of Cleveland and Pittsburg and New York as Hay did can hardly facilitate social climbing. Hay was, in fact, so much bored by the sterility of Cleveland society that he was already devising plans to escape from it. Read as an historical document, the novel seems to say: to what good purpose are better wages for labor and more dividends for capital likely to be devoted among a people where an increase of money brings an increase of vulgarity? The germ of *The Bread-Winners* may have come from the seclusion of Henry Adams's library as much as from the strikes of 1877.

It is very doubtful whether Hay had set out to write a polemic of any sort. He started to do a Hogarth painting but the moralist, or cynic, in him ran away with the artist. It is true that he recorded the impertinence which the industrial barons of the day pretended to see in the ominous tramp, tramp of the industrial classes across the last quarter of the 19th Century toward better wages, better hours, better protection of health and life. He also portrayed the bewilderment and alarm of those not parties to the struggle but victims of the conflict. If Hay offered no remedy it should in all fairness be recalled that the vast majority of his fellow citizens were equally devoid of ideas.

The worst that can be said for *The Bread-Winners* is that the author stated vividly a problem which he could not solve. If Hay had married the daughter of a village merchant in Warsaw there is no reason to assume that he would have been any more successful as a social reformer. Those who protested against the novel in 1884 may have belonged to the coming day, but in their own they were a very small minority. Hay, far better than his critics, knew how the great mass of the people were thinking on the industrial question in the seventies.

Neither Jim Bludso nor the father of "Little Breeches" ever carried union cards. John Hay was no prophet of the golden dawn, but he was a faithful interpreter of the gilded age.

The anonymous letters to the *Century* present a different problem. They reveal a man who lacked the courage of his convictions. Hay's feeble effort to continue his disguise by asserting that he, too, was a working-man—common though the argument was in those days and later—was less honest than the book he was defending. One cannot resist the conclusion that Hay wrote anonymously because, having already had one unhappy experience with the critics, he lacked the courage to stand up and take the criticism openly. To be conspicuous was to Hay excruciating torture. A dozen years before he might have led a liberal movement; now he might have led a conservative one: he had no taste to lead anything. He was as sincerely an individualist as his creature Matchin, the carpenter. He presented the unhappy spectacle of a man of forty who had not escaped disillusionment and yet without finding himself, or the way. He knew not whither he was drifting. For practically everything he had written, something else that he had written could be quoted against it.

The recent critics have found it unforgivable that the author had married a rich wife. They should have continued their searches farther. They should have gone back of his marriage to his boyhood home which was culturally superior to that of any of its neighbors, and to a mother and grandmother who cherished in wilderness and prairie the traditions of refinement brought from New York and Rhode Island. Hay failed as social philosopher, as he had failed as poet, not because of his wife, or his mother, or any woman, but because all through life, until near its end, wherever choices were presented he was too inclined to select the easier way.

POETS are often strong partisans, but they are difficult stuff out of which to make loyal party-men. John Hay in 1875 was most of all a poet. As such, as well as freeman of the prairies, he cried for liberty. Whether the shackles were those of dogma, of office routine, or of group action, he carried them with great discomfort. Long ago he had determined that he would wear no man's livery. It remained to be seen whether such a person could come to terms with political party organization and be "regular."

Hay had another quality not usually favorable to political success; his taste as to friends was too selective. Never at any one time in his life did he have more than half a dozen intimate friends, and they changed from decade to decade. This discrimination, with which must be counted an ingrained hatred of sham and political bunkum, would load any one down with formidable handicaps for success in politics.

In the political strife of the tempestuous period from 1858 to 1865 Hay was hardly more than an onlooker. Even when in the midst of it he was detached. During the Johnson administration he was out of the country most of the time. Such opinions as he had were probably those of Seward; the Radicals of the day he viewed with mild amusement. He was in Vienna during the presidential campaign of 1868. To John Bigelow he wrote, July 9, 1869: "In a year or two everybody will be where you are. We are all free-traders at heart, except the pigironical classes. We must start the debt down hill before we can do much with the tariff." [1] There is no record of what Hay then thought of Grant, but it was apparent in Madrid in 1870 that he was becoming dissatisfied with the administration under which he served.

The *Tribune* in 1870 was an independent Republican paper, bending every energy to defeat Grant's renomination in 1872. This was not alone the sentiment of the aging editor, Horace Greeley, but of Whitelaw Reid and the entire staff. In this effort the *Tribune* by no means stood alone among the nominally Republican papers. It was a noble company of the elect editors of the day who banded together to stem

[1] Copy of letter supplied by the late Miss Grace Bigelow.

the nauseating tide of what was called "Grantism"—Samuel Bowles, Joseph Medill, William Cullen Bryant, Henry Watterson, Murat Halstead, John Bigelow, Emil Praetorius, and Oswald Ottendorfer. Such a company, and such a purpose, were wholly congenial to Hay. There was about it the flavor of the noble "Forty-eighters" of Europe whom Hay greatly admired. Led by the magnetic Carl Schurz, a group of crusading German radicals, now American patriots, were campaigning for righteousness. That many of the crusaders were also free-traders did not bother Hay. It was perhaps sufficient that Charles Francis Adams was being put forward to lead an independent ticket. Just back from abroad, Hay had landed in excellent company, and had been provided with a liberal cause in harmony with his own feelings. He despised political corruption.

The famous Cincinnati Convention of 1872 was timed to meet in advance of the conventions of the two regular parties. Its platform proved one which could enlist Hay's hearty enthusiasm. It condemned Grant for careless use of his high office, for abusing it to promote personal ends, and for disregard of the fundamental principles of constitutional government. The platform charged the Republican party with having thwarted investigation and reform, as well as having kept alive the passions of the war. In ringing words the new party called for the supremacy of civil over military power, reform of the civil service, return to specie payments, refusal of further land grants to railroad and other corporations, and the removal of all civil disabilities imposed by reason of the late war. Up to this point Hay had no difficulty.

Then came the nomination of Greeley, his own chief, but also Lincoln's gadfly, whose political ineptitude had reached a climax at Niagara Falls with Hay as its most intimate witness. Two months later at Baltimore the Democratic party endorsed Greeley and his platform, thus making the ticket less Republican than Democratic. Hay left no record of his emotions. After all, the choice in November was to be between Greeley and Grant. To work for Greeley may have been difficult but to follow Grant was impossible. Politics are that way. Group or corporate action of any sort rests on compromise which is bitter medicine for poets and individualists generally. It is hard to realize that the choice between two evils, where there is no third alternative, is the choice between two goods. It is doubtful whether Hay as a regular Republican ever had a more difficult choice than faced him as a bolter in 1872.

Hay's political activity in the Greeley campaign was largely confined to the *Tribune* office, where he shared with Whitelaw Reid, after
Greeley's retirement as editor, the excessively difficult responsibilities
of carrying the paper through the campaign without wrecking a
property as well as a party. In the office Hay was second in command.
During the summer he made a brief visit to Illinois, where he found
the younger members of the family for Greeley, while Milton Hay
worked for Grant: youth and maturity. His letters do not indicate
great ardor or enthusiasm; he could not have been greatly surprised
at the result in November; nor was Greeley himself. Hay finally
escaped the dilemma by not voting at all.

From the status of Greeley mugwump where in later years he described himself as helping to hold up the Republican party by the tail,[1]
Hay passed by easy stages in eight years through that of Blaine half-
breed to party regularity.

The death of Horace Greeley, November 29, 1872, precipitated a
fight for the control of the *Tribune*, which was calculated to keep alive
in Hay the emotions of the ill-starred campaign. Samuel Sinclair, publisher of the paper, sold his twenty shares to William Orton, president
of the Western Union Telegraph Company, who was believed to be
acting on behalf of Roscoe Conkling and others of the old New York
guard, the evil genii of Grant. It was proposed to make Schuyler Colfax, the retiring Vice President of the United States, the editor, thus
bringing the "Great Moral Organ" into the fold of the Conkling Republicans. Just at the moment when the coup was to be executed,
investigations of the *Crédit Mobilier* tarred Colfax with such a broad
stripe that the owners took a second thought for their property interests. The small stockholders were frightened. Orton was unable to
swing the necessary options.

Up to that point Whitelaw Reid had been fighting with his back to
the wall. For Greeley's place he was an avowed candidate, but he had
lacked the necessary financial backing. It was a dramatic moment.
Hay learned of the situation as he was passing east through Springfield,
Ill., early in December. "If there is any attempt to oust him [Reid],"
he wrote to his mother, December 5, 1872, "I shall oppose it with all
the means in my power." A month earlier Hay had been trying to sell

[1] *Letters and Diaries,* II, p. 160.

a share of *Tribune* stock, but when he reached New York Reid arranged for him to buy still another. William Walter Phelps, a warm friend of Reid's, also came to the rescue. More substantial, however, was the help of Governor Sprague, an old Washington friend of Hay's, and the help of Jay Gould, who bought up the opposing options and permitted Reid to realize his ambition to be Greeley's successor. The path of moral reform also is beset with compromise: Greeley for President, and then Jay Gould back of the *Tribune*.

During the contest there was much muck-slinging, especially by the rival papers. Many of the rumors still survive, but into the merits of the controversy it is not necessary to go. It is worth recording, however, that Reid's victory was regarded as a great moral triumph by such a man as Bayard Taylor, who had been one of "Greeley's boys." To John Russell Young, also an old *Tribune* man, but now lined up with Ben Butler and Grant, Taylor wrote jubilantly, from Switzerland, January 23, 1873: [1] "The *second* revolution inside the *Tribune* accords with my own ideas of what the paper should be *now,* and what it should seek to become. Reid and Hay, together, will not be likely to make any serious mistake; to a certain extent they complement each other. The news that the Sinclair, Orton and Colfax arrangement was overthrown, was the best I have received for many a day. We live in an age of little principle and less faith, but I never more firmly believed in something higher than interest and expediency than just now; and I am willing to stand or fall in that belief."

The tribute was all the more impressive because half of Bayard Taylor's modest fortune was in *Tribune* stock.

No doubt Hay felt as Taylor did. The cohorts of evil had won in November, but within the *Tribune* they seemed to have met their just deserts. From that time forward the political views expressed by the *Tribune* were, in general, though with exceptions in detail, the views which John Hay approved. Many of them were, in fact, his own, for he continued during more than twenty years an active correspondence with Reid, and he also continued his contributions, political comment as well as literary criticism.

Whitelaw Reid was not by temperament a mugwump. It was not possible to put the *Tribune* immediately on the back track and make it into an administration paper. Nor did either of the young men desire

---

[1] *John Russell Young Papers,* Library of Congress.

such a course. The "third term" was coming over the horizon and so the paper continued, as independent Republican, to oppose "Grantism." The next opportunity came in the State campaign of 1874 when John A. Dix, who had followed Bigelow at Paris, and under whom Hay had served for a brief period, was pitted against Samuel J. Tilden, fresh from his Tweed Ring prosecutions. Dix shilly-shallied on the "third term" issue, and never declared himself as unequivocally as Reid wished. The paper therefore supported Tilden in spite of his soft money plank, and the latter, when elected, was frank to acknowledge that the *Tribune* support had been a decisive factor. The sentiment of the *Tribune*, however, was less for Tilden than against Grant. Hay voted for Tilden.

The New York campaign of 1874 marked the definite close of Hay's career as an independent. Even an independent cannot escape compromise.

The next year Hay moved to Cleveland. The reason was purely personal. Probably he would have gone no more willingly if he could have foreseen that in the following nine presidential elections Ohio would supply no fewer than six successful candidates. It was, in fact, by far the best State for a man to take up residence in, if he had in mind a political career. It is now by no means a rash guess that John Hay might have been a President of the United States if in 1875 he had seen his opportunity and had been willing to pay the price. No doubt such an ambition then would have seemed to him preposterous. He does not appear to have had any thought of active politics.

Hay arrived in Ohio just as the State Republican Convention was meeting in Cincinnati to nominate Rutherford B. Hayes, after an interval of retirement, for a third term as governor. The previous year the Democrats had carried the State by 17,000, electing thirteen out of twenty Congressmen. The gubernatorial campaign of 1875 was therefore of national interest. The Republican platform adopted at Cincinnati seemed to Hay "almost perfect," probably because it endorsed resumption of specie payments and did not favor a third term for Grant.[1]

Such a platform paved the way for Hay's return to the fold. As for Hayes, Hay was less enthusiastic. His latest biographer, Eckenrode, thinks that in 1872 Hayes had been at heart a liberal Republican. He

[1] Letter to Reid, June 3, 1875.

had, however, felt the inhibitions of party regularity and in the end had not only supported the party platform but had even campaigned vigorously for Grant's re-election. Eckenrode remarks that most of Hayes's speeches in that campaign were "specious and insincere." [1]

The best that Hay could say for the candidate was, "I suppose Hayes to be a good sort of man." Others felt the same way, but even Carl Schurz, whom Hay had found a glorious figure in the old White House days, and who had been a comrade of the Greeley campaign, was persuaded to go into the State and speak for the Republican ticket.

Next to the issue of political corruption, and now overshadowing it, was the question of an inflated currency. Three years earlier the Greeley platform had contained a hard-money plank, and the *Tribune* was a resumptionist paper. Euclid Avenue was a hard-money street, naturally; creditors did not relish the idea of being paid at seventy or fewer cents on the dollar, and much preferred $1.40. Hay made no pretenses at being an economist, but he had lived abroad on a letter of credit long enough to know the consequences of soft money to international credit such as Euclid Avenue was committed to maintain.

On the other hand, a political campaign viewed from the editorial office of a metropolitan paper is one thing, and it is quite another viewed from a ward in a corrupt city. The difference is like that in looking through the two ends of a spy-glass. In the *Tribune* office one could take a large view of things; in Cleveland Hay was faced with the nasty condition of ward politics, and with what he regarded as the bovine quality of the average voter's intelligence. Hay was not yet quite able to accept Ohio politics with equanimity. "I am in a profound disgust about the campaign here," he wrote to Reid on September 24, 1875, probably in response to a request for an article on Ohio politics. "These bellowing, howling hounds expect to carry the State, and I have not heard of any Democrats who will bolt. . . . Think of this State—with half the Republicans and all the Democrats inflationists at heart, and carrying on a campaign on the bald issue whether the nation shall be a liar and a thief or not. I don't like the job you propose to me of skinning that skunk."

Thus Hay viewed Ohio politics and statesmen. The Republican success in 1875 awakened Governor Hayes's lively presidential ambitions. An astute political sense would have dictated that Hay attach

[1] H. J. Eckenrode, *Rutherford B. Hayes*, pp. 93–95.

himself to the Hayes chariot if he wished to hold office in the next administration. It is unlikely that Hay gave much thought to the situation. He was still a citizen of the world who merely happened to have a residence in Ohio. He was without ambitions which he regarded as political and, as for Hayes, he was not the kind of a man with whom he was accustomed to spend his time. It is not surprising, therefore, to see Hay turning away from Hayes in the spring of 1876, but it is with some astonishment that one finds him enrolling himself under the banner of James G. Blaine.

"I am only anxious for myself to have a man on one ticket or the other," he wrote to Reid March 14, 1876, "for whom I can vote without nausea." A month later, however, he had cast aside all indifference and wrote enthusiastically: "If anybody wants a better pair of candidates than Tilden and Blaine, the two most prominent politicians of the two parties, he must wait till he gets to heaven—and finds an absolute monarchy. Better men than these are not given to republics."

To what extent Hay may have followed up this conviction and busied himself in Cleveland to advance the interests of Blaine, thereby opposing Ohio's favorite son who had the endorsement of the state machine, is unknown. It is evident, however, that he received the news of the nomination of Hayes with sorrow. To Blaine, he wrote, June 17, 1876: [1]

"It is a bitter disappointment to all of us, but still we can see that you received the greatest personal tribute yesterday which has ever been given to a public man in this country. Without a single machine vote, in the face of the most energetic machine work, you had not only your three hundred and fifty-one votes, but also the cowardly good-will of the Ohio and the Pennsylvania delegations, three-fourths of whom would have voted for you if they had dared defy the machine lash."

Poets and political machines do not easily adjust themselves to each other.

Thus Hay began political life in Ohio, aloof from the machine, contemptuous of many people, and more sorrowful than happy over the fact that a favorite son was being elected President.[2] Local politics

---

[1] Gail Hamilton [Mary Abigail Dodge], *James G. Blaine,* p. 418.

[2] In his opinion of Hayes, however, Hay did not stand alone, even among the intelligentsia of Cleveland. "We knew him as a man of high character," wrote James Ford Rhodes, "with a fine sense of honor, . . . but we placed no great faith in his ability."

were forbidding. They cried for reform. The city was in the grip of demagogues to whom Hay paid tribute a few years later in biting paragraphs in *The Bread-Winners*. He was appalled at the indifference of Euclid Avenue, but unlike Mark Hanna who was looking out upon the same scene, Hay was not the sort of person to go out into the muck of the ward, city and county, to organize a reform. Least of all could he bring himself to fight fire with fire, as Hanna did, buying votes where necessary, in the interests of better government.[1]

Hay turned to his history, and poked fun occasionally at Hayes. He referred to him, sarcastically, as "this model reformer," and once when Hayes had ventured to reprove Gov. Shelby M. Cullom of Illinois for his views on silver legislation, Hay remarked to Reid: "He is not goddlemity and governor of Illinois both." [2]

Within two years after the election of Hayes, Hay had reason to assume toward the Administration and the President a different attitude. In December, 1878, Bayard Taylor, newly appointed minister to Berlin, died at his post. The position was offered to Whitelaw Reid, who, in declining, brought forward the name of Hay. The suggestion met with discouragement. The President had already expressed an unwillingness to make use of Hay. "He wants the Ohio places for his friends," Hay remarked acidly. Now, William M. Evarts, Secretary of State, to whom Reid had made the suggestion, elaborated the difficulty. Hay lacked "political standing." This remark was immediately reported to Hay, who modestly recognized its truth but added, plaintively, that he would like "a second-class mission uncommonly well." [3]

Not long after this Hay met, through Reid, William Walter Phelps in New York. Urged by both Reid and Phelps, Hay returned to Ohio, resolved to take Evarts' hint and bestir himself. In August of that year he sent the *Tribune* some paragraphs of a speech he had made by way of "Shermanizing a little." The speech had been made in the strongest Democratic ward in Cleveland and had been very well received. Soon he was making a speech nearly every night. They were having a "red hot canvass." One Saturday evening he addressed a mass meeting of 5,000 people on the Public Square. "Tell Mr. Phelps he

James Ford Rhodes, *Historical Essays*, p. 246. Subsequently both Hay and Rhodes came to have a higher opinion of Hayes's ability.
[1] Herbert Croly, *Marcus Alonzo Hanna*, pp. 114–15; 136.
[2] Cortissoz, I, p. 389.
[3] Hay to Reid, March 30, 1879.

bullied me into it," he wrote to Reid. Yet in the midst of his "Sherman-izing" he found time to write to Blaine, September 11, congratulating him on his success in the Maine elections, in the following words: [1] "Pass greatly on! Thou that hast overcome! You have won the most prodigious personal victory of the time."

Hay never really enjoyed speech-making. The preparation of a speech tore him to pieces and the delivery was equally taxing. Natur-ally critical, he may have found it difficult to abandon the critic's attitude. However, he was out to acquire political standing. A political speech was in the nature of a literary trick, and there was no literary trick which Hay could not acquire with facility. One speech led to an-other until at length Hay was presiding at a political mass meeting to introduce "Zack" Chandler, the same who had been dragged out of bed on election night in 1876 to send the famous telegrams to make certain that in South Carolina, Florida, and Louisiana, no unnecessary vote for Tilden should be counted. If it is a little difficult to imagine John Hay declaiming the following paragraph, we cannot doubt the *Tribune* for October 9, 1879, especially when we know that Hay him-self sent in the speech:

Reeking with the contact of repudiators and thieves, they yet dare to accuse their betters of malversation in office; and with slander and perjury, to strike in defiance the spotless shield of that party which has reduced the debt a thousand millions, and given us, through an honest resumption, a credit unpar-alleled in history.

The adjectives in the speech were equally applicable to Philip II and Napoleon III. And, after all, could it have been any harder to introduce "Zack" Chandler in 1879 than it had been to write editorials for Greeley in 1872?

Hay had found another use for his powers of invective. His imagina-tion now dwelt with indignation upon the wrongs which the Democratic party was inflicting upon the freedman in the South. He ignored the part which President Hayes had played by withdrawing the Federal troops. His old passion for liberty, lighted in Europe if not earlier, flamed again, and in a speech at Royalton, Ohio, and reported in the *Tribune,* October 15, 1879. He closed as follows:

We think that we have done all that men could be asked to do in the way of reconciliation. With not a traitor hanged or punished for his treason; with

[1] Gail Hamilton, p. 475.

no restraints even upon the most persistent slack-jaw in the land; with free license for all of them to insult and revile the Nation which has pardoned them; with the liberty to set up in their own states whatever devilish caricature of free government they choose; we feel that we have done all that the most Quakerish forbearance could require. And now in addition they ask us to consent to sit by in silence and smile approval while they tear from the statute book every vestige of those righteous laws, by which we tried to secure the fruits of freedom and nationality after the terrible war into which the rebellion of Democrats had forced us. If they ask us to consent to riot and murder in one section, and to the employment of hired bands of ruffians in another, to trample under their brutish hoofs the last sacred thing we have saved from their lust, the free ballot-box, then it is time to call a halt.

"We think"; Hay had identified himself forever with the Republican party. Not with Conkling, never; but he had been able to go as far as "Zack" Chandler, which was at least as far as might reasonably be expected of a poet of reform.

The team-work between Hay and Reid was perfect. Hay sent in the speeches; Reid gave them a national audience. No longer could it be claimed that Hay was without political standing. "Col. Hay has come out of his retirement," said the *Tribune*, October 2, "to take part in the Republican canvass." He was modestly confining himself to ward and township meetings in his own county, but Reid did not fail to point out that few young men were so well equipped for a political career as this brilliant secretary of Abraham Lincoln, a distinguished diplomat, and a former editor of the *Tribune*. Reid was glad to report that the Republicans of the Twentieth Ohio District were thinking of running Hay for Congress the following year. He was regarded as of peculiar availability for he was free of all cliques and had no political debts to pay.

Another one of those dazzling triumphs equal, in some ways, to the literary success of 1871. Four years earlier John Hay had come to Cleveland a relative stranger. No apprenticeship in politics for him, no standing in line waiting for seniors to be moved off. Hay never started at the bottom of anything. He never had to. With one leap he could be a candidate for Congress in a district where election was practically certain. In the United States such combinations of literary and political success were amazing, the only similar one that comes to mind being that of Henry Cabot Lodge who that same year was preparing to turn from teaching at Harvard to serve an apprenticeship in the State legislature. But that was in Massachusetts.

Mr. Evarts' skepticism was now removed. The President himself began to feel differently about Hay. In October the Hays entertained William Dean Howells and his wife in their beautiful home on Euclid Avenue. The President and Mrs. Hayes came up from Fremont for the reception. Hay could entertain as well as he could speak or write. Such a man now appeared useful. Just then Frederick W. Seward, who began as Assistant Secretary of State with his father in 1861, and who had returned to the post in the Hayes Administration, resigned. Evarts offered the position to Hay. It was a better offer, at least a more important one, politically, than the Berlin mission which Evarts had withheld six months before.

Hay hesitated, even refused. Reid renewed his urging. Hay agreed to go to New York and talk the matter over. On the eve of his departure from Cleveland he wrote to Howells, November 5; "I can't write that article. I am too chivied and worritted. I have to go to New York tomorrow to talk with Reid in behalf of the State Department and give my reasons for not accepting,—and woe is me! I fear my reasons will be considered frivolous and vain. In that case I shall have to accept and I stand like a hydrophobiac on the edge of a bath tub. It is enough to make a man perish with self-contempt, to see such vacillation and lack of self-knowledge."

It was a case for the psychologists—a mind at war with itself.

Hay did as he feared, accepted the appointment, and was sworn into office November 1, 1879.[1] He served seventeen months, resigning just after the Garfield administration came into office, March 31, 1881. He established a home at 1400 Massachusetts Avenue, renewed his acquaintance with Henry Adams, plunged into the approaching presidential campaign, and performed without special distinction the functions of his office.

The pre-convention campaign of the Republican party in 1880 bristled with difficulties, especially for an Ohio politician with an af-

---

[1] Nov. 1, 1879 was the date of his oath of office, according to the records of the Department of State. The fact that Hay declined Evarts' offer on Oct. 28, that he changed his mind only after a trip to New York where he met Evarts in Reid's library, probably November 7, and the further fact that Hay's appointment was not announced in the *Tribune* until November 15, raise the amusing question as to whether Hay's oath of office, without which his salary could not begin, was not dated back. See Cortissoz II, p. 9. We are reminded of the 48-day transit expense account when Hay returned from Vienna in 1869, *ante* p. 85.

fection for Blaine. John Sherman, Secretary of the Treasury, whose resumption of specie payments was one of the best claims of the party to be continued in power, was an active candidate for the nomination. The Ohio State convention in April passed resolutions putting him forward as the favorite, though somewhat cold and unemotional, son. Grant, just back from his trip around the world in the hands of John Russell Young, was the candidate of Conkling and the stalwarts. Blaine, thwarted in 1876 by Conkling and his own "turkey-gobbler" speech, was again the idol of the halfbreeds, which numbered such men as Tom Reed, Wayne MacVeagh, and Carl Schurz.

Notwithstanding the April endorsement, Ohio was by no means solid for Sherman. The state appeared, at times, to be almost evenly divided, nearly half being for Blaine. On the first ballot at Chicago nine of the Ohio delegates cast their votes for the "plumed knight." This was a mistake, as John Sherman afterwards pointed out.[1] The nine votes for Blaine so outraged the Sherman delegates that even when it became certain that they could not nominate their man, and when a united Ohio delegation voting solidly for Blaine, would have given him the majority, the Sherman men would not yield. Whether Hay had any share in this blunder is not apparent from any records which remain. At any rate Hay saw his favorite ride again to defeat.

There is something puzzling about Hay's fondness, even affection, for Blaine. The *Crédit Mobilier* business, the Mulligan letters, the rather tortuous politics which had characterized Blaine's entire Congressional career, his contempt for civil service reform, appear never to have shaken Hay's faith. But, for that matter, neither did they shake the faith of William Dean Howells. When *Twenty Years in Congress* was published, Hay wrote, June 21, 1883: "The book puts you easily and securely in the front rank of American men of letters" —an extraordinary judgment in which Hay's opinion, detached from the heat of politics, seems absurdly enthusiastic. Blaine was the only political leader who ever bewitched Hay.

Out of the Chicago convention emerged James Abram Garfield, the Republican candidate. Hay and Garfield were about the same age and they liked each other. That made it easier, for now Hay could say "we" with fewer reservations. He was a deep-dyed Republican, committed by a dozen public speeches, by conspicuous office-holding, and, unlike

[1] John Sherman, *Recollections of Forty Years*, p. 611.

Schurz, never quite easy in the rôle of reformer. In the last five years, in such odd times as he had, he had been reviewing the history of the Democratic party from the days of Pierce and Buchanan. The record stirred his indignation, and he so presented it in the second volume of *Abraham Lincoln: A History*.[1] Hay's party convictions were greatly strengthened by his historical studies. His great speech of the Garfield campaign, "The Balance Sheet of the Two Parties," delivered July 31, 1880, in Mark Hanna's opera house, and reported at full length on an entire page of the next day's *Tribune*, was largely historical. Hanna loaned the opera house, rent free, for the occasion. The Cleveland *Leader* reported that "a perfect storm of applause greeted Cleveland's honored son" as he came upon the platform. He was introduced as "the cultured and honored Assistant Secretary of State," and the speech was subsequently printed as a campaign document.

"The sure way to get civil words from everybody in Cuyahoga County, at last," he wrote to Reid, "is to refuse to run for Congress. I will keep it up." The more he refused, the more they wanted him. He had already determined to resign with the change of Administration.

Hay's speech, which opened the campaign in northern Ohio, had been carefully prepared. It had several patches of rhetoric such as had characterized his speeches of the year before, but evidently he was trying earnestly to set the tone of the campaign at a more dignified pitch than was characteristic of the period. Having asserted his belief that the Republican party had "governed this country honestly and on the whole wisely for twenty years," he launched into an examination of recent history. He urged that the debate be confined to facts and principles, that personalities be eliminated. Garfield and Hancock both were "men who enjoy the love and esteem of their friends. Between now and November they both will be charged with plenty of petty little infamies, but nobody will believe a word of it all. The Democrats know that General Garfield is an able, patriotic and honest man of great capacity, unsullied character and blameless life. The Republicans know that General Hancock is a gallant soldier and an accomplished gentleman. Both of them have private characters without stain; both have rendered signal services to the Republic. All the mud that can be thrown at them will defile only the hands that throw it."

The conclusion of the address was an exhortation to young men.

[1] For a discussion of the division of authorship between Hay and Nicolay, p .137.

Stripped of their rhetoric, these paragraphs were a statement of Hay's own political convictions, and as such, form a fitting close to this chapter:

In concluding, I have one word to say to the young men of this State—to those who are just beginning their civic life, who are just casting their first vote in a national election. Many of you are Democrats through some accident of association, without having maturely weighed the history and principles of the two parties. I ask you to look back for twenty years and see upon which side the continuing honor and glory lie. Which party elected Abraham Lincoln? Which party opposed, vilified and killed him? Which party freed the slaves? Which built the Pacific Railroad? Which saved the Union and the honor of the flag? Which sustained the financial integrity of the nation, and made its credit the best in the world? If it be right to regard with pride the fulfillment of your duties as citizens, look around you and see who boasts that he voted for Breckinridge in 1860. Who brags that he cast his first vote for Vallandigham? What father tells his children that he labored to put Buchanan in the White House?

. . . Why should young men choose to cast in their lot with a discredited and soiled record; with a party which only asks of the present the plunder of office, and of history, only oblivion? With what noble thought, with what high enterprise, has that party been associated in the last quarter of a century? What purpose but that of blind obstruction has it served? I firmly believe that it has no space left for repentance. Its place is fixed in history. . . .

This is no fit fellowship for brave and magnanimous youth. . . . The national glory and national welfare have been in Republican keeping for twenty years, with the results you see. In the ranks of that party are enlisted the greater portion of the virtue and intelligence of the land, while its counsels are hallowed by the patriots and martyrs of the great war. Its past is luminous with the story of beneficent achievements; its future is as bright with promise as the radiance of the morning stars.

Thus John Hay came to rest in the Republican party from which he ten years before had been more estranged than separated.[1] Before this could happen the party had had to change from what it had been in Grant's day; but Hay, also, had changed.

He never again wrote as good verse as he had written before he became a "regular" Republican.

[1] There is a tradition, unsupported by evidence, that a committee of politicians visited Mr. Stone and intimated that he would be expected to contribute $20,000 if his son-in-law were nominated for Congress. (Thayer, I, p. 437). The story does not, on the whole, seem very plausible.

Abraham Lincoln: A History, comprises 4700 pages, about one and one half million words. As biography, it was longer than any essay ever before undertaken by any writer. As history, it was twice the size of Green's *English People,* longer than Gibbon's *Roman Empire,* and equalled only by Bancroft's *History of the United States.* Few historians had ever before written to such a scale, although Henry Adams and James Ford Rhodes were then approaching it. Where others covered several centuries of the life and thought of nations, Nicolay and Hay confined themselves to a quarter of a single century, chiefly to the life of a single man, and gave most attention to a half of a single decade. It was one of the many contradictions of Hay's career that he, whose whole life was characterized by turning from one interest to another, rather than by sustained effort in any one direction, should have been joint author of this monumental work in ten volumes.

The project was not born full-grown; it grew under the hands of the authors, grew also with the lengthening shadow of their hero, as the nation moved onward from 1865. While the two young secretaries were still with Lincoln there came to them the idea of some day writing a book. Hay kept, intermittently, a diary; Nicolay kept memoranda. The President approved and permitted the secretaries to retain some papers of personal or historic interest. Yet for several years the project appears to have lain in their minds as merely "the Lincoln book."

"Nobody talks turkey as distinctly as we could wish in relation to the Lincoln book," wrote Hay from New York to Nicolay in Paris, March 5, 1867. This was in the dark days of job-hunting when Hay all but tramped the streets seeking congenial employment. One cannot give him too much credit for withstanding at that time the temptation to turn out some cheap pot-boilers such as he might easily have sold for a week's board. "They say the market is glutted," he continued. "That [book] will be, after all, I fear, a labor of love that we will do when we get rich and idle."

The next week in Chicago he saw "Bob" Lincoln, who thus far had declined to give up to any of the persistent would-be biographers the key to the boxes containing his father's papers. Robert Lincoln also had a simple sense of the dignity of his father's memory and did not wish to cheapen it with cheap books. He did, however, go so far as to express the hope that some day he might have the assistance of Nicolay and Hay in putting the papers in order. The time was not ripe for the big book; Abraham Lincoln was not yet the great national hero, by the side of Washington. "You had better not come home until you are kicked out," Hay advised Nicolay, "and our crazy friends in the Senate have legislated all the dead beats now in office into an eternity of bread and butter."

It was another four and one-half years before any serious efforts were made. Meanwhile, Hay had won his literary triumph in New York, and Nicolay had for a brief time edited the Chicago *Republican*. "I am convinced that we ought to be at work on our *Lincoln*," wrote Hay, November 22, 1872. "You might just as well be putting in your time collecting material as not. I don't think the time for publication has come, but the time for preparation is slipping away. I wish you could have spent a week or so at Auburn before it was too late.[1] Gideon Welles has a mass of important matter but he is using it all himself in the *Galaxy*. Fox [2] would tell you a great deal worth knowing. So would Sanford.[3] Judd [4] ought to be thoroughly interviewed, and all the Springfield luminaries."

Collecting material in 1873 for history was a far more formidable task than it is today. Interviews proved untrustworthy and were abandoned. On the other hand, libraries were few, poorly stocked, and badly catalogued. Historical societies had not yet begun to collect correspondence systematically, if at all. There were no manuscript collections of importance on the war outside of the official archives of the government. Nicolay and Hay had, in fact, to make a library before they could make a book. The senior secretary addressed himself to this initial task, and, as the years went by and Hay was in a position to do so, the latter financed the purchases. In 1872 Nicolay was appointed Marshal of the Supreme Court, a post very favorable for the prosecution of the work. Robert Lincoln turned over the Lincoln papers, with

[1] William H. Seward died at Auburn, N. Y., October 10, 1872.
[2] Gustavus V. Fox, Assistant Secretary of the Navy under Gideon Welles.
[3] Probably Henry Sanford. He, representing Col. E. S. Sanford, President of the American Telegraph Company, was in the party which accompanied Lincoln from Springfield to Washington in 1861. N. & H., III, 310.
[4] Norman B. Judd, Illinois politician, also in the Lincoln party.

the reservation that he should be permitted to review the manuscript. Nicolay became the librarian and the engineer of the great enterprise.

As the material expanded the project grew in proportion. The next ten years were the reminiscent decade. Memoirs of the war poured forth from a hundred pens; and then the apologias. War books became the vogue and were much sought after by publishers.[1] Old men's memories, however, are treacherous, and too easily lend themselves to special pleading. The appearance of each new book added to the task of the young secretaries, now no longer young.

"I am kept riled constantly by the lies of McClellan, Joinville & Paris. They have built up an impudent fiction which I fear the plain truth will never destroy. And the Century is going to give McC. the vast influence of its million readers," wrote Hay, April 13, 1885. A few weeks later, May 31: "It makes me so mad to read the maunderings of the McClellan crowd, Swinton, McC., himself, and Paris, that I fear I will have to stop reading them. It affects me physically—makes me nervous—to see them lie so about Lincoln. Even Webb[2] who tells the truth about McClellan all the way through, winds up by abusing Lincoln and Stanton like pickpockets for not supporting him better. Is there any chance to have the truth listened to?"

One thing led to another and in the end the biography became a history, and thereby the troubles were increased.

The differences between biography and history cannot be reconciled, not even in a million and a half words; they are structural. Biography deals with the life and work of an individual; history is concerned with the broad currents of human thought and action upon which the individual is borne along and to which he may make contributions. But the contributions which even a Lincoln may make are but a small part of the current itself. Vast forces, which were remote from Lincoln's life, underlay the war: physical forces—geography and climate; economic forces; spiritual forces. The very stars in their courses warred with each other, and the whole creation groaned. A biography, yes; that was relatively simple. A history, no; one cannot hold a telescope to one eye and a microscope to the other, and have trustworthy vision. *Abraham Lincoln: A Chronicle* would have been

[1] The Century Company alone was reported to have made more than a million dollars in the publication of its numerous war books. Robert Underwood Johnson, *Remembered Yesterdays*, p. 190.

[2] Alexander S. Webb, *The Peninsula: McClellan's Campaign of 1862.*

better. As one critic remarked, the frame became too big for the picture.

In the eighties of the last century historiography in the United States was itself between two worlds. Just passing was the method which required a selected point of view, a party or a personal loyalty, which, once adopted, made the writing easier, and often far more interesting, but which tended to over-simplification of the facts. It cut the cloth to fit a selected pattern. Too many facts were left over. Just beyond was the modern historical scholarship which, in addition to its scorn of secondary sources, sought detachment, objectivity, and held itself as rigidly as mortals may to inductive logic. Nicolay and Hay were practical men with no academic theories. They adopted what seemed to them a simple method which would take them straight to their goal. It merely happened that the method they improvised belonged partially to both the earlier and to the later school. They had a hero and were therefore committed to writing a hero-tale. They were attorneys for the defense. They belonged to the Republican party. On the other hand, Herbert Baxter Adams, fresh from the German seminars, in his classroom at Johns Hopkins, could have taught very little about conscientious search of historical sources to John George Nicolay, Bavarian born, whose formal education had hardly reached beyond the discipline of the village print-shop and the country editor's office. Furthermore, it was a rare student who came into Adams's classroom after five years of such life abroad as both Hay and Nicolay had lived. Nor was he likely to find any scholar with Hay's ready pen. It is significant that two of the most notable contributions to American history in the following twenty years came from the searches of three men, one in Washington and two in Cleveland (James Ford Rhodes being the third), all of whom began as rank amateurs.

Embedded in an amusing letter from Hay to Charles Francis Adams, December 19, 1903, one finds the canon of historical scholarship which guided the biographers twenty years before. Adams had been inquiring about the truth of some Lincoln legend:

These stories have lost much of their sparkle to me in the constant succession of them which have come across my observation for the last twenty years, and there is apparently no end to them. Of course, we do not wonder at them in the case of professional liars like A. K. McClure, who has written several volumes of reminiscences of Lincoln, with whom I really think he never had two hours' conversation in his life; but no one seems to be immune by character or reputation from this malady of inventing interviews with great personages. When Nicolay and I came to Washington we thought we should have great advantage in personal conversation with Lincoln's contemporaries in regard to the important events of his time, but we ascertained after a very short experience that no confidence whatever could be placed in the memories of even the most intelligent and most honorable men when it came to narrating their relations with Lincoln. We stopped at once asking questions, because it placed us in a dilemma of either being compelled to report a lot of worthless fiction, or of giving grave offense to our friends by declining to do so. The example worked upon us so powerfully that in our *History*—which you justly characterized some time ago in one of your essays as unreadable by mortal man—we did not set down a single fact from our personal recollection, nor in the course of those ten volumes did we quote one word of Lincoln of which we had not a written memorandum made at the time.

But, after all, the thing which strikes me most is that all these lies and legends run in the direction of the truth. I have rarely seen a Lincoln lie that was not intended to enhance his reputation, and which did not have more or less influence in the direction of a truthful appreciation of him. One cannot help feeling that, after all, Hercules must have been something of a hustler.

Hay delighted in the degree of anonymity which came from joint authorship, perhaps because previous experiences led him to dread responsibility. He also had enough of the instinct of the showman to appreciate the value of what intrigued the curiosity of the public. He repelled all efforts to discover how the preparation of the history had been divided between the two authors, and it was almost certainly Hay himself who wrote into the "Authors' Preface": "Each has written an equal portion of the work; while consultation and joint revision have been continuous, the text of each remains substantially unaltered. It is in the fullest sense, and in every part, a joint work. We each assume responsibility, not only for the whole, but for all the details, and whatever credit or blame the public may award our labors is equally due to both."

In view of the fact that Hay had the superior literary reputation, this was a handsome statement; honest, no doubt, but also generous and magnanimous. It might be possible to show from papers still extant what chapters were first drafted by Hay, but such an exercise could not be very profitable. In general, Nicolay was the research man and the political historian; Hay was the biographer and the stylist. He, for example, made the first drafts of the early chapters on the life in Illinois which was so vivid to him, while Nicolay appears to have made the first sketch on the Compromise of 1850. In the revision, however, the style as well as the material was rubbed down and fitted so tightly that the lustre of Hay was largely lost, and Nicolay's material was simplified. To the completed task Hay had given fewer hours than Nicolay. He was slow to begin and he was interrupted by ill-health, by political life, by business cares, by trips abroad, and by the writing of *The Bread-Winners*. On the other hand, when once started he worked furiously, and few could equal his rapidity of composition. His most unremitting efforts were in the year and a half (1885–86) which preceded serial publication in the *Century*.

As the task dragged over the long years it wore down both authors, and palled on Hay. They had become the guardians of the Lincoln tradition, an increasing responsibility. The work was a grind. The writers became irritated. Each wrote intemperate letters, not to each other, but to others, especially to the publishers, letters which the other either refused to send or had to explain. There are many such letters from Hay, the same kind of letters which later he used to write about Senators and Ambassadors. Letters of this sort never meant to Hay what they seemed to mean to readers who saw them in cold type. Hay liked to paint with a full brush. In his more reflective moods his literary sense and his courtesy came to his rescue. The following long letter, pencilled August 10, 1885, fairly illustrates both the spirit and the method by which the collaboration was carried forward:

I return herewith the Gilder correspondence. There will be no difficulty whatever in beginning the series—if ever—next fall (1886). The only contingency in which we should not be able to keep up would be death. If we live we can do it.

The reason why I wanted you to criticize that chapter with the utmost severity is this—I dictated every word of it. I found myself breaking down with the nervous fatigue of writing & copying. I therefore hired a stenographer —a dull young Englishman, who has nothing in the world but a handwriting. I always thought I could not dictate—but I found the only way was to take time and not hurry; to go back,—erase, start fresh &c, just as if I was writing —and not much faster. It is a vast gain. After he writes out the notes, I go all over them again with great care.

As to your criticisms—you can put in all the things you think lacking, or make a note and I will do it next fall: strike out, or reduce to footnotes whatever you think superfluous. Do this without hesitation and I will do the same with yours. An outside judgment on those points is almost sure to be right.

As to my tone towards Porter and McClellan—that is an important matter. I have toiled and labored through ten chapters over him (McC). I think I have left the impression of his mutinous imbecility, and I have done it in a perfectly courteous manner. Only in "Harrison's Landing" have I used a single injurious adjective. It is of the utmost moment that we should *seem* fair to him, while we are destroying him. The Porter business is a part of this. Porter was the most magnificent soldier in the Army of the Potomac, ruined by his devotion to McC. We have got this to consider. We are all alone in condemning him. I don't count John Logan's company, for historians. Even Palfrey, who takes the hide off McClellan, speaks of "Porter's perfect vindication at the hands of the Board." A big majority of the American people believe him innocent; all the Democrats, all the mugwumps, which means all the literary folks, all the Southerners, & half the Republicans of the North. We believe him guilty; but I don't think we need go farther than say so, dispassionately. A single word of invective, I think would be injurious to us, rather than to him. It would be taken to show that we were still in the gall and bitterness of twenty years ago.

Gilder was evidently horrified at your saying that Lee ought to be shot; a simple truth in law and equity. I find, after a careful reading of a dozen biographies and all his own reports that Stonewall Jackson was a howling crank; but it would be the greatest folly for me to say so. I am afraid I have come too near saying so, in what I have written about him. He is a "saint and a hero." General Black said so, in a speech the other day—Gen. Black of Ill., Comr. of Pensions.

The war has gone by. It is twenty years ago. Our book is to be read by people who cannot remember anything about it. We must not show ourselves to the public in the attitude of two old dotards fighting over again the politics of their youth.

I confess I learned something from the criticism of your book.[1] All the reviews acknowledged its merits of style, accuracy, and readableness—but nearly every one objected to its tone of aggressive Northernism. This was a surprise to me. I read it in Ms. and thought it perfectly fair and candid—but I am of that age, and inbred with all its prejudices.

We must not write a stump speech in eight vols, 8mo.

We will not fall in with the present tone of blubbering sentiment, of course. But we ought to write the history of those times like two everlasting angels— who know everything, judge everything, tell the truth about everything and don't care a twang of their harps about one side or the other.

There will be one exception. We are Lincoln men all the way through. But in other little matters, let us look at men as insects and not blame the black beetle because he is not a grasshopper.

Salmon P. Chase is going to be a nut to crack.

So is Stanton.

[1] *The Outbreak of Rebellion*, in Scribner's "Campaigns of the Civil War Series."

I am sick abed—but the Dr. thinks I am gaining on him and will be out of his hands this week.

Regards to Mrs. Nicolay and Hélène.

Yours faithfully,

J. H.

P. S. Destroy this letter. It would be too great a temptation to any reporter who should pick it up.

Hay had undertaken the business negotiations with the publishers and revealed a firm grip on business matters. At length the Century Company and Harpers were bidding against each other, greatly to the advantage of the authors, although it never could be said that the remuneration received for both serial and book rights was commensurate with the labor spent. Serial publication began in November, 1886, and continued each month for more than four years. No editor would dare mortgage his pages that way in these days, but it was different then, when people had fewer time-saving devices and more time. There is still, in many an old attic from Maine to California, a dust-covered stack of those old numbers of the *Century,* put there years ago by Grandma who thought that perhaps the children some day would like to read them. But the children never did.

Half, or less, of the manuscript appeared in the magazine, most of the military chapters being omitted because the *Century* had already covered that ground in the various war series in previous years. To the authors the criticism of the currently published portions was valuable, though sometimes torturing. "We shall not have a friend left on earth by next fall," wrote Hay. "If you can see your way to soften your *tone* toward old Jeff—though I don't suppose you can—it would be politic. Let the facts make him as despicable as he is—*we* do not want to appear to hate and despise him. J. H.

"But we do, and I suppose we can't keep it from sticking out."

The fact that serial publication began during a Democratic Administration did not make the situation any easier. The *Century* editors were nervous and not infrequently pleaded for moderation. Hay had some sympathy with them, but felt that their chief difficulty was that they were all at heart mugwumps—a group for whom he now had great scorn. The book was, in fact, a good deal of a Republican document, a by-product of which had been Hay's campaign speech at Cleveland in the summer of 1880. As Hay's political convictions hardened (Nicolay's were already fixed) it was impossible to keep the Republicanism from sticking out. It was not the primary aim of the history to make Republicans proud of their party, and to gather in the new voters each year, but it served to accomplish such a purpose. The book was having that effect as late as 1902, when Roosevelt, up at Oyster Bay, read it. "After reading your volumes," he wrote to "Dear John," July 22, 1902, "I do congratulate myself that my father was a Republican and that I am a Republican. It seems to me it would be a dreadful thing to have to live down being descended from Vallandigham; and I should mortally hate to have had men like Seymour or McClellan for ancestors"—which were almost the words of Hay's appeal twenty-two years before to the young voters of Ohio.

On the other hand, whatever the feelings and convictions of the authors, they had allowed Abraham Lincoln's gentle spirit to shine through, and in the same letter President Roosevelt wrote, as in the mood in which one comes from church: "At any rate, it has made me of set purpose to try to be good-natured and forbearing and to free myself from vindictiveness. . . . In the little work, the easy work, of these days of peace and prosperity, I see on a small scale much that Lincoln saw in the supreme years of the nation's life struggle. Mrs. Josephine Shaw Lowell is an utterly unimportant annoyance; and I doubt if Wendell Phillips was relatively much more of an annoyance to Lincoln."

It was strange, indeed more than strange, significant, how the Lincoln theme had again awakened the moralist in Hay—he who did not like to meddle with moral ills. He wrote furiously to do justice to a slandered friend, to set a nation right. In a mood not out of harmony with that in which he had come back from Europe in 1870, crying for freedom and hating Napoleon III, he now found himself writing a tract. He became the apostle of the Republican party, so to be regarded to the end of his days.

A later biographer of Lincoln, Nathaniel Wright Stephenson, declared that "their Lincoln is exasperatingly conventional, always the saint and the hero, as saint-heroes were conceived by the average American in the days when it was a supreme virtue to be 'self-made.' " [1] Well, the authors were conventional men; one of them was, as truly as Lincoln himself, "self-made"; and the other author hardly less so, yet

[1] *Cambridge History of American Literature*, III, 378.

with a different result. A more generous judgment came from the late John Spencer Bassett, one of the best of American historical scholars, a Southerner and a Democrat. He wrote in 1921: [1] "In completeness of treatment, clearness of statement, and fair discussion of the men and problems that Lincoln encountered, it was one of the best historical works of the generation in which it was written." Such partisanship as the book contained was evidently more apparent to a politically sensitive reader at home than to the foreign observer. Bassett's estimate is in accord with that of a contemporary reviewer in the *Spectator* (London), May 2, 1891, who wrote: "We must congratulate the editors on the tone of moderation and fairness they have displayed throughout."

Among John Hay's most discriminating critics was his old Cleveland friend, James Ford Rhodes, who, in his earlier historical writings, traveled over the same ground which Nicolay and Hay covered. Many years after Hay's death Rhodes wrote: [2]

Hay was not a trained historian in the way of knowing thoroughly the masters of the art. He did not read with rapt attention Gibbon, Macaulay, Parkman or any other historian except Henry Adams. He was apt to have at hand some high class French novel or Memoirs. . . . Although Hay did not possess the power of generalization of Gibbon he had two qualities invaluable for a historian—that of narration and a skepticism that influenced in a marked degree his judgment of men and of events. . . . Hay was a partisan. . . . Nicolay and Hay made Lincoln out a saint.

"No man," Hay wrote in a private letter, "can be a great historian who is not a good fellow." A "good fellow," a genuine man was Hay in every respect.

The publication of *Abraham Lincoln: A History* marked the end of the major phase of Hay's literary work. It also marked the beginning of the major phase of his political career. To Democrats it doubtless may have appeared that *Abraham Lincoln: A History* was an ermine mantle to cover the faded and unlaundered "bloody shirt"; at any rate Hay became the Republican laureate.

[1] *Ibid.*, p. 182.
[2] *The McKinley and Roosevelt Administrations, 1897–1909*, pp. 121–23.

JOHN HAY had just turned forty-one when he became Assistant Secretary of State in November, 1879. He served for seventeen months and then went immediately to New York where, in the absence of Whitelaw Reid, he was acting editor of the *Tribune* for six months. At the age of forty-three he was free and he did not again hold any office, except his directorship in the Western Union Telegraph Company, until March, 1897, when, in his fifty-ninth year, he became ambassador to England. Of this intervening period Hay spent a total of about sixty months, five years, in literary work on *The Bread-Winners, Abraham Lincoln: A History,* and, with Nicolay, in editing the speeches, letters, and state papers of Lincoln which were published in two volumes in 1894. After making the most generous estimates as to the amount of time devoted to productive literary work, one finds about ten fallow years. Some portion of this time is chargeable to illness, but it is plain that, notwithstanding the periods of furious labor on the history, John Hay was leading a very leisurely life.

It was during those years that Hay became a man of affairs. His father-in-law, in the last years of his life, traveled a great deal in search of the health which was denied him, and in these periods Hay had charge of some of Mr. Stone's interests. The settlement of the latter's complicated and somewhat scattered estate, in the summer of 1883, immediately after the return of the Hays from nine months in Europe, led the son-in-law into many and diversified financial affairs both in real estate and in the stock-market. In the latter Henry Adams, who knew little of the spirit of adventure which belongs to the prairie, thought he was playing with an "edge-tool." [1]

"I had a season of sweet refreshment with John Sherman the other day," wrote Hay to Adams four years later. [2] "He says there is no dear

---

[1] "Financially we grub along and talk poor, but as no one here need spend money unless he likes, the loss of thousands of millions has little outward effect. No improvement need be expected until things have got settled to a new economic bottom. Most of us are really better off when the great properties shrink. I am sorry for your Wabash, but conservative people here avoid Mr. Jay Gould and expect him to take their money if he can get it. John Hay plays with that edge-tool, but I don't. . . ." Henry Adams to Charles Milnes Gaskell, an English friend, Sept. 21, 1884; *Letters of Henry Adams,* pp. 360–61.

[2] *Letters and Diaries,* II, p. 136, Cleveland, Ohio, Nov. 7, 1887.

property in Washington; it is cheap at any price. He does not believe in
suburban property. I agree with him. Neither of us owns any."

In real estate and in stocks Hay succeeded as he had in politics, and,
at an earlier day, in letters. In the spring of 1888, when his part of the
Lincoln history was about complete, he reported: [1] "I am up to my eyes
in the greasy details of money-making and find that I am prospering
as do the wicked." Two months later he added: [2] "I have made so much
money this year—by Harrison's victory over Uncle John—that I can
afford to be generous." The reference is to the defeat, in the Republican
nominating convention in Chicago in June, 1888, of John Sherman,
whom Hay supported.

In the spring of 1884 Hay and Adams purchased, to quote with some
amusement the only slang which seems to have been preserved from
an Adams pen, "a swell piece of land which looks across a little square,
something like Portman Square, to the White House, where our Presidents live." [3] Hay, being in Adams's eyes the "capitalist," took the
larger lot on the northwest corner of Sixteenth Street. Building began
almost immediately. The purchase was an excellent investment.

The change of residence, early in 1886, from Cleveland to Washington, marked the beginning of a new phase in the life of John Hay. In
Cleveland, as Amasa Stone's son-in-law, he had been grafted on to a
civilization to which he did not belong and which left him ill at ease. In
Washington he could order his life as he pleased. The very much lighter
tax-rate of the District of Columbia gave him a freer hand, while the
association with Henry Adams, to which reference will be made in the
following chapter, resulted in the most intimate friendship of his life.

For the next ten years John Hay would have presented a suitable
theme for John Bunyan. He had built a house to be gay in, but to a man
who has cast off most of the responsibilities which give zest to life,
gaiety is elusive. Without a profession, without an occupation, without
any clearly defined objective in life, he attempted to be gay. He tried
society, travel and life abroad, association with Henry Adams, all the
time dabbling more or less in politics, but never attending to anything
for long. The gaiety which he found soon tarnished in his hand and long
before the decade was finished he was numbering his days and waiting

[1] *Op. cit.*, p. 148, May 28, 1888.
[2] *Op. cit.*, p. 152, July 14, 1888.
[3] Adams to Gaskell, May 18, 1884; *Letters,* p. 357.

to die.

The Washington to which the Hays came offered a more rewarding society than Cleveland, but it was not a national capital in the sense that Paris, Rome, and London were capitals, and it could not satisfy John Hay very long. It was a city of only about 150,000, of whom one-third were negroes. James Bryce observed that there were there no national leaders of finance, industry, commerce, or of the professions; few men of letters, no artists, and hardly any journalists.[1] What was called the "society" of Washington was a small group of polished people who constantly met one another. Bryce found it no less agreeable because it had a peculiar flavor; so far from aspiring to political authority, it deemed it bad form to talk politics.

"The richest people live in the quietest way," wrote Cecil Spring Rice,[2] who came to the British Legation in 1887 and immediately began to write letters which contained vivid pictures of Washington, "and only spend money on entertainments and flowers—not in huge houses and gorgeous carriages." He noted the absence of snobbishness, but he, as well as Joseph Chamberlain, was impressed with the rampant dullness. Spring Rice's description of an afternoon tea sounds very much like John Hay's description in *The Bread-Winners* a few years before, of an evening party in Cleveland. He wrote:

Now, these teas are wondrous things. You call at a house on the lady's day, together with a monstrous horde of persons from the uttermost parts of America. The lady says she is glad to see you and then asks your name. She then passes you on to another lady in a low dress who takes you to have tea at a table served by a young lady of her acquaintance from Buffalo or Little Rock, Arkansas. The ladies are often very pretty and charming; always rather amusing. I asked the one from Little Rock if it were a large town? She said, "Oh yes, there were two germans there." (i. e. Cotillion clubs, by which she measures the size of the cities.) I asked her afterwards if it were true that ladies in the States were often engaged to three men at a time. She said she was herself; that was why she didn't want to go back.

It was the newcomers from Buffalo, Little Rock, and Chicago, arriving in the late eighties and early nineties, who gave a new direction to the social life of Washington, and, for that matter, to the life of such other social centers as New York and Newport. Something was

[1] James Bryce, *The American Commonwealth*, II, p. 858.
[2] Stephen Gwynn, Editor, *The Letters and Friendships of Sir Cecil Spring Rice*, I, pp. 84–85.

happening to the national life as well as to Washington. One is tempted to resort to statistics. In twenty years prior to 1880, the Federal government gave away to corporations and individuals nearly 150,000,-000 acres of land. Perhaps these figures are sufficient. The population and wealth of the nation began to roll up. Almost every figure employed to describe the state of the nation in 1860 had in the next thirty or forty years to be multiplied by two, by three, by four, or even by five. No such ratios of increase were ever known before. wealth, wealth, wealth.

Out of the sturdy, yeoman stock which broke up the "unshorn prairies," or ministered to the needs of these pioneers, emerged a new generation of sons and daughters, particularly the latter, who, with their mothers, felt about the prairies just as John Hay had felt in 1859. They demanded society, culture, traditions, which they could not supply and which they sought in the Eastern cities and resorts. Spring Rice described the new aristocracy in New York as "those whose fathers had made money," and of the passing show at Newport he observed: "They are all strugglers in society." [1] The Americans, not all of them with names easily recognized as American, were climbing, some of them faster than others.

It was not for the company of such people as these that John Hay came to Washington. Over a column by its Washington society reporter a New York newspaper carried some headlines about "the gay life of Lincoln's Secretary in the capital" to whose entertainments came all the notables of Washington. It stated that the Hay receptions and dinners had "almost revolutionized the social functions of the Washington season." That was the way it looked from the outside. Inside the Hay home it was different. Over the library door were bronze portraits of William Dean Howells and Henry James. There was also a painting of the latter, done by La Farge when James was twenty-one. Nor could the visitor miss the masks of Lincoln, one by Volk in 1860, and the other by Mills in 1865.[2] A nonconformist by nature, Hay accepted the ritual of society, studied respectability, appeared at the Leiters' balls, and even went to White House receptions, but his soul abhorred any kind of "crush."

[1] *Op. cit.*, pp. 90, 108.
[2] There is a description of Hay's library in *Authors at Home,* edited by J. L. and J. B. Gilder.

John Hay's ideal in this period was to be a gentleman and a man of culture. "His natural propensity for culture," wrote James Ford Rhodes,[1] "was fostered by the reading of books and by mingling in the best society. Having a notable aptitude for acquiring knowledge second-hand, he used this knowledge in his talk with wonderful skill. Always meeting interesting people, he absorbed incidents that in turn set off his own conversation. He loved wit and humor, and any manifestation of them was to his latest day a passport to his favor. He was a remarkable dinner-table talker and, in discussing the subject, a man of wide experience could only think of two shining lights of Boston and Cambridge who were his equals."

There was in Washington a stratum of this kind in which Mrs. Cabot Lodge and Mrs. Don Cameron were the reigning hostesses. Here one might find traditions and culture which had matured under the shadow of great institutions and literary personages, such as the prairies did not yet sincerely appreciate or desire. This smaller group had a civilized way of living which left it in no necessity to study the smart patterns of what was coming to be called "Society." Here, in addition to Lodge, Hay could find Cecil Spring Rice, Theodore Roosevelt, who became Civil Service Commissioner in 1889, and a few kindred spirits. Henry Adams did not "go out" much, but he was always just off-stage. Hay was more at home with such people, but there was the difficulty that the men he found there were living active lives while he was merely searching for good conversation. More and more John Hay turned to England for the satisfaction of his social hunger.

Hay's introduction to English society appears to have been supplied in 1882 by Henry Adams, who passed him on to Sir John Clark and Sir Robert Cunliffe. "We arrived in England the end of last July," Hay wrote Nicolay, March 8, 1883,[2] "spent a few weeks in London and then went north. Saw Lincoln, York, Edinburgh and Aberdeen, then went to visit a Baronet in the Highlands named Sir John Clark; passed a delightful week with him, then went to the shore of the Northern Ocean at Inverness. Thence down the Caledonian Canal to Oban, Staffa, Iona. Then back to Hastings where we had left the children during all these philanderings. We went up to London again after that; next to North Wales, to visit another Baronet and

---

[1] *The McKinley and Roosevelt Administrations*, p. 125.
[2] *Letters and Diaries*, II, pp. 77–78.

M.P., Sir Robert Cunliffe. At his house we met the Judge Advocate General in Gladstone's Government, Mr. Osburne Morgan, M.P., who invited us to visit him, which we did & passed a pleasant day or two in an Inigo-Jones house in the mountains of Wales. Then we went on a regular debauch of English Cathedrals: Hereford, Worcester, Gloster, Wells, Salisbury, without once taking breath; and after that we broke for Hastings again; and after a week of rest by the summer sea, we gathered up the whole caboodle and went over to Paris."

During this visit to Europe Hay renewed his acquaintance with Henry James, whose preference for life in England rather than in the United States was already the subject of much hostile comment in America. The criticism incensed Hay, who wrote to Howells: [1] "Of all vices I hold patriotism the worst when it meddles with matters of taste."

The Hay household which was established at 800 Sixteenth Street in Washington in 1886, was organized on a modified British pattern— not because it was British, or smart, or expensive, but because John Hay liked to live that way. Such living was, in his life, equivalent to the poker and whiskey which were more characteristic of his native land. At one end of the table sat an aristocrat by taste if not by birth; opposite sat a puritan who could be as uncompromising about whom she would receive as was Queen Victoria herself. The Hays avoided Newport.

After 1883 John Hay returned to England frequently. Through Adams he had come to know Spring Rice and the latter also passed him on to his friends. To Ronald Munro Ferguson, later Lord Novar, Spring Rice wrote in 1887: "I hope you will meet John Hay; if not, I shall in any case take you to see him at Cleveland, Ohio, or in Washington, as he is a brick." [2] As Assistant Secretary of State in 1880, Hay had come to know Henry White,[3] and a few years later in London, where White became a secretary of the American Legation, he renewed the acquaintance. White also opened doors. "I lunched with the Whites," wrote Hay to his wife,[4] "to meet the P.P.S. (Presidential Princesses) [5] Present: Lord and Lady Aberdeen, Lady Ribblesdale,

---

[1] *Op. cit.*, II, p. 76, Dec. 20, 1882.
[2] Gwynn, I, p. 71.
[3] Allan Nevins, *Henry White*, Chap. 6.
[4] *Letters and Diaries*, II, p. 226, June 18, 1891.
[5] Evidently Mrs. James Robert McKee, and Mrs. Russell B. Harrison, niece and daughter-in-law, respectively, of President Harrison, who were in London that season.

(Margot Tennant's sister), Knowles,[1] Mr. and Mme. de Bille, Danish minister, Lady Jeune, and one or two others. I took down Lady Aberdeen & sat between her and Lady Ribblesdale. It was very pleasant and broke up early as luncheons always do here. I saw Mrs. McKee at White to get her a chance to see the Queen at the Ponsonby wedding. He seemed affable and evasive, but will probably do it. He usually does. . . .

"Last night there was a grand dinner and reception at the Legation for the P.P. Present at dinner: Lord and Lady Albemarle, Lord and Lady Alcasta, Belgian and Swedish ministers, Sir W. and Lady Plowden; of Yankees: the Emerys, White, Mrs. Adair, Bradley Martins, Camerons, Blaine, Smalleys &c. I took down Mrs. Adair. On my left was Mrs. Bradley Martin, who has asked me to dinner and opera tomorrow night. After dinner there was a rather large reception. The American colony in force and some nobility and gentry. The house opens up very well and the whole entertainment was in excellent style."

Transatlantic marriages also helped to enlarge Hay's circle of English friends. Mary Endicott, daughter of Cleveland's first Secretary of War, married Joseph Chamberlain; Mary Leiter married George M. Curzon. By the Chamberlains and the Curzons, Hay not infrequently was entertained in England. Andrew Carnegie purchased a castle in Scotland and Hay went there. Too deeply rooted in America to follow Henry James to England to live permanently, Hay became more and more sympathetic with James's point of view.

Deferring for a later chapter the discussion of the influence on Hay's political views, it remains to be observed here that the gay social life of neither Washington nor London brought happiness. If we may judge from his letters Hay was, in fact, utterly miserable most of the time. There were moods in which he even thought he would enjoy the realization of the old Omaresque dream of a home in the wilderness.

In the summer of 1888 the Hays and Clarence King made a tour of the New Hampshire lakes with a view to purchasing land for a summer place, and eventually decided upon Lake Sunapee. King, whose instability was the most marked characteristic of his business relations, dropped out of the deal, leaving Mrs. Hay, who had to think

[1] Knollys [?]

of the summer needs of her vigorous, growing children, to sustain interest in the project. Her husband, viewing at closer range the prospect of a cabbage-garden, assented with some misgivings to the wilderness location. As Henry Adams and John La Farge were preparing for their tour of the South Pacific, John Hay, always regretful that he did not join them, started building at Sunapee. From Boston, July 17, 1890, he wrote to Adams: [1]

I have no excuse for writing to-night except that you said that you had not my new address, which is, to wit: Newbury, New Hampshire. Thither I go at early fowl-crow to-morrow, to plunge into a barbarism profounder than that Stanley came across in Jimjamjumbo. My desire to go to the Pacific with you increases at every new exhibition of the bellicose with my children; and yet I feel more and more that my duty lies here—to keep them from massacring each other. . . .

I do not know what my poor little wretches will do at Newbury;—they are looking forward to a season of summer opera-bouffe, instead of the deadly repose we have planned for them. I went out today and bought Del [2] a carload of fishing tackle which he will never learn how to use. He did not even seem to care for the shopping. In my day, buying the hooks and lines, and digging the bait was fun enough, even if you caught no fish.

A few weeks later Hay had somewhat modified his opinion about the New Hampshire wilderness, which, in later years, was to be his refuge, and which at length afforded his tired eyes their last earthly view. To Adams he wrote: [3]

Mrs. Hay has once more proved her superiority to me in practical sagacity. This sojourn which I regarded with horror has turned out rather agreeable than otherwise. I do not mind the country fare. The children seem very happy. They have even more amusements than they can manage. They fish and row and swim. They colonize the desert islands in the lake. They climb the hills. They quarrel and fight and have a good time generally.

I cannot tell you how my heart sinks at the thought of your going away without me. I recognize it as the last ringing of the bell. I now feel that I shall never go west, and thence east. I shall never see California nor the Isles of the sea. But we have resolved to begin building at once, and I must be here during the next three weeks. I am a worthless creature, destitute of initiative.

In the next few years Hay wrote many letters in the vein of the last sentence quoted above. His divided nature was again at war.

With so much leisure on his hands one might have expected Hay

---

[1] *Op. cit.*, p. 195.
[2] Adelbert Stone Hay; the other children were Helen, Alice, and Clarence Leonard.
[3] *Op. cit.*, p. 197.

to return to writing, but for creative work in the field of literature he was now cumbered with too many cares, and things. "I thank you for your kind word about my verses," he wrote to "My dear Henry" in 1887.[1] "They are not fresh, but have been kicking about the place for twelve years. There will be no fresh ones—once in a decade I may fish out an old one and have the pleasure of hearing a friendly critic say what progress they exhibit, and of hearing some scorpion contemporary hiss that I am falling into dotage." The drudgery of the final work of completing the history, although he employed competent assistants to help in the proof-reading and the verification of the citations, left him flat, and with the conviction that his creative days were over. In 1890 he collected his verse and brought out a new edition. Several poems which had appeared in the edition of 1871 were omitted, and others were added, among which was "The Stirrup Cup." It is a surprise to discover that this verse was first published in *Scribner's* in May, 1881, but moods of depression which this verse expresses were common, and the times in which Hay believed that he had but a short time to live were frequent. The poem was as authentic of John Hay as "Jim Bludso" had been of the Mississippi river-boating days. In 1905 Talcott Williams, in other respects a severe critic of Hay's literary work, called it "his one poem of the first quality." [2]

> My short and happy day is done,
> The long and dreary night comes on;
> And at my door the Pale Horse stands,
> To carry me to unknown lands.
>
> His whinny shrill, his pawing hoof,
> Sound dreadful as a gathering storm;
> And I must leave this sheltering roof,
> And joys of life so soft and warm.
>
> Tender and warm the joys of life,—
> Good friends, the faithful and the true;
> My rosy children and my wife,
> So sweet to kiss, so fair to view.

[1] *Op. cit.*, p. 109, May 12, 1887.

[2] "Through all his life he held lightly the prizes of life, and what he did he did easily, or not at all. His folk verse was the rarest of quality. The 'Stirrup Cup,' so generally reprinted at his death, his one poem of the first quality, will be in every future anthology for its eerie suggestion. The author of 'Leonore' won fame for less." *Book News*, August, 1905.

So sweet to kiss, so fair to view,—
The night comes down, the lights burn blue;
And at my door the Pale Horse stands,
To bear me forth to unknown lands.

After 1890 he wrote a few sonnets, but found it impossible to apply himself to longer and more sustained writing. In 1894 Edward L. Burlingame, editor of *Scribner's,* asked him to write a review of Bret Harte's later work. After leaving the letter unanswered for ten weeks he replied: [1] "The reason I did not answer it at once is that I dallied with the notion—it was very agreeable to me. But it is no use. I am too old. I can nevermore write anything, as a matter of enjoyment. I have not the critical faculty and—lots of other things I lack, which it would be painful for me to write and tedious for you to read. I may as well stop short and say I am very sorry I can't do it."

In 1890 the *Century* for September carried a sonnet of Hay's, "Love's Dawn." "I am rather too old a bird to be singing in this strain," he explained to Gilder.[2] When the editor returned it with the suggestion that one line contained an incorrect number of syllables, Hay replied: "Your ear is all right—not so long, perhaps, as some editors. Pronounce 'heaven' in one syllable, and there you are. If you prefer 'sky,' why 'sky' be it. I have a preference for heaven, being a Presbyterian." Gilder yielded to Hay, but the editor was metrically right.

"I have been in wretched health since arriving here," he wrote Adams from London, whither Mrs. Hay, having taken things in hand, had sent him in the spring of 1891,[3] "—had influenza, followed by every other fiendish complication you can imagine, ending in fainting fits, which the great diagnostician, Broadbent, says is nerves and not heart—as if that made it any more amusing. I would not have mentioned so dull a subject except to account for the fact that I have no news to tell you. I do not go to Court, nor anywhere among the mashers. I told you, also, to let you know that if you want to see me alive, you had better get a hustle on you and come home. . . ."

Returning in July, he went to New Hampshire, thence to Cleveland, and after a week of duck-shooting to which he devoted himself reli-

---

[1] *Letters and Diaries,* II, p. 341.
[2] *Ibid.,* II, p. 191. Hay at first asked that the sonnet be printed anonymously, but seems to have consented to the use of his name.
[3] *Ibid.,* pp. 220–21, June 4, 1891.

giously each autumn, he returned to Washington, still low in spirit. "I do not want to lie to you," he wrote to Adams.[1] "We are too near Mount Vernon and the cherry tree for that. I cannot offer you any inducements. We are as dull as Chelsea. . . . You never saw us so dreary as we are. The dips who used to be amusing are gone or dead. Springy still survives, though he has had the grippe—but he is going to Japan any minute. . . ."

At Newbury the following summer, Hay continued in the same vein:[2] "We live a languid, vegetable life. Everybody asks me:— 'What do you *do?*' and the question leaves me speechless. We come here to escape doing anything. I shall never do anything again. It comes as near being amusing as I can now attain." The following February Washington was "as the dry-suckedest orange you ever saw —until your return. It is pathetic to see our little attempts to be gay. . . ."[3]

After a visit to the World's Fair at Chicago in 1893 the Hays went abroad for a year. From Rome, Hay wrote to Adams:[4]

Since I wrote last, nothing has happened to me, save that, impelled thereunto by a daughter who cares more for her amusement than my repose, I have been to Court and made a leg to the Queen. I do not know how I acquitted myself, but trust that, in imitating as well as I could remember the reverences I have seen you and King make to the beautiful and great in H Street, 1603, I did you no discredit. Her majesty was very gracious—and afterwards expressed herself in regard to my family in language I have carefully kept secret from my wife and daughter for fear they should shake me and "go off with a handsomer man."

The following May, from London, he reported:

I go out daily to lunch or dinner, and semi-daily to tea—the soul within me withering for pure bore—because I hope a little glimpse of what London is like may amuse Helen, or at least be something to have known hereafter. The *enfant de fin de siècle* is hard to amuse—perhaps the *meminissi juvabit* will be the best hold after all. She does not care for great functions, except to put them in her diary. She is bored by the great and the good, the few specimens she meets; but she does uncommon well like to come across a boy from Cleveland—which she does every five minutes from Naples to Liverpool— or a girl from Dobbs Ferry. There is one hopeful sign about her. She does not

[1] *Ibid.*, p. 231, Dec. 17, 1891.
[2] *Ibid.*, p. 242, Aug. 12, 1892.
[3] *Ibid.*, p. 251.
[4] *Ibid.*, p. 277, Feb. 5, 1894.

object to standing with me in a corner of a palace, and seeing the glittering show pass by.

It was Mrs. Hay and the children who kept him going through these ever recurring periods of melancholy.[1] The life he was deliberately leading was, after all, hardly suitable to a man of his talents. As the older children, Helen and Del, emerged from childhood, as they came to assume more and more their places by his side as individuals rather than as mere offspring, he began to think of what he had to hand on to them. Through the children there could be a transference and a prolongation of the life which in him he believed to be drawing to a close.

When they returned from Europe in the summer of 1894 it was Mrs. Hay who again stepped in quietly to give her husband's life a new interest. "After a week of struggle against fate I have succumbed," he wrote to Adams.[2] "Even indolence gives way to a stronger God, and Mrs. Hay has convinced me that it is best for Del that I take up my *pilgerstab* again and go to the Yellowstone."

With more enthusiasm, in fact, with greater satisfaction than he had shown for anything in years, he viewed his daughter's literary gifts, and sought to pass her on to his old editorial friends. To Burlingame, editor of *Scribner's*, he wrote: [3] "My daughter has written a few things that seem to my not impartial taste good enough to print. I send you a sonnet, knowing that your conscience is more powerful than your friendship—and that, if you do not like it, you will not hesitate to send it back to me."

John Hay was trying to hand down the torch which, in his own hand, had already grown dim.

In these dull years, for which ill health is a partial though not a complete explanation, Clara Stone, rather than John Hay, became and remained the hero. To such a degree was this true that it becomes proper to close this chapter with an extract from an intimate letter

---

[1] It is important to add that this emotional conflict and melancholy appears to have been reserved for letters and, possibly, for Henry Adams. It was not disclosed to John Hay's family or household. There he was always the gay, sympathetic, indulgent parent and host, especially attractive to young people. To so great an extent was this true that some of those who knew him best in those years, upon reading these pages in proof, have learned for the first time of this other mood which was being recorded in letters.

[2] *Ibid.*, 298, July 12, 1894.

[3] *Ibid.*, p. 352, April 10, 1895.

"The Fells," Hay's summer home on Lake Sunapee, New Hampshire. The site was selected in 1888 by the Hays and by Clarence King. The house was built in 1891, the architectural style being somewhat suggestive of Mt. Vernon.

The Washington homes of John Hay and Henry Adams, designed by Henry H. Richardson, completed in 1886, and now demolished, were a famous show place in their day. The entrance to the Hay residence was 800 Sixteenth Street; that to the Adams house, shown at the left, was 1603 H Street. Contrary to report, there was no door in the party wall.

to his wife, probably written from London, June, 1891, in which her part in his life is tenderly recognized:

I want the days to pass and bring the 1st, so that I can feel that every hour brings me nearer to my beloved ones. I am so weak and good for nothing. I hope your presence and your love will be the medicine that will make me well again. I feel stricken with remorse some times to think how much you have done for me and how little I have done for you. And yet I know it will continue so until the end. I shall bear the ever increasing load of obligation and shall do nothing to lighten it. Yet, after all, you would never have met with a man who could love you more or appreciate more fully your sweet and noble qualities. But that does not make my obligation less. It merely increases it. For seventeen years your true heart, your rich and noble nature, your beauty, has been mine, and have made me happier than it is possible for most men ever to be. And I cannot think what I have done, more than anybody might have done, to make you happier, my darling. If Heaven grants me a return to health and to life, it shall be my study in the future to try to find some way of adding to your happiness. I am not half good enough for you— but I do love you with all my heart and nobody could love you more. God bless and guard you and bring us together again.

IN so far as John Hay's life, between 1880 and 1897, had unity or coherence, outside of his home, it was in the "Five of Hearts," a select association originally comprising Henry Adams, Mrs. Adams, Clarence King, Mrs. Hay and himself. More a symbol than anything else, it seems to have come into being in the winter of 1880–81. It was abruptly reduced to the "Four of Hearts" by the death of Mrs. Adams, December 6, 1883, and then still further narrowed by the infrequent visits to Washington of Clarence King. Ultimately the "Five of Hearts" consisted only of John Hay and Henry Adams taking a brief walk up Sixteenth Street each afternoon at five o'clock and returning to have tea with Mrs. Hay.

The "Five of Hearts" was not so important as it seemed. It aroused the curiosity of the public because the public was excluded from its mysterious tea-table rites, but to its members it was merely an amusing name. Its note-paper, official pin, and the tea-set with the five-of-hearts design, were hardly more than adolescent, and for that reason added to the gaiety. As a group it produced nothing except subjects for the gossip of those who passed under the H Street windows and wondered why it was so masonic. The group sought no influence collectively, and had none either in the life of the nation or of the nation's capital. There is even a grave question whether its net influence on two of its members, Hay and King, was not destructive rather than helpful. Its atmosphere was too highly charged with Adams's pessimism and cynicism to be healthy. And yet, what a canvas the group presents!

If it were possible to add to an intimate biography of John Hay, that of Clara Stone, Henry Adams, Marian Hooper, and mix it up with a dash of the almost unbelievable life of Clarence King—doing it as Thackeray or Mrs. Humphry Ward would have done such a group in English society—the product would be an incomparable chapter of American social history: Henry Adams, scholar, recluse; Marian Hooper, clever, a good sport, a man's woman, childless; Clara Stone, a woman's woman, mother of four children, conventional, regular at the meetings of the missionary society, buying her Christmas presents in August, an American matron of the Western Reserve, whose presence in any group carried assurance that it was respectable; John Hay, who escapes all classifications except that of amateur; and, Clarence King, a man of fashion, good fellow, scientist, engineer, writer, improvident, unreliable, and, after his death, known to have been leading so incredible a double life that his name was never again mentioned over the "Five of Hearts" teacups. King's portrait at length could find shelter, the gift of Hay, only in the Geological Survey which had been King's best mistress and then his monument. To fill in the story, add Don Cameron, Mrs. Cameron, the Lodges, the Leiters, father, mother, and daughters, George Curzon, the Endicotts, Joseph Chamberlain, Whitelaw Reid, and William C. Whitney. All this against the background of the Cleveland and Harrison Administrations. That was America.

It is plausible, even probable, that John Hay and Henry Adams first met in Washington in the early part of 1861, perhaps at the salon of Mrs. Eames, to which Henry's brother, Charles Francis, was accustomed to go,[1] or at the home of Congressman Samuel Hooper, to whose daughter Anne, Hay was rumored engaged, and whose niece, Marian, married Henry Adams in 1872. Probably also they met again in the American Legation in London in 1865, '67, or '68, when Hay was passing to or from Paris or Vienna, and stopped to pay his respects to Henry's father, the American minister, by whom the young man was cordially received. Henry Adams was seven months older than the new secretary of the Legation in Paris. The two should have had something in common, for Henry had already for four years held the corresponding position in London. Yet the meetings seem to have made too little impression on Hay to have been recorded in either his diary or in any letters now extant, nor does Adams appear to have recalled them in later years. In the autumn of 1868, after Hay had gone to Vienna, Adams settled down in Washington to adopt what he thought was a career of journalism. It consisted, in part, of writing huge "fire-crackers" for English reviews, only the very faint detonations of which resounded in America. In 1870, when Hay was forming his connection with the *Tribune*, a more vulgar style of journalism than would have suited Adams, the latter was entering upon his duties

[1] Charles Francis Adams, *An Autobiography*, pp. 91, 103.

as editor of the *North American Review* as a side issue to his work as instructor in history at Harvard. The next year, due, no doubt, to the young editor's interest in geology, the *Review* carried a notice,[1] several pages long, of "Mining Industry," the third volume of the series of reports of the Geological Exploration of the Fortieth Parallel, of which Clarence King was in part the author. Notwithstanding Adams's interest in belles-lettres and in European politics, he took no notice of "Jim Bludso of the Prairie Belle," of "Sunrise on the Place de la Concorde," or of *Castilian Days*. In those years Hay and Adams, although they may have eaten at the same tables, were at work on different levels.

Clarence King appears to have been the bond between Hay and Adams in the friendship which blossomed overnight in Washington, in the season of 1880–81. Four years younger than Adams, three and a half younger than Hay, educated at Yale, entirely escaping military service in the Civil War as did Adams, and as Hay almost did, Clarence King also had a fastidious side to his nature and there was in him the spirit of adventure which the others both admired and lacked. In 1863 King set out across the continent, intending to make the journey on horseback from the most western rail-head at St. Joseph, Missouri. Arriving in California after many adventures, and equipped with a "Bible, a Table of Logarithms, and a volume of Robertson's sermons,"[2] he joined the state Geological Survey. In 1867, he became the actual, though not the nominal, director of the famous Fortieth Parallel Survey, the appropriation for which he had lobbied through Congress the previous year.

King's fame as explorer, hunter and athlete, spread through the mountains and was, no doubt, heightened by the silk stockings, low shoes and unwrinkled suit in which he received his guests in camp.[3] Henry Adams, amateur geologist, in Wyoming in the summer of 1871, found him "a bird of paradise rising in the sage-brush."[4]

"King had everything to interest and delight Adams. He knew more than Adams did of art and poetry; he knew America, especially west of the hundredth meridian, better than any one; he knew the professor by heart, and he knew the Congressman better than he knew the pro-

---

[1] *North American Review*, July, 1871.
[2] *Clarence King Memoirs*, p. 317.
[3] *Ibid.*, p. 345.
[4] *Education of Henry Adams*, pp. 311, 312.

fessor. He knew even women, even the New York women, which is saying much." The latter was a subject upon which John Hay was not uninformed. Sharing the same room, the same bed, Adams and King "talked till far towards dawn." Wit, youth, information, manners: King seemed to Adams an avatar of all desirable graces.

Out of King's experiences on the Fortieth Parallel Survey, came in 1870, *Mountaineering in the Sierra Nevada,* parts of which were published in the *Atlantic* about the time of Hay's Spanish essays. Like *Castilian Days,* the book was so good that it has been kept in print for sixty years. Thus King joined the literary circle of which Hay and Howells were members. In the field of literature, to a much greater degree than Hay, King elected to remain an amateur. "He was," wrote Howells, "above everything indifferent to literary repute. He would have preferred not to own the things he wrote, and keep only for his reward the esthetic delight he had in doing them." [1] Having won the affection of Adams in 1871, King appeared in New York three years later and became an enthusiastic admirer of Hay.[2]

In 1878 King assumed the directorship of the newly created United States Geological Survey, which was assigned to the Interior Department under Carl Schurz. The latter, in turn, a friend of Hay at that time, was an intimate of Adams, in whose house at 1607 H Street he seems to have lodged during some portion of his term as Secretary.[3] When Hay came to Washington the following year as Assistant Secretary of State, he found King there. Adams was in Europe that season, but the next year the Adamses took up their residence at the address above mentioned, in the house the threshold of which marked the entrance, according to James Truslow Adams, of the "most noted *salon* this country has evolved." [4]

King remained in Washington through the balance of the Hayes Administration and, as Hay did, resigned shortly after Garfield came into office. Thereafter, King charged through life, now rich, now poor, a brilliant mining engineer but a poor keeper of his own vineyard, one of the strange spirits for whom such a world as this was evidently not

---

[1] *Clarence King Memoirs,* p. 141.
[2] He is believed to have been the author of the appreciative biographical sketch of Hay in *Scribner's* for April, 1874; and again in 1886 he was selected to write for the *Century,* October, 1886, "The Biographers of Lincoln."
[3] *Letters of Henry Adams,* p. 356.
[4] *The Adams Family,* Boston, 1930, p. 327.

made, until, broken in body and mind, he died in tragic loneliness at Phoenix, Ariz., the night before Christmas, 1901.[1]

"Once in a great while," Hay reported to Sir John Clark,[2] "he gives us a day—never more than that—in Washington, and then there is a Jubilee among the Four of Hearts—even the vacant chair seems less gloomy when he is there."

"It warms my heart to hear you speak of King, though he gives us so little of himself," wrote Hay to Howells.[3] "He is now in Cuba looking at mines for millionaires. He handles vast interests but cares so little for money that he gains very little. A touch of avarice would have made him a Vanderbilt. A touch of plodding industry would have made him anything he chose. Yet I fear he will die without anything except to be a great scientist and the sweetest-natured creature the Lord ever made,—but, come to think of it, that's something."

Thus Clarence King comes into and passes out of this narrative— the friend of two inhibited men, whose glorious impulses were their vicarious adventures.

Poor King! In him was the blood of those hardy pioneers, gentlemen rovers, of the early China trade. His father had sat with D. W. C. Olyphant in what the other traders derisively called the "Amen Corner" in the factories of old Canton. An uncle had fitted out an expedition and, with S. Wells Williams and Dr. Peter Parker aboard, had sailed away to open Japan to the Bible and to trade, fourteen years before the arrival of Perry in Kanagawa. King's father had died prematurely, and by the time Clarence was of age, there was nothing left but a love of adventure and the volume of Robertson's sermons to tie the son up to his heritage. He had been born too late to be a merchant prince of old Canton with a summer palace at Macao. He should have become a Leland Stanford, a Henry Huntington, or a La Farge, or, perhaps, a Henry Ward Beecher. At any rate, he missed the way. That would have endeared him to Hay and Adams. Too little sure of themselves, they welcomed him into a select circle of those who had retired from the game, and the graces of the respective homes, where he was indulged and mothered, relieved but did not satisfy his manifold affections.

King's last years were often assuaged by Hay's generosity, and there remained after his death an unopened Christmas box of delicacies, packed probably by Mrs. Hay's own hands. King was an irregular and fitful correspondent but in one of his last letters he attempted a not entirely frank self-examination which helps to illuminate the "Five of Hearts" and to explain why King had been its much loved member:

Pasadena, California
August 22 [1901]

My dear Hay:

The check from the Del fund, and your most touching letter came without delay, but I have been so weak and so harried by fever that I have only had a few minutes in which I could possibly write and these I divided between Mrs. Hay and Mother. To Mother I have not written for seven weeks before.

I receive from six to ten letters a day, none of which I can answer and I should think there were a bushel of accumulated communications of one kind and another. I pick out a few of the most important and struggle with them.

Of your generosity and kindness to me I am always thinking, and always grateful. It seems superhuman to me and perhaps it is. In my present condition of uncertainty of folded hands and days of reflection I have been trying to understand why a man as well endowed with intelligence as I, should have made such a failure of many matters as I have.

During the last six or seven years I have constantly lifted my technical work and had at last a practice that yielded enough to cover my ten or twelve thousand of expenses of my dependents and myself. Two thousand has covered my own cost of life and you know that it is not much to keep a decent position with. I have check stubs for $275,000 spent on my family in the last 35 years but besides that I ought to have made abundant money. But I fear that I stayed too long in pure science and got a bent for the philosophical and ideal side of life too strong for any adaptation to commercial affairs.

I might have taken a college position and abandoned the family to sink. But really whenever the moment came, I could not do it and struggled on my wavering way.

I believe I could have done better in pure literature, but the door seemed always shut in my face.

Now of course every activity is prevented. Till this fever or I die out, I can only wait and hope.

My doctor is far less hopeful than at first, but every now and then he brightens up and talks of recovery. He thinks a year or so will test the fever question and he seems hopeful that I may gain that fight and come out into a period when I could write a work, but he fears that I may be detained several or many years in a lung climate.

If so (and we should know next April) I think I shall go and live in

Arizona. It is better than any part of California and is not so far from my life associations as to prevent my coming into touch now and again. But these are golden dreams. I can't help indulging them because they give me a hope of seeing you now and then. Of course they are all dreams, and the wide-awake view is that a month hence I go to Phoenix to try the very best position in America and apply the best test for the future.

I am trying to be patient till then.

Forgive this sad ramble of dull talk, but I have no one else to say it to. God bless you and heal the wounds of soul, and hold up your hand in the splendid work you are doing.

Affectionately,

C. K.

One cannot refrain from wondering again what kind of a man John Hay would have been, if he had, like King, remained unmarried, and been deprived of the stability which Clara Stone gave to his life.

Dear as King was to Hay, he was, after all, only an episode in a life of which Adams was actually a part. The latter appears to have been the only person, outside of his intimate family, whom John Hay was ever able easily to bring himself to call by his first name.

"My dear Henry," wrote Hay from New York, at the time of Mrs. Adams's death,[1] "I hoped all day yesterday and this morning to hear from you, and thought it possible you might summon King and me to be with you at the last. But I suppose you had gone north when I sent my despatch. I return to Cleveland tonight.

"I can neither talk to you nor remain silent. The darkness in which you walk has its shadow for me also. You and your wife were more to me than any other two. I came to Washington because you were there. . . ."

The new house into which the Hays moved early in the following year, together with the Adams house of the same design, of similar materials, and under the same roof, was significant, in the social as in the architectural history of Washington.

Lafayette Square was, of course, dominated by Hoban's broad-porticoed White House, which suggested open-handed agrarian hospitality. This theme had not been carried out in the varied designs of the houses which flanked the Square, east and west, in a way which would suggest that the Senators, and others, who lived in them, were in any degree the vassals, or even the supporters of the man who lived

---

[1] December 9, 1885; The Brunswick, New York. *Letters and Diaries*, II, p. 98.

in the white manor-house across the avenue. On the other hand, they were graceful houses, properly subordinated to their impressive neighbor, and there was about the Square an air of generous living in keeping with Hoban's conception. Latrobe's little white Byzantine St. John's Church, set at the east corner of Sixteenth Street on the north side of the park, was as the private chapel of the manor-house, and yet a symbol of the proper separation of Church and State, and a due subordination of the one to the other. After the war a few ugly red brick houses had crowded in, but Lafayette Square had not yet wholly lost the character of the "President's Park," by which the older residents of the city still knew it.

Opposite St. John's Church, opposite, also, the White House, now rose Richardson's lovely dark red brick adaptation of a Romanesque design for a private residence. In neither color nor style did it offer any compromise to either the little church across the way, or the big white house across the park. Its deeply recessed doors, shadowed by the low, Romanesque arches, carried the intimation of a well-guarded and discriminating hospitality which was new in Washington. Its windows let in too little light and looked out, not on the street, but over the heads of the passers-by, and the line of vision carried also over, rather than to, the White House. There was, in contrast to the other houses around the Square, less openness, and just a trace of scorn for Southern, or Western, traditions. It was apparent that there lived people who were not accustomed to unpack their treasures, or their hearts, in public. After the plans had been approved, John Hay hardly saw the rising structure until it was completed, but Adams and his wife had remained at 1607 H Street, next door to the house the latter was destined never to occupy, to watch over the construction, as owners with creative impulses are apt to do.

The houses, when completed, were as conspicuous on the square as their owners were in Washington; conspicuous because their individuality obtruded into a sleepy Southern town. Although designed by a New Orleans-born architect, they were, in fact, like a new document of New England Federalism, fashioned too late for inclusion in the collection which Henry Adams had published in 1877. The houses were as uncompromising as the papers of the Hartford Convention which in 1814 defied the Federal Government and proposed a revision of the Constitution to restore the sovereignty of the Essex Junto. They

varied the architecture of the square in somewhat the way in which the White House would have interrupted Boston if it had been built on Beacon Street to face the Common. From the library windows Adams could look out across the park to reflect on democracy's neglect of the well-born and the intelligent, and Hay could look over toward the room he used to occupy in the Lincoln days, and grow bitter about the "corruptions, the self-seeking, the cowardice" which had rejected John Sherman and brought to the Executive Mansion a Benjamin Harrison, and later returned the fat, toiling Cleveland with the four chins, and the pretty wife.

It was about this time that Cecil Spring Rice, then a young secretary at the British Legation but later better known in the United States as the British Ambassador at Washington during the World War, began writing letters to England, about his friends, old and new in America: Theodore Roosevelt, Henry Cabot Lodge, Adams, Hay, William C. Whitney, Senator Don Cameron, Whitelaw Reid, and the people he met at Newport, which had, he thought, the vulgarest society in the world, "the refinement of vulgarity." [1]

He was impressed with the whiskey, the poker, the stock-market conversation, the opulent wives, and the drunken sons. The letters reflect the growing fear of the laboring classes and of the Catholic vote —a fear which appeared also in *The Bread-Winners*. Spring Rice observed how wealth was not, as in England, being related to the land, how the rich who went to Washington, to New York, and to Newport, though recently raised from the soil, had fled from it and from their own people. This fact carried for him a warning for British aristocracy. He found it difficult to get those who were in politics to talk about the corruption but those outside talked freely and had a "bitter despair in their minds" which was hard to describe and not pleasant to listen to. He thought the whole Adams brood, meaning the children of Charles Francis, were making a "sort of profession of eccentricity," but that Henry was a "rather interesting sort of cynic." "Next door is the house of John Hay, the poet, who drops in to talk and chat and argue and compare notes; the best story-teller I have ever heard, and such a good sort, too." Spring Rice became very fond of Adams, and

---

[1] "An intelligent and agreeable fellow has turned up here at your legation; about the last place one looks for one. His name is Spring Rice and he has creditable wits." Adams to Gaskell, May 8, 1887; *Letters*, p. 383.

of Hay, but he wrote that there was "something rather melancholy about the talk of educated men here." The Spring Rice letters give one a very good idea of how America looked in 1887–95 from the Adams and Hay libraries overlooking Lafayette Square.[1]

"One friend in a lifetime is much; two are many; three are hardly possible," wrote Adams of his meeting with King in Wyoming.[2] "Friendship needs a certain parallelism of life, a community of thought, a rivalry of aim." In his novel, *Democracy*, he amplified his definition of the basis of friendship with a comment on the two sisters, Mrs. Lightfoot Lee and Miss Sybil Ross. He wrote: "The keenest psychologist could not have detected a single feature or quality which they had in common, and for that reason they were devoted friends."[3]

During the first seven or eight years of their intimacy both men were engaged in the writing of history, but while Adams was historically minded, and had a gift for generalization, Hay was more a journalist turned historian, who wrote only about the times through which he had lived, and about the people whom he had known. Both interrupted their historical work to write fiction, where Adams again disclosed a reflective habit of mind, and so presented his characters that they spoke for themselves, whereas Hay too obviously intruded with his own opinions. *Democracy* was a caricature; *The Bread-Winners* was a tract. Hay's historical generalizations were likely to be brash and violent, as when he described Andrew Jackson as the most injurious person in American history.

One hesitates to say that Adams was more thoughtful than Hay, but it is evident that they thought about different things and grappled differently with their ideas. Adams was interested in the significance of the past as it might throw light on the future; Hay was more concerned with the "now." "During a long acquaintance I never heard

[1] James Bryce confirmed the statements made by Spring Rice. In *The American Commonwealth* he commented on "a certain apathy among the luxurious classes and fastidious minds, who find themselves of no more account than the ordinary voter, and are disgusted by the superficial vulgarities of public life." These educated and wealthy classes, he noted, "find no smooth and easy path lying before them. Since the masses do not look to them for guidance, they do not come forward to give it. If they wish for office they must struggle for it, avoiding the least presuming on their social position." He added, "The idle rich of America, who, though relatively few, are numerous enough to form a class in the greatest Atlantic cities, seem by no means the happiest class in the country." John Hay's name appears in the list of those to whom Bryce made acknowledgments in his preface. It is difficult to believe that the author did not have Hay, and perhaps Adams, in mind when writing the sentence quoted above.

[2] *"Education,"* p. 312.

[3] Henry Adams, *Democracy,* p. 15.

him talk of historians," wrote Rhodes,[1] "except of his friend Henry Adams, but he had at his tongue's end what we used to call belles-lettres and his conversation there was a profit and a delight." In the field of history Hay was a dilettante in about the same degree that Adams, as a Secretary of State, would have been a doctrinaire. Hay's had become a practical mind.

One would also hesitate to assert that either of the two was a stronger character than the other. It is not evident that, at the end of twenty-five years, either had materially altered any important conviction because of the views of the other. Both men were skeptics, and while Adams had the sounder critical judgment, Hay was probably a more trustworthy adviser in matters of immediate moment. They met, not to agree and nod approval, but to pitch into each other, to engage in dialectics, to score points. The tea-table was likely to provide the intellectual equivalent for a very fast game of hand-ball. The correspondence was, at times, on a similar plane and, for that reason, has often been taken too seriously. It amused both to see one or the other put in the wrong. For example, a paragraph of a letter from Hay in Paris, April 25, 1894: [2]

I shall read of the progress of Coxey's army with new interest now that I know you are in Washington. Perhaps they will spare my house because it adjoins yours. You, of course, are known throughout the country as a Democrat and an Anarchist and an Unemployed. Your house will be safe anyhow; so you might as well stand up on my steps while the army passes, and shout for "Chaos and Coxey" like a man. . . .

It cannot be shown that at the end of the relationship Hay was in any respect another sort of man than he had been before 1880. Adams was a free-trader, a Democrat with leanings to mugwumpery, and admired Blaine only for his "powers of invention"; Hay remained a protectionist and a Republican with fast hardening convictions. The bitterness and despair which Spring Rice noted and which appear in the letters of both men, are the qualities and conclusions of onlookers and spectators who lacked optimism because they were actually taking no part in the game. Both men appeared to be ardently interested in current politics, but neither had felt deeply enough to retain his legal residence in a state to which he could go home to vote.

[1] *History of the McKinley and Roosevelt Administrations,* pp. 121 ff.
[2] *Letters and Diaries,* II, p. 286.

If the sole reason why Hay took up his residence in Washington had been because of his desire to be near Adams, then the latter could have been set down as one who, unconsciously, had betrayed his friend to a lotus-land—"easy, irresponsible Washington."

"As Hafiz sang—'How sad were the sunset, were we not sure of the morrow!'" wrote Hay, as Adams and La Farge started for the Pacific,[1] "and that is just our fix. That pleasant gang which made all the joy of life in easy, irresponsible Washington will fall to pieces in your absence. You were the only principle of cohesion in it. All the elements will seek other combinations, except me, and I will be left at the ghost-haunted corner of 16th and H."

One cannot fail to detect in the growing volume of letters from Hay to Adams, with their salutations, "Dearly Beloved," "Apple of Mine Eye," "Light of Mine Optics," "Guide and Philosopher," "My Own and Only One," "Très Cher," and again "My Beloved," a note of almost effeminate dependence strangely in contrast with both their radically differing views and Hay's poise and habits of decision so soon to be disclosed in his official career. The entire relationship with Henry Adams presents one of the most striking contradictions in Hay's complex life.

Perhaps the most important service which Adams did for Hay was to pass him on to his English friends.

[1] *Letters and Diaries,* II, p. 194, July 12, 1890.

WHEN in 1880 John Hay definitely decided not to run for Congress, and when in the same year he also declined Garfield's offer of a position as the President's Secretary, Hay believed that he had definitely turned his back on politics. A few years later, by the transfer of his legal residence to the District of Columbia, it seemed that he had burned his bridges behind him. In taking his citizenship out of Ohio, in fact, almost surrendering his citizenship except for the right to secure a passport, he forswore not only his chances for elective office, but also his influence in State politics, where alone one may expect to approach the political side of national affairs. Hay could not foresee that he, still a young man, was thus depriving himself of the resources to make life interesting when the Lincoln book was finished, but thus it turned out.

Hay's relation to Garfield seems to have been more intimate than that with either McKinley or Roosevelt, although the two latter reciprocated with more munificent offers of position. To some extent Hay inherited his enthusiasm for Garfield from Amasa Stone, who had long been a generous supporter and who contributed frequently in the summer of 1880 to both the public and private Garfield chests. Only seven years younger, with kindred literary tastes, Hay felt himself in the position to assume the rôle of candid friend both during the campaign and in the cabinet-making period. They were on terms of social intimacy and Garfield appears to have invited Hay's suggestions and to some extent to have depended upon his judgment. "I see you have given up your house for the summer," Hay wrote on June 8, congratulating him on the nomination. "If you come back here for the close of the season, I can give you a comfortable room at my house, 1400 Massachusetts Ave., where you can see as much or as little as you choose of the moth-world which lights attract." [1]

"Beware of your own generosity," Hay warned on October 18,[2] "on the 2nd of November, *you* ('not Lancelot nor another') are to be made

---

[1] *Garfield Papers*, Library of Congress.
[2] Theodore Clark Smith, *James Abram Garfield*, II, p. 1045.

our President. . . . You do not need the whispered admonition of the
ancient monarchs, 'Remember thou art mortal!' It will pay you to keep
a cheap friend to drone continually in your ear, 'It was *you* who were
nominated at Chicago and elected by the people.' "

After the election Hay busied himself in behalf of Sherman, then a
candidate for his old place in the Senate, and for Blaine, who next to
being President desired to be Secretary of State. In pleading for Garfield's support of Sherman, he wrote: [1] "It seems to me indispensable
that Mr. Sherman should be elected Senator. If he should be defeated
for that place, the injury would be irreparable, even by you. To offer
him a seat in the cabinet, after Governor Foster had beaten him for
the Senate, would not comport with your dignity. As to Ohio's representation in the Cabinet, if you would not consider it impertinent to
mention such a thing—I should certainly say the State requires no
such representation. We have the President—the Supreme Chief Justice, an Associate—the General and Lt. Gen'l of the Army, and the
country can get along very well without an Ohio man in the Cabinet.
. . . I ask and want nothing. I expect to do whatever I can in Ohio for
the next few years for your administration and the Republican party,
and if anybody ever mentions my name to you, you may know it is
without warrant. I wish I could have taken off your shoulders a few
other citizens, who are good fellows enough, but whose only fault is
that they are too numerous."

Hay's most earnest pleadings were for Blaine. "Since you have
given me warrant to write to you with freedom," he wrote,[2] "I will
say a word—which may be taken only for what it is worth—about a
matter of which your mind must be very full of at the present.

"It is the opinion of many of the most judicious of your friends that
Mr. Blaine will be the best possible appointment which can be made
for the Secretary of State. Of course I can tell you nothing about *him*.
In two important points of view, 1. his ability to transact the work
of the office, and 2. his standing in the party and before the country,
I know of nobody who can be compared with him, leaving Mr. Evarts,
of course, out of view. His brilliant, original, and versatile mind will
find the fullest scope in the work of the department and I should think
his presence in the Cabinet would always be suggestive and helpful.

[1] December 6, 1880.
[2] December 22, 1880.

"Of course there would be criticisms made, on the part of the people who do not know him as well as you do. But among political circles I think his appointment would be extremely acceptable, and in the country at large he has many warm friends. I was talking of the matter with Mr. Evarts the other day, and he said unreservedly that he thought Blaine would make a brilliant and successful administration of the Department, comparing most favorably with Clay's.

"I may say that in a recent private conversation with Mr. Blaine the subject was touched upon and he spoke with a good deal of frankness in regard to it."

At length, he also put in a word for his old friend, Carl Schurz, whose frame of mind was evidently not quite plumb with the Garfield policy on appointments.[1] "I think no harm and some good might come of it," Hay wrote, "if you would ask Mr. Schurz to visit you and talk things over. He is full of hearty good will, but if things should not go his way, he will feel a little as if he were not much regarded, and I should greatly regret having him going out to St. Louis in that frame of mind. You know of course the desire of his heart. Whether you can gratify it or not, it might be advisable to have a full and free talk with him. I write this of course without his knowledge and solely in *your* interest. . . ."

In such letters as these, and there were many of them, Hay disclosed himself as a practical politician. Garfield heeded many of Hay's suggestions, but the best he had to offer for Hay himself was the post of Private Secretary, which the latter promptly declined.

"If I could share your own view of my fitness for the place," Hay replied, "I should be inclined to sacrifice all considerations and go to work. But I cannot. The contact with the greed and selfishness of office-seekers and the bull-dozing Congressmen is unspeakably repulsive. The constant contact with envy, meanness, ignorance and the swinish selfishness which ignorance breeds needs a stronger heart and a more obedient nervous system than I can boast."[2]

Garfield tried again, but Hay was firm. He realized, however, that this refusal involved his elimination from political life in the approaching administration, for he had already refused to run for Congress

[1] February 16, 1881.
[2] T. C. Smith, II, 1070–77.

in Ohio.

In the campaign of 1884, notwithstanding his unfailing enthusiasm for James G. Blaine, Hay took no very active part. "I did not intend to do anything but pay my subscription," he wrote to Howells,[1] "but I was caught the day I got home, and made to preside at the biggest mass meeting I ever saw in the Square the other night. It looks to us favorable to Blaine. President Hayes lunched with me the day I got home; he is hearty in his support of Blaine, though they have never been friends." In Hay's eyes Grover Cleveland and Tammany were identical, and he viewed the Mugwumps with alarm. The fact appears in a letter to the Reverend Edward Everett Hale:

> I have taken so much comfort from your admirable letters and other utterances during this unprecedented campaign, that I must write and express my gratitude for them in behalf of a great many silent Republicans. I have looked with dismay, all this season, at the antics of men I have been accustomed to respect, until I would begin to doubt whether I had not lost my own reason or conscience, if it were not for the direct and straight-forward speech of men like you, and Hoar and Evarts. I think there is a vast Katzenjammer preparing for many of our friends.

In 1888, Blaine having eliminated himself from the contest, Hay favored the nomination of John Sherman who was then for the third time the official choice of the Republican party of his state, but who, neither in 1880 nor in 1884, had been able to poll in the convention the votes of an undivided Ohio delegation. Sherman's lack of magnetism and lack of a following, wrote Hay to Reid,[2] would be "worth millions to the Presidency, if he were elected. He is thoroughly fit for power. Then, if we must be beaten, Sherman is the best possible man to be beaten with. It won't hurt the party much, and it won't hurt him at all."

Hay attended the Chicago convention in 1888 not as a delegate but as a worker for Sherman, and sitting in the gallery, lifted up his voice "in shouts for Uncle John," but to no avail. "Benjamin Harrison got there, and I suppose I must vote for him. I will keep myself up to the task by thinking of Cleveland, and occasionally reading an editorial in the *Nation*."[3] On the same day he wrote Sherman a long letter, the

[1] *Letters and Diaries*, II, p. 89, Sept. 16, 1884.
[2] *Letters and Diaries*, II, p. 144, March 16, 1888.
[3] To Adams, June 25, 1888. *Letters and Diaries*, II, p. 150.

next to the last sentence of which is a little puzzling in view of Hay's consistent enthusiasm for Blaine since 1876: [1]

I suppose you, with your usual unselfish magnanimity, care very little for this result but it is excessively bitter to me. The thing which I cannot get over is this: during the week I spent at Chicago, I talked with a great many delegates and never found one who did not say "Sherman would of course make a better President than anybody in the field." But they always treated this evident fact as a purely secondary consideration. What can be more disheartening than that? To say that a great Convention is not looking for the best man, and that the highest qualities of character and statesmanship are of no advantage to a candidate. I spent hours in conversation with delegates who stupidly insisted that you could not carry their states, without giving a single reason why you could not, and while admitting that in their opinion you would make the best possible President. Why they should assume that the people have no sense or conscience, that the man universally known as the best man for the place could not get votes as easily as a man universally regarded as second-rate, is a mystery I cannot fathom.

I will not go into details of the darker aspects of the case; of the corruptions, the self-seeking, the cowardice which were everywhere apparent.

I am inclined to think the best men can never again be chosen. Long and illustrious service rouses so much of envy and hatred among lower natures, as to make conventions cowardly.

But they can never tarnish or blot out the record of your life which will live forever in the history of your country. You have done the greatest service to the nation that any man of this generation has been able to do. From 1865 to 1888 there is no one approaches you. But the deliberate rejection by the great party of the best, and their deliberate choice of the second best, is beyond expression humiliating and discouraging.

Hay's bitter disappointment may have been in some degree personal, for it is a fair guess that if Sherman, instead of Harrison, had been nominated and elected in 1888, John Hay, rather than Robert Lincoln, would have been the next American Minister to London. Hay's political aspirations were being continually thwarted by the failure of the candidates whom he supported. In 1880 he might have gone to London, and if not there, certainly to some good diplomatic post, if Blaine instead of Garfield had been elected; in 1884 the Democrats came in; four years later Harrison was not a friend of Hay's and Blaine, as Secretary of State, was unwilling or unable to help There was a tacit agreement with both Blaine and Whitelaw Reid that when the latter should resign as American minister in Paris, a

[1] *Sherman Papers*, Vol. 451, Library of Congress.

post to which he was appointed by Harrison, Hay would replace him. But when Reid resigned to accept the nomination for the Vice Presidency in 1892, Blaine was out of the Cabinet, and Senator Hoar stepped in to demand the place for T. Jefferson Coolidge, who was appointed.[1] After Harrison, there intervened another Democratic administration, before Hay had even an opportunity to be considered for appointment.

There is in the Hay papers an undated memorandum of a conversation with the President, probably Harrison, which appears to show that in 1889 Hay was the intermediary to persuade Whitelaw Reid to accept the appointment of Minister to Paris when the latter was ambitious to go to London. The memorandum is interesting also as an example of the methodical way in which Hay, in many ways so unmethodical, preserved important records:·

> The President sends for me
> His embarrassment & annoyance
>   Always intended to offer &c
> Objections to England
>   *Attitude of* TRIBUNE
>   Either Salisbury would not like it
>   or
>   The *Tribune* would be muzzled
> The two places equal in dignity
>   France the more desirable
>   Urged it as a personal favor to himself
> I replied:
>   Certainly all three points
>   Said Reid would not like it, but wd support the Admn with vigor as if—
> Saw Blaine— After full conversation, he was inclined to think Reid would do better to accept.
> Arrived in New York, reported all above conver- and added Blaine's recommendation & then said
> It might be possible for your friends to bring such pressure on President but better to make him your obligé—

"It is odd to live in a small city like this," Hay wrote to Edwin A. Abbey, the painter, on January 21, 1889,[2] "and see the world at a distance, and be like a dead man, if dead men can read the newspapers —and be as out of it as Julius Caesar."

[1] Benjamin Harrison to Wm. A. Russell, June 2, 1892. *Harrison Papers.* Library of Congress.
[2] *Letters and Diaries*, II, p. 162.

While their relations were outwardly friendly Hay had no very high regard for Harrison and in one of his familiar letters to Adams a year later he wrote: [1] "Give Spring Rice my love and fond regrets! Give the Goddess of your breakfast table my worship and duty! Give the President three years' warning!" Hay was drifting back into the mood of 1867, when he had been pursuing Seward for a "fat office." Before the second Cleveland administration was half over, he seems to have decided that at the first opportunity he would step in and claim his reward as laureate of his party. From London, where he was suffering from boredom, he wrote to Adams, May 28, 1894, in a vein not wholly jocular: "I think I must take office again when we get youalls out." [2]

There is at least a slight intimation in a letter to Adams, dated August 4, 1896, that Hay, looking back on the twenty-five years which had preceded the nomination of McKinley, regretted that he himself had not ordered his affairs with more political wisdom: "I have been reading Shelley," he wrote. "He seems to have had a certain faculty in writing verse. If it had not been for that, he would have made a good candidate for the Presidency." Hay had, however, disqualified himself less by the verses he had written, than by escaping all the boredom, and some of the taxes, of Ohio.

In the autumn of 1895 he returned to the great American pastime of president-making under more favorable auspices. In October, he was in Cleveland and "talked some politics," [3] quite probably with Mark Hanna, whom, though a fellow-townsman, he had never known well. "I think," wrote Hay, "McKinley is much 'forrider' than a few months ago. The faithful think Foraker is pulling straight, and there are *anguilles sous roches* that betoken an early collapse of other booms." Hay returned to Washington a McKinley agent, and during the winter did some errands at the Capitol in behalf of Ohio's newest favorite son. He went to England in May so confident that he addressed to the London *Times* a letter, printed June 1, in which he predicted McKinley's nomination and attempted to refute a Smalley dispatch which had asserted that McKinley was for free silver. "He will be nominated in June and elected in November as the result of a singularly spontaneous movement of the voters of the country, against

[1] *Op. cit.*, p. 182, November 4, 1889.
[2] *Op. cit.*, p. 289.
[3] *Op. cit.*, p. 368.

the violent opposition of some of the most powerful politicians of his own party, whose apparent objection to him is that they may not find him sufficiently pliable for their own purposes. This alone is sufficient testimony to his possession of unusual qualities. We who know him, regard him as a man of extraordinary ability, integrity and force of character, and have no hesitation in predicting for him an administration in a high degree wise, pure, politic and magnanimous."

The still unsettled issues of the Venezuela dispute, and the apparent disposition of Lord Salisbury to regard the Cleveland-Olney assertions lightly as claims which a Republican administration would repudiate, provided Hay with another political opportunity, and also supplied information of importance in determining the degree to which Hay's English friends had made him an Anglophile.

Henry James described the Venezuela message as "the American outbreak," which had darkened all his sky.[1] He thanked God that he had chosen to live away from home, and became the more determined to remain in England. "The explosion of jingoism there," he wrote, "is the result of all sorts of more or less domestic and internal conditions—and what is most indicated, on the whole, as coming out of it, is a vast new cleavage in American national feeling—politics and parties—a split almost, roughly speaking, between the West and the East. There are really two civilizations there side by side—in one yoke; or rather, one civilization and a barbarism."

John Hay was never either jingo or "tail-twister," but this time he was numbered among James's barbarians. He took a line which must have commended itself even to Henry Cabot Lodge—and, no doubt, to McKinley. He approved the broad principles asserted by the Democratic administration and felt confident that the Republicans would not retire on the Monroe Doctrine. In conversation with Sir William Harcourt, Bryce, Curzon, and Chamberlain, he urged that the British government reach an agreement with the United States before the American elections, and he reported his conversation immediately to Richard Olney in the following letter:

R.M.S. *Teutonic.*
July 31, 1896.

Dear Mr. Olney:
    The day before I left London I had a long and very interesting conversation

[1] *The Letters of Henry James.* Edited by Percy Lubbock. 2 vols. N. Y. 1920. I, 242.

with Sir Wm Harcourt on Venezuela, which, followed, and was the result of, one I had had the day previous with James Bryce. In neither case did I seek the interview—and in neither case, I hope I need not say, did I assume any representative character, or any means of information not open to everybody. Sir Wm Harcourt spoke unreservedly, as the leader of the opposition—and though nothing was said as to my repeating the conversation, I felt as if I ought confidentially to let you know one thing he said.

He expressed his gratification at the improved tone of the negotiations between the two countries, and said that you were perfectly right in your claim as to "settled districts"; that in an action for ejectment it was no defense that a wrongful occupier had built a house on his neighbor's land; that he had already let the Government know his views in the matter; that he had not wished to embarrass them by a public discussion while negotiations were in progress, but that he was using all proper means of pressure to induce them to come to an agreement with us at the earliest possible moment. He then asked my opinion as to the Presidential canvass. I told him I thought McKinley would be elected. He asked what effect this would have on the negotiations, if they were not completed before next March. (It has been intimated that Lord Salisbury desired delay in the hope that the next administration may be less exacting in its contention than the present.) I told him I thought any such calculation would be a great mistake; that the public sentiment of the United States was virtually unanimous in the support of the administration's action in this question; that no steps backward would be taken by McKinley and that only omniscience could guess what Bryan would do, if he got in.

He was anxious that I should let Mr. Chamberlain and Mr. Curzon know this view, and I accordingly conveyed to both of them, before I sailed, my impression that time was an element of considerable importance in the matter.

From what I have been able to gather in conversation I infer that most of the leading men are convinced that Lord Salisbury's tone a year ago was a mistake, and that our attitude, is on the whole, reasonable. Everybody wants the matter settled if it can be done without damage to the pride and prestige of England. Chamberlain seems afraid of making a precedent which may be injurious hereafter in Canada—and they all dread arbitration since Geneva.

I beg you will not think I have been meddling in what does not concern me. I said little or nothing myself, but the things that were said to me were so interesting that I thought I ought to communicate a word or two of them to you.

Please let me know this has reached you. My address is Newbury, New Hampshire.

As we draw to a close this narrative of the somewhat aimless decade which preceded Hay's return to political life, we marvel. Some men might have turned to better account the ten years from 1886 to 1896;

some men might have done so, but as a matter of fact, in political life few men, aside from Theodore Roosevelt, did. Many, with more ambition, more industry, and more ambitious wives, set out to do more, and actually did much less. The nearest to a philosophy of life that John Hay had been able to fashion was that its sequence of events was in the nature of a chain of accidents. The theory found in his own life as substantial support as could be discovered for such an hypothesis. Hay had disregarded every rule of political expediency, and had cast aside most of the copy-book rules for personal success in the United States, and yet in the next five years, by the death of Vice President Hobart in 1899, and then by the death of McKinley in 1901, Hay was to become twice even second in the order of succession to the Presidency itself. Once only one diseased life, and again only a reckless one, stood between him and the great office.

John Hay owed his position in life to his association with Abraham Lincoln; his position in American history he owed to his friendship with William McKinley. And yet, but for their official positions, it seems unlikely that Hay would ever have known either of them intimately. McKinley was not, any more than Lincoln, the kind of man Hay was accustomed to pick for a friend.

McKinley fell in the category of men whom Hay usually described as dull. In fact, he appears to have conceded as much to a representative of the London *Chronicle*.[1] "It is difficult to describe Mr. McKinley in a picturesque manner," he is quoted as having said. " 'Happy is a nation,' a French writer has expressed it, 'whose annals are dull.' A man like McKinley is all on one side—there is nothing to be said against him." Hay emphasized, however, that McKinley was "distinguished by great moral earnestness."

No one has yet done for McKinley, the politician, what Nicolay and Hay did for Lincoln. A generation after his death we still lack the information to determine how much he was beyond being the very competent politician whom every one recognizes. Theodore Roosevelt's petulant contemporary outburst that he had no more backbone than a chocolate éclair has today as little currency as the notion, born in the heat of the campaign of 1896 and sustained for some years by Davenport's cartoons, that he was Mark Hanna's man. William McKinley wore a mask but from beneath it there protruded a very square

[1] The interview was reprinted in the New York *Tribune*, June 15, 1896.

jaw. His manner was that of one who had early retired into his closet
and so thoroughly rehearsed the rôle he had determined to play that
in public it became his own character. Probably few men, and no
women, ever got behind the mask. Hay may have come as near to it
as anybody when he wrote to Henry Adams, October 20, 1896: [1]

I spent yesterday with the Majah. I had been dreading it for a month,
thinking it would be like talking in a boiler factory. But he met me at the
station, gave me meat, and calmly leaving his shouting worshippers in the
front yard, took me up stairs and talked for two hours as calmly and serenely
as if we were summer boarders in B—— at a loss for means to kill time. I
was more struck than ever with his mask. It is a genuine Italian ecclesiastical
face of the XVth Century. And there are idiots who think Mark Hanna will
run him.

I leave town today to see if there are any ducks in the world. If so, I shall
spend a week or two in the marsh, and then hie me to you. You are making the
mistake of your life in not reading my speech. There is good stuff in it—to
live and to die by. If you read it in a reverent and prayerful spirit, it might
make you a postmaster.

You are not interested in political news. If you were I would give you a
political pointer. The Majah has a cinch—and don't you forget it.

The address referred to had an amusing history. Late in September
Hay had intimated to President Charles F. Thwing, of Western Reserve University, of which Hay had been a trustee ever since the gift
of Amasa Stone in 1880, that he wished to be invited to address the
student Republican Club. He wrote that he might not be able to come
in person but that, with the invitation in hand, he would be provided
with an opportunity to print the address and have it circulated. An
invitation from the faculty and students was immediately forthcom-
ing. The address was delivered October 7—delivered in the form of
several thousand pamphlets from the job press of the Cleveland
Leader—"The Platform of Anarchy." "The word 'address,'" he explained in a letter to Dr. Thwing, "is non-committal and does not necessarily connote the living voice." The faithful *Tribune* on the same
day carried extracts from it with the following introductory paragraph:

"Cleveland, Oct. 6 (Special)—Immediately on the opening of
Western Reserve University for the fall term President Thwing, at the

---

[1] *Letters and Diaries*, III, p. 78.

request of the faculty and students of that institution, invited Colonel John Hay to address them on the political issues of the hour. He responded today in an address, from which the following passages are taken." The *Tribune* also commented on the speech editorially, and hailed Hay as belonging in the front rank of political orators, but neither in the pamphlet nor in the *Tribune* was there any hint that the author, far from being in Cleveland that day, was actually still at his summer home on Lake Sunapee.

The pre-inaugural relations of McKinley and Hay were characterized by reserve on both sides. Hay neither asked for, nor received, any promises. In the matter of appointments McKinley kept his own counsel to the end. Notwithstanding Hay's services in Washington in the winter of 1895–96, and possible contribution to Mark Hanna's pre-convention funds; notwithstanding, also, a subsequent campaign contribution which may not have been so large as might be inferred from reading the *Education of Henry Adams*,[1] or the "Platform of Anarchy" speech, or the visit to Canton mentioned above, or another on January 20, Hay was without personal assurances from McKinley as late as February 25, and had, in fact, been doing all that he could to secure the post at London for Whitelaw Reid.[2] The nomination of Hay as Ambassador to the Court of St. James's was actually not sent to the Senate until March 16. Obviously there had been no "deal." On the other hand, that he desired the position above all others in the gift of the President, there can be no doubt.

"I did not pay McKinley's debts," wrote Hay to William L. Stone, an old college friend and fraternity brother.[3] "I never called him 'William' in my life, nor did he ever call me 'John.' Our intercourse has always been of the most formal character."

It should not be inferred from the reserve with which the two men dealt with each other that there was any lack of sincere feeling. The development of the friendship proceeded by easy stages. Rhodes, who knew both well, stated [4] that "McKinley and Hay took to one an-

[1] p. 324.
[2] Thayer, II, 154–55.
[3] Copy supplied by Mr. Louttit, from an old auction sale list. Location of original letter not known. While the assertion about the McKinley debts is verbally accurate, there is no doubt that Mr. Hay was one of the contributors to the fund by which these debts were liquidated.
[4] *McKinley and Roosevelt Administrations*, p. 124.

other, drawn together by an innate sense of refinement, for McKinley appreciated culture." The President-elect, a good public speaker, but not a man of letters, no doubt admired a writer. Was not Hay the Republican laureate?

Chapter XVI

JOHN HAY arrived in London April 21, 1897, to serve as Ambassador not quite seventeen months. They were the happiest months of his life. At last he had found gaiety, mixed with enough of serious purpose to satisfy all sides of his nature. His health, while by no means perfect, was greatly improved. The note of frustration and despair disappeared from his letters. All his varied experiences of more than half a century had combined to prepare him for the rôle to which he had been assigned, and he carried it easily.

In several respects Hay had his usual good luck.

The school of American political thought which holds that the most certain way to reach a friendly understanding with John Bull is to begin by giving him a stiff punch in the nose finds some measure of support in the Venezuela incident which closed November 12, 1896, with the approval by Secretary Olney of a proposed treaty of arbitration between Great Britain and Venezuela. "The impression that the Americans were pining for British friendship and affection," thought Mr. Olney, reviewing the subject in 1899,[1] ". . . was effectively, even if somewhat rudely, dispelled." The way was thus cleared, he believed, for the development of a genuine cordiality, based on respect. It should not be overlooked, however, that both Great Britain and the United States had reached, or were approaching, positions where they had need of each other. Henry Adams thought that Germany was scaring England into American arms. It was equally true, on the other hand, that the United States, drifting into war with Spain, and so soon to take up in earnest the question of an isthmian canal, needed a transatlantic friend; required, in fact, an understanding with England, especially about the Caribbean. If it was Hay's luck to appear at this favorable moment, it was equally the good fortune of his government to have in London just the right sort of person to give direction to the new turn of affairs.

Among John Hay's good qualities, to be placed next to his modesty, was his unfailing good taste. He did not overdo things. The situation

---

[1] *Olney Papers.* Library of Congress. November 20. To Maurice Low.

called for that quality above all others. His predecessor, Thomas F. Bayard, had, in the Democratic Convention of 1884, polled the highest number of votes next to Cleveland. Bayard had then served as Secretary of State. Having for four years directed the foreign relations of his government, he was, when he went to London, hardly in the mood to receive rather than to give instructions. He was over-confident, and past his prime. The "long wash" of his "unhesitating orotundity" of speech, may have, to use Hay's words, "knocked the British public silly," but it had drawn from Congressmen a vote of censure, and had not been very convincing to the British Foreign Office. The latter had preferred to transact business through Sir Julian Pauncefote, who had been in Washington since 1889. Bayard overplayed his part; he was an easy man to follow.

The selection of a literary man for the American representative in London was greeted with satisfaction. Such a choice does not often occur, for the holder of this most important of American diplomatic posts must also be rich. Hay was not rich as riches were beginning to be counted in America, but he was well able, at 5 Carlton Terrace, to maintain an adequate establishment, and he had the good taste not to overdo the display. His card of introduction to the British public was that he was the author of the *Pike County Ballads* and co-author of the Lincoln history. In British eyes he was characteristically American, a best product of American civilization. Probably no other American envoy in London ever started with half so large a list of friends—Curzon, Chamberlain, Harcourt, Bryce, and many others—among the people of importance.

In one other respect Hay was particularly fortunate. Henry White, given the choice between going to Madrid as Minister and to London as First Secretary, chose the latter. White had served under Lowell, Phelps, and Lincoln.[1] Shrewd, tactful, devoted, he knew the routine work of the embassy and he knew his England even better than Hay knew it. The appointment of White gave Hay a very free hand.

Although the period of Hay's service in London must be regarded as the most important since the days of Charles Francis Adams, the Embassy was not very busy. Only two important subjects, bimetallism and the fur seals controversy, required attention in the first year, and in the handling of both Hay shared the responsibility with envoys

[1] Nevins, *Henry White,* 51 ff.

specially named for the purpose.

The Republican party had come into power on a platform "opposed to the free coinage of silver, except by international agreement with the leading commercial nations of the world," which it pledged to promote. The outgoing Congress, by an act of March 3, 1897, authorized the President to call an international congress, or to send commissioners to Europe to seek an international agreement on the silver question. The special envoys appointed were Senator Edward O. Wolcott of Colorado, former Vice President Adlai E. Stevenson, and Colonel Charles J. Paine of Massachusetts. The project was not quite so chimerical as it now seems, for there was in Europe, and more especially in France and England, a substantial group of leaders who favored bimetallism and were actively seeking an international agreement along the lines suggested in the Republican platform.

Upon arrival in London Hay began to gather information on bimetallism and, May 20, reported that the subject aroused little or no interest. Balfour, First Lord of the Treasury, was the most conspicuous silver protagonist; Salisbury was open-minded; there was some silver sentiment in the Midlands; but the "City" was against it, as were also Chamberlain, Harcourt, and such important papers as the *Times* and the *Chronicle*. Hay, although thoroughly committed to the gold standard, prepared an impartial survey of the situation which did not, even to the extent of a single adjective, disclose his personal opinion. The despatch, however, was not at all encouraging and the President, having read it, returned it to the Department of State with the instruction that it was not to be given out in any form. The special envoys visited France and then came to London where Hay helped them to see the necessary people, but even Wolcott was soon discouraged. The tide of affairs was running fast in the other direction.

"We have not yet received our answer on silver," wrote Hay to Adams, Oct. 20, 1897,[1] "but I *know* what it is certain to contain— some sinuosity of words, but the substance a categorical negative. With that we go back to France; she shrugs her shoulders and backs out. We go home."

Three weeks earlier he had written to Mrs. Hay: "Wolcott has come back without his wife. He is still hopeful, but confidentially I think nothing will be accomplished. England is very cross about

[1] *Letters and Diaries*, III, 100.

the Bering Sea—the more especially because this time *they* are in the wrong, and they know it. Every morning the papers are full of abuse of America and everything American."

The Bering Sea controversy concerned the preservation of the seal herd which resorted each summer to Pribilof Islands. While Hay's part, as ambassador, in the long negotiations between the United States and Great Britain from the eighties to 1911, was very small, it was his most important negotiation in London.

The demand for sealskin coats, without which no American lady in the nineties considered herself well dressed, caused, first and last, a great deal of trouble to governments. Seals resorted to breed each spring on the Pribilof and Commander islands in the North Pacific Ocean. The islands belonged, respectively, to the United States and to Russia. For the purpose of regulating seal hunting, and to prevent the extermination of the herd on the Pribilof Islands, the Treasury Department, under authority of an act of Congress, leased to the Alaska Commercial Company, a California corporation, an exclusive concession which limited the number of seals to be killed each year, and the manner of killing. The industry became profitable and attracted the nationals of other governments, notably the Canadians, who, excluded from the American islands, hunted the seals in the open sea. It was alleged that the pelagic sealers were taking many females in search of food for their young. The herd was being decimated, therefore, not only by the pelagic sealing but also by the consequent starvation of the young seals on the islands. The regulations for the protection of the herd were thus being thwarted and American observers feared early extinction. Back of the agitation for more effective protection for the seals was the combined interest of nature-lovers and the American seal fishery.

The effort of the American Government to prevent pelagic sealing first took the form of a not very modest assertion that Bering Sea was included within the territorial waters of the United States, and that the alleged Canadian poachers were consequently liable to arrest and seizure. This claim, having been rejected by a board of arbitration at Paris in 1893, was abandoned in favor of the more reasonable project to regulate pelagic sealing by an international agreement between Russia, Japan, the United States, and Great Britain, the latter acting on behalf of Canada.

As early as May 10, 1895,[1] the American Government proposed to Great Britain the project of creating a commission of the four interested powers to investigate the facts and to propose suitable remedies. Russia and Japan were known to be favorable but England withheld assent. The alleged reason was that the evils complained of did not exist; the real reasons seem to have been that Canada did not wish to enter a conference where she was certain to be out-voted, and preferred to reserve the controversy for settlement at some more favorable season when a concession relative to seals might be traded for a substantial consideration, perhaps for a reciprocity treaty.

The McKinley administration renewed the often repeated request for a conference. Secretary Sherman broached the subject to Sir Julian Pauncefote, and Hay also took the matter up with the Foreign Office. He urged an immediate *modus vivendi* to become effective for the approaching season, and also a conference of the four powers.[2]

The progress of the negotiations was not hastened by the publication, in the New York *Tribune,* of a long, rasping instruction to Hay, over the name of Sherman, but from the pen of John W. Foster, who had followed Blaine as Secretary of State under Harrison, and who had been retained by McKinley as adviser in the fur seal matter. Hay appears to have entered a mild protest at this breach of etiquette. Sherman was at loss to explain how it happened, and McKinley gently urged that in the future the Department be more careful. In May Foster was made "Ambassador on Special Mission" to conduct all correspondence and negotiations relative to the matter and immediately sailed for London. Hay became, therefore, only partially responsible for the course of the subsequent exchanges with the Foreign Office.

On the seventh of July Hay renewed his request for a conference of the four powers. Three weeks later Lord Salisbury consented to "a meeting of the experts nominated by Great Britain, Canada and the United States" "to arrive, if possible, at correct conclusions" respecting the facts. Nothing was said in this note about Russia and Japan, nor was there any reference to the American proposal that the conference should also propose suitable remedies. Salisbury had thus given a very limited acquiescence, but in his reply Hay

[1] *Foreign Relations*, 1895, pp. 610 ff.
[2] *Foreign Relations*, 1897, p. 272.

expressly assumed that England was assenting to the proposed conference of the powers which Hay had previously urged.[1] Hay's answer to Salisbury was, in fact, similar to his reply to Russia two and a half years later with reference to the Open Door note, the difference being that in the latter instance Russia acquiesced in Hay's interpretation, whereas in this case the Foreign Office pointed out, Sept. 22, that it had never agreed to a conference of the powers, and referred Hay to Salisbury's limited acceptance of July 28. Secretary Sherman undertook to defend his ambassador's interpretation of the correspondence but the British held fast. Hay appeared to be incensed and wrote to Foster: [2] "I was never so surprised in my life as when they objected, at the end of September, to Russia and Japan. I had always thought of English diplomacy as overbearing and pigheaded, but I never imagined it was tricky and tortuous. But when they suppressed my note of July 29, and then represented me as trying in September to have them include Russia and Japan in the conference, I had to remodel my ideas of their straightforwardness."

To Adams, Hay wrote: "My own dear Salisbury has gone back on me and says that he was joking when he agreed to a conference. It seems Our Lady of the Snows has sat on him again." [3]

A review of the correspondence, now cold for so many years, leads to the conclusion that while England and Canada were obviously pursuing a dilatory policy and acting in not the best of faith, in this particular incident the new American ambassador and the special envoy had been caught in an act of diplomatic prestidigitation. The episode is thus described at length for two reasons. It formed the preface for Hay to a long series of negotiations with Canada which continued through several years while he was Secretary of State. It also illustrates how difficult it was for him to take a defeat. All his life he had avoided situations which demanded matched play; he was unaccustomed to being beaten.

John Hay's most important services in London were less in the field of negotiation than in reporting and in the not easily defined duties of representation. His journalistic experience was invaluable. Being ambassador was, to some extent, like being an editor.

[1] *Ibid.*, p. 301.
[2] J. W. Foster, *Diplomatic Memoirs*, II, 184.
[3] *Letters and Diaries*, III, p. 96.

Col. Hay in 1897 at the time of his appointment as Ambassador to the Court of St. James's. For purposes of comparison there is shown at the right the subject twenty-three years earlier, at the time of his marriage.

The original, from a retouched enlargement by Pach, is in the office of J. Pierpont Morgan.

The Cabinet of President McKinley in 1899. The names are, left to right: President McKinley; Lyman J. Gage, Secretary of the Treasury; John W. Griggs, Attorney General; John Hay, Secretary of State; John D. Long, Secretary of the Navy; James Wilson, Secretary of Agriculture; Elihu Root, Secretary of War; Ethan A. Hitchcock, Secretary of the Interior; Charles Emory

He could sit at his desk, take the morning papers, skim them for the significant items, recall the conversation at a dinner the night before, and prepare with his own hand a vivid picture of the political events which were likely to be of interest to the Secretary of State and to the President. Hay's despatches prepared in this way were models, and the fact that he did not trust their composition to subordinates indicates that he liked to do them. They were greatly enriched by what he gleaned from his very active social life.

'The new ambassador was immediately a social success. The position offered him just the sort of society that he liked. He had an unerring eye for people of importance and rare gifts to make his presence desired. In the summer of 1897, after Mrs. Hay and the children had returned to America for a brief respite, he started on a round of visits to country houses in Scotland. He reveled in the civilization which lived in castle halls lighted by ancestral portraits from the hand of a Reynolds or a Romney. Invitations came in so fast that he could have prolonged his tour until Christmas. Everywhere this son of the American frontier was welcomed for his personal charm and sparkling conversation. He fitted in as though he belonged. What a man! America has produced few like him.

Hay had for public speaking a dislike so great that the anticipation of a speech not infrequently induced a fever, and yet it was still another form of literary expression in which he excelled. The obvious limitations on ambassadorial speech-making are so many that there remains little to talk about. Before Hay had been in London three weeks he had refused no less than twenty-six invitations to speak, but he did accept some and the addresses he delivered, all brief, greatly added to his fame. The speech at the unveiling of the bust of Sir Walter Scott in Westminster Abbey, May 21, 1897, was in the vein of the best American literary tradition. His simple reference to his father's life in Kentucky, and the contrast of Scott's portrayals of romantic life with the rude realities of pioneer living, were captivating:[1]

In this most significant and interesting ceremony I should have no excuse for appearing, except as representing for the time being a large section of Walter Scott's constituency. I doubt if anywhere his writings have had a more loving welcome than in America. The books a boy reads are those most

[1] *Addresses of John Hay*, New York, 1906, pp. 53 ff.

ardently admired and the longest remembered; and America reveled in Scott
when the country was young. I have heard from my father, a pioneer of Kentucky, that in the early days of this century men would saddle their horses
and ride from all the neighboring counties to the principal post-town of the
region when a new novel by the author of "Waverley" was expected. All over
our struggling states and territories—in the East, where a civilization of slen-
der resources but boundless hopes was building; in the West, where the stern
conflict was going on of the pioneer subduing the continent—the books most
read were those poems of magic and of sentiment, those tales of by-gone
chivalry and romance, which Walter Scott was pouring forth upon the world
with a rich facility, a sort of joyous fecundity like that of Nature in her more
genial moods. He had no clique of readers, no illuminated sect of admirers, to
bewilder criticism by excess of its own subtlety. In a community engaged in
the strenuous struggle for empire, whose dreams, careless of the past, were
turned in the clear, broad light of a nation's morning to a future of unlimited
grandeur and power, there was none too sophisticated to appreciate, none too
lowly to enjoy those marvelous pictures of a time gone forever by, pleasing
and stimulating to a starved fancy in the softened light of memory and art,
though the times themselves were unlamented by a people and an age whose
faces were set toward a far-different future.

It would be difficult, indeed, to devise a more felicitous sentence
than the following: "The man who blew so clear a clarion of patriotism lives forever in the speech of those who seek a line to describe the
love of country."

In January, 1898, with his family, he tried to make up a party to
spend his sixty days of annual leave on the Nile. He invited Henry
James and his old friend, Sir John Clark, neither of whom was able
to go. Henry Adams, however, accompanied him. Before he returned,
March 17, the correspondence between the United States and Spain
over Cuba had reached a stage where war seemed very probable.

The last six months of Hay's residence in England is chiefly significant for the introduction which it gave him to the study of some of
the major problems which he was to face as Secretary of State.

As he was leaving for London in 1897, Hay wrote to Adams in
one of those letters which are not to be taken seriously: "I have
half a mind to hasten the day [of return] by giving my candid opinion
of Congress at a Lord Mayor's dinner. Bayard's vote of censure, of
which he is so proud, would be nothing to it." Instead, at the Lord
Mayor's Easter dinner, April 21, 1898, he made a political speech
of importance—the only political address he made while ambassador.

The subject was "A Partnership in Beneficence"; its haunting refrain was the sharing of the white man's burden. One paragraph may be quoted:

Perhaps I may be pardoned if I say a word about my own country. Knitted as we are to the people of Great Britain by a thousand ties, of origin, of language, and of kindred pursuits, it is inevitable that from time to time we should have occasions of discussion and even of difference. We hear sometimes that we are thought to be somewhat eager and pertinacious in the pursuit of our own interests. If this is so, I can say, I hope with no impertinence, and in a spirit rather of pride than of contrition, that it merely goes to show of what stock we are. But this truth is unquestionable—that for now nearly three generations of men there has been peace between us and friendly regard, a peace growing more solid and durable as years go by, and a friendship that I am sure the vast majority of both peoples hope and trust is to be eternal. The reasons of a good understanding between us lie deeper than any considerations of mere expediency. All of us who think cannot but see that there is a sanction like that of religion which binds us to a sort of partnership in the beneficent work of the world. Whether we will it or not, we are associated in that work by the very nature of things, and no man and no group of men can prevent it. We are bound by a tie which we did not forge and which we cannot break; we are joint ministers of the same sacred mission of liberty and progress, charged with duties which we cannot evade by the imposition of irresistible hands.

Holleben, German ambassador in Washington, coupled the speech with what he alleged to be Henry White's hurried and secret mission to Washington, but which was simply his annual leave, arranged for even before Hay went to Egypt, and scented mysterious omens.[1] The speech was merely Hay's confession of political faith, the gist of convictions which had now thoroughly matured, uttered without suggestion from Washington, but not without realization that the words would be heard in Europe. To that extent he was an Anglophile.

Hay was a day-to-day man; he was not accustomed to sit down and ponder the fundamental significance of the events which went by him, and it seems to have been in his usual frame of mind with reference to such matters that he viewed the approach of the war with Spain. "You and I had better have no opinion about the Spanish War, except the President's," he wrote, April 2, by way of caution to Mrs. Hay, who was in Paris. "He has done everything man could

---

[1] L. B. Shippee, Germany and the Spanish-American War, *American Historical Review*, July, 1925, p. 762.

do to avert it. If it comes now, it will not be his fault." His opinion
was not sought by the President in the turgid days preceding April
11, when the latter sent his famous message to Congress, nor at any
other time, with a single exception noted below. Hay remained close
to the Embassy, and resumed the preparation of reports in his own
handwriting. These reports touched nearly every subject, from the
possibility of a European coalition for interfering with the disposition of the Philippines to the not unrelated subject of the ambitions
of the Powers in the Far East. But he refrained from expressing his
personal opinions as to terms of peace. It may be doubted whether
he had opinions on the subject; he was thinking.

Joseph Chamberlain one evening (May 7) in his own house asked
Hay frankly whether the evacuation of Cuba was the sole condition of peace. Hay was wholly without information and cabled the
inquiry to Washington. It was not until June 3 that he received from
Secretary William R. Day, who succeeded Sherman, April 26, an outline of the terms which the President, personally, would be willing to
approve. The telegram was as follows:

Strictly Confidential.

The President, speaking for himself, would be inclined to grant terms of
peace on the following basis:

First. The evacuation of Cuba and delivery of title and possession of the
Island to the United States to restore and establish order and hold until a
stable government [is] established. United States to protect Spanish subjects
their lives and property while in possession.

Second. United States not demanding any money indemnity for the war,
Spain to cede Porto Rico to the United States in lieu thereof. The United
States to take care of the just and lawful claims of citizens of the United
States arising out of the Cuban insurrection and the present war.

Third. Philippine Islands to be allowed to remain with Spain except a port
and necessary appurtenances, to be selected by the United States, shall be
ceded to the United States.

Fourth. Granting to the United States an island in the Ladrones with harbor
for a coaling station.

These terms will be acceptable to the President at the present juncture,
saving further sacrifice and loss of life. Prolongation of the war [may] change
this materially.

Day.

This information was transmitted to Lord Salisbury on June 6,
but nothing came of it. Meanwhile the President began to modify

his views on the Philippines. On June 14, Day telegraphed: "Since my telegram to you third instant conditions have so changed that paragraph three [as to Philippine Islands] will probably have to be modified. The insurgents there have become important factor in the situation and must have just consideration in any terms of settlement. It is most difficult without fuller knowledge to determine as to disposition of Philippine Islands."

Hay was not slow to catch the drift of the President's thought and, after conference with Salisbury, was able to assure the President that no one was likely to offer any objection if the United States were to retain a "permanent foothold in the Philippines." It was not until July 27 that the President, through the Department of State, invited Hay's comment. Day then telegraphed:

"Have you any reason for revising your views about the terms of peace which were submitted to you in my telegram of June 3rd, and of which in a letter to the President you expressed approval? The President will probably make answer to Spain's general proposal the last of this week.

"Telegraph fully."

The Ambassador suggested no modification as to Cuba and Porto Rico, but proposed, with reference to the Philippines, a "strong guarantee of fair treatment of natives" and a prohibition against either leasing the islands or alienating them without American approval. "I may add," he concluded,[1] "that the British Government prefer to have us retain the Philippine Islands, or failing that, insist on option in case of future sale."

The exchange of telegrams is given in full as an indication of how slowly the President's opinion was forming and more particularly to show by what steps from June 3 the American Government was advancing to the position which it took October 26 when, at the direction of the President, Hay sent the memorable telegram to Paris, instructing the Commissioners to retain the Philippine Islands for a territorial possession of the United States. The Ambassador, by disposition a conservative but now surveying the world from the wider vantage-point of London, was taking the advanced position.

It has been the purpose of this narrative to present a realistic portraiture of John Hay. No effort has been made to show him as a

[1] July 28, 1898.

hero when he was not. His was a soul often in travail not wholly pleasant to observe. If out of the travail there had not come important contributions to American history the tale would have been hardly worth recounting. In the end Hay's life became one of personal achievement to a rare degree, for, in an age characterized by over-coming others, he overcame himself. His brightest personal quality, however, was one which he did not have to achieve; it was always his. He was a modest man. McKinley, immersed in political life where modesty is not highly valued, beset by office-seekers to whom such a grace is unknown, was in a position to have peculiar appreciation for such a quality.

The British Government wished to make an impressive celebra-tion of the completion of sixty years of the reign of Queen Victoria, which came shortly after Hay reached London as Ambassador. Through the British Ambassador in Washington,[1] it was hinted that a special mission of congratulation from the American Government would be welcome. Mr. Sherman replied promptly that at an early date a reply would be made through Mr. Hay. Two weeks later Pauncefote again brought the matter to the attention of the Depart-ment of State which still delayed the disclosure of its plans. On May 12, Hay brought up the question. He stated: "I am aware that it is not in the tradition nor the habit of our country to compete with other powers in matters of display or ceremony." He suggested that, following the precedent of ten years before, he, as ambassador, be specially appointed as envoy to present the President's felicita-tions to the Queen. The British Government appears to have been pressing for an answer and two days later Hay asked for cabled in-structions. Notwithstanding these repeated joggings of the Depart-ment it was not until eleven days later, May 21, eight weeks after Pauncefote had first introduced the matter, and only a month before the Jubilee ceremonies, that Hay was informed of the decision of the American Government. It was proposed to send a delegation consist-ing of Admiral Joseph N. Miller, General Nelson A. Miles, represent-ing the Navy and Army, respectively, and "two eminent civilians," all of whom were to be associated with Hay as head of the special embassy.

The following day Hay received a telegram indicating that the

[1] March 30, 1897.

President was in trouble. It contained the information that, if it were agreeable to Hay, the President would like, in place of the two civilians, to send Whitelaw Reid "to cooperate at the Queen's Anniversary and to be the bearer of his [the President's] message." Obviously the President was now trying to create a special position for the owner of the *Tribune,* but the plan did not fit the situation, for Hay had learned that the Queen would receive only a single envoy. This regulation, Hay replied, would create an invidious position for Mr. Reid, who "coming so far, with special commissions, would naturally feel aggrieved at being relegated so entirely to the background." Hay therefore heartily endorsed Reid, and begged that his own name be omitted entirely. The President, at first not quite comprehending the situation, replied that such an arrangement would not do, and that rather than excuse Hay from the special mission, he would prefer to send no special ambassador from the United States. Further reflection by the President seems to have led him to realize that Hay was offering the only possible way out which would leave Whitelaw Reid in an agreeable mood, and Hay's proposal was therefore adopted.

"The *Tribune's* editorial references to the administration have seemed to take on a new color since the Special Ambassador received his appointment and took his departure," wrote John Addison Porter, the President's Secretary.

The Special Embassy proceeded to London and established itself in almost regal splendor. Hay's sense of humor did not desert him and he wrote to Adams:[1] "The sight of a worthy human being happy is comforting to the soul, and I have seen my friend Whitelaw sitting between two princesses at supper every night, for a week running, and I now may intone my *nunc dimittis.* His rapture has the *aliquid amare* that the end must come, but the memory of it will soothe many an hour of *ennui* at Ophir Farm." Reid himself appears to have been quite unconscious that he had selected a somewhat inopportune moment for collecting on the debt of gratitude which Hay owed him, first for giving him a place on the *Tribune* in 1870, and then for keeping at Hay's disposal the columns of the paper for more than twenty years. On Hay's part the episode marked the chilling of an old friendship. There was never a rupture, but after the Jubilee,

[1] July 25, 1897.

Hay appears to have viewed Reid as one whose desire for office and conspicuous preferment had made him almost insane. One ventures that Hay's conduct in London at the time of the Jubilee had much to do with making him Secretary of State, and may also explain why Reid did not replace Hay in London.[1]

Under date of May 29, the President wrote to Hay the longest letter which, up to that time, he had written to any one. He made grateful reference to the Reid appointment. "Let me assure you of my appreciation of your friendly cooperation in arranging for our representation at the Queen's Jubilee. Mr. Reid is of course delighted with his appointment and must recognize the courteous manner in which you have paved the way for his appearance at this interesting function."

The remainder of this letter, from which the above paragraph is quoted, is added to show, on the one hand, how tongue-tied and commonplace the man with the mask could be, and, on the other, how genuinely Hay had won the President's confidence.

Dear Colonel Hay:

I was very glad to receive your letter and especially to learn of your reaching England under such pleasant circumstances. Certainly your reception was very gratifying, not only as a compliment to yourself, but reflecting credit on the country. Your speeches were models of good-taste in every respect and they have been read with a feeling of pride here.

Please present my compliments to Mrs. Hay and tell her of my appreciation of the courtesies extended to her by the Queen, which I judge were advisedly made especially cordial to both of you.

You have my confidence that you will take whatever may seem the wisest course in regard to the bimetallic conference. The details of the visit of our Commissioners will doubtless reach me through yourself and others in due time. The conservative course which you have mapped out for yourself in regard to attendance upon public functions and the making of speeches will, I am sure, only gain you a greater standing with the people in the end. Arbitration as well as bimetallism is a matter in which good progress ought to and perhaps will be made in the not distant future.

The bright and beautiful cool weather which has continued still here in Washington this spring is a great boon to all of us who are burdened with official work. Mrs. McKinley's health and my own continue excellent. . . .

My time for personal letter writing is very limited now-a-days as you may readily imagine; and for this reason this letter is I believe the longest I have

---

[1] The correspondence relative to the Reid Embassy is partially printed in *Foreign Relations*, 1897, pp. 249–52; the unpublished portions, referred to above, are in the archives of the Department of State, and in the Hay Papers.

sent to any one, but I want you to write me often.

With kind regards and best wishes,

Faithfully yours,

William McKinley.

Not content with a single reference to the Reid affair, on July 27 the President returned to the subject in another long letter. The President was evidently deeply touched, and this time gave a vague intimation that Hay's conduct should not go unrewarded. "Mr. Reid will, I suppose, soon be back here and will probably tell me personally of his experiences. The generosity and delicacy with which you have treated him could not have been exceeded by any one and will in the end I am sure strengthen your own position with the people of both countries, if this were possible or needed, which it is not."

In the summer of 1898 the Camerons went to England and took a house in Kent where was reëstablished from time to time all that was left of "The Five of Hearts" and its friends. Henry Adams was there and John Hay made of it the equivalent of a summer embassy. It was to this house that Henry White on August 15 brought the telegram from McKinley inviting Hay to return and become Secretary of State in place of Day, who was to be one of the commissioners to the peace conference at Paris.

Hay appears to have drafted two replies, a declination and an acceptance. A copy of the former, in Hay's handwriting, found in the Hay Papers, reads:

"I received your despatch with mingled emotions of affection, gratitude and sorrow. It would have been the dearest wish of my heart to be associated with you in that way, but my health will not permit it. I will hold this place through the winter or resign immediately, which ever will be most convenient for you."

Instead, after much debate, he sent the following:

"Your despatch received. I am entirely and most gratefully at your disposition. But I fear it is not possible to get to Washington by September first. I am suffering from an indisposition, not serious but painful, which will prevent my moving for some little time. I shall require several days to break up my establishment and get away. If about four weeks delay could be granted me I could be there by first of October. It might increase the influence and prestige

of Mr. Day if he went to Paris as Secretary of State. If the need
of a change is urgent and it would ·be inconvenient to wait for me,
I hope you will act without reference to me."

The two draft telegrams present in the most graphic way the great
underlying conflict which had embroiled Hay's life for forty years:
on the one hand, love of ease; on the other, sense of duty. The two
texts do not require elaboration. Somewhere in him was a hero whom
he had once portrayed as the man who could "hold her nozzle against
the bank till the last galoot's ashore," and whose "ghost at length
went up alone in the smoke of the Prairie Belle." Now, at the age
of sixty, his own chance had come. He faltered, but only for a moment. The decision which he had once assigned to Jim Bludso he
made his own.

> "He seen his duty, a dead-sure thing,—
> And went for it thar and then."

For almost seven long years, a period of service which ranks John
Hay sixth among all the Secretaries of State, only Madison, Monroe,
John Quincy Adams, Seward, and Fish having served longer, with
no personal ambition to gratify, always engaged in a running fight
with ill health, John Hay served his time. Granted a delay by the
President, he assumed office September 30.

"You don't know how oddly I feel about your coming," he wrote
to Mrs. Hay, October 19. "I am longing to see you and yet I feel so
dull and worthless I almost dread to have you come and plunge into
this life of dreary drudgery. It is going to be vile—the whole business. The men are bad enough—their wives are worse. All the fun
of my life ended on the platform at Euston. I do not mean by that
that England was so uproariously gay—but this place is so intolerable."

In the Cabinet Hay was to sit next to McKinley, on the latter's right; upon the death of Vice President Hobart, fourteen months later, he was to become next in the order of succession to the head of the table.

In assuming his duties as Secretary of State, Hay had more good luck; he came just at the time when his services would be most welcome. The senile John Sherman had been a pitiful figure. William R. Day, who followed Sherman for five months, was already on his way to Paris as the head of the Peace Commission. As a fellow townsman of McKinley's, Day had enjoyed the President's confidence, but it could not be claimed that as Secretary of State he had been a notable figure. Sherman and Day, like Bayard, were easy men to follow.

"Your commission is signed, sealed, and recorded," wrote Alvey A. Adee, Second Assistant Secretary of State, September 23, "awaiting only the filling in of the date in order to effect its delivery. The cuss-words await your pleasure." Hay and Adee were old friends. The latter had served as private secretary to General Sickles in Madrid while Hay was Secretary of the Legation in 1870. When Hay resigned in the summer of that year to enter, as he supposed, newspaper work in Chicago, Adee succeeded to his place. Shortly before Hay became Assistant Secretary of State under Evarts, Adee was transferred from Madrid to Washington where he was appointed a clerk in the Department of State. In 1882, when Adee received his first major promotion, to the place of Third Assistant Secretary of State, Hay had telegraphed, July 12: "God bless you, my boy; the country is safe."

The President greeted Hay warmly. "He seems well and strong, but says he feels tired," wrote Hay to his wife that evening. "He scared me by saying he would not worry any more about the State Department. He has evidently been Secr. of State for the past year. Reid's famished hunger for office is perfectly insane. I will give you details when I see you."

The next day, September 30, Hay was sworn into office by Justice Harlan in the presence of the Cabinet. Then he sat down to his first cabinet-meeting, which he found dull, and went back across the street to "Mr. Mullett's masterpiece," [1] in the south end of which he was to have his office for just short of seven long years. The clerks filed solemnly past him and shook hands. Adee fluttered about to make him comfortable and to tell him funny stories.

In the mail was an autographed photograph of the Prince of Wales. Twelve days later John Hay came upon his sixty-first birthday.

In those days the Department of State was a small and relatively private affair. Aside from a few laborers there was a staff of about sixty people, among whom perhaps eight were carrying the load. It was an antiquated, feeble organization, enslaved by precedents and routine inherited from another century, remote from the public gaze and indifferent to it. The typewriter was viewed as a necessary evil and the telephone was an instrument of last resort. The organization was hardly adequate to the new responsibilities of the United States as a world power, but the increased demands had arisen so suddenly that there had been no time to prepare to meet them. Nor were they met in Hay's time; the new Secretary of State, although not unlearned in business, was almost wholly without experience in business routine. It had been nearly twenty years since he had even made a pretense of sitting at a desk and keeping office hours. The refurbishment of the Department of State, and of the diplomatic and consular service, had to await the coming of a better administrator, Elihu Root, who followed Hay in office, in 1905.

Although eventually Hay came to the point where he could carry his responsibilities, especially the petty ones, with a fair degree of ease, at first they irked him severely. "I am immersed in business and should be as cross as a bear, if I had any one to scold," he wrote to Mrs. Hay on the third day. "I went to the Department at 10:30 this morning and could not catch up with my work. I shall try 9:30 hereafter and see how that will work. I do not think I can help you much in social matters this Winter. It looks as though all my time would be taken up with business." Two days later he reported

[1] Hay's compliment to the architect of the State, War, and Navy Building which has been recently in danger of being robbed of Mr. Mullett's marks in order that it may join the chaste company of Greek temples in which so much of the government business is transacted.

that he was disgustingly busy. "From 9:30 to 5:00 are my hours at the Department, and of course it will be much worse when Congress meets."

Personal relationships were almost the sum of life to the new Secretary. He was very dependent upon the people about him, not so much dependent for personal services as for agreeable companionship. To be intimately associated with those whom he did not like was little less than torture. It is appropriate, therefore, at this point to sketch in the other principal figures who in the next few years were to walk the stage by his side.

First of importance among those upon whom he relied was Adee.

By sheer competence Alvey A. Adee made himself a personage in American history. If the British Government could be epitomized as a justice of the peace with at his elbow a clerk who knew the law, the direction of American foreign relations might have been similarly represented as a procession of Secretaries of State with a continuing Second Assistant Secretary who knew the routine and was able to tell them what they ought to do. The office was created for William C. Hunter in 1866, who for fourteen years previously had been Chief Clerk. When Hunter died in 1886 Adee moved up to his place, but when Adee died thirty-eight years later, it required a dozen people to take over his work, and it never could be said that even then the place had been filled. Hunter and Adee were the incorporation of whatever continuity there was in American foreign relations—and there was a good deal—for about three quarters of a century. When Hay became Secretary his second assistant was fifty-six years old, in his prime.

Adee had a peculiar literary gift which greatly increased his usefulness in the Department. His ordinary prose style was terse and of marvelous clarity. He was also a good imitator and could so merge his personality with that of his superior that no one could detect in the final draft where Adee's red-inked interlineations had been inserted. Hay and Adee began their literary collaborations in Madrid, where they joined in the authorship of a short story, "Life's Magnet," which appeared in *Putnam's* in August, 1870.

"I write today, to ask you to look at a little nightmare in the August *Putnam's*," Hay wrote to a literary friend, David Gray, on July 25, 1870: "The plot is mine, the execution my young friend

Adee's. I think even you, with your partiality for your poor servant, will admit that it is better executed than conceived. I confess I was greatly tickled with it. He wrote it after about fifteen minutes dictation from me, as to the general run of the story. He makes nice verses too, like Luca Giordano, in everybody's style. He can twitter like young Tennyson and maunder like old Browning in a style it would do your heart good to hear."

Hay found his old friend in charge of the Department. During the summer the President had proposed to Adee that the latter should be moved up to the position of First Assistant Secretary in the place of John Bassett Moore, who went to Paris as the Secretary of the Peace Commission. Adee modestly begged the President to leave the appointment open until Hay should arrive. The President had also telegraphed Hay that the latter would have an opportunity to express his preference. The offer to Adee was not renewed and David Jayne Hill was appointed to the vacancy. In 1902 Doctor Hill went as minister to The Hague, and was replaced by Francis B. Loomis. The Third Assistant Secretary, when Hay arrived, was Thomas W. Cridler, and after 1901, Herbert H. D. Peirce, a Lodge appointee. None of the appointments could be described as Hay's personal preference. He took those whom the President selected, and depended upon Adee to see that everything went right. In all but name Adee was the permanent Under Secretary of State. He distributed the work, reviewed the outgoing correspondence before the signature, and became the pivot about whom revolved all departmental activities. He did not escape the usual fate of handy-man; he was always liable to be taken for granted. Hay, who was well aware that most of the dull and disagreeable work fell to Adee, called him Cinderella.

"Cinderella finds himself relegated to the ash heap as usual," the Second Assistant wrote one day [1] at the end of a hard summer when he had reason to feel that his colleagues had forgotten him. He added that one man did not return from lunch until 3:55. "My afternoon lost, the days are too short now for a paddle on the river without an early start, which I can never manage to get." The canoe, the bicycle, and good books, were his only diversions. If he had convictions or ideas of statesmanship, they were never too obtrusive to prevent him from serving loyally a procession of Republican, Demo-

[1] To Hay, Sept. 27, 1904.

cratic, Republican, Democratic, and then Republican chiefs. It was his job to carry out the decisions of the Secretary, and if, in presenting the choices for decision, he sometimes shuffled the cards so that only one choice was possible, so much the more credit to his ability.

Adee was the kind of man who does not often go wrong. Each summer Hay tried to take about two months at Lake Sunapee. Adee was then his faithful daily, even hourly, correspondent. Something of the confidence which Hay had in his assistant's judgment comes out in a letter just before the relief of the beleaguered legations in Peking in the summer of 1900. From Newbury, whither Hay had gone after all but collapsing in Washington, the Secretary wrote: [1] "I only hope you will not be burdened with many such days of work and anxiety while I am gone; but I can not tell you how comfy I feel in my mind to know that you are on deck with an intimate knowledge of the tiller. . . .

> For Heaven's sake, take care of yourself.
> "Princes and Lords may flourish and fade,
> A breath can make them as a breath has made"
> But one Adee is all we have in the pantry."

Suffering then from the malady of which another acute attack five years later caused his death, Hay wrote three weeks later:

The carrion press has evidently made up their minds that I am too long a-dying and have been trying all day to hurry me up with visits and telegrams, etc. I refuse to see reporters and they take their revenge after their kind. The fact is I am rubbing along *sin novedad*. I am neither sick nor well, but clearly incapable, at the moment, of travel or of serious work. I am filled with remorse and grief that it should be so, but *que voulez-vous?*

It is incomprehensible to me that Hill should not long ago have cut his leave to go back to Washington, to divide with you the work and the Kudos you are gaining. It is the biggest job the State Department has been engaged on in our time and insures you already a bright page in our history. Only I dread every day to hear the news of your breaking down from overwork.

At the end of September, Hay, still unwell, decided that he must return. "Perhaps with a spoonful of quinine per day I could get on," he wrote. "I wish I had your indispensable ability to think and work,

[1] Aug. 11, 1900.

but I must patch up the old wreck and keep her afloat until March with your help."

Not a few of Hay's contemporaries were inclined to feel that his not infrequent illness was actually less serious than it seemed in his own estimation. They were quite wrong. Added to an old malady was a new one, the combined effect of which must have been to leave him with even less stamina than in his earlier years of relative idleness. The wonder is that he lived as long as he did.

"You waste your precious time referring such a thing to me," Hay wrote on another occasion.[1] "How often have I told you, you can't go wrong if you try. If it were not that I believe your judgment is better than mine in these things I should not be here." To have such an appreciative chief made Adee's position easier, but the inference is not to be drawn that the assistant actually did the work for which the chief took the credit. Adee could imitate Hay's signature, but very few important documents went out from the Department without Hay's express approval. The Second Assistant Secretary looked upon Hay with such admiration as one craftsman has for a better one.

"I have been so pestered that I feel that my attempt to draft a reply to Jusserand is not creditable—but such as I have I give thee," wrote Adee, February 3, 1903. "I am sure you could do much better with one hand tied behind you and your foot in your hip pocket. Why not try it? My brain is mush today." Hay, in turn, often threw his drafts over to Adee for editing and amendment, but in a crisis, or in any difficult negotiation, there was never any question as to which of the two men was more sure of himself. Some of Hay's ablest papers were written out with a pencil up at Lake Sunapee when he was far removed from the possibility of conference with any of his advisers. To give Alvey A. Adee his long-belated due in no way detracts from the fame of the chief whom he served with so much loyalty and personal affection.

Among the Cabinet members Hay was most closely associated with Elihu Root, who became Secretary of War in the summer of 1899. Hay had suggested Root's appointment to McKinley, although the two men had never been closely related before. Between Hay and Root there grew up a sympathy and understanding without which there could have been a great deal of friction. During the period of

[1] July 21, 1903.

transition, before the relations of the United States to Cuba, Porto Rico, and the Philippines had been defined by law, and in China in 1900, where diplomacy had to be supported by military force, the two men, had they exhibited less regard for one another's judgment and sensibility, might easily have worked at cross purposes. It is as much a compliment to the one as to the other that they never did.

Soon after Root's entry into the Cabinet the rumor spread so insistently that the two men were at odds that Hay became greatly disturbed. With a view to correcting abroad a wrong impression which might embarrass impending negotiations, Hay wrote to Henry White, September 9, 1899:

"A fantastic lie is going the rounds in the Western papers that there is a struggle *à outrance* going on between Root and me as to which shall boss the islands. There is not a shadow of truth in it. There is no dissension in the Cabinet in any quarter. It has been enormously strengthened in its original form and is now a very smooth running and practical machine."

It was the intention of McKinley to transfer the administration of the new island possessions, as soon as possible, from military to civilian hands. But for the President's death there would have been created in October, 1901, and placed in the Department of State, a bureau of insular affairs. That this project could have been so far advanced was a tribute, on the one hand, to McKinley's confidence in Hay, and, on the other hand, to the harmonious relations of the Secretaries of State and of War.

"It will not be very long, I suppose," wrote the President, July 22, 1901, "until Cuba and the Philippines will come into the Department of State, and we already have Hawaii and Porto Rico. . . . I suppose if we organize the bureau under you, that Congress will give us the necessary legislation. I believe that some such bureau in your Department would be of invaluable service." A few weeks later Hay visited the President at Canton, where McKinley appears to have given approval to the final plans for setting up the new office. Hay then hastened to assure Root that he was not seeking to rob the War Department of its responsibilities. Root had some reservation in his approval but, from his letter of September 4, it is clear that there was a perfect understanding between the two men:

I beg you not to let your kind heart be troubled by any faintest apprehension that I shall feel anything but approval of the Bureau of Insular Affairs. I think that both for the name of it and the substance the insular business should be got out of the War Department as early as practicable and the earlier the process begins the better. . . . Of course, so long as we have to continue a measure of military government in the Philippines and are unable to prescribe a definite line between civil and military authority there, it is useful to have both sets of officers subject to the same department so that neither can hope for backing against the authority under which the other acts. A good deal of patience is necessary even in a single department to keep the peace in public. Man, both civil and military, is such a jealous and pernickety animal. I hope, however, that this condition of unstable equilibrium will soon be over and the whole business can go where it belongs under civil control in the nearest approach we can make to a Department of Colonial Affairs.

The assassination of McKinley terminated the project. In one of the earliest cabinet meetings under Roosevelt the difficulties hinted by Root appear to have been elaborated in a long discussion. To Charles H. Allen, recently governor of Porto Rico, whom McKinley had expected to name as the head of the new bureau, Hay reported:[1]

"In what he [Roosevelt] said and what other members of the Cabinet said, he seemed to develop as he went along a fear that there might be a possibility of friction and complications between the civil and military authorities in the Philippines as a result of the establishment of the Bureau, and he hardly seemed to think it was worth while to establish it simply to deal with questions referring to Hawaii and Porto Rico. . . . He regards it as a necessity in the future, and regards you as the best possible man to have charge of it, perhaps with a more independent jurisdiction than we have been talking about."

The friendship between Hay and Root remained unbroken. After one of Hay's political speeches Root wrote: "I didn't think anything could increase my affectionate admiration for you: but your speech has. It was delightful. I knew the disturbance of the nebula in Perseus meant that some one had stolen his sandals. You did it and hitched your words to them."[2]

Root also sympathized with Hay in his troubles with the Senate, although Root himself, as Hay's successor, pursued toward that body

1 September 21, 1901.
2 November 20, 1901.

a very different policy. To a dinner invitation Root once replied to Hay:

> "Missus says yea
> And we'll not stay away
> From your mahoganay
> Next Tuesday
> Eighth of May
> > Damn the Senate
> > Root."

When rumors of Root's retirement as Secretary of War in 1903 reached Hay he urged Roosevelt to accept his own resignation in order that Root might be placed in the Department of State. This episode may more logically be related in a subsequent chapter detailing the relations of Roosevelt and Hay. It is appropriate, however, to add here the letter which Root wrote to Mrs. Hay, July 19, 1905, immediately following the announcement of his appointment as Hay's successor:

I have come to Washington to take office as Secretary of State and I find myself shrinking from it as if it were some breach of friendship. I cannot think of the office apart from Mr. Hay and it seems like thrusting his memory aside to permit myself to be called Secretary of State, but indeed it is not that, dear Mrs. Hay. Affection and sorrow are uppermost in my heart and the deepest sympathy with you and sense of loss myself and for all the circle of friends. Of course no one can fill his place here. It cannot be filled. Other men may hold the office, but his place was what he made it and it can no more be filled than the place of John Quincy Adams or of Daniel Webster can be filled.

It is the cause of melancholy and satisfaction to me that I am sure my accession to the office would have Mr. Hay's approval, for often, when we used to compare notes of weariness and discouragement in office, he would insist that he should resign and that I should take his place. Then I would scoff at him and we would grow cheerful again and go on with our work. It is a satisfaction, too, that we should have talked so much over most of the questions of our diplomacy and most of the great things Mr. Hay did as Secretary and that I have gained from him some of his points of view and method of treatment and spirit.

The relations, official and personal, of Hay and Root reveal again, as in the case of Adee, a magnanimity which goes far toward explaining why John Hay was held in deep affection by his friends. If Hay was ever jealous of one of his fellow men, no trace of evidence remains in any written record.

To a degree almost equal to his reliance on Adee and Root, Hay depended also upon the British Ambassador in Washington. Sir Julian Pauncefote [1] followed the indiscreet Sackville-West in Washington in 1889. He knew his way about the city almost as well as Hay did. Ten years older than the Secretary, he had been a practicing lawyer before he entered the service of the British Government. After wide and varied experience in Hongkong and then in the Leeward Islands, Pauncefote had entered the Colonial Office in London, transferring thence to the Foreign Office, where he became Permanent Under-Secretary of State. His most distinguished service, before coming to Washington, had been in the succession of conferences leading up to the settlement of the status of the Suez Canal. Stated more broadly, it might be said that he was an expert on neutral waterways, a fact which probably explains why he was retained by his government so long in Washington, pending the settlement of the isthmian canal question. Pauncefote was also prominently identified with the cause of arbitration as a method of settling international disputes. Hay usually selected his friends for a light touch which Pauncefote lacked, but the friendship which grew between the two men was one of the most substantial and productive in Hay's life. The personal relationship was so intimate that it no doubt contributed greatly to the ill-founded rumor that the official relations of the two countries which they represented were equally close. Hay owed so much to Pauncefote that it is difficult to see how, without such a friend, he could have accomplished all that now remains to his credit. [2]

Abroad Hay leaned mostly on Joseph H. Choate, who followed him as Ambassador in London in February, 1899. This assertion may surprise many who have come to identify the American Embassy of this period in London with Henry White, who was not infrequently Chargé when important incidents arose. White and Hay were very close friends and the correspondence which passed between them [3] is an important source of information for the diplomatic history of the period, but the Choate-Hay correspondence is more important. For small matters Hay used White, whose personal relations of long

[1] After Aug. 18, 1899, Lord Pauncefote.
[2] R. B. Mowat, *Life of Lord Pauncefote.*
[3] See Allan Nevins, *Henry White: Thirty Years of American Diplomacy.*

standing were extremely valuable, but in the tedious and difficult negotiations over the Alaska boundary, the canal, and similar matters, Choate's long experience in the law, his standing at home, and his genial personality, made him a stout defender of his country's rights, and a formidable advocate of the contentions he was instructed to support. Hay's and Roosevelt's fondness for White should not obscure the fact that Choate was probably the ablest American Ambassador in London since Charles Francis Adams. The combination of Hay and Pauncefote in Washington, with Choate, White, Chamberlain, and Balfour in London, was congenial.

With Horace Porter in Paris, with Andrew D. White and Charlemagne Tower in Berlin, with Robert F. McCormick and George Von L. Meyer in St. Petersburg, Hay had no very important relations. W. W. Rockhill had been appointed American Minister at Athens, but Hay had him brought back to Washington because of his knowledge of Far Eastern affairs. Rockhill was made Secretary of the Bureau of American Republics, but his usefulness to Hay, to which reference will be made in its proper place, was in matters Chinese.

There remains to be mentioned the friend upon whom Hay most of all depended, President McKinley.

In thirty short years William McKinley has become one of the most obscure major figures in American history. A facile public speaker, he was a poor letter-writer, and such letters as he wrote have never been available for careful study. Meanwhile, the reminiscence-writers, often with the best of intentions, have had their day. A recent critic has described McKinley as "at best but a soft, easy-going second-rater," who "had never an idea nor an inspiration, no independence," and who "was the tool of the interests and answered the beck and call of Mark Hanna." [1] Such description applies, perhaps, to the mask, but not to the man.

There is a mystery about the relations between any President and any Secretary of State which the public can never resolve. Under the Constitution the President is specifically charged with the direction of foreign relations. Few Presidents, even those who have been willing to trust most to their advisers, have ever sought to evade this responsibility. Certainly McKinley did not.

[1] Walter F. McCaleb, *Theodore Roosevelt*, p. 112.

A contrast is often drawn between McKinley and Roosevelt in their attitude toward foreign affairs. Mr. Thayer stated, in his biography of Hay, that the latter "used to tell his friends that President McKinley did not send for him once a month on business, but that he saw President Roosevelt every day." [1] With all due deference to Mr. Thayer, who wrote at a time when he could have the advantage of personal interviews with many contemporaries who have now gone, the writer is convinced that the statement conveys a quite erroneous impression. It is true that Roosevelt more often concerned himself with details which McKinley would have left to others, and that he interfered more, and with less courtesy; that he was less eager to take advice; but, there was no major policy or negotiation in which Hay did not as earnestly and persistently seek the advice and consent of McKinley, as later he did of Roosevelt. No doubt the contemporary fame of Hay profited greatly from the popular opinion that McKinley was nothing more than a skillful domestic politician. No specific foreign policy was ever attached to McKinley's name, but it is clear that he kept a firm hand on the direction of foreign relations. McKinley was a good listener, but behind his mask of amiability there was self-discipline and decision of character. Long experienced in the school of domestic adversity, he leaned on no one, but he knew how to use such diverse gifts as those of Mark Hanna and those of John Hay. He was eager for their service but he did the bidding of neither.

McKinley and Hay worked together in much the same spirit, although without the same levity, as Hay and Adee. They amended each other's drafts and consulted each other's judgments. It was characteristic of the President, having struggled with a note, to send it over to Hay with the instruction "add or take away. I want it put right." On the other hand, McKinley was equally quick to see where Hay's ready pen had led him astray, and did not hesitate to correct him; always, however, with a deference and courtesy which made Hay his devoted admirer.

The management of appointments to office bothered Hay more than any of his other duties. He found it convenient to repeat very often that such matters were in the hands of the President and beyond his control. On the day of his arrival in Washington he found his

[1] Thayer, II, p. 297.

desk cluttered with requests from Warsaw to New York for appointments to office. A horde of office-seekers dogged his steps.

"I have absolutely not a single place at my disposal," he wrote to Representative J. M. Dalzell, on October 10, "and, so far as I know, shall not have during the time I hold this office." To William Dean Howells he wrote two days later, "Judge Day cleaned off the shelf before going to Paris. . . . I was told, when I came here, that there were two appointments under the personal control of the Secretary—but Mr. Sherman wanted one & his claim could hardly be denied, and the President took the other." An early comer in search of office was his old friend, Whitelaw Reid, whose importunities raised an exceedingly embarrassing situation. To him he wrote on December 26, 1898: "After you had gone Saturday I felt with some remorse that I may have seemed to you less confidential than it has been my life long habit to be with you. There are two explanations of it which I owe to you.

"First I hate to be the occasion of strife among friends. If I had mentioned in detail the important personal influences which have been urging the President during the last month or two, men who have been intimately associated with you socially and politically, you would have regarded the action as lacking in friendship and in candor. *They* do not regard it so—they speak of you with the same regard and affection as ever; but you, naturally, would take a different view of their action and it was for this reason I did not go into details, and,

"secondly, So long as I am in this place, which I cannot be for long,—although I came to it all most unwillingly, I am bound in common decency to a loyal observance of every obligation to the President and cannot discuss either his actions or his motives, even to my dearest friends."

He always wanted to have Henry White appointed to an Ambassadorship, and had Italy particularly in mind, but as in his own case only a few years before, there was no politics in such an appointment to such an important office. Having tactfully urged White's appointment upon the President, and in vain, Hay wrote his friend: [1]

I cannot complain of the President's action in this or in any other matter. He has been most generous and liberal ever since I have been here; he has allowed me an absolutely free hand in the important work of the Department,

[1] August 23, 1900

supporting and sustaining me in the face of all sorts of opposition in Congress and elsewhere. So long as he gives me this generous support in public matters I am unable to make points with him in regard to personal appointments, and, although I give him my opinion with great frankness in regard to such matters, I have not controlled a single important appointment in the State Department since I entered it.

"I am more and more convinced," he again wrote White on March 18, 1901, "that no exercise of patronage is ever of any use to an Administration. If all appointments could be made automatic, it would be a good thing for Presidents." In the same vein he also wrote: [1]

"All other branches of the civil service are so rigidly provided for that the foreign service is like the topmost rock which you sometimes see in old pictures of the Deluge. The pressure for a place in it is almost indescribable."

Perhaps Hay somewhat overstated his impotence in the matter of appointments. Roosevelt subsequently claimed that he did. But it was not characteristic of him in his dealings with the President to insist on, or even to urge, his preferences.

John Hay had a stern sense of duty.

"I am plagued by the foul fiend flibbertigibbit," he wrote to Adee, August 10, 1899. "I cannot give myself up to rest and be thankful, so I have written to the President to let me come over there [Westport, New York—a very arduous trip from Lake Sunapee], to bore him a few hours about Alaska and Samoa and China and Nicaragua and the other outlying nurseries of woe and worry."

When Hay left London in 1898 it was with no expectation that he would be Secretary of State for more than the remainder of McKinley's first term. He presented his resignation March 13, 1900, immediately following the attacks on the first canal treaty. The President declined to accept it and added: "As in all matters you have taken my counsel, I will cheerfully bear whatever criticism or condemnation may come." [2]

By the following November Hay had become so much a part of the political situation and was so bound to McKinley that resignation was not to be thought of. At the cabinet meeting after the election the President made a little speech "saying the victory was as

[1] To Professor George P. Fisher, July 2, 1902.
[2] Thayer, II, p. 228.

much ours as his, saying that he could not afford to part company with us, and asked us all to remain with him for the next four years. It was one of the most touching and dignified things I have ever known him to do." [1] The Secretary was more than enmeshed in office; he had become fond of it.

Most of all Hay was drawn to McKinley by his personal qualities. He was a "good" man, Hay used to repeat. The President was also a gentleman, as Hay himself always sought to be, and in the concluding lines of his memorial address on McKinley in 1902—perhaps Hay's best speech—he spoke from the heart when he said: [2] "No one but must feel his devotion for his country renewed and kindled when he remembers how McKinley loved, revered, and served it, showed in his life how a citizen should live, and in his last hour taught us how a gentleman could die."

This was the stage and these were the characters who set forth the next act of the drama of the United States as a world power. The actors knew in a vague way that they were making history.

[1] To Adelbert Hay, Nov. 14, 1900.
[2] Addresses, p. 175.

UNDER McKinley, Hay served not quite three years; under Roosevelt, a little less than four. The former was the genuinely creative period; by September, 1901, the major foreign policies were all well defined. It remained for the Roosevelt administration only to apply the accepted principles. Hay's work has, logically, the two phases, corresponding to the two administrations.

Throughout the period from 1898 to 1901 the foreign policy of the United States turned on the nature of Anglo-American relations. Everything else was relative to agreements which had to be reached with Great Britain.

John Hay early acquired and always retained the reputation of being an Anglophile, and yet, when his work is appraised, it is found that, aside from those Secretaries of State who happened to hold office during the liquidation of the wars of Independence and of 1812, he secured from England greater concessions to American advantage than any of his predecessors in office.

He obtained the security of an unbroken Alaskan coast-line; a clear title to the exclusive possession of Tutuila, one of the best harbors in the South Pacific; the right by treaty for the United States to build and defend the Panama Canal; and the acquiescence of England to American paramountcy in the Caribbean Sea. These concessions were accompanied by the hearty good-will of England in the transfer of the Philippines to American sovereignty; and, in China, substantial support, until the formation of the Anglo-Japanese Alliance in 1902, of the doctrine of the integrity of the Chinese Empire.

In return the American Government conceded a couple of islands on the Alaskan coast; yielded equality of rates through the proposed canal; and surrendered in Samoa a tripartite agreement which had already proved unworkable. There were no other immediate considerations. Hay stood firm for American neutrality in the Boer War— an advantage to the power which controlled the seas—but it is difficult to discover what alternative choice there could have been. It was not a concession to apply the traditional American policy of neutrality, although it may have been worth something to England that Hay did not push the American doctrine of the rights of neutrals to its logical last conclusion.

It may be freely admitted that the Secretary had back of him, and pushing him to lengths to which he would not have gone voluntarily, an uncompromising Senate, and an aroused nationalism; that in the final settlement of the Alaska boundary question, he had the strenuous, though undesired and probably unnecessary, support of Roosevelt; that he had the advantage of finding England in a political situation in which it was more profitable to give than to receive; and, that he had rather better than ordinary good luck in a conjunction of events which no individual could control or direct. On the other hand, he was the agent in these transactions then considered highly profitable. In the negotiations he neither uttered nor wrote to England any harsh words to leave a sting, although the same may not be said of his comments on American politicians. While England was retiring step by step in Alaska, in the Caribbean, at the Isthmus, and in the Pacific, John Hay was regarded as the best American friend the British ever had. Daniel Webster in 1842 had secured less for his country; Seward and Fish prepared the way for Hay but they won less, and at the cost of much ill-will; Olney also was an indispensable precursor for Hay, but it was reserved for the latter to reap the substantial benefit, while at the same time pouring oil on the wounds which Olney's slashing stroke had laid open. It is no slight achievement to drive your adversary back step by step, and at the same time win not only his respect but his love. If John Hay was an Anglophile, it cannot be maintained that he placed British interests before those of his own country, and as for being amiable and courteous toward an opponent, was not that the wiser, even the indispensable, way?

The problem in statecraft presented to Hay at the close of 1898 was, if not easy to solve, simple enough to define. The oldest, the most popular, of American foreign policies had been to crowd the transatlantic Powers out of the Western Hemisphere. One by one the European states had been retiring for more than a century. The nation was born in a conflict which resulted in the surrender by Great Britain of all but the most northern of her Atlantic sea-board. Thenceforward through the decades the United States had held fast to the

policy of edging the old world out of the new. With the purchase of
Louisiana, France disappeared from North America. In 1868 Russia
followed. Thirty years later, by force of arms, the United States
separated Spain from the last relics of her old possessions in the West.
Meanwhile, Great Britain, although yielding a little here and there,
had taken her stand on the 49th parallel in the north, and, in the
south, held a cordon of naval bases which served her nearly as well
in the Caribbean and the Gulf of Mexico as Gibraltar, Malta and
Egypt, in the Mediterranean. In the region of the Isthmus, in addition to a naval base, she had very important canal rights secured by
treaties. Under an old convention England had transit privileges by
the northern route, across Nicaragua, as good as any possessed by
the United States. Furthermore, by the famous Clayton-Bulwer Treaty,
Great Britain had made with the United States an engagement that
neither the one nor the other would ever obtain or maintain for itself
any exclusive control over any canal which might be built. When
the treaty was signed in 1850 it represented a distinct gain for the
United States for at that time British capital alone could have built
a canal. Half a century later the conditions had changed. England
had no intention of entering upon such a project, while the United
States was not only able, but eager to take it up. Thus, with the
passing of years, by solemn agreement with both Nicaragua and with
the United States, as well as by virtue of several naval bases, which
could threaten and almost control all lanes of approach to the Isthmus,
England held the keys to any interoceanic canal which might be
built.

It fell to John Hay to advance the old policy a little farther—to
give England another push toward the Atlantic Ocean.

Turning to the Pacific and Far East, Hay found another set of
problems.

The oldest economic policy of the United States in foreign affairs
was the demand for most-favored nation treatment for her merchants.
After the recovery from the panic of 1893, the United States rapidly
developed a surplus of exportable goods for which markets were believed to be needed. Again, the problem was easily stated, but not
simple of solution. The Far East, particularly China, promised expanding markets, but these outlets for American produce were
threatened by British and European monopolies which, in China,

seemed to presage the creation of spheres of interest from which the American might be excluded entirely. The United States, never prepared or willing to underwrite a commercial policy with military force, needed political support for a commercial open door. The most dependable source for this help was Great Britain. Thus England again held the key.

Without the concurrence of England the United States could not escape from the treaty of 1850; without the active cooperation of England the United States could expect in China only opposition and, eventually, commercial defeat. Whatever the Continental rivalries, the entrance of a strong commercial rival in the Far East was a threat to every over-populated, surplus-producing European state. It was John Hay's major task to reach such an agreement with England as would permit the United States to continue its policy, not only of edging the old world out of the new, but also of assuring its merchants a reasonably free field of competition in the old world's most alluring market.

The approach to British favor was not rendered easier by the fact that no sooner had the United States extended its sovereignty over its new insular possessions than it brought them under the operations of its coastwise shipping laws, and thereby took away from British maritime interests profitable shipping which had belonged to England for generations, even for centuries.[1] The first fruit of British support of the new American expansion was a restriction on British maritime privileges. England had helped to call into being a new rival.

The famous convention of 1850 contained in the first article some undefined geographical terms which gave rise to the suspicion that there had been a lack of candor. Great Britain joined with the United States in an engagement never to erect or to maintain any fortifications commanding the proposed Nicaragua canal, or "in the vicinity thereof, or occupy, or fortify, or colonize, or assume, or exercise any dominion over Nicaragua, Costa Rica, the Mosquito coast, or any part of Central America." A casual reading of the declaration would lead to the inference that England thus engaged to remove herself entirely from the region of the proposed canal. It was in this sense that the

---

[1] For British protest in the case of Hawaii, *For. Rel.* 1898, pp. 382–83; for similar protests in regard to Porto Rico: Pauncefote to Hay. Nov. 16, 1898, Dept. of State.

Senate understood the engagement when it advised ratification of the convention. After the treaty had been signed and sent to the Senate Sir Henry Bulwer had notified Mr. Clayton that the British Government did not understand that Belize, or British Honduras, was a part of Central America, and that it was not included within the scope of provisions of the treaty. Mr. Clayton acquiesced in the British interpretation, but the Bulwer communication, although known to the chairman of the Foreign Relations Committee, was not submitted to the Senate formally, and when the latter took action on the treaty, most of the Senators appear to have been in ignorance of the qualifying note. The British Government eventually carried out the terms of the treaty as they had interpreted it, and in 1860 President Buchanan, in his last annual message, declared that the final settlement of the British Honduras question was "entirely satisfactory" to the American Government. Many Americans felt, however, that too many cards had been dealt from the underside of the pack, and that actually advantages had been withheld from the United States which the plain language of the treaty appeared to confer.

Furthermore, in 1850 the Monroe Doctrine was quiescent in American foreign policy. Under the provisions of the treaty the United States joined with Great Britain not merely in guaranteeing the neutrality of the canal, but also in the agreement to invite other nations to make a similar engagement. Such an international guarantee was subsequently believed to be a clear violation of the fundamental principle of the Monroe Doctrine, in that it invited the transatlantic powers to participate and, potentially, to interfere in the Western Hemisphere.

The bargain which the United States made in 1850 had, in fact, displaced Great Britain from any exclusive control of any proposed isthmian canal, but for this advantage the United States, as it appeared at the close of the century had paid well; it, also, had forsworn its liberty to acquire exclusive control. The net result was to leave England where she could play a "dog-in-the-manger" rôle. She had no desire or intention to build a canal, but she could prevent the United States from building except under the provisions of an international guarantee outlined in the convention of 1850. Even the denunciation of the treaty, however, would have left England still with canal rights in Nicaragua under her treaty of 1860, a treaty to which the United States had once given full approval. The unilateral abrogation of a treaty is, in the family of nations, usually regarded as a major scandal. It was Hay's most immediate task in his first year as Secretary of State to find some alternative which would, on the one hand, give the American people what they desired at the Isthmus, and, on the other hand, preserve intact the national honor.

There was in England no very serious objection to the building by the United States of a canal. It was, however, estimated that the military effect of such a waterway would be equivalent to doubling American naval strength.[1] It seemed to the British Cabinet inappropriate that Great Britain should make such a concession to the United States until the relations of the latter with Canada had been put on a basis above the possibility of such continual wrangling as had characterized their history for a generation. Canadian-American relations had rarely been worse than when John Hay became Secretary of State.

In February, 1899, the Joint High Commission, created nine months before to settle a dozen outstanding questions, went on the rocks. The Canadians were unwilling to agree to any decisions until the Americans would yield on the boundary between Alaska and British Columbia in the region of the Lynn Canal. The Canadians demanded a port and a corridor to British territory. Failing that, they were disposed to insist upon arbitration of the American title to the territory itself. Back of the intransigent attitude of Canada was resentment at a long procession of Republican tariffs which gravely affected Canadian prosperity. Thus Hay's efforts to reach an agreement with Great Britain over a canal had come to be entangled with Canadian local politics. The problem was formidable. The old world method to meet such a situation would have been either a reciprocity treaty with Canada, which to Republican priests of high tariff was anathema, or an Anglo-American understanding to offset the Triple Alliance of Germany, Austria, and Italy, on the one hand, and the Franco-Russian Alliance on the other. By such an arrangement England, entering upon the Boer War, and needing friends, could have secured such substantial advantages that she well could have afforded to make concessions on the Alaska coast, in the Caribbean, in China, and also in the Pacific.

[1] Mowat, p. 247; Parliamentary Papers, 1901, XII, 1050.

John Hay believed profoundly in the reasonableness of the American contentions both at the Isthmus and on the Alaska coast. Although in his letter to John W. Foster, already quoted, he had implied that in the fur seals controversy British policy seemed to him not only "overbearing and pigheaded," but also "tricky and tortuous," such an outburst of petulance was never repeated. Hay had never followed Blaine into the ranks of the "tail-twisters," perhaps because forty or fifty years before he had found little congenial company among the Irish and German immigrants in Illinois. On the contrary, he believed in the British sense of justice and fair-play, and was willing to stake the fortunes of his country on this belief. He looked upon England with affection as the mother of his race. At some unknown time, probably several years before he became ambassador, Hay framed the following sonnet, now published for the first time:

> Hail to thee, England! Happy is the day
>   When from wide wandering I hither fare,
>   Touch thy wave-warded shore and breathe thine air,
>   And see, as now, thy hedges white with May.
> Rich memories throng in every flower-gemmed way;
>   Old names ring out as with a trumpet's blare;
>   While on, with quickened pulse, we journey where
>   London's vast thunder roars like seas at play.
> To thee, the cradle of our race we come—
> Not breaking fealty to a dearer home—
>   To warm our hearts by ancient altar-fires;
> Thy children's children, from whatever skies,
> Greet the high welcome of thy deathless eyes,
>   Thou fair and mighty mother of our sires!

The sentiment of this sonnet, together with the opinions expressed in the address, "A Partnership in Beneficence," at the Lord Mayor's dinner in 1898, indicate the manner in which Hay approached England. The last paragraph of the brief address is as follows: [1]

It may be trite and even tedious for me to refer again at this distance of time to the mighty pageant of last June, but I may ask leave to recall one incident of the naval review, which will long be remembered by those who saw it. On the evening of that memorable day, when all the ships lay enshrouded in darkness, the commander of the *Brooklyn* ran up the British and the American colors, and then at a given signal, turned upon those two kindred flags the brilliant rays of her search lights. In that high illumination

[1] *Addresses of John Hay,* pp. 79–80.

shrined in clear radiance far above the obscurity that hid the engines of destruction and preparation for war, those friendly banners fluttered, proclaiming to the navies of the world their message of good will. The beauty of the scene lasted but a moment; it passed away with much of the splendor and magnificence that adorned the historic day; but may we not hope that the lesson and inspiration of that spectacle may last as long as those banners shall float over the seven seas, carrying always in their shadow freedom and civilization?

The suggestion of an Anglo-American understanding had met with immediate response.

Three weeks later Joseph Chamberlain carried the thought a little further in his famous Birmingham speech of May 13, in which he said of the relations between the United States and England: [1]

"I don't know what the future has in store for us; I don't know what arrangements may be possible with us; but this I do know and feel, that the closer, the more cordial, the fuller, and the more definite these arrangements are, with the consent of both parties, the better it will be for both and for the world—and I go even so far as to say that, terrible as a war may be, even war itself would be cheaply purchased if, in a great and noble cause, the Stars and Stripes and the Union Jack should wave together over an Anglo-Saxon Alliance."

At the close of the Spanish-American War, Chamberlain elaborated still further the idea, in words which may have been suggested by the Hay speech already quoted. "The United States of America, if you have regard to its potential resources, is already the greatest of civilized States, with its immense population, chiefly of Anglo-Saxons, upwards of 70,000,000 of intelligent citizens, and if we are assured of the friendship of the Anglo-Saxon race, whether they abide under the Stars and Stripes or under the Union Jack, there is no other combination that can make us afraid." [2]

That there was some actual correspondence between the speeches of Hay and Chamberlain is proved by the letter which Hay wrote to Lodge May 25, in which he said: [3]

"It is hardly too much to say that the interests of civilization are bound up in the direction the relations of England and America are to take in the next few months. The state of feeling here is the best

---

[1] Dennis, *Adventures in American Diplomacy*, p. 122.
[2] *Ibid.*, p. 122.
[3] *Letters and Diaries*, III, p. 124.

I have ever known. From very quarter the evidence of it comes to me. The Royal Family, by habit and tradition, are most careful not to break the rules of strict neutrality, but even among them I find nothing but hearty kindness and, so far as is consistent with propriety —sympathy. Among the political leaders on both sides I find not only sympathy but a somewhat eager desire that the 'other fellows' shall not seem the more friendly. Chamberlain's startling speech was partly due to a conversation I had with him, in which I hoped he would not let the opposition have a monopoly of expressions of good-will to America. He is greatly pleased with the reception his speech met with on our side and says, 'he don't care a hang what they say about it on the Continent.' "

Even if prompted solely by motives of political expediency, just as the United States was entering upon the war with Spain, Hay's address could have been set down as a very clever stroke. The Hay and Chamberlain speeches together carried a warning to Europe to stand aside. There had been, however, no stage-play. Hay expressed only his settled convictions, and it became the substance of his policy toward England after he became Secretary of State—a partnership of beneficence.

Hay regarded the liberation of Cuba, the extension of American rule to Hawaii, the acquisition of the Philippines, the building of the Panama Canal, as works of beneficence similar to the extension of the Pax Britannica over India, Egypt, and South Africa. Seeing in the American motives which led to this expansion nothing ignoble or unworthy, but rather a fine expression of the American spirit, he was not disposed to find ignoble or selfish motives in British policies. The two countries needed each other and Hay was eager to carry a coöperative policy with England to any point short of a repudiation by American voters which would have placed a Bryan in the White House.

An alliance with England, however, ran contrary to all American traditions; it was, in Hay's words, "an unattainable dream." Even the slightest suggestion that such an arrangement was contemplated was seized upon by the Democrats to bid for support not only from Irish- and German-American voters, but from "tail-twisters" every-where. Hay, who personally might have viewed an alliance with no alarm, was immediately placed upon the defensive.

"An attempt is made in the Ohio Democratic platform to excite the prejudice of certain classes of voters against the present Administration by accusing it of an alliance with England," wrote Hay to Colonel Charles Dick, the chairman of the Ohio Republican Executive Committee, September 11, 1899, in an open letter which was considered so important as a campaign document that it was circulated as a pamphlet by hundreds of thousands. "The people who make this charge know it to be untrue; their making it is an insult to the intelligence of those whose vote they seek by this gross misinterpretation. . . . There is no alliance with England nor with any power under heaven, except those known and published to the world, the treaties of ordinary international friendship for purposes of business and commerce. No treaty other than these exists; none has been suggested on either side; none is in contemplation. It has never entered into the mind of the President nor of any member of the government, to forsake, under any inducement, the wise precept and example of the Fathers which forbade entangling alliance with European powers."

The letter secured such wide international publicity that Hay hastened to write to Henry White: [1] "You will see there is nothing in it incompatible with the most friendly relations with England. I simply refute the Democratic platform charge that we have made a 'secret alliance with England.' This charge was having a serious effect on our Germans and it had to be denied. The fact is a treaty of alliance is impossible. It would never get through the Senate. As long as I stay here no action shall be taken contrary to my conviction that the one indispensable feature of our foreign policy should be a friendly understanding with England. But an alliance must remain in the present state of things an unattainable dream."

It was not merely that an alliance with England was impossible; any agreement was difficult. Hay explained his difficulties to Choate in an irritated letter.[2] "The Democratic Press evidently thinks there is some political capital to be made by denouncing any arrangement with England and they, in common with a large number of German newspapers, are ready to attack any treaty with England, no matter how advantageous to us, as a hostile act towards Ireland and Germany. The Democratic Convention of Iowa has adopted, as you will

[1] September 24, **1899.**
[2] August 18, 1899.

doubtless see before this reaches you, resolutions in this sense, which seemed too ridiculous to treat seriously; but all these senseless charges indicate the intention of the opposition to make a party matter of our relations with England, and to oppose any treaty we may make with that country."

To Henry White, in the same vein, he added on September 9: "Whatever we do, the Bryan party will attack us as slaves of England. All their state conventions put an anti-English plank in their platforms to curry favor with the Irish (whom they want to keep), and the Germans whom they want to seduce. It is too disgusting to have to deal with such sordid liars."

The situation was, viewed in retrospect, even more ominous. Hay complained of the two-thirds rule of the Senate as to ratification of treaties, and, of the Bryan party in American politics, the success of which promised to Hay nothing short of anarchy. As a matter of fact, the force of the new nationalism which was then rising in the United States was greater by far than the Senate or the Bryan party. Popular feeling was running high after a successful war; the Americans had whipped Spain; and, "by jingo," if other powers stood in the way of what seemed purely American affairs, they too could be whipped. Such a spirit, vainly deplored by the peace advocates, was sweeping the nation with all the power of a mass psychology. Spain had stood in the way; Spain had gone down. Now England stood in the way; let England beware!

Thus Hay was placed between the grindstones. The growing pressure for a canal, added to the accumulation of unsettled questions with Canada, ground against the equally unyielding demand that, in reaching an agreement with England, there be no concessions, no slight surrender of an American interest.

An approach in another temper, a few more Venezuela messages, might have secured concessions, for England was unquestionably in a tight place with a far flung line of defense and almost a continent leagued against her. Even of this there is no certainty. But, as we look back upon it now, how much wiser and more statesmanlike was the approach which Hay chose! The sentiments he entertained for England were genuine and sincere; their reiteration was worth more than a fleet of battleships.

In addition to Hay's affection and admiration for the English people, there was the added advantage that during his many private visits to England, and while Ambassador, he had won for himself a degree of respect and confidence which the English people do not usually yield so readily. He had made a deep impression on Queen Victoria, who had not hesitated to show him special preference, as well as to laugh at his wit. King Edward liked him equally well. Following the death of Hay's son, Adelbert, in June, 1901, the King sent a message of personal condolence. To this Hay could reply as follows, in language which wholly lacked presumption:

July 12, 1901

To His Majesty,
    The King,
    Sir: I beg to be allowed to return my sincere thanks to your Majesty for the kind and gracious message I received on the occasion of my beloved son's death. I am indebted to the Royal House of England for many kindnesses, but for none more than these gracious words of sympathy in the time of our deepest sorrow.
    My family join me in these expressions of gratitude, and I remain,
    Sir,
    Your Majesty's obliged and faithful Servant,

John Hay.

When Balfour became Prime Minister of Great Britain in July, 1902, Hay as an old friend wrote [1] to "My dear Balfour" that "I presume I am the last person in the civilized world to congratulate you on your accession to the most important official post known to modern history." This placing of the position of Prime Minister of England above that of the President of the United States gave great offense to Theodore Roosevelt when he happened upon the letter six years later. The latter is understood to have expressed the opinion that if Hay really thought the position of Prime Minister more important than that of President, he was foolish; but to give expression to the thought in writing to the English Prime Minister while he was American Secretary of State was worse than foolish.

No doubt Roosevelt was right. But it was out of such personal relationships and such convictions as these that John Hay made his "bricks without straw"; and sometimes greatly to the profit of his country.

[1] July 29, 1902. *Letters and Diaries*, III, pp. 254–55.

THE adjustment of the Alaska boundary controversy has a double importance in this narrative. The material interests involved were not great but, in the sequence of events, the settlement of the vexed question was a major factor in Anglo-American relations. Furthermore, Roosevelt, however generous he may have been in his praise of Hay while living, after the latter's death claimed the credit for this settlement.[1] In an evaluation of Hay's statesmanship much, therefore, depends upon whether Roosevelt's claim can be sustained.

By the Alaska Purchase Treaty of 1867 the United States acquired in North America whatever territorial rights had formerly belonged to Russia. In Southeastern Alaska those rights had been defined, supposedly, by the treaty of 1825 between Russia and Great Britain. The line therein described, however, started from a point which subsequent surveys showed not to exist, and proceeded from crest to crest of a mountain range which never was. The negotiators of the Russo-British treaty had been aware that they were dealing with quantities relatively unknown and had, therefore, amplified the definition of their intent with what turned out to be the most absurd provision of all, namely, that where a line from crest to crest would be more than ten marine leagues from the sea the boundary should, instead, run parallel to the sinuosities of the coastline and not more than ten leagues from it. The Alaskan coast in this region is split by innumerable islands, large and small, and further broken by long narrow bays, or canals, as they are called, which reach far back toward the top of the continental water-shed. It is geometrically impossible to draw parallel to such a jagged line another ten leagues distant which will not cross and recross itself like the tracks of a man lost in the snow. On the other hand, the intent of the treaty was reasonably clear: Russia had sought to exclude her rival from the coast and from navigable water. Great Britain, in turn, in 1825, protested but acquiesced. The area in question then seemed nearly worthless.

Three quarters of a century later Southeastern Alaska was seen to

---

[1] See Chapter XXIX, "Roosevelt and the Alaska Boundary."

be important. Fish, lumber, and more especially gold, had changed the situation. The Canadians, struggling heroically to develop an empire of their own, felt bitterly about that long strip of coastline which shut them off from tidewater. They needed at least a corridor to navigable water and, failing to get that, were disposed to challenge the interpretation of the treaty in such a way as to call in question the territorial rights of the United States to a large part of the area itself. The discovery of gold in the Klondike intensified the bitterness. The new gold-fields, for the most part, lay on the Canadian side of the water-shed, but access to them was by three trails which started at the coast and proceeded inland through what was claimed as American territory. As the gold seekers swarmed in from all over the world there came to be more and more involved the questions as to which government should administer the disputed area, and whether the tariff and coastwise shipping laws of the United States were applicable. The latter rigidly excluded from the coastwise trade vessels of British registry. Prospectively there was also involved the American tariff on Canadian lumber. Thus, an area which had once been supposed to be worthless was developing to a point where it touched the conflicting economic interests of the British Columbian and the American ports on the Pacific Coast from San Francisco northward. Indeed, the interests of the entire northwest of the United States were more or less involved.

In turn, political matters, party politics, entered the controversy. Alike in Canada as in the United States, the party in power could not afford to alienate the political support of the regions whose economic interests were affected. To be more specific, in the presidential election of 1900 it was expected that McKinley would need the votes of the Pacific and Northwestern states. Any slight concession to Canada by the American government would be an effective weapon in the hands of the Democrats. The political situation in Canada was very similar. In each instance the party in power was required to preserve a record which would show that it had been the stalwart defender of the material interests of the voters. Rarely will one find a better illustration of how a question of vast international importance, the building of an inter-oceanic canal across the back-bone of the Western Hemisphere, may trail off into local politics.

In the meetings of the ill-fated **Joint High** Commission five different proposals had been made for the settlement of the Alaska boundary question. The American commissioners offered to give the Canadians for fifty years the use of Pyramid Harbor, whence started the famous Dalton Trail over the passes to the Yukon, with the provision that the strip might be under British administration, but that the port should remain under the operation of the coastwise shipping laws of the United States. The Canadians were not satisfied with this offer and demanded two modifications. They wished to have what amounted to perpetual occupancy, and to have the port opened to vessels of British registry. Failing to secure these concessions, the Canadians proposed that the entire question of the territorial rights of the United States be referred to an arbitrator precisely as the American government had, only a half dozen years before, required that Great Britain arbitrate with Venezuela. The American members were disposed to accept the principle of arbitration but objected to the application of the terms of the Venezuela reference. They therefore put forward the idea of an "arbitral board composed of three eminent jurists upon each side" to determine, not the legal right of the United States to possession of the disputed area, but rather the true meaning of the terms of the treaty of 1825. It was further suggested that in such a tribunal the decision should be by majority vote. This was, substantially, the plan finally adopted in 1903, but in 1899 the Canadians were still unsatisfied and insisted that the proposed commission of jurists should allot the territory in the same manner as the Venezuelan territory was being divided.[1] No agreement being possible in the Joint High Commission, the Canadians took the position that they would not consent to the settlement of any of the other questions. The commission therefore adjourned, never to meet again.

The *impasse* was coincident with the consideration by the British Cabinet of the first Hay-Pauncefote treaty for an isthmian canal. Lord Salisbury was reported to have remarked, tartly, that he could not help contrasting the precarious projects and the slowness of the Canadian negotiations with the rapidity of the decision proposed in the canal matter.[2] Thus Hay was required to go more deeply than had been expected into the boundary question, in order to remove the obstacles

[1] The foregoing summary is based on the report of Senator Charles W. Fairbanks, an American member of the Joint High Commission, to Hay, March 25, 1899. Department of State, Miscellaneous Letters.

[2] Mowat, p. 274.

to the consideration of the canal treaty.

There was, in fact, in the Alaskan situation early in 1899 a degree of urgency which can scarcely be overstated. A stream of adventurers was pouring into a disputed area where the public order was always in danger. Local sentiment ran high. At any moment a clash of local administrations might create an incident which could have easily involved the peaceful relations of the United States and Great Britain. The desire for Canadian annexation was by no means dead south of the border.[1]

In addition, it was evident that sentiment was growing for the denunciation of the Clayton-Bulwer Treaty and for the defiance of Great Britain. Only a few weeks before the adjournment of the Joint High Commission the United States Senate had passed, January 21, by the overwhelming vote of forty-eight to six, Senator John T. Morgan's Nicaraguan Canal bill, calling for an American controlled canal. Late in February, seeing that his bill could not pass the House, Morgan obtained in the Senate an amendment to the Rivers and Harbors bill, by a vote of fifty to three, providing $10,000,000 to begin building the canal. Such sweeping majorities indicated a growing impatience with Great Britain for having once secured from the United States a promise never to obtain for itself any exclusive privileges at the isthmus. Just at that moment came a piece of luck. Morgan's enthusiasm for the Nicaraguan route had stirred the advocates of the Panama route to frantic activity. The lobby set up by the new Panama Canal Company, which had something to sell to the American government, came ludicrously enough to the rescue of imperilled national honor. The lobby defeated the Morgan amendment in the House and had substituted for it a provision to create a new canal commission to study all possible routes and report back to Congress on the whole subject.[2] The developing contest over the route to be selected meant delay, giving Hay the opportunity which he needed to smooth out the boundary question and get the British government to approve his canal treaty. The Walker Canal Commission did not make a report to Congress until November 19, 1901, and did not make a final report

[1] The annexationists had even secured the following veiled endorsement in the Republican platform of 1896: "We hopefully look forward to the eventual withdrawal of the European powers from this hemisphere, and to the ultimate union of all English-speaking parts of the continent by the free consent of its inhabitants."

[2] See *The Story of Panama*; Hearings on the Rainey Resolution before the Committee on Foreign Affairs. 1913, p. 226.

until the following January.

The significant phases of the adjustment of the Alaskan boundary are three: early efforts, which were soon abandoned, to effect a permanent settlement; a provisional settlement, which eventuated in the agreement of October 20, 1899; and, the final determination, which was postponed until 1903.

Hay first tried to devise a means for an immediate permanent settlement.

The Secretary shared the conviction of the American members of the Joint High Commission that the Canadian claim to the territory, a claim which had never been made officially until after the commission took the boundary question under consideration, was trumped up. As early as January 3, while the commission was in session, in a letter to Henry White bitterly complaining that Lord Herschell, the only British member of the commission, was disclosing an unwillingness to be fair, Hay had said: "We are actually driven to the conclusion that Lord Herschell put forward a claim that he had no belief or confidence in for the mere purpose of trading it off for something substantial, and yet the slightest suggestion that his claim is unfounded, throws him into a fury." [1] The sudden death of Herschell in Washington on March 1 removed one obstacle to agreement, but the Canadians remained uncompromising.

The British Ambassador, as a member of the British delegation to the Hague Conference, was soon to be in London on his way to and from The Hague. He was fully aware of the serious nature of the situation and appears to have had not much more confidence than Hay in the justice of the Canadian demands. The Secretary depended upon Pauncefote to convince the British Foreign Office and, in anticipation of the conference which would take place in London, sent to Choate, April 19, 1899, a formal instruction and a draft of a treaty. The instruction, with which was enclosed a copy of the Fairbanks report, already summarized, stated clearly why the American Government was unwilling to adopt the terms of the Venezuela reference for Alaska. The two questions were radically different in that in the one case England had for many years been occupying land in spite of the repeated and persistent protests of the Venezuelans, whereas in Alaska there had never been any question except as to the manner in which

[1] Nevins, *White*, p. 189

the specific provisions of the treaty of 1825 should be interpreted. In the judgment of Hay the only points at issue were two. First, what crests of mountains were to be followed? Second, where the line so drawn would give the United States a *lisière* of more than ten leagues, was the parallel line to be drawn from the headlands of the long, narrow inlets, or from the tidewater marks at the remote ends?

The draft treaty proposed by Hay was a project, not for arbitration, but for a "commission of jurists of repute," three on a side, decision by majority vote, to determine the meaning of the early treaty. "This, it will be noted," wrote Hay to Choate, "is substantially the proposition submitted by Lord Salisbury to Secretary Olney for the adjustment of the Venezuela dispute." [1] Nine days later Hay also initiated with Choate the correspondence looking toward a provisional settlement; but it will be simpler, for the moment, to follow a little farther the exchanges with reference to the proposed commission of jurists.

The doubtful point in Hay's proposal was that it did not take into account the possibility that a commission with three on a side might divide evenly and end in a stalemate. Both Pauncefote and Choate raised this question. The scheme was really adapted from the Olney-Pauncefote arbitration treaty upon which the Senate had failed to act. In reply to a query from Choate on this point Hay, with apparent reluctance, replied on May 1 that in case of disagreement the commission might be empowered to agree on a seventh member who would then act in the capacity of referee. Choate and Pauncefote conferred in London and on May 12, the American Ambassador inquired whether Hay would agree to a commission of five. Choate's telegram was referred to the President, who decided to accept the plan. "I am inclined to think that the proposition is as good as any we can secure," wrote McKinley to Hay, May 14. The project, thus modified from the form in which Hay had first presented it, went to the British Cabinet. The Canadians, who had to be consulted, would not consent unless the United States would agree in advance that whatever the decision of the tribunal, Pyramid Harbor would go to Canada. [2]

"It is as if a kidnapper, stealing one of your children," wrote Hay to Choate, [3] "should say that his conduct was more than fair, it was

---

[1] April 19, 1899. Dept. of State.
[2] May 18, 1899. Choate to Hay, Dept. of State.
[3] June 15, 1899.

even generous, because he left you two"; "two" being Dyea and Skagway, which lay at the foot of the other two passages over the mountains to the gold-fields. The Canadians were willing to concede them to the United States provided they could have Pyramid Harbor. The effect of such an arrangement would have been to give Canada a corridor down through American territory to the tide-water. The corridor, of course, would have bisected Southeastern Alaska.

The progress of the negotiations was not encouraging but Hay had, incidentally, won his first point. The Canadians were willing to separate the boundary question from the other matters before the adjourned High Commission. At the same time the Foreign Office was left in no doubt that the United States would decline to settle on any such basis as Canada proposed. Nevertheless, on July 3, Lord Salisbury, at the request of Canada, formally submitted the counter-proposal that the entire question be referred to arbitration on terms similar to the Venezuela reference.

In the negotiations thus far narrated there is nothing notable except that in 1903 the two governments actually adopted the plan of a tribunal of six which Hay and Pauncefote had devised four years before. Hay's immediate success was not in the proposed treaty for a final delimitation of the boundary, but in effecting a provisional settlement, a *modus vivendi*, thus making it possible to take up the canal question which, meanwhile, hung in abeyance.

The anxiety in which Hay was working appears in a long letter to Choate, April 28. It is also a complete statement of the situation:

I would like to add a word or two, in this private and confidential manner, to the instruction I sent you a few days ago in regard to the present aspect of our negotiations with Canada.

By a memorandum of the 4th of February, 1899, I find that the British Ambassador called upon me that day, and, after discussing several pending matters, talked of the state of the negotiations in the Canadian Commission. He deplored the possibility of a failure of the negotiations, and seemed to think that the most dangerous point of all was the matter of the Alaska Boundary, and he suggested that it might be possible to leave that single point to arbitration, on the lines of the arbitration treaty agreed upon between him and Mr. Olney, by a tribunal of jurists, the decision of which would not bind either party unless agreed upon by a large majority. He thought all the other matters might be arranged by the mutual concessions which were then—and still are—in sight. If this were done, the British Government, he said, would have no hesitation in agreeing to the modification of the Clayton-Bulwer Treaty, and to the sweeping away of all the objectionable features of the Treaty of 1818, which would clear the entire slate of all subjects of discussion.

The draft of the treaty I sent you is founded on the General Arbitration Convention of 1897, agreed upon between Mr. Olney and Sir Julian Paunce-fote, but it is even more favorable to Great Britain than was that document, which provided for a Court or Board of three judges from each nation on all boundary questions, and that the decision should not be final unless five arbitrators should unite in a decision. See Article VI (Foreign Relations of the United States. 1896. page 239). The draft I sent you, you will see, provided that a vote of two-thirds of the full Board should be sufficient.

The matter of the Alaska boundary is becoming a matter of great anxiety to us. Soon after the close of negotiations between our Commissioners and those of Great Britain, Sir Julian and I took up the subject of a *modus vivendi* on the Alaskan frontier pending the full settlement of the question, and substantially agreed upon a provisional boundary, beyond which neither party should assume jurisdiction, and without prejudice to the claims of either party in the final settlement of the boundary. He transmitted a copy of my note, which accepted the propositions of his note, written last July, to Canada and to England. Lord Minto called a meeting of his council, which immediately rejected our proposition, on the ground that it gave us more territory than we had a right to claim. Knowledge of this decision of the Council was communicated to me confidentially by Sir Julian. He could not communicate it officially because the matter had been referred by Canada to England and had not yet reached him from the Foreign Office. Of course, we were greatly disappointed by this unexpected rebuff. Our disappointment was increased by the dispatches from the Governor of Alaska, who insists that the Canadian Mounted Police are encroaching upon our territory everywhere along the boundary and that the miners who have taken up claims in the disputed territory are in great anxiety lest they should be ousted from their holdings by the operations of the British Columbia alien acts.

I saw Sir Julian again, and, making another slight concession as to the boundary line, I asked if he could not induce the Dominion Government to effect a suspension of the British Columbian acts as to the miners working in the disputed territory until the matter of the boundary could be settled between the two governments. He sent to Canada and to London what appeared to me a very reasonable and satisfactory telegram on the subject, but to this we have had no reply.

You will infer from this that the whole matter is in a most unsatisfactory state, which has a tendency to become worse every hour. I do not believe that we are asking anything unreasonable, and I am sure that if the matter depended on direct negotiations between the United States and England, it would be very speedily and satisfactorily settled, but we are driven to the conclusion that the Canadians do not wish any settlement, that they preferred the present risky and unsettled state of things to any decision which would leave them open to attack from the Opposition, as having shown a lack of spirit and a lack of regard for Canadian interests, in their negotiations with the Americans. I do not see that any thing is to be gained by calling the Conference together again. I should fear that the same scenes would reproduce themselves, and the same fruitless result would follow. Especially—and this I say to you in the utmost confidence—especially should we deprecate the filling of Lord Herschell's place on the Commission by another lawyer, who would come with the intention of making the most of his case as an advocate, instead of with the purpose of settling the matter in a spirit of mutual fairness and moderation. Unless the two Governments can come to a sort of agreement beforehand, it would be simply a waste of time to call the Conference together again.

You are by this time probably aware of the great difficulties that surround the arrangement of any controversy in which Canada is concerned. The Dominion politicians care little for English interests. Their minds are completely occupied with their own party and factional disputes, and Sir Wilfrid Laurier is far more afraid of Sir Charles Tupper than he is of Lord Salisbury and President McKinley combined; while the habit of referring everything from the Foreign Office to the Colonial, followed by a consultation of the Canadian authorities by the Minister of the Colonies, produces interminable friction and delay. I hope it may be possible for you in your conversations with Lord Salisbury to cause him to feel the desirability of finding, if possible, some arrangement of these troubles, which, though intrinsically insignificant, are likely at any moment to embitter the relations of our two countries, solely in the interest of the warring factions in Canada.

The negotiations for a provisional line halted just where the proposed treaty was held up; the Canadians wanted Pyramid Harbor.

"There is little room for negotiation or for argument," wrote Hay to Choate, June 15, "if they [the Foreign Office] have adopted the Canadian contention that we have no more claim to Dyea and Skagway than they have to Pyramid Harbor. We have occupied the ground about the head of Lynn Canal, and the Russians before us, since 1825 We settled and built Dyea and Skagway without a hint from any quarter that they were not on American territory. . . . There is absolutely nothing on the face of things to show that they are not as much our territory as Sitka or San Francisco. . . ." It is apparent that as Hay moved on into the fag-end of the year, before his summer rest, his nerves were becoming taut. To his old friend Smalley, American correspondent of the London *Times,* he wrote irritably, and probable not quite accurately, June 1, that, as for Pyramid Harbor, the Canadians had never set foot upon that region, "never raised a tent or moored a canoe there."

Hay stuck grimly to his point and gradually forced the Canadians back to a provisional line twenty miles above Pyramid Harbor. Notes were exchanged October 20; that phase of the matter was disposed of. Hay had scored a complete victory; he conceded practically nothing.[1]

It was during the summer of 1899, while Hay was stubbornly forcing the Canadians back beyond tidewater in Alaska, that the Democrats of Ohio improved the opportunity to insert into the party platform the charge that Hay had entered into a secret alliance with Great Britain. From Newbury Hay wrote the ringing denial already quoted in part, and paid to have it printed for general circulation. The letter was in the vein of his earlier political speeches, and we may add another excerpt:

". . . It is hard to take such a charge seriously," he declared, "and if it is taken seriously, how can it be treated with patience? In the name of common sense, let me ask what is the duty of the government, if not to cultivate, wherever possible, agreeable and profitable relations with other nations? And if with other nations why not with that great kindred power which stands among the greatest powers in the world? What harm, what menace to other countries is there in this natural beneficent friendship? Only a narrow and purblind spirit could see in it anything exclusive. It is a poor starved heart that has room for only one friend. It is not with England alone that our relations are improved. We are on better terms than in the past with all nations. . . ."

The assertion in the last sentence appears to have been well within the truth.

The campaign charge, that in the *modus vivendi* with England Hay had betrayed American interests, was carried over into the presidential campaign the following year. To Choate Hay poured out his soul, August 22, 1900 as follows:

"No sane man—and you are one of the sanest I have ever known—can appreciate the stupid[ity] and the malignancy of our Anglophobes. It is not merely by the Yellows, the Irish and the Tammany people—they are a matter of course—but by far the worst of the lot is the *Sun,* which claims to be supporting McKinley, and whose furious attacks upon the State Department from time to time scare our

[1] See *For. Rel.,* 1899, pp. 320 ff. for a reasonably full presentation of the correspondence and for a map.

managers out of their five wits. Just now they are having all colors of fits over our *modus vivendi* in Alaska. That was, as you know, one of the best bargains for us ever made. I do not want to publish to the world the details of an engagement some of whose features are as yet incomplete, and it is abominable form for a Government to brag of its diplomatic success, so I must let the tempest of dust and foul air blow itself out. Any form of regular diplomatic work is rendered impossible by the conditions of our political life. Other countries can negotiate with us, and when an agreement is reached the work for them is done. For us it is only begun. It takes ten times the energy, the labor, the care, the wear and tear of nerves to convince our Committee of Foreign Relations and the majority of our people that we have not betrayed the country and that they will not lose votes by the treaty. . . . But as it cannot be cured, somebody must endure it. It is for each successive Secretary of State to decide for himself when he has enough."

The reasons why a Secretary of State is rarely in a position to defend himself were still further elaborated in a letter to Perry S. Heath, of the National Republican Committee.[1] "We made an arrangement which was altogether favorable to us, the best arrangement we could possibly have made, much better than anybody on the General High Commission imagined possible; but that very fact makes it excessively awkward for the State Department to be quoted in the matter. The boundary line between British territory and Alaska is not yet settled. No measures have yet been agreed upon for settling it. There is a vast extent of disputed territory which the Canadians claim, the whole of the Lynn Canal, we also claiming the whole of it and thirty miles beyond. Nobody who knows anything about the case thinks we have any just claim on the Chilkoot and White Trails beyond the passes; yet the boundary we assign on the map is considerably beyond those passes . . . Now it is out of the question for us to go into the full merits of the case. We cannot admit to the world, either in a document signed by me or by the Republican Committee that we are putting forward claims that we think are more than we are entitled to. . . ."

So much for one phase of Hay's Anglophilism.

We return now to the concurrent discussions for a permanent settlement.

Soon after the British Government made its formal proposal that

[1] August 23, 1900.

the terms of the Venezuela arbitration be followed in the Alaska dispute, an alternative suggestion was made which came to nothing but which is of some importance because of the correspondence which followed. The latter gives us a glimpse of the relations of Hay, on the one hand, toward the President and Cabinet, and, on the other, toward the Foreign Relations Committee of the Senate. The proposal, really an adaptation of a scheme which had already been discussed in the meetings of the High Commission, was that the American Government should grant to a British syndicate a lease of a small area at Pyramid Harbor, together with a right of way for a railroad to the Canadian border. In forwarding the proposal Choate pointed out that the effecting of a lease would in itself involve an admission by the British Government of the validity of the American title to the territory.

Hay thought well of the proposal and, after discussion in the Cabinet, it was approved by the President. The Secretary felt, however, that before going farther in the matter it would be well to consult some of the members of the Joint High Commission and the Foreign Relations Committee. There he met with discouragement. General Foster, of the Commission, was opposed to compromise. "No one," he wrote, "with any knowledge of the spirit of the British Government, can believe that if it were convinced that this claim was a good one, it would ever abandon it for half a square mile of leased land at the head of the Lynn Canal." [1] Senator Cushman K. Davis, chairman of the Foreign Relations Committee, answered promptly, and also in the negative. To the latter Hay replied in a letter which betrayed his irritation: [2]

I have received your kind letter of 31st July. It is very discouraging—the more so, as I have no doubt that your opinion is perfectly just. You know the Senate better than anybody, and you are thoroughly acquainted with public opinion also.

I share your view of the utter baselessness of the Canadian claim to Alaska. No impartial court would entertain it, but where shall we find the impartial court? We are so sure of our case that we are not willing to put it in jeopardy before some chance arbitration. If it were as clear as the sun in heaven—as I think it is—the fatal tendency of an arbitrator to compromise would almost certainly give Canada more than we are now talking of—a lease of a bit of ground, of which we should retain the fee, the flag and the sovereignty. This, I am convinced, is the best that can be done. And this,

[1] Memorandum without date in Dept. of State Archives.
[2] Hay to Senator Davis, Aug. 4, 1899.

you think, is impossible.

To drop the matter here means a great deal, which you have doubtless considered as much as I have. We have twelve questions—mostly Canadian —to settle with England. None of them will be settled until this one is. The Clayton-Bulwer arrangement also goes by the board. We shall be left in the state of dull hostility, varied by commercial reprisals. The friendship between the two countries, of which nobody has spoken so wisely and eloquently as you have, will prove short-lived and derisory.

It was a great blunder in Sir Wilfrid Laurier to talk about war. Of course what he meant was that war was impossible and therefore we must have arbitration. But the word, War, should never be used except by philanthropists and soldiers. It is positively indecent in the mouth of a diplomat.

It seems to me that in leasing them these terminal facilities for a railroad, the whole boundary question will be decided in our favor forever. The very act of granting a lease implies unquestioned possession.

But you know more law and politics than I do, and your opinion has great weight with me.

It was not a perfectly temperate letter. The situation was on Hay's nerves. His state of mind comes out even more clearly in his letter of August 18, 1899, to Choate:

Our position in regard to Arbitration is not free from embarrassment. We are absolutely sure of our right. We think that before any high court of law we should not have any difficulty in proving our case, but an arbitration is not a court of law. The Arbitrator has an almost universal tendency to compromise. We own the whole of the Lynn Canal: the Canadians claim nearly all of it. In that state of things, unless the terms of the Arbitration are so strictly guarded as to make any "splitting of the difference" impossible, any European Arbitrator would almost certainly give the Canadians a foothold on the coast—as a "measure of equity and good neighborhood."

And yet it places us in an awkward position to refuse Arbitration. The English frankly say, "you forced us to accept arbitration with Venezuela and now you deny us the same treatment you compelled us to grant that little power." Of course we can show the difference between the two cases, but the public, on either side, takes but little account of these details. We are put in an ungracious attitude.

It is for this reason that I received with much pleasure the suggestion of the lease of a bit of ground and the right-of-way for a railroad, which Lord Salisbury made to you, with the implied assent of Canada. I at once laid it before the President and the Cabinet, and they are all agreed that if the details can be satisfactorily arranged, it would be a reasonable solution of the matter. I was tempted to wire you immediately to the effect and to authorize you to begin the negotiation, but I thought it prudent to invite some expression of opinion from the leading members of the Committee of

Foreign Relations in the Senate. To my great chagrin I received the enclosed letter from Senator Davis, whose acquaintance with the Senate is accurate, and whose integrity and friendship to the President are alike unquestioned. I wrote in the same confidential way to Mr. Frye, who has not yet answered my letter—a fact as significant as Mr. Davis' communication.

Now, the irreparable mistake of our Constitution puts it in the power of one-third of the Senate to meet with categorical veto any treaty negotiated by the President, even though it may have the approval of nine-tenths of the people of the nation. If it be true that the Democrats as a body are determined that we shall make no arrangement with England, we shall have to consider whether it is expedient for us to make a treaty which will fail in the Senate, or wait for a more convenient season.

For my part, I should have no hesitation in making a treaty on the basis of a lease and right-of-way and taking the chances of the Senate throwing it out, if I could foresee the effect it would have on the vastly important election of next year. The President has no great desire for re-election, and is ready to take the consequences of any action he may think to the advantage of the country without regard to the effect upon himself. His last words as I left him yesterday were, "If you think best, go ahead and conclude a treaty on those lines." But I cannot help thinking very seriously of what may happen, if by the loss of one or two northern states, we should risk the unspeakable disgrace of making such a creature as Bryan President.

You can understand with what distress I have written this letter. After a year of labor and anxiety we have gotten from England a proposition which was worth the year's work. The way to an honorable and advantageous settlement was open to us—and a blunder of our Constitution-makers gives a chance to the worst third of our Senate to stop the way. An irreparable blunder—for though every intelligent Senator sees that this two-thirds rule paralyzes the majority of the Senate in its most important function, yet sees that it doubles his individual value when he happens to be in the minority and none of them is willing to give it up.

From the standpoint of international good will Hay was probably right in his assumption that the lease of a railroad terminal and the right of way on the Lynn Canal would have been a better solution of the Alaska boundary question. He was, however, wholly wrong, presumably, in his assumption that nine-tenths of the people in the United States would have approved of it. The increase of popular control over foreign policies does not necessarily tend to promote international peace. Quite the reverse: democracies are even harder bargainers.

Hay's attitude toward the Senate, as it appears in these letters, is already well known. The same kind of criticism crops up repeatedly in Henry Adams's *Education*. Both men had been feeling that way for many years. It should not be overlooked, however, that McKinley, instead of cautioning his Secretary not to arouse the antagonism of the Senate, as we might have expected him to do, was actually supporting and even encouraging Hay in a course which was sure to end in conflict. The astonishing aspect of Hay's relations with the Senate is that McKinley, an old parliamentarian and seasoned politician, seems to have been no wiser.

In the letters already quoted there has appeared at length Hay's objections to arbitrating the boundary question. Arbitration is apt to mean compromise rather than justice, and seems to be of limited usefulness. The "have-nots" are likely to have an advantage over the "haves," regardless of the justice of the claim. The more plausible project, the lease, being out of the question, Hay turned again to his original proposal, a tribunal of jurists to determine the meaning of the treaty of 1825. The correspondence proceeded slowly.

"I think it may be as well if you do not accelerate the progress of the negotiation for a few weeks," wrote Hay to Choate, August 4. The Secretary was thinking of the approaching elections. On October 20 the provisional line was agreed to by a formal exchange of notes. That relieved the situation. The November elections were encouraging. At length, January 22, 1900, the American Ambassador in London presented a voluminous reply to Lord Salisbury, demolishing the Canadian contention for arbitration on the Venezuela pattern. The matter rested for twenty months. Delay was the master stroke.

There remained now only one more point for Hay to gain—approval by the British Government of the canal convention which had already been waiting in London for nearly a year.

"I wish I could believe that Lord Salisbury would let the Clayton-Bulwer Convention go through, independent of Canadian matters." Hay had written to White.[1] In January Salisbury was still reluctant but, having again consulted the Canadians, he agreed. "I think you must give Canada a long credit mark for this," wrote Choate.[2] The first Hay-Pauncefote treaty was signed in Washington February 5, 1900.

As for the Roosevelt claim to honor in the Alaska matter it is sufficient, for the moment, to point out that most of the work and anxiety

[1] September 9, 1899.
[2] Feb. 7, 1900.

connected with the settlement of the boundary came during the long summer of 1899, when Theodore Roosevelt was still in Albany. In the sequence of events it was the treaty which Hay refused to sign and the *modus vivendi* which he secured in that summer which are important. Of Hay's share in the treaty of 1903 we shall write in due course. The friends of John Hay will find no embarrassment in conceding that the final settlement carried the heavy boot-marks of McKinley's successor in office.

IT is common to date the emergence of the United States as a world power from the Spanish-American War. Potentially we were then a world-power, but actually it was during the period of the Boer War, from October, 1899, to June, 1902, that the American government made its position recognized and secure. It was not wholly accidental that these thirty-two months were so important in American history. Speaking somewhat cynically, the conflict in South Africa provided a favorable opportunity for dealing with England. During this period the United States either concluded, or brought to an advanced stage of negotiation, practically all the diplomatic questions in which it was essential to American interest that Great Britain either make concessions or extend its good will.

The American Government, in its attitude toward the Boer War, departed in no way from its traditional policy toward transatlantic political affairs. This policy had been restated only a few months before, July 29, 1899, in the reservation which the American delegates at the Hague Conference attached to their signatures on the convention for the settlement of international disputes. This reservation read: "Nothing contained in this convention shall be so construed as to require the United States of America to depart from its traditional policy of not intruding upon, interfering with, or entangling itself in the political questions or policy or internal administration of any foreign State. . . ." On the other hand, the personal sympathy of John Hay for the British in South Africa was probably no inconsiderable factor in his success in dealing with England on other matters of more immediate interest to the United States. Furthermore, his sympathy revealed the man to such a degree that the Boer War became an important incident in Hay's life.

To begin with, unlike so many of his countrymen, John Hay was not what might be called an "under-dog" man. He had not been conspicuously a protester, or a crusader, or a friend of lost causes, save for his anti-monarchical and anti-clerical prose and verse in the early seventies. In American life he had associated himself with those who have, rather than with those who have not. In England, his friends were perhaps not exclusively Tories, but at least always among the ruling classes: Curzon, Chamberlain, Balfour, Harcourt, the bankers, the landed gentry. Not lacking in sentiment in his personal relations, Hay was not given to sentimentality. The harrowing details of the Cuban concentration camps do not appear to have disturbed him in 1896 any more than he had been stirred thirty-five years earlier by the evils of slavery. Hay was not conspicuously a humanitarian. He had great regard for wealth and power such as the British Empire exemplified.

"It is wholly illogical," he wrote to Choate, Jan. 3, 1900, "but nevertheless in accordance with the observed workings of human nature, that the less the Boers need sympathy, the more they get. If England had no reverses she might have done as she pleased with South Africa. But as she has had two or three setbacks, the welkin rings with outcry against her, flavored with a brogue, and the lower breed of politicians begin to join in the outcry. A smashing victory would quiet everything considerably but I gravely fear the effect of another British defeat."

Hay believed in the British Empire. It was a cardinal principle of his statecraft that, as he put it to the German Ambassador on January 2, 1900, the "continued existence of the British Empire, even though somewhat humbled," would be of greater advantage to the world than its downfall.[1] With prophetic vision he remarked: "If the existence of the British Empire should be called in question there is no knowing what constellation might then make its appearance among the powers."

The most active and troublesome advocates in America of the Boer cause were German and Irish immigrants for whom, as a class, Hay had often expressed his distrust. It probably appealed to his sense of humor that the Irish were even willing to support in South Africa a government so aggressively Protestant that Catholics were by law excluded from holding office.[2]

Hay's personal interest in the war was directly enlisted when, without solicitation on his part, and even greatly to his surprise, the President decided to send Adelbert, Hay's son, to Pretoria as consul general. The appointment of this young man, only a few months out

---

[1] Dennis, p. 125.
[2] Hay never publicly made use of this fact, but he had been supplied with a memorandum, presumably from British sources, on the religious intolerance of the Boer laws.

of Yale, to so responsible a post, was to the father a shock as well as
a surprise. Hay was excessively devoted to his children but Del, as he
was always called, the father had not understood. Now the President,
who had taken the opportunity to know the boy, gave him a degree of
confidence which Hay had withheld. It shocked the father thus suddenly
to learn that he had overlooked the good qualities of his own son. The
discovery seems to have provoked an emotional reaction in which were
mingled haunting remorse with bursting pride. Hay's known sympathies
in the war were by a critical public assigned to the son, and protests
began to pour in that the newly appointed consul general was hostile
to the Boers.

These allegations, which Hay did not recognize as just in his own
case, even more deeply enraged him when directed at his boy. In
replying to such protests he did not disguise his feelings. To an old
acquaintance in London, an ardent advocate of the Boers, he wrote: [1]
"He [Del] is absolutely neutral and impartial in his feelings, as I
surmise he has been in his actions and his expressions, and I am getting
rather tired of insinuations to the contrary. As to my own position,
there ought not to be any mystery about that. We are strictly neutral
in this controversy, and as to sympathies, I am too busy sympathizing
with my own country to waste emotions on others."

The charges persisted and six months later, in a letter to Senator
James McMillan,[2] he set forth a general defense of Del. "I hardly
know how to answer your last question except to say that the question
embodies a lie. My son was appointed in the place of a man who was
a sneak and a coward, purely because he was neither. A letter written
from Pretoria, and recently printed, from Richard Harding Davis, an
ardent Boer sympathizer, says, 'Nobody in Pretoria knows with which
side Mr. Hay sympathizes,' which simply shows he had been doing his
duty and not shooting off his mouth. . . . The men who tell these lies
know they are lying and lie simply to annoy."

Shortly after Del's arrival at Pretoria, he forwarded by telegraph,
March 10, 1900, an official request of the Boers urging intervention
with a view to the cessation of hostilities. Similar requests were made
to European powers. The President directed that the substance of the
telegram, with an offer of good offices, be conveyed to the British

---

[1] To John E. Milholland, Jan. 22, 1900.
[2] July 3, 1900.

Alvey A. Adee, Second Assistant Secretary of State, in conference with Secretary Hay in the latter's office in "Mr. Mullett's Masterpiece." Nearly thirty years before they had written together a short story which was published in *Putnam's Magazine*, August, 1870, under the title, "Life's Magnet." (See p. 199).

John Hay's facility as a phrase-maker, compared with Grover Cleveland's similar gift, was portrayed by Clifford K. Berryman, the famous Washington political cartoonist. This cartoon was redrawn for Col. Hay, and its presentation led the Secretary to offer Mr. Berryman a consular post abroad in order that the latter might continue his art studies. Original in the collection of Clarence L. Hay.

government. Lord Salisbury promptly and courteously declined to accept an intervention of any power. The offer of good offices was, in fact, hardly in keeping with the spirit of the reservation to the Hague Convention already quoted, and some regarded it as a very clever trick on Hay's part. Such an offer made and rejected, not only left the record clear, but placed the American government in a position where it could reply, as the Secretary frequently did afterwards, that there was nothing further that the United States could do.

President McKinley, facing the Presidential campaign of 1900, in which the Democrats were freely charging that the United States had a secret understanding with England, quietly supported his Secretary of State in his Boer policy, and it remained unchanged under Roosevelt. On January 29, 1902, following an appeal to the President from the Boer representatives in the United States on behalf of some captured Boers in South Africa, the Department issued a statement which recalled the offer of good offices and added: "The President is convinced that at the present time no other course is open to him than that which this government has hitherto consistently pursued."

Hay's own feelings remained unchanged throughout the war.

In 1902 a campaign was started in this country in the interest of the Boers to persuade the American government to protest against the concentration camp in South Africa. Senator Lodge enclosed a letter from one of his constituents to which Hay replied with some asperity: [1] "It is extremely difficult to answer such a letter without exposing oneself to the charge of Anglomania or utter heartlessness. The Boer women and children are in the Concentration Camps simply because their husbands and brothers want them there, and as to the war with all its hideous incidents and barbarities, it will stop the instant Botha and deWet wish it to stop; and, in any case, there is no reason why the Government of the United States should take it upon itself to stop the war in which it has less concern than any nation in the world. But nothing of this can be said to a gentleman of Mr. Robbins's state of mind, and I am afraid this letter will be of no use to you except to help fill your waste basket."

To Charles M. Walker of the Indianapolis *Journal* Hay expressed himself further with reference to the concentration camp: [2]

[1] February 19, 1902.
[2] March 10, 1902.

As to the general subjects of these concentration camps, I have never said a word in public, and do not propose to. I am not the attorney of the British Government to defend their acts. There is, of course, great suffering and loss of life, but it ought to be remembered that when Lord Kitchener and General Botha met some time ago to discuss terms of surrender, Lord Kitchener appealed to General Botha to spare the farms and houses of surrendered Boers, and promised on his part not to disturb the families and farms of Boers fighting against them. This, General Botha refused to agree to and declared he was entitled to ask every man to join or if they did not do so, to confiscate their property and leave their families on the veldt. After this, in the opinion of Kitchener, he could do nothing to bring in the families of friendly burghers for protection but, as I said before, we are neutral in this fight, and have nothing to say on either side.

Toward the close of 1900 occurred a peculiar incident, illustrating not only Hay's attitude but also the degree to which President McKinley was giving his personal attention to matters of foreign policy, and, at times, restraining his not always discreet Secretary of State. There seemed at the moment some possibility that President Kruger, who had taken refuge in Holland, might visit the United States. Obviously his presence in America would have been an embarrassment to the administration. Foreseeing this, Hay addressed a private letter, Dec. 3, 1900, to the American Minister at The Hague, Stanford Newel:

A good many thoughtless and some malicious people are sending letters and telegrams to President Kruger inviting him to visit this country. It is not desired that you should take any official action in regard to the matter, but I would be glad if you could, discreetly and indirectly, have the impression conveyed to President Kruger that a visit to America would be of no advantage to him. He would have, at private hands and by private organizations of all sorts, a flattering reception, but the demonstrations in his favor would be almost entirely confined to opponents of the Administration, and the object of them would not be the interests of President Kruger nor of the Transvaal Republic, but merely the expression of political hostility to President McKinley. We have already done all we are permitted to do in the way of using our good offices for mediation. Our offer having been declined, our function, by that act ceases, and could not possibly be renewed.

No sooner had the letter been sent than the President, realizing that, if its substance were to become known in the United States, it might create troubles greater than those it sought to avoid, prevailed upon Hay to withdraw it. In explaining the situation Hay again wrote to

Newel at the close of the year. After explaining that McKinley thought that "an absolutely quiescent attitude would be better," Hay continued: "I write now to say that I wish you would consider it as not written, and that you will be good enough to return it to me with this one. I have not changed my opinion in regard to the matter. I still think a journey of President Kruger to this country would be a great inconvenience both to him and to us, and would do no good, and, although I know of no one who differs with me in this opinion, they seem to think that I had better not give you any directions in regard to it." [1]

The Boer War renewed the old discussions of international law as to the rights and duties of neutrals. There were the questions of the definition of contraband, "continuous voyage," "ultimate destination," and the immunity of private property at sea. The British were determined to prevent the entrance of foodstuffs into the Boer country. They met Ambassador Choate in a friendly spirit and assured him of their willingness to pay claims, but intimated that as for neutral rights, their interest was not in legal theories but in winning the war. Hay likewise was no theorist, and appears to have taken no personal interest in the representations. He did not allow the discussions of legal theory to run out into long legal briefs. When Great Britain offered a solution by agreeing to purchase outright such captured goods as were shown to have been the property of American citizens, the incident was closed.[2] The broad question of the rights of neutrals to send goods not contraband to neutral ports adjacent to a belligerent area remained unsettled except as it was wrapped up in the renewed determination of the naval powers by increased armaments to seek control of the seas.

The other legal phase of the war concerned the right of Americans to sell horses and mules to the British government for use in South Africa. Boer sympathizers sought to show that for the American government to permit such sales was a violation of American neutrality. Such protests irritated Hay and he expressed his views in many letters. Toward the close of the war, in response to such a protest, Hay drafted a reply which serves in a comprehensive way as the expression of his views: [3]

I have received your letter of the 4th of April. There ought not to be any doubt in any intelligent mind of the position of this government. It can show

---

[1] December 21, 1900.
[2] Annual Message, Dec. 3, 1900. *For. Rel.*, 1900, p. xxix.
[3] April 7, 1902.

no partialities, in case of any foreign war, between the combatants. Its sympathies and interests are all with the people of the United States. It is governed by the statutes of the United States and the law of nations, and, within the limits thus fixed, it works for the interests of the American farmers, American manufacturers, and American merchants. It seeks, in every proper way, to extend the market for their goods and products all over the world. They have a perfect right to deal with everybody, whether belligerents or not. We should be glad to see our people furnish remounts to every army in the world, to feed and clothe them, and to supply them with everything they need. This policy was inaugurated under the Administration of Washington, and has been adhered to for more than a century.

The draft was shown to President Roosevelt, who added in pencil, "In 1812 it was even adhered to at the cost of war."

The notable quality of Hay's handling of the Boer War questions is that, although when dealing with the various unofficial or official representatives of the Boers he maintained a suave and courteous manner, he was, in fact, as his private letters reveal, indignant and irascible. He could see no redeeming virtue in the Boers' defiance of England, and as for their American sympathizers, he regarded their motives as usually partisan, unworthy, and insincere. Looking forward to an early British success, he wrote to Del as early as July 1, 1900, about coming home. "I imagine after the war is over and the British rule established, you will hardly care to stay much longer. You can then do what seems most attractive to you for a while. We should be glad to see you here, but do not insist on your returning immediately. You can come back, if you prefer, by Suez, Egypt, Turkey, Greece, Italy & France. There will be no objection, even on the part of those filthy curs of Tammany, I should think, to your visiting England after you are out of office,—and the elections are over. I think we are going to larrup them well this fall, but even if they win, we shall be independent of them."

There is no slightest evidence that Hay ever seized upon the moment when the British were hard-pressed in South Africa or in Europe to demand a concession to American advantage in Canada, the Caribbean, the Pacific, or China. The British Foreign Office must have known that Hay was as keenly interested in British success as the most ardent British supporter of the war. For that very reason it was easier for the British Government to yield to Hay's steady and persistent requests. It was a happy accident in Anglo-American relations that it was so, for the Americans were deadly in earnest and meant to have what they wanted, whether England liked it or not.

IN seeking the consent of the British Government first to modification and then to abrogation of the Clayton-Bulwer Treaty, John Hay felt more deeply than is usually appreciated, that the national honor was at stake. Unlike many members of Congress, he believed that, until England should consent to a different agreement, the Convention of 1850 must be regarded as in full force and binding upon the United States not to obtain an exclusive privilege or to erect fortifications at the isthmus.

President McKinley agreed with his Secretary, but in his annual message of December 5, 1898, he was cautious, and treated the canal question as though it were a purely domestic one. He referred to the canal as indispensable and as imperatively required. He asserted that it should be controlled by the United States alone, and urged Congress to take some definite action.

Two days later Hay directed Henry White, who was then Chargé in London, to broach the subject to Lord Salisbury. Hay also stopped short of conceding British rights, but pointed out that, while many public men in America went even so far as to argue that the treaty was obsolete, he did not at the moment desire to revive or entertain any controversy on that point.[1] The President, explained Hay, thought that it would be more judicious to approach the British Government in a frank and friendly spirit of mutual accommodation, and to ask whether it might not be possible to secure modification of the provisions of the Clayton-Bulwer Treaty. The President hoped that he might take it for granted that the British government not only had no wish to prevent the accomplishment of this great work, but that they felt a lively interest in it and appreciated the fact that the benefits of its successful achievement would be to the advantage not only of England and America, but of all commercial nations.

On the same day, however, probably to allay the excitement created in London by the President's message, in an interview with L. F. Moneypenny, a British journalist, Hay appears to have given positive

[1] *Diplomatic History of the Panama Canal,* pp. 1–2.

assurances that the President's words were not to be interpreted as "implying any intention to override the neutrality provision of the Clayton-Bulwer Treaty." [1] A perfect understanding also existed between Hay and Pauncefote. There is even an intimation in the Hay papers that two days before the annual message Hay transmitted to the British Ambassador the *projet* of a new canal convention. On December 3, Hay sent Pauncefote the inquiry: "Will you kindly look over this project of a convention and let me know what you think of it?"

Lord Salisbury received the overtures in a friendly spirit. He was much gratified by Hay's letter to White, and wished to know exactly what "modifications" in the Clayton-Bulwer Treaty the American Government desired. The only definite conviction that Salisbury mentioned was that the canal, when constructed, should be open to the ships of all countries on equal terms.[2] In a private letter to Hay on December 23, White amplified his official report with a summary statement of Salisbury's views: "The Prime Minister quite realizes (1) that the canal can only be built by a Government, that no company can be expected to undertake it alone, and that it is desirable that it be built; (2) that it is better for it to be under our protection than that of any other power—and better, in the abstract, under the protection of one than of two or more Powers; (3) he is of the opinion—and said so privately to me—that the canal is of comparatively little importance to England now that they have the Suez Canal." [3] Evidently Lord Salisbury did not think the retention of the existing treaty rights a matter of serious importance to Great Britain.

Thus the way seemed open for a treaty settlement and Hay wrote optimistically to Senator John T. Morgan, December 27, 1898: "I do not look forward to any protracted negotiations." Two months later, however, there came the great disappointment. The British Cabinet refused to consider the canal treaty until the United States had come to some agreement with Canada over the ownership of some glaciers in Alaska. Negotiations were thus delayed nearly a year.

There were in all what amounted to three drafts of the Hay-Pauncefote Treaty—the one which the British Cabinet first approved;

[1] Moneypenny to Hay, Dec. 7, 1898.
[2] *Dip. Hist.*, pp. 3-4.
[3] Nevins, *White*, p. 145.

the draft as amended by the Senate, which was rejected by England; and, the treaty which was ratified in 1902.

The first draft incorporated the provisions of the proposed agreement in three very simple articles. One of them clearly stated that the United States might construct the canal and might enjoy the exclusive right of providing for its regulation and management. Another article set up seven rules for the application of the general principle of neutralization which had been agreed to in the Clayton-Bulwer Treaty. It was stated in the text that those rules were "substantially" those which had been embodied in the Suez Canal Convention of 1888. One rule declared that the canal should be free and open, in time of war as in time of peace, to all nations on terms of entire equality. Another, while allowing the United States to maintain a police force, prohibited fortifications. The other rules dealt with the limitations on the use of the canal by belligerents. The third article of the treaty provided that the two signatories should invite all other Powers to adhere to the treaty. In short, the new convention amended but did not repeal the Clayton-Bulwer Treaty.

The simple language of the first and third articles suggests that they were drafted by Hay, although no evidence has been found to prove it, while the rules quite certainly represent Pauncefote's contribution.[1]

In transmitting the draft to London, January 13, 1899, Hay explained to White in a private letter which was no doubt designed to be shown to Salisbury: "We desire no advantage, and I am sure we take none in this arrangement. Our only object is to make it possible for the Government to take charge of and build the canal without in any way violating our international obligations to England." The Secretary expressed the hope that England would approve the draft, without amendment, and, promptly, for the Senators were becoming impatient and getting themselves "balled up in their own eloquence."

[1] Nov. 14, 1898, Hay wrote to Richard Olney to learn what, if any, conversations he had with the British Ambassador about the Clayton-Bulwer Treaty. Olney replied the following day that when the supposed unfriendliness of England to the building of the Nicaragua Canal was urged by some Senators as an objection to the Olney-Pauncefote General Arbitration Treaty, he had some informal and unofficial conversation with Sir Julian. "The result," wrote Olney, "was a decided impression on my part that Great Britain was anxious to have the canal built, did not care whether the United States built it or not provided English ships were allowed the same privileges in the canal as the ships of any other nation, and would be willing to amend the Clayton-Bulwer Treaty accordingly. It was suggested that the international conventions now governing the possession and use of the Suez Canal should be taken as the basis of such amendment."

The British authorities could find no fault with the draft but, as already explained, would not authorize their Ambassador to sign it until the Alaska boundary matter had been cleared up.

The creation of the new Isthmian Canal Commission with Rear-Admiral Walker as chairman changed the situation in Congress. It was expected that the commission would require from one to two years to make its report. Therefore, although the *modus vivendi* for the Alaska boundary was effected October 20, 1899, Hay did not immediately seek to reopen the canal question. Probably he expected so soon to follow the temporary agreement with a permanent settlement that it was intended to delay the Hay-Pauncefote Treaty until the Alaska matter had been finally adjusted.

The idea of an American-built trans-isthmian canal had so completely captured the imagination of the American people that as soon as the Fifty-seventh Congress opened for its first session in December, 1899, it was apparent that further delay of the treaty would be hazardous. The nation was bursting with self-confidence and with energy which, if not diverted to some peaceful enterprise, might very likely express itself in a less creditable or constructive way. The project of the canal was coming to have the value of a moral equivalent for war. Congress was reluctant to wait for the report of Admiral Walker's "million dollar commission." The Senate had, in the previous session, revealed itself as overwhelmingly in favor of an immediate decision with a view to the early inauguration of work on the Nicaraguan route. Congressman Hepburn introduced a bill into the House to appropriate whatever sum of money might be necessary "to excavate, construct, and protect" a canal from Greytown to Brito, i. e., through Nicaragua. There was in the House a large majority known to be in favor of it, and no question as to the Senate. The bill both ignored England and was contrary to engagements of the Clayton-Bulwer Treaty.

Hay watched the situation anxiously and became convinced that it would not be safe longer to delay the negotiations on the Hay-Pauncefote Treaty, the draft of which had already been lying in London nearly a year. He prepared a private letter to Ambassador Choate, under date of January 15, 1900, and then delayed it a week in order that Pauncefote might also prepare a report to Salisbury to reach London at the same time. After recalling that the draft treaty had "received the approval of everybody" the year before, he pointed out that the Alaska matter was now temporarily settled, and that Congress was not likely to pay any attention to the Convention of 1850 when once it was thoroughly convinced that the American people demanded a canal. He went on:

The reasons for such an arrangement are more imperative than ever and the matter is approaching a stage in America which really requires something definite to be done. You will remember that last year, the Congress, in apparent despair of an agreement between the two Houses on the comparative merits of the Hepburn and the Morgan bills, passed all at once, with very little deliberation I am bound to say, the bill for the creation of a commission to examine and report upon all possible routes across the Isthmus. To do thoroughly the work assigned to them, this Commission will require at least a year, and probably two. Now, both Houses seem to have grown impatient at this prospect of delay which was rendered necessary by their own act. Mr. Hepburn has introduced a bill for the immediate construction of the canal, which, if it passes the House, Mr. Morgan is quite sanguine he can carry through the Senate. This bill is in many respects highly objectionable, especially as it absolutely ignores the Clayton-Bulwer Treaty, and, in fact, in many features, is an absolute violation of it. I think we should be in a most unenviable attitude before the world if that bill should pass in its present form. My own position would be one of very especial awkwardness, and would raise very serious questions as to what would personally be required of me. I think we ought to make an effort to arrange the matter through diplomatic channels, so that at least the administration would have its skirts clear of any complicity in a violent and one-sided abrogation of the Clayton-Bulwer Treaty.

Two or three facts seem evident enough. The canal is going to be built, probably by the Nicaragua route. Nothing in the nature of the Clayton-Bulwer prohibition will finally prevent the building of the canal. As soon as Congress is convinced that the people of the country demand the construction of the canal, it will be done. It will be a great benefaction to the entire civilized world. It is hard to say whether we or England will profit by it most. It would be a deplorable result of all our labor and thought on the subject, if, by persisting in postponing the consideration of this matter until all the Canadian questions are closed up, England should be made to appear in the attitude of attempting to veto a work of such world-wide importance; and the worst of all for international relations is that the veto would not be effective.

England was left with no reasonable alternative. The treaty was unobjectionable. The attempt longer to use the canal question as an inducement to concessions to Canada meant two things: American defiance of England at a moment when British prestige was already imperilled in South Africa; and, probably, Hay's resignation as Secretary of State, with a return to the old and very popular tail-twisting policy. Just before midnight, February 3, Hay received a private telegram from Choate stating that by direction of the British Cabinet, Pauncefote had been instructed to sign the canal convention.

President McKinley's letter two days later transmitting the treaty to the Senate was somewhat unusual in form in that it included no letter of explanation from the Secretary of State. If it was Hay's modesty which prompted him to omit explanations, he was ill-advised, for the correspondence thus opened with the Senate seemed unnecessarily abrupt, especially in view of the fact that in the negotiation of the treaty the members of the Foreign Relations Committee do not appear to have been taken into the confidence of the Secretary. Hay was at first in high spirits, confident that the convention would be easily and perhaps unanimously approved. He was gradually disillusioned.

From the report on the treaty by Cushman K. Davis, Chairman of the Foreign Relations Committee,[1] it is apparent that Davis shared Hay's alarm lest the Clayton-Bulwer Treaty be abruptly abrogated. More than half of the fifteen pages of this report were devoted to arguments to prove that the Convention of 1850 was still in force.

"It is manifest," declared Senator Davis,[2] "that the Clayton-Bulwer Treaty was regarded by our government as the peaceful solution of a very grave situation in 1850 that we were not prepared to accept as a *casus belli*, having just emerged from a great and expensive war with Mexico. It was then felt by the American people that the attitude of Great Britain in her Central American policy was distinctly aggressive toward the United States and was unjust, overbearing, and dangerous to the future of our country, and much of that sentiment still strongly affects our people. But they cheerfully accepted the treaty of April, 1850."

The Senator argued that to abrogate the treaty would be distinctly disadvantageous to the United States since under its provisions England was inhibited from claiming exclusive rights in Nicaragua under her treaty of 1860: "The right to a footing in Nicaragua, thus acquired by Great Britain, is full of peril to this Republic." In the Hay-

[1] Sen. Doc. 268, 56–1, Mar. 9, 1900.
[2] *Ibid.*, p. 7.

Pauncefote Treaty, England had agreed that the restrictions as to the exclusive control of the canal imposed by the Clayton-Bulwer Treaty should continue to bind her, while the United States would be released from them.

Senator Davis then commended the neutrality provision of the new treaty. "It is right in its moral features, in its impartiality, and, above all, in the tendency to decrease the resort to war." The Senator pooh-poohed the objection that the treaty prohibited fortifications, and appended a statement by no less a personage than Admiral Dewey who declared that to fortify the canal would simply result in making it a battle ground in case of war. "The real danger to the canal, from the absence of fortifications," declared Davis, "is so slight and improbable that its discussion appears to be unnecessary."

The Foreign Relations Committee, however, recommended one amendment to bring the neutralization rules completely into line with those of the Suez convention. It was proposed to add that these rules should not apply to "measures which the United States may find it necessary to take for securing, by its own forces, the defense of the United States and the maintenance of public order."

The minority report, presented by Senator Morgan, likewise argued that the Clayton-Bulwer Treaty was still in force and that it should not be abrogated. The proposed reservation seemed to the minority "entirely superfluous and unnecessary." And so it seemed to Hay.

In Congress the situation became unmanageable. Initially the impression was allowed to slip out that the treaty constituted an abrogation of the Convention of 1850. A motion in the Senate to remove the injunction of secrecy was defeated, but some Senator, notwithstanding, supplied a copy to the press. Led by the New York *Sun*, the opposition began to roll up until something resembling a mania was created.

"What folly," cried Congressman Hepburn, "to bring in this treaty at a time when every authority on international law, every one posted on international treaties, and every one familiar with the provisions of the Clayton-Bulwer Convention regarded the convention as obsolete." The very act of signing the new treaty seemed to Hepburn disloyal, for to sign was to give virtual recognition to the validity of the old treaty.[1] The House was already practically a unit for a fortified canal such as the Hepburn Bill proposed.

[1] New York *World*, February 13, 1900.

"As if not satisfied with the gash made fifty years ago in the Monroe Doctrine," declared the *Sun*, "the negotiators of the new treaty actually ask the Senate to vote to go farther and call over to this side of the Atlantic all the new Powers of Europe to assist Great Britain in coercing us should we ever be desperate enough to attempt to control in war the canal which we shall have built and paid for." [1]

Four days later the *Sun* carried on the front page Governor Roosevelt's famous statement against the treaty, and followed it up on the 14th with an editorial appeal to Hay, in the vein of a journalistic day that was passing, to correct his "stupendous blunder, honestly perpetrated."

John Bassett Moore sprang to the defense of the treaty in a long communication to the New York *Times*, March 4, 1900, which was subsequently reprinted as a pamphlet by the Department of State. His article is important as showing how completely Hay's treaty incorporated the historic policy of the government. "There is, in reality," Moore asserted, "but one question at issue, and that is whether the exclusive control of the canal for purposes of war is so essential to our national safety that we should discard the advantages that would accrue from its neutralization and devote ourselves to the accomplishment of the opposite policy."

Moore argued that the principle of neutralization was in harmony with the historic policy of the United States of opposition to monopoly; that the conception of an inter-oceanic canal between the Atlantic and the Pacific as a great common highway of nations, open on equal terms to all, was also in line with the other great policy of the United States, the freedom of the seas. Moore cited a long list of American statesmen who had taken the view with Henry Clay that the benefits of the canal "ought not to be exclusively appropriated to any one nation." In the treaty of 1846 with New Granada, now Colombia, the United States had guaranteed "the perfect neutrality" of the isthmus. In transmitting this treaty to the Senate, President Polk said that it was confidently expected that similar guarantees would be given to New Granada by Great Britain and France. He added, "the interests of the world at stake are so important that the security of this passage between the two oceans cannot be suffered to depend upon the wars and revolutions which may arise among different nations."

[1] New York *Sun*, February 8, 1900.

It was this principle of neutralization which in 1900 seemed so objectionable to a growing section of the American people; yet prior to that time it had rarely been questioned. It was approved by Marcy in 1856 and by Cass in 1858. Four years later Seward went so far as to instruct the American representatives at London and Paris to invite those governments to join with the United States either alone or jointly in the protection of the Isthmus of Panama against a local revolutionary movement. Declared Seward: "This government has no interest in the matter different from that of other maritime powers. It is willing to interpose its aid in execution of its treaty, and for the benefit of all nations." In 1867, in a second treaty with Nicaragua, the United States renewed its guarantee of neutrality. In 1877 Hamilton Fish issued a circular instruction which contemplated securing the accession of the principle maritime powers to a new canal treaty with a view to neutralization.

It was not until 1884 that a contrary opinion appeared. On December 1 of that year Secretary Frelinghuysen signed a convention with Nicaragua to effect a perpetual alliance with Nicaragua to "protect the integrity of the territory of the latter." No provision was made for neutralization. The treaty was submitted to the Senate in 1884 but was not approved, and the following March, President Cleveland withdrew it. Cleveland maintained that the treaty provision was "inconsistent with such dedication to universal and neutral use," and would "entail measures for its realization beyond the scope of our national policy or present means."

In concluding this summary Moore stated: "It is superfluous to add that no matter what our future policy may be, these stipulations [of the first Hay-Pauncefote Treaty] embody our historic policy in respect of the inter-òceanic canal."

John Hay was nearly sixty-two years old. Child of the prairies though he was, he had never caught the spirit of the "rough riders." He had always been a conservative, never a man of adventure, and now, because he so often was repeating the assertion to himself he was an old man. If he had failed to catch the vision of the great American Empire of the next century, he had failed in company with an illustrious fellowship which included McKinley and his cabinet, Cushman K. Davis, and most of the elder statesmen. But his critics charged that the Secretary of State had been too zealous to safeguard

British interests—as zealous as Clayton, Marcy, Cass, Seward, Fish, and Grover Cleveland!

Fundamental in the growing opposition to the treaty was a new and youthful spirit of imperialism which also manifested itself in the presidential campaign of 1900. The Democrats tried to make of it a partisan issue but in the end dared not take the other side of the argument. The Republican platform of June 22, 1900, declared for "the immediate construction, ownership, control and protection of an isthmian canal by the Government of the United States." The Democratic convention, meeting July 4, although pretending to boil with indignation over Republican imperialism in the Pacific, declared strongly for the Monroe Doctrine, and condemned "the Hay-Pauncefote Treaty as a surrender of American rights and interests, not to be tolerated by the American people." So much for the logic of party platforms on issues of foreign policy. By December it was a foregone conclusion that the treaty was due for still further changes.

Two more amendments were recommended by the Foreign Relations Committee and many more were proposed from the floor of the Senate. The two approved by the Committee were passed. One of them declared that by the new convention the Clayton-Bulwer Treaty was "hereby superseded." The second cut from the treaty entirely the article requiring the signatories to invite the other Powers to adhere to it. The neutrality provisions were retained, as was the prohibition against fortifications, but the United States was left as the sole guarantor of the neutral use of the waterway. Obviously the elder statesmen and the new school imperialists had reached a compromise. The amended treaty was, in fact, less acceptable to the new school of thought than the new draft which Hay submitted a year later. Ratification with the amendments was advised December 20, 1900.

Two days later Senator Lodge issued a prepared newspaper statement, intended, perhaps, to assuage Hay's bruised feelings, but containing an assumption of Senatorial prerogatives which must have been to Hay like salt in an open wound. Lodge asserted that, the Senate being a part of the treaty-making power, "treaties sent to it for ratification are not strictly speaking treaties, but projects of treaties. They are still inchoate." The next sentence was little less than an official insult to the Secretary of State. "In the exercise of the undoubted rights, without the slightest reflection upon any one, and without a shadow of hostility to a friendly nation, the Senate, *continuing the negotiation* begun by Mr. Hay, offers three new propositions to England." [1]

In a private letter to Choate, December 21, 1900, intended, presumably, to be shown to Lord Salisbury, Hay gave his version of the history of what happened:

From the moment the first opposition developed itself I had no hope of the treaty going through intact. As soon as the Senate assembled it was evident that a combination of two or three groups of recalcitrants could command more than a third of that body. The people opposed to any canal; those whose support had been acquired by Panama; those who wanted to hurt the President *sans en avoir l'air;* those who wanted me out of the Cabinet; and the craven time-servers who think it is always good politics to attack England; and a certain number of honest and narrow-minded patriots who know no better—all together numbered enough, in the opinion of our friends, to kill the treaty, if they were not squared. Our friends were persistently misled. They were sure that the Davis Amendment would satisfy everybody—but the moment it was adopted, a swarm of new ones came up—from which the Republican leaders adopted two, which they thought relatively innocent. They submitted them to the President, who asked me to meet a committee consisting of Lodge, Aldrich, and Foraker, at the White House. They told their story—that the treaty would be rejected if these additional amendments were not adopted; that with these amendments, they could not only carry the treaty through, but could prevent any hostile legislation pending further negotiations with England. The President said the treaty was right as originally drawn, ought to be ratified without amendment; but as this seemed impossible we were willing to do our best to persuade the British government to accept the Davis Amendment; but that he did not think they could accept the other two. Upon which Lodge said "That puts the onus of rejecting the treaty on England!" But they all agreed that if the treaty were rejected now, it would be impossible to prevent the violent repudiation of the Clayton-Bulwer Treaty by act of Congress. To this proposition the President made no reply, leaving to the Senate itself the responsibility of its action. But, to give you an instance of the incapacity of these men to gauge the opinion of their own body, the very next day Lodge was beseeching the President to send for Morgan and beg him to refrain from canal legislation pending the settlement of the treaty matter.

Hay went on to state that he believed that the Senate amendments deformed and disfigured the treaty—that they took from it much of the grace and value of the concession which Great Britain had made. "But beyond the matter of taste and good manners I consider them

[1] New York *Sun,* December 22, 1900; italics supplied by the writer.

of little moment. They give no additional advantage to us; they demand no sacrifice from Great Britain. The Davis Amendment is a mere *brutum fulmen;* it leaves intact the provision against the fortification of the canal; it reserves to us in vague terms the right which can never be exercised. The omission of the IIId article hurts nobody but ourselves. It deprives us of the enormous advantage we should have in a universal guarantee of the neutrality of the Canal, and does not in any way injure Great Britain. . . ."

"As to the attitude of the British Government—it is not to be questioned that they have a perfect right to reject the amended Treaty if they think best," continued Hay. "They generously gave us our release from the Clayton-Bulwer Convention, in the terms we ourselves suggested. *We* have suffered a rebuff at the hands of the Senate; it is our dignity that has suffered, and not that of England. If Great Britain should now reject the treaty the general opinion of mankind would justify her in it. If our Congress should then go forward and violently abrogate the Clayton-Bulwer Treaty by legislative action—which is to be apprehended—we shall be putting ourselves hopelessly in the wrong, and not, so far as I can see, injuring England, except to the extent that the interruption of friendly relations will injure us both. The President's veto cannot prevent this, as both Senate and House show two-thirds against him in this matter."

Hay closed his letter with an appeal to the good nature of Lord Salisbury to ratify the Convention as amended. He hoped that England would say: "Take your treaty, Brother Jonathan, and God send you better manners." "If you can persuade our friends to take this view, you will have done a great work for civilization and righteousness." The letter, with its superficial analysis of the objections to the first draft of the treaty, and its imputation of low motives, did not disclose the Secretary of State at his best.

Choate, who of course had been less under fire, took the situation more calmly. In summarizing the comments in the London press he wrote to Hay:[1] "As you will see, they will take it good-naturedly, but at the same time with an eye to business and a clear idea of the actual situation. They fully realize and more clearly than the Senators themselves appear to do that it isn't possible for the Senate by any vote to

[1] Dec. 15, 1900. See Senate Doc. 746, 61–3, presented by Senator Root, for many letters, private as well as official, between Hay and Choate.

force upon you or the President, or upon Great Britain, any amendment that you or they don't approve of; that England made great concessions last spring in assenting to your treaty, getting nothing in return; that if the Senate doesn't wish to avail itself to these great concessions, it has a perfect right to refuse them; but that the alternative is the continuance of the Clayton-Bulwer Treaty in full force. Of course, the action of the Senate has created a most unpleasant impression upon the public mind here—but I hope that they may yet recede, with some view to the law and the Constitution, and ratify the Treaty as you made it. We can wait for the canal, but we can't afford to put ourselves in the wrong."

In spite of Hay's urgent plea Lord Lansdowne acted deliberately. Some of the Senators, becoming impatient and being eager to place the burden for the failure of the treaty upon Great Britain, charged that the British government was really hostile to the building of the canal. The Secretary assured them that the last surmise was wholly incorrect and thought that they ought at least to give the British time to bury their dead Queen.

Pauncefote kept his poise. "I have not had a single word from London on the subject," he wrote to Hay,[1] "and it is best not to worry over it. I believe it will come out right by and by, and it is very important to gain time for the most fervent spirits to cool down." It is also significant that at this time Lord Lansdowne, to whom Lord Salisbury had relinquished the Foreign Office after the British elections of 1900, extended for still another year Lord Pauncefote's term of service in Washington.

Hay made one more appeal through Choate:[2]

I am sorry to say that General Morgan, who was the strongest friend we had in the Senate and who defended the treaty in its entirety from beginning to end, is now led by his anxiety to see work begun on the canal during his own lifetime to demand immediate action on the Hepburn Bill. He excites himself to such an extent with his own eloquence that he is led to demand an immediate cessation of diplomatic relations with England, if any objection is made by England to whatever we may do in regard to the canal.

I judge from occasional paragraphs in the newspapers that the matter is receiving due consideration at the hands of the British government, and I feel, as I said before, that I need add nothing to what I have already said

---

[1] Quoted in Hay to Choate, Jan. 11, 1901.
[2] January 11, 1901.

to you in regard to it. It is more a case for your trained faculties as a lawyer and a man of the world to work with than a matter of definite official instruction. I have gone over it very thoroughly with Lord Pauncefote, and I think he is altogether in favor of an acceptance of the amendments en bloc as a choice of evils. It is certain that if the amendments are rejected, we shall have a very disagreeable state of things between the Executive and the Senate. This, of course, is a consideration which can have and should have no weight with the British government. They are not concerned with our internal wrangles, but I really think that for them the most judicious, as well as the most magnanimous course, would be to accept the amendments and save worse friction hereafter.

But Hay's earnest appeals were in vain.

In March, His Majesty's Government, by a memorandum from Lansdowne left at the Department by Pauncefote, notified the American government that they were unable to accept the amended treaty and preferred to retain unmodified the provisions of the Clayton-Bulwer Convention.[1] Lord Lansdowne's reply was courteous but firm. The American government had, through official channels, proposed a convention and England had accepted it without change. The abrupt action of the Senate in proposing abrogation of the Clayton-Bulwer Treaty without a word of preliminary negotiation was plainly resented. Then the Foreign Secretary placed his finger on what was by no means the least significant meaning of the proposed abrogation. Under the treaty of 1850, the two powers had engaged never to colonize or assume or exercise any dominion over any part of Central America. With the treaty abrogated both powers would resume their freedom of action. There is just a hint in the Lansdowne note that England suspected that under the guise of securing an American canal the United States was attempting to clear the way for conquest in Central America.

That this point had been discussed is evident from the speech of Senator Morgan in an executive session, December 8, 1901. He said: "The question is put to me by Senators whether the Hay-Pauncefote Treaty revokes the prohibition alleged to be expressed in the Clayton-Bulwer Treaty against our acquiring dominion over Costa Rica and Nicaragua hereafter."

"The change," remarked Lansdowne, tartly, "would certainly be of advantage to the United States, and might be of substantial im-

[1] *Dip. Hist. of the Panama Canal*, pp. 11–17.

portance." [1] Perhaps he was remembering the famous prediction of William H. Seward. Lansdowne did not dwell upon the point, and passed on to the main objection. What had become of the magnanimous, grand idea of a neutral waterway between the two oceans?

When Hay had recovered from the shock of the Senate amendments, his further handling of the negotiations with England was above criticism. He tried his best to secure approval for the amended treaty. When London withheld its assent, he turned at once to the discovery of some new formula which would satisfy both the American and the British objections. Nothing in his career more clearly reveals the practical bent of his mind. He was not a theorist, nor was he greatly concerned with general principles. If the American people had outgrown the national ambitions of 1850, he was willing to do his part in giving expression to new ones. Having had the advantage of hearing a very full discussion of the first treaty, he was clearly in a position to draft a better one.

"I do not think the omission of Art. 3 [the guarantee of other Powers] is to be regretted by either England or ourselves," wrote Adee, April 8, 1901, in submitting a first sketch of a new convention. "The chances are ten to one that Germany, or any power which may sometime clash with us, would not be a party to such a guarantee." Hay appears to have accepted this view; the new draft was carefully phrased to make the United States the sole guarantor.

The question of fortifications was more delicate. Adee recommended that the subject be passed silently. "I have always thought," wrote Adee, "that the greatest danger to the canal may lie in its attempted seizure or destruction by Central American insurgents. This we should guard against."

"Suppose the canal had been built and working, in April, 1898,' continued Adee, "when we went to war with Spain, would not Spain have bribed or stirred up her Cent. Am. sympathizers to blow up a lock or otherwise obstruct the canal? The same thing might happen should we ever get into a squabble with Venezuela or Colombia.'

In the new draft the dangers to which Adee referred were met by the insertion of the provision that the United States should be at liberty to maintain such "military police" along the canal as might be necessary to protect it against "lawlessness and disorder."

[1] *Ibid.*, p. 15

On April 27, 1901, the Secretary sent Choate a new project for a treaty. With the permission of the Department, Choate showed it in London to Senator Lodge who appears not to have been freely consulted by Hay in the drafting, and Lodge approved the treaty enthusiastically. His own final contribution consisted of four words which, amusingly enough, had the effect if they had any meaning at all, of still further clarifying British rights. The new treaty conceded every demand: the American Government could not only build and operate, but also defend an Isthmian Canal.

Meanwhile, by the death of President McKinley, September 11, 1901, Theodore Roosevelt became President of the United States. The treaty was signed in Washington, November 18, 1901, and ratification was advised by the Senate, December 16. Happily, the new President was never to be called upon to decide what course he would take in case Great Britain should refuse to agree to the abrogation of the hated Clayton-Bulwer Convention.[1]

The day after Christmas, Hay wrote to White, "You will have seen by the newspapers of the rapid and prosperous journey of our treaty through the Senate. Cabot, who felt himself particularly responsible for the wreck of the last one, put his whole back into promoting this one. The President was likewise extremely zealous in rounding up the bunch of doubtful Senators, and the treaty at last went through with no opposition, except from the irreconcilable cranks. 72 to 6 was near enough unanimity." [2]

Thus, after many discouragements, Hay accomplished his big work with reference to the Canal Treaty. He saved his country from unilateral abrogation of the Clayton-Bulwer Convention. He retained throughout the negotiation the sympathetic support of Pauncefote, Salisbury, and Lansdowne. Perhaps another could have done as well, but it is doubtful whether so much could have been accomplished by one who was not in the position to write the friendly letters which he could write to King Edward, or a letter in which he told Henry White, September 24, 1899, at the beginning of the Boer War, to "say many things for me to our friends at the F. O. and to Mr. Balfour—in fact, many more things than I have any business to say."

---

[1] As late as Mar. 27, 1901, he had favored denunciation. *Roosevelt-Lodge Letters*, I, p. 485.

[2] Nevins, *Henry White*, p. 159.

"I HAVE had my diplomatic reception—," wrote the Secretary to his wife, one day early in October, 1898, "they were mostly dagoes & chargés." Hay and his friends had the one generic term for the Latin Americans. In those days the best diplomatic representatives from Latin America came to Washington rarely, if at all. They found the European capitals more civilized. In Hay's long residence in the city, he had few close associations with Latin Americans, and regarded them lightly. Like the Boers, in his estimation, many of them were among the peoples for whom the "partnership of beneficence" was devised.

"The real duties of a Secretary of State seem to be three:—" he wrote cynically to Adams, August 5, 1899; "to fight claims upon us by other States; to press more or less fraudulent claims of our citizens upon other countries; to find offices for the friends of Senators where there are none." [1] The claims which he so disliked to press, and often did not press, were usually in Latin America. As for the offices which he was expected to find, especially in South America, it seemed to him that the Senators were searching the Keeley cures to fill them.

Much confusion arises from lumping together all the nations south of the United States under a racial category—Latin America—rather than dividing them geographically. In the formulation of American foreign policy, as in so many other respects, the states in and bordering on the Caribbean Sea are so much a separate and geographically immediate group that to call them Latin American is not to classify them by their chief characteristic. The names of neither McKinley nor Hay were ever associated with a major Latin American policy, but in the Caribbean it was quite otherwise. Dividing the policies of the Administration into three broad groups—Transatlantic; Pacific and Far Eastern; and Caribbean—the last named was by far the most important.

The Caribbean policy of President McKinley was to make the United States the paramount power from Key West to the Isthmus.[2]

---

[1] *Letters and Diaries,* III, p. 157.
[2] "The Nicaraguan Canal should be built, owned, and operated by the United States; and by purchase of the Danish Islands we should secure a proper and much needed naval station in the West Indies." Republican platform, 1896.

This policy was revealed in four major actions: the annexation of Porto Rico; the declaration, by the Platt Amendment, of a protectorate over Cuba, together with the stipulation that the United States would require from Cuba a sufficient number of coaling stations and naval bases to enable the protector both to defend itself and to protect the island; the Hay-Pauncefote Treaty, by which foreign powers were eliminated from any control of the projected isthmian canal; and, the attempted purchase of the Virgin Islands from Denmark. With all of the territorial settlements incident to the restoration of peace with Spain, Hay, as has already been pointed out, was in full accord, but the decisions as to Porto Rico and Cuba were made before he became Secretary of State. The diplomatic relations of the United States with Cuba were not inaugurated until May, 1902, when H. G. Squiers assumed his duties at Havana as American Minister. President McKinley's project to create in the fall of 1901 a bureau of insular affairs in the Department of State having failed because of his death, the policy of the United States toward Cuba continued to be directed from the War Department by Elihu Root, and subsequently, from the White House by Theodore Roosevelt. Hay was frequently consulted, as, for example, in the drafting of the Platt Amendment, but it does not appear that to the basic policy he made any contribution.[1] Hay's part in the Caribbean was in the Canal treaties—six negotiations in all: the first and second Hay-Pauncefote Treaties with Great Britain; the subsequent negotiations with Nicaragua and Costa Rica for canal rights to the Nicaraguan route; with Colombia, and eventually with Panama, for the southern route; and, in the attempted purchase of the Virgin Islands. None of these negotiations was completed under McKinley, but Roosevelt made no addition except in the final transactions with Colombia and, at the end, in the recognition of Panama. The Hay-Pauncefote Treaties having already been reviewed, there remains, therefore, the attempted purchase of the Danish West Indies and the early negotiations with Nicaragua and Costa Rica, to exhibit John Hay's contribution to American policy in the Caribbean.

However timid the Secretary may have been about demanding from Great Britain a full relinquishment of her canal rights, and, however he may have at first adhered to the policy of his predecessors with

---

[1] Root to Hay, Jan. 11, 1901; Dennis, *Adventures in American Diplomacy*, ch. 10, "Cuba and the Caribbean."

reference to an international guarantee for a neutralized waterway, he was in full accord with the proposal that the United States should become without delay the paramount power in the Caribbean. The proposed purchase of the Virgin Islands, negotiations for which were initiated several weeks before the first Hay-Pauncefote Treaty was sent to the Senate, represented a major step in the attainment of this objective.

The panorama of territorial expansion spread out before John Hay in his first eighteen months as Secretary of State would, perhaps, have been more terrifying, had it not been that Hay was so often walking in the steps of an old idol. William H. Seward purchased Alaska; John Hay fought to conserve its boundaries. Lincoln's Secretary of State had a vision of expansion in the Pacific, the first step of which was to acquire Hawaii as well as Alaska, with its long bony finger of islands reaching almost to Asia; his disciple supplemented the plan, after Hawaii had been taken, by adding Samoa. Seward visioned a southward movement of the United States below the Rio Grande; Hay signed the treaty which conveyed substantially sovereign rights at the Isthmus. Seward was in favor of American expansion in the Caribbean; sitting at the same desk, thirty years later, his youthful admirer, no longer young, saw Cuba become an American protectorate and saw Porto Rico an American possession. So in the case of the Virgin Islands. Seward signed the first treaty to purchase two of them. In those days the American people lagged behind their prophet; the Senate failed to ratify the treaty. Hay had the satisfaction to draw his old master's treaty out of the files, dust it off, add a little to it, sign it, and have it ratified by the Senate within four weeks after it was presented. Hay was merely picking up the threads of a pattern already old in history. With the slavery question eliminated, it is at least plausible that John Quincy Adams, of whom also Hay was a disciple, would have approved; certainly the statesmen of Manifest Destiny would have; and so would have Hay's younger idol, James G. Blaine. Doubtless the Secretary would have preferred to have the project viewed in the long perspective rather than merely as a favorite scheme of Henry Cabot Lodge. As recently as March 31, 1898, the Senator had, on behalf of the Foreign Relations Committee, presented a report and a bill, authorizing the purchase.[1]

[1] Senate Report No. 1, Executive, 57–1. To accompany S 4303. Lodge's arguments were:

The revival of the effort to acquire the Danish Islands was enveloped in some suspicion. The Republican platform of 1896 advocated the purchase. A little later there appeared in Copenhagen an American citizen of Danish birth, Niels Grön, who professed to be in the confidence of eminent Republicans. He represented that a sum, say $500,000, placed at his disposal, would be sufficient to secure the coöperation of the United States Senate. The Danish Foreign Office later declared, falsely, that it had declined to have any dealings with him. He was reported, at any rate, to have succeeded in raising some portion of the sum from bankers and Danish sugar planters.[1] From the outset it was assumed in Copenhagen that it would be necessary in Washington to corrupt public officials in order to accomplish the sale. The activities of Mr. Grön upon his return to the United States were guided by this assumption. Before he disappeared from the picture several prominent Americans, including Henry H. Rogers of the Standard Oil Company, Charles R. Flint, who was interested in shipping, Cornelius N. Bliss and John D. Long, Secretaries of the Interior and the Navy, respectively, and even the President's brother, Abner, were more or less soiled by their relations with Grön.[2] Professor Tansill has ascertained that while the Danish committee put up only 5,000 kroner, it was agreed that the honorarium for negotiating the sale of the islands would be ten per cent of the purchase price.

Before returning to the United States, Mr. Grön placed in charge of the Copenhagen office of his firm one Walter Christmas, a Danish subject who, having been court-martialed from the Danish Navy, had added considerably to his ill-repute by other adventures. In November, 1899, Christmas appeared in New York and was able to secure from reputable bankers a letter of introduction to John Addison Porter, McKinley's secretary. As "Captain W. Albee Christmas Dirckinck-Holmfeld" he desired an interview with the President "on a matter of importance." [3] From that date onward the machinery of

So long as the islands are in the market there is danger that some European power will purchase them, which would be an infraction of the Monroe Doctrine; and, their military value, as Captain Mahan had pointed out, could hardly be overestimated. Cf. Charles Callan Tansill, *The Purchase of the Danish West Indies*, p. 213.

[1] Jan. 4, 1900; Laurits S. Swenson, American Minister at Copenhagen to Hay. A confidential letter in the Hay papers.

[2] Tansill, pp. 215 ff. House Report No. 2749, 57–1.

[3] Senate Report, Executive M. 57–1, Jan. 27, 1902. Tansill devotes a chapter to Christmas.

the American government moved with such celerity, even with such undignified haste, that within three weeks Secretary Hay had ordered Henry White from London to Cophenhagen on a secret mission to confirm the statements made by Christmas. Four weeks after receiving White's full report, a refurbished draft of Seward's old purchase treaty was on its way to Denmark to be presented through official channels for the approval of the Danish Government.[1]

Christmas represented that he was authorized by the Danish Government to make known to the United States that Denmark was no longer able to hold the islands, that they were for sale, and that Denmark would ask for no money payment whatever, but would require that the United States assume the debt of the islands—St. Thomas, St. John, and St. Croix—to the amount, more or less, of three and a half million dollars. As is usual in real estate transactions, there was hinted that if the United States did not respond to the offer, probably some other Power would be glad to have them. The mysterious envoy stated that the islands would be offered in succession to several European powers until a buyer could be found.[2]

"Mr. Christmas brings no credentials whatever," explained Hay to Henry White in the letter of instructions directing the latter to proceed to Copenhagen; "he is not even introduced by his Minister; he explains this by saying that the Danish Government, having sustained a severe rebuff from the U. S. Senate in Mr. Seward's time, cannot initiate new negotiations on this subject without being assured of the reception they are to meet with. I have thought the matter of sufficient importance to ask Captain Christmas to call at our Embassy in London and to make himself known to you.

"My purpose is, if it suits your convenience, and that of our Ambassador, to ask you to go to Copenhagen, in the strictest privacy, and to have an interview with the Danish Minister of Finance which Mr. v. Christmas professes to be able to arrange for you. Without committing this Government to any definite action, you will, if practicable, ascertain the intentions of the Danish Government in regard to the Islands; the exact terms they will require, in case this Government wishes to take them over: the debt of the Islands, its amount and character, where held and how payable."

[1] *For. Rel.* 1917, p. 462.
[2] Hay to White, Nov. 28, 1899.

Hay requested from White a brief résumé by cable and a fuller report by mail. So great secrecy was to be employed that White was not to make his presence known to the American Minister. The mission was to be regarded as unofficial, but this injunction was seriously compromised by the fact that White's expenses were to be borne by the American Government.

When Mr. Swenson complained to Hay in a personal letter of the irregularity of the proceeding, the Secretary replied, somewhat ingenuously: [1] "There has been a swarm of men about the State Department; some of them have got access even to the President on one pretense and another, and some have been introduced to me by men of the highest personal and financial standing." Hay wished to verify Christmas's statements and yet be in a position to "say truthfully that no communication had passed between the two Governments."

Christmas lost no time in proceeding to London and presenting himself to the Embassy. With Henry White he arranged a rendezvous and, on December 20, substantially making good his representations to Hay, Christmas was able to introduce White to the Danish Minister for Foreign Affairs and Marine. Somewhat more cautious than Christmas, the latter nevertheless confirmed the statement that the islands were for sale and intimated that a payment of between four and five millions would be sufficient. White telegraphed a report, December 22, and followed it the next day with a long despatch.[2]

To the telegram Hay replied promptly: "I suppose I shall get your letter with the details of your Copenhagen trip about the beginning of next week. But I shall not wait for that to thank you for your telegram which was exactly what I wanted, clear, comprehensive and satisfactory throughout. The President was delighted with it, & old Adee said once more, 'White is the most valuable man in the service,' to which I replied, 'A qui le dites-vous?' You were the only man I would have asked to undertake such an errand, and it was done precisely as I wished." [3]

Hay's most important task was to rescue the project from suspicion

---

[1] Swenson to Hay, Jan. 4, 1900; Hay to Swenson, Jan. 19, 1900.
[2] *For. Rel.* 1917, pp. 457 ff.
[3] Nevins, *White,* p. 147. It is interesting to observe that the statement, so often credited to Roosevelt, as to White's preëminent value in the diplomatic service, appears from this letter to have been current with Adee long before it was repeated by Hay or Roosevelt.

and scandal: "Of course, we cannot prevent the Government of Denmark from being plundered by adventurers and loose fish," he wrote
to the American Minister in Copenhagen, "but I can assure you that
on this side there will not be one cent to divide among them." [1] Meanwhile, through Senator Lodge, Captain Christmas had received intimations that his further services were neither required nor desired.[2]

The negotiations for the purchase proceeded only after Hay had
consulted fully with both Senators and Congressmen. Possibly the
Secretary was already being made to realize that he had too much
ignored Congress in the negotiations of his first canal treaty. The
relatively recent action in the case of the annexation of Hawaii naturally suggested a method by which a possible Senatorial opposition
could be avoided. Why not annexation by joint resolution of both
houses, which required only a majority vote, rather than by a treaty
which required the approval of two-thirds of the Senate? "I feel
reasonably sure of a majority of both houses," Hay continued to
White, "and equally doubtful of two-thirds of the Senate. But of
course I had to talk with Senator Davis first. So I went to him and
put the case squarely, which procedure offered the better chance of
success. I could see that he felt as I did—that a joint resolution was
preferable. But being a Senator he could not at once bring his mind
to pass over the Senate." Evidently the idea of a joint resolution was
soon abandoned for on January 29, 1900, the draft treaty was on its
way to Copenhagen, accompanied both by an official instruction from
the Secretary of State and a personal letter to Minister Swenson, giving minute orders as to the way in which the draft was to be presented
to the Foreign Office.

"You may say to his excellency, the Minister of Foreign Affairs,"
concluded the instruction,[3] "in the event of his entertaining this proposal in the friendly spirit in which it is put forward, that it is thought
desirable to bring the matter in definite shape before the Senate at an
early date, and that if the subjoined draft is substantially accepted
I would be prepared to sign it with the Danish Minister at this capital
on his receipt of telegraphic authority to that end." Again, haste.

The Secretary was evidently being crowded. To the urgency of those

[1] Hay to Swenson, Jan. 19, 1900.
[2] Christmas to Hay, Feb. 3, 1900.
[3] *For. Rel.*, 1917, p. 463.

who still expected to make a personal profit was added the enthusiasm of the naval group. In the opinion of naval strategists the acquisition of Porto Rico, far from strengthening the American position in the Caribbean, had actually weakened it. In a war with any one or more of the European naval powers the United States Navy would not be strong enough to maintain itself in Porto Rican waters, isolated twelve or fifteen hundred miles from any home port, without a well-fortified naval base for which Porto Rico itself did not seem to offer the necessary conditions. The desired base, argued the strategists, should be in the Virgin Islands which, as Hay pointed out in his official instruction to Swenson, were "virtually a geographical offshoot" of Porto Rico.

"In view of the Isthmian Canal and the German settlements in South America, every additional acquisition in the West Indies is of value," declared the General Board. "The farther east the acquisition, the greater the value as against aggression from European bases; the farther south the acquisition, the greater the value for aggressive action on our part against localities in South America." The power most feared was Germany. Much consideration was being given to the evidences of Germany's aggressive colonial and naval policies.

The fear of Germany should not divert our attention from the fact that, actually, the naval power in the Caribbean whose influence it was proposed to offset was Great Britain. In the early part of 1900 Hay, and the Administration, were still committed to an international guarantee for a neutralized canal, incorporated in the first Hay-Pauncefote Treaty. On the other hand, correlated closely with that policy was another, that the United States, in the place of Great Britain, which had enjoyed that advantage for, literally, centuries, was to be the paramount naval power in the adjacent waters. The point is significant. The "partnership of beneficence" policy involved a division and a reapportionment of naval responsibility in which Great Britain, isolated from the Continent, at war in South Africa, would leave the Caribbean to the United States.[1]

Probably we do not go wrong in assuming that among the arguments for haste in effecting the purchase of the Virgin Islands at that time, when the first canal treaty was receiving its baptism of fire in the Senate, was the desire of the Secretary of State to present in full

[1] John H. Latané, *American Foreign Policy*, Chap. XXIII.

the well-rounded plan which was being evolved. The two treaties would have helped one another. With an American naval base in the Virgin Islands, with others in Cuba as the American Government already contemplated, the fortification of an isthmian canal, which so eminent an authority as Admiral Dewey, President of the General Board of the Navy, had regarded as impractical, might seem less important to Senators.

The Danish Government, however, could not be rushed. In March the ministry fell and the government which replaced it, never very secure, was reluctant to go forward with a project which might offend Danish pride and cost the new ministry precious prestige. Nothing was accomplished before the American Congress adjourned and it was not until the latter part of August that Hay, from Lake Sunapee, asked Adee to call in John Bassett Moore to examine the Danish objections and to redraft the treaty.[1] These objections, in part, related to encumbrances which Denmark wished to transfer, and to the uncertainty as to citizenship rights of Danes in the islands after the transfer, but the main obstacle was financial. The negotiations came more and more to resemble the conversations which preceded the purchase of corner lots on Euclid Avenue in Cleveland. Hay's first offer was $3,500,000. As the date drew near for the reassembling of Congress, he raised the tender, November 16, to $3,750,000, and, in a confidential letter to Swenson the next day, authorized $4,000,000 for a "perfectly clean transaction," that is, for one free of the encumbrances.[2] Hay had been dealing in real estate for nearly forty years. Nevertheless, although he was perfectly familiar with the technique, he had made the initial mistake of permitting the Danish Government to know that it had a very eager buyer. Furthermore, the Lodge Bill of March 31, 1898, had proposed to authorize no less than $5,000,000 for the purchase.

Another year went by with nothing accomplished. In August, 1901, Swenson being absent on leave from his post, Hay, in despair, sent Henry White the second time to Copenhagen where his intrusion was again resented by both the American Minister and the Danish Government. While in Copenhagen White received the news of the death of President McKinley. He was able to do nothing except to report

---

[1] Aug. 23, 1900.
[2] *For. Rel.*, 1917, pp. 474 ff.; and, Hay to Swenson, Nov. 17, 1900.

that the Danes wanted more money. October 4, Swenson informed the Secretary that $5,000,000 would be required; Hay replied with an offer of $4,250,000, which was promptly refused. The Secretary felt that it would be necessary again to "take the sense of the Senate" before meeting the demands of Denmark. The Senate did not care one way or another about a few hundred thousand dollars. "The matter of price will cut little or no figure," wrote Senator C. D. Clark of Wyoming. The other Senator Clark had paid more for his seat than the entire amount in question.[1]

Not until January 24, 1902, three years after the inception of the official negotiations, did Hay have the opportunity to place his signature to the treaty. The Senate without delay advised ratification, February 17. But the Danish Government, as had been clearly foreshadowed for months, was unable to secure the necessary parliamentary approval. Fourteen years later, August 4, 1916, motivated even more than Hay had been by the fear of German aggression, Robert Lansing signed a new treaty with Denmark by which the United States paid $25,000,000 for the islands.

Quite possibly, if he had been at liberty to proceed with less haste, and if he had been a man to whom a few millions of dollars had seemed of less consequence, Hay might have succeeded. The importance of his effort is now purely historical, throwing light on the evolution of American policy in the Caribbean; and biographical, showing how John Hay's thrift, inbred from Warsaw, Illinois, remained with him through plenty, to the end of his days. Never penurious, he was, nevertheless, not conspicuously generous even in his personal affairs. He had been, all his life, accustomed to give freely, but in relatively small amounts.

The blue-prints of American policy in the Caribbean in 1900 called for a rough approximation of the British position in the Mediterranean: an unfortified, neutralized canal, with a series of naval bases to guard the lanes of traffic. Negotiations for the naval bases being well started, a canal treaty with England being before the Senate, Hay turned to the Central American states through which the canal was expected to pass. Behind him were some not perfectly patient men.

---

[1] The private correspondence in the Hay Papers covering the closing phases of the negotiation is extensive. It does not, however, add greatly to what has already been published by Professor Tansill. The official correspondence is in *For. Rel.*, 1917.

Senator John T. Morgan, seventy-six, fearful lest death might overtake him before the Canal was even begun, was one of Hay's most frequent correspondents and callers; with Morgan the canal had become an obsession. Even the President was impatient.

"Senator Morgan is just here," wrote McKinley, September 21, 1900, "and I have had a long talk with him about Nicaraguan matters. He is of the opinion that we ought to make some arrangement with Nicaragua that she will consent to treat with us concerning concessions, etc., without delay. I have already talked with you on this subject, and I know you took some steps in the direction of negotiations, but your illness and the grave questions which have been with us have prevented your prosecuting them to a conclusion. I want you to give the fullest consideration to the suggestions of Senator Morgan, and write me how we can best carry out such suggestions." Morgan felt that some understanding with Nicaragua would act as a leverage with the Senate which had adjourned in June without action on the Hay-Pauncefote Treaty.

Hay had not, in fact, been wholly neglecting the situation. The negotiations with the two Central American republics went forward rapidly and on December 1, Hay was able to sign protocols in which the two governments respectively engaged to make treaties as soon as the President should be authorized by Congress to acquire control of a canal zone.[1] The protocols were vague and there are not sufficient records out of which to reconstruct the conversations. At the close of 1900 the general outlines of the proposed treaties had been determined.[2] The very extravagant demands of the Central Americans were being reduced. The latter were prevented by their constitutions from ceding territory, but they could concede "in perpetuity" certain exclusive rights in a zone from coast to coast. It was contemplated that the United States would have the right to police the area, and, when necessary, employ naval or military forces for its protection. In return the republics were to receive lump sum payments and also "annuities." The amounts were still to be fixed by subsequent agreement, but the two republics were yielding to persuasion. In this latter respect the negotiations were taking the form of another real estate deal.

The final Senate amendments to the Hay-Pauncefote Treaty and

[1] *Dip. Hist. of the Panama Canal*, pp. 572–74.
[2] *Drafts of Treaties*, IV, Dept. of State.

the failure of England to consent to them, interposed delay. Meanwhile the partisans of Panama were beginning to gain ground. Negotiations with Nicaragua and Costa Rica were not resumed for another year and a half, but when canal matters again became active, the outlines of the desired agreement were at hand. It is worth noting, also, that nothing had yet occurred to disturb the friendly relations of the United States with Central America.

In summarizing the material accomplishments of the McKinley Administration in the Caribbean to September, 1901, it must be admitted that the actual results, aside from Porto Rico, and the Platt Amendment, were not notable. On the other hand, the second Hay-Pauncefote Treaty was all but ready for signature. The Virgin Islands negotiations were petering out, but all the ground had apparently been laid for the acquisition of a canal zone as soon as Congress should give its authorization. The hardest, the most tedious, work was over. There remained only to apply the principles which had been worked out. Not the least among these was courtesy.

Furthermore, when we consider the terms of the first Hay-Pauncefote Treaty in relation to the other steps which were being taken to insure the paramount military position of the United States in the Caribbean, the criticisms of the ill-fated treaty, now commonly accepted as valid, lose some, though of course not all, of their force. It should also be remembered that while on Hay's shoulders was loaded the opprobrium for having in his first canal treaty been too generous to England, many other very able men joined with him in fashioning the general plan of which the canal treaty was but a fragment. It is hardly fair to condemn the treaty apart from its context. The concessions in the canal treaty had been more apparent than real. The intent was to displace England as the paramount Power in the Caribbean.

Chapter XXIII   *"God's Language" and the "Cosmic Tendency"*

> Far be it from our principles of state
> On distant reefs and islands to display
> Our power and motives.

THE sonnet from which these lines are taken is undated, and was never published. It is to be found in a most unexpected place—in the private papers of one of the "noble Forty-eighters," Carl Schurz, the German radical, the liberal, the anti-imperialist.[1] The handwriting and sentiment are unmistakably Hay's, but of a period long before he, as Secretary of State, cabled to Paris for the American Peace Commission to demand of Spain the entire Philippine Archipelago; before he negotiated the transfer to American sovereignty of Pago Pago, one of the best harbors in the Pacific; before he sought to purchase the Virgin Islands; before the Platt Amendment was thought of. Before, also, Hay had initiated the long negotiations which culminated in the construction of an isthmian canal, American owned, operated, and defended, to provide an avenue from the newly acquired reefs of the Caribbean to the distant reefs of Hawaii, Midway, Samoa, and the Philippines.[2]

The sonnet marks a stage in the development of the political ideas

[1] *Schurz Papers,* Library of Congress.
[2] The entire sonnet is as follows:

> Thou little isle, afloat in western sea,
> Alluring bait to many a greater power!
> Oh, may we long postpone the evil hour
> When, in our zeal for making thee free,
> We join thee with us. 'Tis a foolish plea
> That thou, who seekest shelter like a flower
> Behind the fortress of a massive tower
> Still our advance guard in the world should be.
> Far be it from our principles of state
> On distant reefs and islands to display
> Our power and motives. It would take the might
> Of untold fleets to guard thee day and night.
> Nay, islet, keep thou in the distance, pray,
> And if thou fain wouldst join us, watch and wait.

This seems to have been inspired by the discussions over the proposed annexation of Hawaii at the time of the extension of the Hawaiian reciprocity treaty between 1885 and 1887.

not only of John Hay but of the American people, on the subject of insular possessions. The fact that the sheet on which the verse was written came into the possession of Schurz gives an added interest. Was the sonnet reminiscent of those far removed days of the Hayes Administration, when Hay and Adams had just found each other, when Schurz was Secretary of the Interior, when Hay, not yet escaped from the mood of his earlier verse and prose, used to find congenial hospitality in the Adams library to discuss European colonial policy? Those years marked the parting of the ways for Schurz and Hay. One moved step by step out from the Grand Old Party through mugwumpery and the *Nation* to the Anti-Imperialist League of 1898; the other slipped uneasily over into the school of younger prophets where he found himself, on the subject of territorial expansion, in the company of Henry Cabot Lodge and Theodore Roosevelt.

We are viewing another phase of Hay's adaptability. Never the prophet, he was always the interpreter of his age, whether it was vexed by Napoleon III, Bismarck, theological upheaval, industrial strife, bimetallism, or, at last, the islands of the western sea. There was no demagoguery in Hay, for that quality implies a desire to win votes or popularity. He desired neither. His harp was one upon which played the winds of the day, sounding forth the inarticulate and unformed wishes of the multitude. No one could count the voices to which he gave words, but in those instances where the purposes and opinions he expressed were submitted to the voters, usually Hay's side won. Whether we call it keeping step with the age or drifting out on a tide, it was Hay's most notable characteristic. He was not much given to philosophizing, but he was by no means unconscious that he was being carried on toward undreamed-of destinations. When he prepared his address for the opening of the Press Parliament at the Louisiana Purchase Exposition at St. Louis, May 19, 1904, he seems to have raised with himself the question of how it happened that he, who had once felt so differently, could for six years past have been agent for American territorial expansion. The occasion was the hundredth anniversary of the first chapter of the westward growth of the United States. "Jefferson was the last man in America of whom we could have expected this departure on the field of illimitable expansion, and Napoleon was, of all the sovereigns of Europe, the least likely to give up so vast an extent of empire." What is it that makes men do what they are least likely to do? "Cosmic tendency," replied Hay: [1]

No man, no party, can fight with any chance of final success against a cosmic tendency; no cleverness, no popularity, avails against the spirit of the age. In obeying that invincible tendency, against all his political convictions, Jefferson secured a conspicuous place in history; while the Federalist politicians, who should have welcomed this signal illustration and proof of their theory of the power of the Government they had framed, through the influence of party spirit faltered in their faith and brought upon their party a lasting eclipse through their failure to discern the signs of the times. . . .

This, gentlemen, is the lesson which we are called to contemplate amid the courts and palaces of this universal exhibition: that when a nation exists, founded in righteousness and justice, whose object and purposes are the welfare of humanity, the things which make for its growth and the increase of its power, so long as it is true to its ideals, are sure to come to pass, no matter what political theories or individual sentiments stand in the way. The common good will ultimately prevail, though it "mock the councils of the wise and the valor of the brave."

Hay was confident that he had been right, and yet had doubts. He could not quite forget the old discussions with Carl Schurz and Henry Adams. On the lips of the Kaiser such words as he had just uttered would have seemed to him as alarming as many of the speeches the German Emperor actually did make. "I know," he added, "what snares lie in this idea—how it may serve as the cry of demagogues and the pretext of despots. Woe be unto the nation which misuses it! but shame and dishonor is also the portion of those who fear to follow its luminous beaconing."

No doubt Hay was in part impelled to his conclusions on territorial expansion by his observations while ambassador in London, and the arguments of his English friends. The annexation of Hawaii, for which the sugar planters and navy officers had watched and waited so impatiently, took place while he was still at the Court of St. James's. Hay had no part in the transaction, but he approved. Spring Rice, then in the British Embassy in Berlin, sent Hay repeated warnings in private letters in the embassy pouch. He harped on the lessons of the Turco-Russian and the Sino-Japanese wars: "Don't let the Americans forget what happened. . . . Those who profited were not those who fought." He believed that Germany was likely to step in at the close of the war with Spain to demand compensations, probably

---

[1] *Addresses;* "The Press and Modern Progress," pp. 249, 250, 253.

Samoa. He urged that Hawaii be annexed promptly, before the close of the war, and not at a time when the action would be confused as belonging to the peace settlement.[1]

From the most responsible quarters assurances poured in to Hay that if Germany were to assert her claims, England would maintain a policy friendly to America. "Therefore, as I say again," wrote Spring Rice on May 7, 1898, "let us try while we can to secure what we can for God's language." Incompletely informed, enveloped in an atmosphere where a lack of candor made even the simplest conversations seem parts of a deep intrigue, Hay came to regard himself as the representative of a nation which was making its first venturesome journey along the Jericho road and certain to meet with thieves.[2] Hay agreed with Spring Rice. "I am extremely obliged for your kind letter. It is so precisely in line with my own ideas that I sent the substance of it to the President."

Thus, to a President who needed little urging, came from across the Atlantic the report that Germany was the power to be feared, while from across the Pacific spread the rumor that Japan was the one which had marked Hawaii for its own. By joint resolution of Congress, July 8, Hawaii passed under the American flag. The cosmic tendency was setting in.

From Hawaii to the Philippines was a long jump. Hay hesitated. He could give unqualified approval, as a part of the peace settlement, to the cession of Cuba and Porto Rico. As a director of the Western Union Telegraph Company, he could see the advantages of a cable station in the mid-Pacific beyond Honolulu, but at first he was reluctant to suggest the retention of more than a single coaling station. A month later, however, he disclosed, July 28, 1898, that his British friends were urging him on. "I may add," he telegraphed, "that British government prefer us retain Philippine Islands, or failing that, insist on option in case of future sale."

During that summer, Spring Rice came home from Berlin with his reports that the Kaiser was seeking to form an anti-American coalition.

[1] Gwynn, I, pp. 246–48, 251, 253. The originals of these letters are in the Hay papers.
[2] The publication of the correspondence of the German Foreign Office in *Die Grosse Politik der Europäischen Kabinette 1871–1914*, particularly Volume 15, has stripped most of the sinister aspects from the German ambitions in the Pacific. "The impartial historian," concludes Professor J. Fred Rippy, after a most exhaustive study, "will perhaps record the view that Germany was fully as 'moderate' as the United States in the Pacific phase of this war with Spain." *Latin America in World Politics*, p. 279.

He conferred with Chamberlain and Balfour; they in turn sent him on a secret mission to Hay. When questioned about it a dozen years later, Spring Rice was somewhat vague in his recital of the details but the import is plain.[1]

"I remember going down to Kent where J. H. was staying with the Camerons (at the Dering's place), and telling him, on behalf of J. C. that he would leave the Cabinet if the decision taken were the wrong one. 'Tell him to see if I am still there and he will know that it is all right.' I asked A. J. B. about it here, and he remembered that the attitude taken by himself and Chamberlain was such that there was practically no doubt as to the decision of the Government."

Thus fortified by the assurances of Chamberlain and Balfour, Hay came home to be Secretary of State. Standing alone he might have lacked the courage to demand the cession of the entire Philippine Archipelago, but with McKinley and the groups which were urging the momentous step, Hay could place himself in full accord. The cosmic tendency had him in its grip.

The next step was Samoa.

The acquisition of Samoa came not by scheming or diplomatic intrigue so much as by patient waiting. Under the treaty of 1872 the United States had a lease of a coaling station at Pago Pago. This treaty had not been terminated by the Berlin Act of June 14, 1889, under which Germany, Great Britain, and the United States had set up a tripartite supervision of the islands. In that act the powers agreed to respect Samoan independence and the free right of the natives to select their own king and to choose their form of government. A German firm had invested heavily and possessed the paramount commercial interests. On the other hand, the Chief Justice, to whose office the Berlin Act had assigned the responsibility of deciding a possible disputed election, was an American. The German consular officer was officious and aggressive; his British and American colleagues would not accept his leadership. There was constant friction. The trouble culminated in the attempt to elect a new king in the latter part of 1898. The election was disputed and the Chief Justice decided against the claim of the candidate who had been supported by the Germans. Up to this point the Department of State had assumed a passive attitude, merely insisting that the Powers must recognize the right of the Samoans

[1] Gwynn, I, p. 253.

freely to elect their own king. On the other hand, the German and British governments were in frequent, not always amiable, conversations. The British Ambassador in Washington repeatedly approached the State Department with suggestions which would have involved more aggressive measures than Hay was prepared to approve. It is difficult to determine whether the power most interested in Samoa was Germany, as Spring Rice had prophesied six months before, or England, which was seeking to forestall any measures her rival might take to acquire a major political as well as economic interest.

As conditions became more complicated in the islands, and as the tension in Berlin and London grew more threatening, Hay slowly relented. At Apia affairs became so bad that the cruiser *Philadelphia* was dispatched to the scene, arriving March 6. The American naval officers promptly supported the king in whose favor the Chief Justice had decided, and, ten days after their arrival, bombarded the forces of Mataafa, the German candidate. On the first day of April a combined American and British landing force was ambushed by Mataafa and several Americans were killed and wounded. The three governments were now required to take some concerted action. Otherwise their representatives at Apia would have dragged them into conflict with each other.[1]

Germany then took the lead, proposing a joint commission with full powers to visit Samoa, investigate the trouble, and restore peace. The United States promptly agreed, and England somewhat more slowly. The commission reached Apia May 13. The American Commissioner, Bartlett Tripp, brother-in-law of Senator Cushman K. Davis, quickly formed the conclusion to which all of the events of the preceding decade pointed, that the tripartite supervision was impractical. He recommended almost immediately that the United States retire from its entangling alliance and reserve for itself the benefits of the original treaty with Samoa. He established very cordial relations with von Sternburg, the German commissioner, already friendly to the United States and subsequently German Ambassador in Washington. The German government was equally of the opinion that the condominium should be abolished. At length the three commissioners signed a unanimous report that "the only system which can assure permanent pros-

---

[1] The correspondence is published in *For. Rel.* 1899, pp. 604 ff. See also *British Documents on the Origin of the War 1898–1914*, vol. 1; and, *Die Grosse Politik*, vol. 15.

perity and tranquillity is a government by one power." Tripp followed
the commission report with an urgent recommendation that the United
States acquire possession of Pago Pago. Hay had only to sit quietly
by. He did not have to wait long. Germany renewed her recommenda-
tions for the partition of the islands and volunteered that the United
States should retain Pago Pago, and the adjacent islets. Salisbury was
agreeable in principle, but did not at first see how two things, there
being only two important islands, could be divided among three.

The conversations between Germany and England then proceeded
independently of Washington, and on Nov. 14 the two powers reached
an agreement by which England retired from Samoa, gave Germany
certain small cessions in West Africa, and took the Tonga and Solomon
Islands. There was never any question as to Tutuila. Hay signed the
treaty December 2, and the Senate promptly advised ratification. A
few weeks later the Senate also approved of a treaty by which the three
Powers referred to the arbitration of the King of Sweden and Norway the claims arising out of the disturbances at Samoa before the
arrival of the Commission the preceding year.

Pago Pago was thus an apple tossed into the American lap in order
that it might cease to be an object of discord between Germany and
England. Viewed as an operation in European politics the settlement
of the Samoan question was a gesture of good will by Germany to
England; viewed from the American side, it was another piece of Hay
luck.

"I came to the conclusion a good while ago," wrote Hay to Henry
White, September 24, 1899, "that the Berlin Treaty could not permanently endure. The tripartite business has given nothing but trouble
and annoyance to us and to England from the beginning. Cleveland,
you know, was most anxious to get out of Samoa altogether. I think
that was a great mistake. We must keep our foothold there in the
interest of our Pacific work. But if we could get out of the tripartite
business and keep Tutuila, I should be very glad. . . . But of course
if England refuses, that ends the matter. There can be no compulsion."

"I was kept quite in the dark up to the last moment," Hay added
to Choate on November 13 following, "as to the arrangement between
Germany and England. The newspapers have announced without the
least reserve that England was to keep Samoa, and Germany to get
the Gilbert and Solomon Islands, or, as the boys with a natural remi-

niscence for the opera bouffe called them, 'The Gilbert and Sullivan.'
I should have been glad if you had squandered a little of the public
money letting me know by telegraph the true state of the case. . . .
Germany, it is true, has been excessively anxious to have the matter
concluded before the Emperor's visit to England, and, in their intense
anxiety, I am inclined to think they have somewhat lost sight of their
material interests in the case. . . . Our interests in the Archipelago
were very meagre, always excepting our interest in Pago Pago, which
is of the most vital importance. It is the finest harbor in the Pacific
and absolutely indispensable to us."

And so on another distant reef and headland Hay placed the sign
of America's power and motive.

Significant events in American history followed one another so
rapidly, as Hay swung out into the new currents of world politics, that
a day by day chronicle of 1899 is bewildering. American foreign policy
was touched with imagination. Hay was not uniformly the initiator,
nor was he ever solely responsible, but in an age of expansion surely
there is something to be said for having a poet to direct the foreign
policy. The ratification of the treaty of peace with Spain gave the cue.
Whether on the side of the angels or not, the Administration was keeping step with what the majority of the American people desired. The
United States now had a "Pacific work." Thence we may follow the
flag one leap farther into the Pacific, to the famous open door notes
about China.

As AN episode in the development of John Hay's career as Secretary of State, the correspondence relative to American commercial rights in China was something more than another piece of Hay luck, but there was in it a considerable fortuitous element. The Secretary was probably as little aware of how the notes would strike the American people as he was when he dashed off "Little Breeches" and "Jim Bludso" nearly thirty years before. Furthermore, it could hardly be claimed that he was the author of the notes. The ballads made him famous over night; the notes revived, as nothing else he had ever done, the fame of those early years. Indeed, the public invested this bit of diplomatic correspondence with the homely spirit of the ballads and recognized in both expressions of high principle: they seemed to breathe the spirit of American faith and philanthropy. That the notes were also the token that American political motives and purpose had advanced from the reefs of the Pacific to the headlands of China in one short year, and were giving concern in half a dozen of the world's great capitals, tickled American vanity.

"Is it impossible for this Government to exert some influence against China's partition? Has that gone too far?" inquired Paul Dana of the New York *Sun*, March 15, 1899. Many people thought so. China was becoming an escape valve for the results of the machine age in Europe. The Western world could produce faster than people could buy. Capital, also, was accumulating more rapidly than ways could be found for its profitable investment. "Markets, markets, markets!" cried Europe in alarm. China, with its swarming millions, without political cohesion or purpose, lacking also defense, and ports, and railways, seemed to offer the most immediate relief. Likewise, China was desired as the not very delicate make-weight to maintain the unstable political equilibrium of Europe. It is now an old story which needs no retelling, how, after the close of the Sino-Japanese war in 1895, the Powers descended upon prostrate China with the voices of friendship and the claws of vultures to demand trade concessions. Russia, France, Germany, England, Japan, all staked out their claims and ear-marked for their own those portions of the Chinese Empire which they proposed to grab when the break-up should take place.[1]

Of the events in China the American government was kept fully informed by its representatives in Peking but it was not until March 8, 1898, that the Department of State was required to make a definite decision. On that day the British Ambassador, immediately following the failure of Salisbury to make satisfactory progress for an understanding with Russia,[2] presented directly to President McKinley a "very confidential" memorandum, inquiring whether the United States would be disposed to join with Great Britain in opposing the Continental Powers in China. The Ambassador pointed out the two probable contingencies, either one of which might require action:

"There are two methods by which Foreign Powers may restrict the opening of China to the commerce of all nations, either by procuring leases of portions of the Chinese coast under conditions which would ensure preferential treatment to the Powers acquiring such leases, or by obtaining actual cessions of portions of the Chinese littoral." [3]

England was evidently alarmed about affairs in China, but the moment was very inopportune in Washington, as Hay doubtless would have advised the Foreign Office, had he been in London. He had not yet returned from his vacation up the Nile. The President had before him the bill which passed the House of Representatives the next day to force his hand by appropriating $50,000,000 for the pacification of Cuba. That was no time to talk about China. McKinley replied immediately that he was unaware that up to that time there had been any occupation of China which promised to interfere with American trade. He saw no reason for the departure of the United States from its traditional policy respecting foreign alliances and European entanglements.

Hay seems not to have been greatly impressed by the President's reply, for a month later he went to the Lord Mayor's dinner at the Mansion House and made his significant "partnership of beneficence" speech. In June, in a personal letter to the President, he reopened the subject of the British proposal, but McKinley was still engrossed with the war and directed Secretary Day to reply that the suggestion

---

[1] Tyler Dennett, *Americans in Eastern Asia,* chap. XXXII.
[2] *British Docs.,* I, p. 16.
[3] *Notes From British Embassy,* March 8, 1898, Dept. of State.

was still inopportune.[1] Day added, however: "The outcome of our struggle with Spain may develop the need of extending and strengthening our interests in the Asiatic Continent."

Meanwhile England, unable to reach an understanding in the East, busily followed one exchange of notes with another to make clear her rights at Weihaiwei, in the Yangtse Valley, and at length, at Kowloon, across the bay from Hongkong. The latter she regarded as a virtual cession of territory.

One other event of some importance in this sequence took place before Hay returned from London to be Secretary of State. Lord Charles Beresford, ostensibly representing the Associated Chambers of Commerce, set out upon his almost royal tour of the Far East. Before his departure he had a conference with the American Ambassador to unfold his plan. Hay advised him to consult with the Americans along the way. On November 20, 1898, Beresford reported from Shanghai that everywhere he had found Americans "most sympathetic to the idea of a Commercial Alliance with England based on the Integrity of China and the open door for all nations' trade." He hoped also that the British and American financiers would combine to develop the railways and other commercial enterprises in China. He spoke hopefully of his efforts to induce the Chinese government to create an efficient and well organized army under European officers. Beresford rushed on to Hankow and in a letter begun there, nine days later, and finished in Hongkong harbor, reported again that the Americans with whom he talked had been "in sympathy with the views I communicated to you before I left England. As America has got over 50% of the import trade with the north part of China, it is imperative for American interests as well as our own that the policy of the 'open door' should be maintained. I have every hope that in the near future the suggested Commercial Alliance between Great Britain and America with reference to the 'open door' in China may become an absolute fact."

These blithe assurances that the American government could be thus easily detached from its traditional principles of statecraft are amusing, but also of some importance in showing the degree to which Hay was being faced with the problem of how to prevent the partition of China. In a more sober vein Rounsevelle Wildman, consul-general

[1] Day to Hay, July 14, 1898.

at Hongkong, added some information in anticipation of Lord Beresford's arrival in Washington.[1] After stating that Beresford based "all his hopes of keeping the door open by enlisting the sympathies of America during his trip across the Continent," Wildman went on:

He led me to believe that England as a nation would admit the right of the United States to place a preferential tariff on American goods imported into the Philippines, and would hold up our hands against the criticism of the rest of the world that we had occupied the Philippines for mercenary rather than humanitarian motives. However, he will talk this all over with you.

No one in this Colony believes for a moment that American goods could be successfully imported into the Philippines if any form of the open door policy was adopted by the Islands. To England and Germany would fall 75% of the trade. Under the old Spanish preferential tariff, Spain had less than 13% of the entire trade of the Islands. Distance, freight rates, tariffs and the price of home labor are against the possibility of our competing with these nations.

Personally, I do not believe that at present our trade with China guarantees any great expense on our part towards aiding England to maintain the open door policy in China, for until the Nicaragua Canal is opened, I fear that our only exports to China will remain oil, flour, and cotton.

The outlines of the proposition emerge from these somewhat casual letters. In Chinese affairs England was looking for a friend. However, the British policy in China suggested the expedients of a bareback rider who had mounted two horses going in opposite directions. Salisbury wanted an open door for trade with all China but he also wished to have a sphere of special privilege. Now, having from the scramble in China extracted an uncertain share of the cessions and concessions, England desired American support to prevent the closing of the door to British trade in those parts of China which had fallen to the other Powers. The motive, however, was not exclusively economic; Russia was the nation from which England had most to fear, not only in China but also all across Asia and eastern Europe.

Those not well acquainted with American political sentiment are loath to believe that the time will never come when the American government will abandon its old policy of avoiding political alliances. In 1898 it seemed, as it had seemed so many times since then, that the turning point had come, that some form of close association with one or more transatlantic powers for a common political purpose was

---

[1] Wildman to Hay, Jan. 6, 1899.

inevitable. Beresford was not alone in his light-hearted enthusiasm. The British government, notwithstanding the rebuff in 1898, still clung to the idea that the logic of events in China would force the United States into more intimate relations with England. Overtures were renewed early in January, 1899. On the eighth of that month, in a personal letter, Pauncefote, by instruction of the Foreign Office, urged that the American government join England in a joint protest against the extension of the French Concession in Shanghai. Lord Salisbury felt that if the protests were made jointly their force would thereby be much increased.

"I am aware," argued Pauncefote, "that it would be a departure from the usual practice of your government . . . who, I believe, adopt the form of identic representations in preference to conjoint action, but the departure in the present instance might be justified by the special community of interest arising out of the new condition of affairs in China."

Much as Hay might have liked to yield the point at the moment when the Hay-Pauncefote Treaty was waiting approval in London, he was obliged to refuse. " 'Give and take,' the axiom of diplomacy to the rest of the world," Hay wrote,[1] "is positively forbidden to us, by both the Senate and the public opinion. We must take what we can and give nothing, which greatly narrows our possibilities."

Lord Beresford, after a more or less spectacular trip across the continent, arrived in Washington, February 21. In his honor that day Hay gave a luncheon for fourteen to which he invited many Senators, some army and navy officers, and, with that tact which never deserted him on such occasions, he included also "Speck" von Sternburg of the German Embassy. Beresford hurried back to England and rushed through the press *The Break-up of China,* in which he elaborated to some hundreds of pages the arguments which he had set forth, from Hankow to Washington, for a foreign-officered Chinese army, international patrol of Chinese rivers, a general reform of the Chinese Government and, of course, the "open door." But on top of his plan, like oil on water and not more easily disguised, floated the continuing spheres of influence and interest of Russia, Germany, France, and Great Britain. The publication of the book served to keep alive, even to increase, the discussion of the expected partition of the Empire.

[1] To Whitelaw Reid, Sept. 20, 1900. *Letters and Diaries,* III, p. 193.

John Hay had in the Far East the accentuated personal interest which grows out of frustrated desire. Persistent traveler though he was, circumstances always seemed to prevent a tour of the East which had captured his imagination many years before he became Secretary of State. One of the great disappointments of his life had been that when Henry Adams and John La Farge, like "school-boys on a lark," [1] set out upon their pilgrimage in the Pacific in 1890, he had remained at home. Adams did not on that occasion visit Japan and China, but from Sydney he wrote to Henry Cabot Lodge: [2] "On the whole, I am satisfied that America has no future in the Pacific. She can turn South, indeed, but after all, the west coast of South America offers very little field. Her best chance is Siberia. Russia will probably go to pieces; she is rotten and decrepit to the core, and must pass through a bankruptcy, political and moral. If it can be delayed another twenty-five years, we could Americanize Siberia, and this is the only possible work that I can see still open on a scale equal to American means."

It may never be possible to prove it to the satisfaction of the historian, but the guess is ventured that Henry Adams, in the opinion expressed above, which was no doubt reëxamined and discussed many times in the H Street houses during the next few years, laid the basis for Hay's Far Eastern policy. If this guess is correct it represents not only an exception to the general statement that Adams had relatively little influence on Hay, but also a substantial contribution by Adams himself to the political development of the modern world. Hay never even visited the Pacific Coast until 1901, when he accompanied McKinley on his last speech-making tour through the Southwest and up to San Francisco. The inability to have observed the Far East with his own eyes may have released Hay's imagination and may have given to the political situation in 1898–99 an emphasis possibly even stronger than if his earlier desire to visit those areas had been realized.

Next to Adams as the Secretary's instructor on the Far East was W. W. Rockhill. The latter, upon his return from Peking where he had begun his diplomatic career as a Secretary in the American Legation in 1885, had been a welcome guest at the Adams breakfasts. Rockhill had supplemented his brief political experiences in China and Korea by several years of study and exploration in Mongolia and

[1] *Letters of Henry Adams*, p. 429.
[2] *Ibid.*, p. 511.

Tibet; he knew and could support Adams's opinion about Russia in the East. In the second Cleveland Administration Rockhill served first as Chief Clerk in the State Department and then as Third Asst. Secretary. By President McKinley he was appointed Minister to Greece, Rumania, and Serbia, where his letters to Hay indicate that he was restless and unhappy. That the latter respected his ability and judgment is evident from the fact that Hay would have preferred to have him return to the Department as First Assistant Secretary of State in 1898. Rockhill resigned at Athens early in 1899 and, through Hay's influence, was made Director General of the Bureau of American Republics, now the Pan-American Union. From that position he became the Secretary's principal adviser on Far Eastern questions, supplying the personal experience which Hay lacked, but shaping the policy along the broad lines which Henry Adams had indicated as early as 1891.

As for the open-door notes, two other influences should be noted: the zeal of American manufacturers for the newly discovered market in Manchuria and in North China; and Alfred E. Hippisley, an Englishman who had served in China in the Inspectorate of Maritime Customs. Of these two factors the first needs only to be mentioned for it is well known: Hippisley, however, emerges from the dim background to which he has previously been assigned, as one who played a really important part. The notes so long assigned to Hay and then to Rockhill, were in substance, the Hippisley notes.

Late in July, after having already had a conference with Hay, Hippisley laid before Rockhill a suggestion which, within six weeks, became the kernel of the famous notes of September sixth. He pointed out that the spheres of influence in China must be accepted as facts, but something, he thought, might be done to prevent the creation within these spheres of preferential tariffs. A little, at least, might be saved out of the imminent wreck.

"I venture therefore to suggest," wrote Hippisley,[1] "that the United States lose no time in calling the attention of all the Powers to the changes now taking place in China, and—while disclaiming any desire on her part to annex territory—in expressing her determination not to sacrifice for her annually increasing trade and of the rights and privileges she has secured by treaty with China: and, to assure this

---

[1] Enclosure in Rockhill to Hay, August 3, 1899; also in the Hay Papers, Rockhill to Adee, August 19.

end, that she obtain an undertaking from each European Power that all the Chinese treaty tariff shall without discrimination apply to all merchandise entering its sphere of influence; and that by any treaty, ports in them shall not be interfered with." Unquestionably, here, not very felicitously expressed, is the substance of the open-door notes.

"This is, I think," continued Hippisley, "all that can be attempted now that events have reached the length they have; but it would do much."

When objection was made, presumably by Adee, that it would be politically inexpedient for the United States to make any proposal that could be twisted by critics of the administration into any resemblance of a policy cooperative with, or dependent upon, Great Britain, Hippisley replied on August 16:

My object in urging prompt action on the lines of my note of the 25th ult. was precisely to forestall any suggestion likely to prove injurious to the Administration that it was following the lead of or leaning towards England, by inducing it to take the initiative itself; then if England took similar action, she would follow America's lead. I think it would be suicidal for America to drift and do nothing for another year. My latest advices from Peking say: "the activity of the Russians in Manchuria is simply wonderful. . . . The Russification of Peking and North China will proceed as rapidly as has that of Manchuria." These are precisely the districts which are the great consumers of American textile fabrics, and I don't for a moment believe that the American manufacturers will sit by with folded hands and see these districts closed without making an effort to retain them. Pressure will therefore be brought to bear upon the Administration and it may have no option but to take some such action as I have suggested, with possibly, however, the difference of following instead of leading England.

Here, therefore, lies the secret of the origin of the famous open door notes which, for good or for ill, stated to the world American policy toward China for the next generation and, perhaps, until some distant day when the nations of the world will try with arms to realize what note-writing is not likely in this instance to obtain. By Hippisley's arguments Hay appears to have been convinced. Within two weeks, August 28, from the Holland House in New York, at the Secretary's request, Rockhill forwarded to Newbury a memorandum from which the notes were written, with slight verbal changes. In another week they were on their way to be presented in the great capitals of the world.

We should not overlook the fact that this declaration of policy in 1899 was limited in scope. Both Hippisley in his letters, and Rockhill in his memorandum, accepted the spheres of influence as accomplished facts which could not be changed. The notes were designed to forestall an emergent situation, to safeguard American commercial interests in event of China's partition. Apparently Rockhill and Hay in 1899 were both prepared to acquiesce in whatever steps the Powers might take, provided they did not disturb American commercial rights. Rockhill's recommendation, completely accepted by Hay, was a direct request that the Powers give the following formal assurances: (1) that they would in no way interfere within their so-called spheres of interest with any treaty port or with vested rights in it of any nature; (2) that all ports they might open in their respective spheres would be either free ports, or that the Chinese treaty tariff at the time in force would apply to all merchandise landed or shipped, no matter to what nationality belonging, and that the dues and duties provided for by treaty would be collected by the Chinese Government; and (3) that they would levy no higher harbor dues on vessels of other nationalities frequenting their ports in such spheres than would be levied on their national vessels, and that they would also levy no higher railway charges on merchandise belonging to or destined for subjects of other powers transported through their spheres than would be levied on similar merchandise belonging to their own nationals.

"In other words," explained Rockhill, "we should insist on absolute equality of treatment in the various zones, for equality of opportunity with the citizens of the favored powers we cannot hope to have, in view of the well-known method now in vogue for securing privileges and concessions, though we should continually, by every proper means, seek to gain this also."

The notes were addressed to England, Germany, and Russia. Subsequently France, Italy, and Japan were also approached. Each Power was invited to give formal assurances that in its sphere the rights outlined by Rockhill would be recognized. No treaty or joint action of any sort was contemplated. Thus by simple agreements in language which any one could understand the American Government sought to bind the Powers to respect some of the rights which China had granted to all under her fundamental treaties. As for technique, it was simple, straightforward, shirt-sleeve diplomacy. The Powers were placed in a position where direct refusal was all but impossible.

The answers were, without exception, in some greater or less degree evasive. Great Britain would make no pledge about Kowloon, but as for Weihaiwei and all territory hereafter to be acquired by lease, or otherwise, and similarly as to all spheres of interest then held or to be acquired, the requested declaration was made, contingent upon a similar agreement by the other Powers. Germany would agree if the others would. Russia was so evasive as to leave the entire proposal deflated. Count Mouravieff replied on December 30: "As to the ports now opened or hereafter to be opened to foreign commerce by the Chinese Government, and which lie beyond the territory leased to Russia, the settlement of the question of customs duties belongs to China herself, and the Imperial Government has no intention whatever of claiming any privileges for its own subjects to the exclusion of other foreigners."

Even this wordy statement, in which Russia had as clearly excepted her leased territory in Manchuria as England had excepted Kowloon, was qualified by the requirement that the other interested Powers should make similar declarations.[1]

Notwithstanding these qualifications and hedgings, Hay calmly announced in a circular March 20, 1900, that all the Powers had assented to his proposal and that in each case he considered the assent "final and definitive." What began as straightforward diplomacy thus ended in diplomatic prestidigitation such as Hay had tried once before in London in the fur-seals correspondence and failed to accomplish. It would have taken more than a lawyer to define what new rights had been recognized, or required, or even what had actually been said, but such comment is beside the point. These notes had not been put forward by a lawyer as a contribution to the law of nations but by a publicist to crystallize public opinion.

Hay was well aware that Mouravieff's response was worth very little. "Our object is now to give the widest significance to the Russian reply of which it is capable," he wrote privately, January 22, 1900, to Charlemagne Tower, American Ambassador at St. Petersburg:

Without running the risk of bringing upon ourselves a contradiction of our assumptions, we want to take it for granted that Russia has acceded to our proposals without much qualification. If it were safe for us to quote Count

[1] The final replies are published in *For. Rel.*, 1899, pp. 128–42.

Mouravieff's expression to you in conversation, which you reported to us, that Russia will do whatever France does, that, coupled with the full and definite acceptance of our proposition by France would be sufficient to interpret the answer of Russia in a fuller sense than its mere text would warrant. We do not want to run the risk of Russia refusing to be bound by that oral promise given to you to do whatever France does. . . .

I was very much interested in your despatches which preceded the final one, in the temper which Count Mouravieff showed, and the slight tinge of resentment there was in his words at being forced into a corner and compelled to reply categorically to our proposals. I had the same experience here with Count Cassini. He protested rather vehemently at one time against the extent of what he called our "demands," saying, "You do not yourself see the vast portée of them." I did not choose to contradict him, but I thought I saw the portée of them perfectly well. . . . I am convinced that Cassini would have stood out against us here almost indefinitely if I had not by my instruction to you shifted the field of discussion from here to St. Petersburg.

I think we may all congratulate ourselves on a most fortunate outcome of the entire transaction, and in this last stage of it I am most anxious to assume every thing possible as being settled, and, at the same time, not give occasion to any protest from Russia in the way of limiting her assent which would give an excuse for any other Power to withdraw from the general acceptance of our proposals, based on the supposition that all the Powers were to agree.

Mouravieff declined to enlarge his original statement. He did not object to having the American government regard his reply as favorable but he was unwilling to have it interpreted in the sense of the less qualified assent from France. He very strongly protested against the expression "open door." Mouravieff asked Tower to write to Hay that he hoped the term would not be employed in connection with Russia, explaining that "it is not a true expression, in any event, for Russia does not intend for instance to throw open the door at Port Arthur." [1]

"The truth is," reported Tower, "that the Russian Government did not wish to answer your propositions at all. It did so finally with great reluctance, but it did so because of the desire upon its part to maintain the relations subsisting between the two countries, which it would not on any account disturb. It went a great way, as Russian diplomacy goes, when it put into writing the answer which you now have. . . There is probably nothing in the whole course of international relations so distasteful to the Russian government as the necessity to bind itself by a written agreement where such course is not absolutely

[1] Tower to Hay, February 12, 1900.

unavoidable."

The Hay notes gave increased currency to a new slogan to which all chancelleries would be required to do at least lip service for a long time. These notes became the starting points for a long series of subsequent agreements and declarations, the effect of which has been to hold the Powers somewhat at bay while China still wrestles with the same internal problems which Lord Beresford published to the world in 1899.

For John Hay, personally, the open door notes did more than all of his more substantial achievements. The phrase itself, although he did not coin it, did not even use it in the notes, adhered to him and by popular imagination was dramatized. "Is it indeed true," inquired Samuel Mather, in amazement, from Cleveland, "that you have secured written pledges from the Great Powers of our treaty rights with China, good in event of complete partition?" [1] The public generally was even less exact: the author of "Jim Bludso" had saved China—that was the way the public took it. By popular acclaim John Hay became a leading statesman of the world. His leadership, thus advertised, made easier all that he subsequently undertook. This man, who all his life had seemed to lack courage, now, by a stroke of the pen, put the Powers on notice. Never before a leader of anything, John Hay became more than any other person, the leader, however unwillingly they might follow, of all the Powers interested in the Far East. He had neither sought nor expected such a portion, and was probably as surprised as we are today, when it was thus thrust upon him. Such are the rich rewards for those who have the prescience to discern the cosmic tendency as well as the true destiny of "God's language." Thomas Jefferson was one who had that gift, and John Hay was another.

The most immediate effect of the open door notes was a strengthening of Hay's position in England.

"I congratulate you very much on your success in procuring declarations from all the great Powers in respect to commerce in China," Choate added to a private letter, January 6, 1900, while he was wrestling with the rights of neutrals in the Boer War. "It has obviously made a great and very favorable impression here."

---

[1] Samuel Mather to Hay, January 15, 1899 [1900].

More material for the bricks which had to be made without straw.[1]
Viewed in the light of their British origin and the other concurrent
negotiations between Washington and London, one ventures the sug-
gestion that the open door notes, together with the acquisition of the
Philippines and Samoa, represented part of the price paid by the
United States to secure the practical withdrawal of England from the
Caribbean.

[1] The figure of speech is from a letter to John W. Foster, June 23, 1900, which is
quoted at length on p. 334. The "straw" which the Secretary would have found it
convenient to use would have involved the concurrence of the legislative branch of the
Government. With little prospect that such action could be obtained, Hay made his
bricks without it, *i. e.*, by offering concessions which did not require legislative approval.
The figure of speech is useful, of course, only when limited to the narrower sense. It
does not imply that Hay was clever enough to get something for nothing.

THE Rockhill memorandum was premised on the "probability of complications soon arising between the interested powers in China, whereby it will be difficult, if not impossible, for the United States to retain the rights guaranteed them by treaties with China." [1]

The vague promises evoked by this very modest request were discouraging, but distinctly heartening must have been the popular approval with which the notes were greeted. The persistent tendency to interpret them for more than they were worth indicated that public opinion might have supported demands for more than Hay had timidly asked in 1899.

Within three months after Hay had acknowledged the receipt of the final answers and declared the agreement in force, the expected complications burst upon the world with unexpected force. The Boxer "uprising," as Hay chose to call it, provided him with an opportunity to advance the statement of policy one long step further. From vague promises of an open door he moved forward to more solid ground, seeking assent also that the powers would "preserve Chinese territorial and administrative entity." Many people thought John Hay was a timid man; his Boxer policy in the summer of 1900 was a very bold stroke.

The events of the Boxer uprising—one of the most dramatic episodes in modern history—are well known. Enraged by increasing taxes, by the failure of crops following a drought, and by the ever-pressing and importunate demands of the foreigners for special privilege, the populace of North China, led by fanatics, and secretly encouraged by the Empress Dowager—Old Buddha, rose to drive the "foreign devils" into the sea. The attack centered upon the missionaries whose annoying demands had been one cause of the outburst, and upon the foreign Legations. The Powers were caught unawares. Before the middle of June the foreigners were driven into the Tartar City at Peking where most of them took refuge in the grounds of the British Legation. Communications were cut off and a siege began

[1] Dennis, p. 212.

which lasted until relief from an expeditionary force appeared over the walls August 14. During the greater part of the time it was believed that many, if not all, of the foreigners had been massacred.

In two important respects the Powers were unprepared to deal with the situation. There was at hand no adequate military to create an expeditionary force. Even more desperate was the lack of any plan, or leadership, adequate to cope with the problem, which, as well as being military, was political. It embraced not merely China, not alone the Far East, but even the peaceful relations of the great Powers of the western world.

In company with the other foreign ministers, Hay at first took refuge in what he chose to describe to Henry Adams,[1] facetiously, as a "craven opportunism." "I do what seems possible every day— not caring a hoot for consistency and the Absolute—and so far, I sleep o' nights, in spite of universal war and a temperature of 99° steady. How long I can stand it is another question. Always doing the thing I know is wrong must be in time ruinous to the Immortal Soul—but that I can charge to the American people whose fault it is."

The opportunism, while it lasted, was required, in part, by the absence of authentic information both from China and from the capitals of Europe, but in greater part by the fact that the Republican National Convention met in Philadelphia June 19, and the Democrats followed at Kansas City July 4. "Imperialism," and the misuse of executive power, were to be the paramount political issues in the United States for the next four months. The Boxer uprising, like the Russo-Japanese War which followed it four years later, and the frequently recurring occasions for intervention by military force in the affairs of Central American states, carried with it the temptation for the Executive to strain, if not to abuse, the discretionary powers conferred upon him by the Constitution.

What Hay would have done if he could have had a free hand, unrestrained by the charges of the Democratic stump-speakers and the pleadings of Republican party managers, is speculative. The tasks which he actually set for himself were to preserve entire freedom of action for the American Government, to hold the other Powers in line for the single purpose of rescuing the beleaguered foreigners and then of reëstablishing order in China. He tried to do it in such a way as

[1] July 8, 1900.

to thwart the suspected ambitions of the Powers to make use of the situation for increasing their privileges, or possessions, in China at the expense of each other as well as of the Chinese people.

Prior to the accomplishment of the relief of the Legations Hay made four moves on the international chessboard, each one favored by the usual Hay luck, which, together, built up his policy.

The first, taken after a Cabinet meeting, was blind, but safe. To the American minister in Peking, E. H. Conger, he telegraphed, June 10: [1] "We have no policy in China except to protect with energy American interests, and especially American citizens, and the legation. There must be nothing done which would commit us to future action inconsistent with your standing instructions. There must be no alliances."

Obviously the telegram was political, like the Perdicaris telegram four years later, and in the interest of harmony and patriotic enthusiasm in the approaching Republican Convention. The message was immediately given to the press.

Of more immediate importance, however, was the action of a very literal-minded American admiral the next week at Taku, below Tientsin, just as the convention was opening in Philadelphia. Admiral Louis Kempff, in command of the naval force which had been ordered to Taku as the first step for the protection of the foreigners, was suddenly confronted with a situation for which his orders made no provision. The other admirals decided, as a precautionary measure for assuring access to Tientsin, to demand the surrender of the Chinese forts below the city. Forty-one years before, almost to a day, and in the same place, the American Commodore Tattnall, confronted by a very similar situation, had cast discretion to the winds, and, with the cry that rang around the world, "Blood is thicker than water," had jumped into the fray. He even helped the British to serve their guns when Admiral Hope lay wounded on the deck. Kempff was of a very different temperament. Orders were orders. He did not feel that he was authorized to initiate an act of war against a state with which his country was at peace. The other naval forces bombarded the forts but Kempff drew aside.[2] The American press, his brother

---

[1] *For. Rel.,* 1900, p. 143.
[2] Telegram, via Chefoo, Kempff to Secretary of Navy, June 20, Secretary of Navy to Secretary of State, June 20, 1900, Dept. of State.

officers, and even the President were disposed, on first reports, to be critical. Both the White House and the Department of State withheld comment, but within twenty-four hours it seems to have dawned on the Administration that Kempff's decision, while less adapted to headlines than Tattnall's had been, was much sounder. The Chinese interpreted the attack on the forts as an act of war and began to close in on the improvised relief expedition which was already well advanced toward Peking. Admiral Seymour was forced to turn back. It was not until the fourth day of the following August that the international force at Tientsin felt itself strong enough to start out again for the capital. Kempff raised a fundamental question: was the United States at war with China? Hay jumped at the question and answered in the negative.

A war with China would, in the United States, call for the assembling of Congress; in Europe it would unleash the hunger for conquest; in China it would consolidate the Chinese people behind the Boxers. Hay drew a fine distinction. The United States was not at war with China; it was, on the contrary, merely gathering a relief expedition to protect American life and property.

The other Powers fell in line. Three days later the admirals at Taku issued a notice to the provincial authorities that they intended to use their arms only against the Boxers and those who opposed the march to Peking.[1] The effect was immediate in China. The two viceroys at Nanking and at Wuchang, on the Yangtse, at once conveyed to Wu Ting-fang, the Chinese Minister in Washington, the assurance that they were able to keep the peace and protect the foreigners in their areas, provided the naval forces did not take the aggressive. Hay replied, June 22, that the President had no intention of sending any American military or naval forces into any parts of China where they were not needed. This information was also immediately communicated to London, Berlin, Paris, St. Petersburg and Tokio. England professed to be following the same policy for localizing the conflict, but, in spite of the requests of the viceroys that there be no naval demonstrations on the Yangtse, decided to send a vessel to each treaty port on the river.[2]

Even as between the United States and England, whose policy was

[1] *For. Rel.*, 1900, pp. 251–52.
[2] China No. 3, (1900), pp. 66–67.

most nearly in accord with Hay's, there was this subtle difference already appearing, that the American Secretary was trusting a little more to persuasion. As late as August 22, the German Emperor was asserting that there was war; [1] he was, at least, legally right. No government declared war on China. Thus the uprising was isolated in the North. It is very doubtful whether any one had the foresight to realize in the middle of June what an advantage was to result from such a course. A month later Hay was disposed to lay great emphasis on it but it would appear, from all available evidence, that the decision was just one of those happy ones which lucky opportunists sometimes stumble into.

"The only thing," he wrote to Adams, in the letter quoted above, "was to localize the storm if possible, and this we seem to have done. All of the Powers have fallen in with my modus vivendi in the Central and South. If any arrangements can be made at all, it can only be by isolating Tuan and Tung fuh Siang [Chang Chi-tung]—and this seems, now, not impossible.

"I need not tell you the lunatic difficulties under which we labor. The opposition press call for impeachment because we are violating the Constitution and the pulpit gives us anathema because we are not doing it enough. McArthur wired Root that taking one regiment from Fil's would lose us the archipelago. But we go on. We shall have our quota at Taku in a few days. All the Powers treat us as a central Hello office, and we strive to please the public.

"If I looked at things as you do in the light of reason, history and mathematics, I should go off after lunch and die, like Mouravieff." [2]

Hay's second move was deliberate, and bold.

While Lord Salisbury was gravely intriguing to secure assent from the Powers for Japan to send twenty or thirty thousand troops into North China for the double purpose of hewing a path to Peking and off-setting the Russians; while Germany was persistently misunderstanding the Salisbury scheme, and planning to claim the leadership because among all the ministers in Peking only the German had been murdered; while France was timidly assenting to any plan so long as it appeared to be agreeable to her Russian ally, Hay came forward

---

[1] *British Docs.*, II, p. 8.
[2] Count Mouravieff, Russian Minister of Foreign Affairs, died of apoplexy June 21, 1900.

with a frank declaration of purpose which was designed once more
to assist China to become her own door-keeper. Underlying the
schemes of all the other foreign offices was the principle of military
intervention on a large scale. Hay's proposal was very different.

The famous circular of July 3, which had been approved by the
President in Canton without the change of a word, repeated the conviction that the condition in Peking was one of virtual anarchy
whereby power and responsibility were practically devolved upon
the local authorities. While proposing to hold the authors of the existing outrages to the utmost accountability, Hay reaffirmed the desire
of the American Government "to remain in peace and friendship"
with the Chinese people. As an earnest of this desire he declared that
it was the policy of the United States "to seek a solution which may
bring about permanent safety and peace to China, preserve Chinese
territorial and administrative entity, protect all rights guaranteed to
friendly Powers by treaty and international law, and safeguard for
the world the principle of equal and impartial trade with all parts of
the Chinese Empire."

Unlike the notes of September 6, 1899, the circular did not require
an answer. The American representatives abroad to whom it was
sent, were instructed merely to communicate its purport to the foreign offices. However, Hay eagerly awaited for responses.

The circular was designed to be heard in three places. Issued the
day before the meeting of the Democrats at Kansas City, it was
prefaced by the statement that the United States was adhering to
the policy toward China which, under very similar conditions, the
Democratic Buchanan Administration had declared at the beginning
of the Anglo-French War of 1858. Hay's declaration offered no opportunity for the Democrats at Kansas City to criticize it. As for
the Powers, the words were carefully chosen and skillfully put together. Without using the words "open door," it affirmed the "prin
ciple of equal and impartial trade in all parts of the Chinese Empire'
—a far stronger phrase than Hay had ventured to use in the notes
of the previous year. The circular went even farther, to the funda
mental proposition of the integrity of China, and a Chinese adminis
tration which in the future would be freed from such European in
terference as had for two generations been encroaching on its liberty
as a sovereign power. It offered a platform on which the Powers could

unite, provided they did not intend to use the opportunity for the promotion of selfish purposes. In the third place, the declaration was designed to consolidate the local authorities in China outside of the Boxer zone and place them in a mood which would make them more useful, ultimately, than all the troops which Europe could scrape together.

This bid for Chinese support would have seemed even more absurd if the world had then known that, on the very day the circular was issued, the Empress Dowager in Peking had stopped the bombardment of the French Cathedral for several hours, not as a respite to the foreigners, but because she and several of her ladies were on a picnic in the palace grounds and the noise of the guns gave her a headache.[1]

For formal responses from the Powers, Hay waited in vain. From none of them did he ever have a direct reply which he cared to publish. Lord Salisbury, quite preoccupied with his plan to draw the Japanese to his side against Russia, saw Choate at the end of a busy day and expressed an emphatic though hurried concurrence, but Hay's circular did not make much impression as a practical measure.[2] Delcassé, in the Chamber of Deputies, July 8, scorned the idea of a declaration of war, but made no mention of Hay.[3] Germany, preoccupied with plans to avenge the murder of von Kettler, discussed with France and Russia a declaration of war,[4] but did not make it, and on the 12th von Bülow declared before the Foreign Affairs Committee of the Bundesrat that Germany desired no partition and regarded as of first importance the maintenance of a good understanding among the Powers.[5] The next day, in replying to the British proposal about Japanese troops for China, Russia substantially endorsed the circular but did not mention it. Count Lamsdorff defined the "fundamental principles which have already been accepted by the majority of the Powers" as "the maintenance of union between the Powers; the maintenance of the existing system of government in China; exclusion of anything which might lead to partition of the

---

[1] Harley Farnsworth MacNair, *Modern Chinese History Readings*, Shanghai, 1927, p. 594.
[2] *For. Rel.*, 1900, p. 345.
[3] France Despatches, July 12, 1900; Porter to Hay, Dept. of State.
[4] *Die Grosse Politik*, Vol. 16, pp. 44 ff.
[5] Germany Despatches, July 13, 1900; Andrew D. White to Hay, Dept. of State.

Empire; in fact, the reestablishment by joint efforts of a legitimate central Government capable of assuring order and security." [1]

Upon receipt of a copy of the text of the Russian statement, Hay felt warranted in giving to the press the text of the circular, with the following comment:

It embodies the views to which this Government has strictly adhered from the very beginning of the present troubles and which the different Powers have one by one taken into favorable consideration. The view announced at the start by the President that we did not consider ourselves at war with the Chinese nation, and that all our efforts should be directed to localizing the disturbances in the Province of Chih-li and keeping them from spreading throughout the Empire by enlisting on the side of peace the powerful Viceroys of Central and Southern China, has now apparently been adopted by all the other Powers. It is too soon to prophesy the ultimate results of this policy, but thus far the indications are all favorable.

The statement also called attention to the fact that there had not been any "formation of groups or combinations of Powers of any sort whatever." The relations with France had been particularly cordial.

So far, so good.

On July 11, Hay had another inspiration, or intuition. The Chinese Minister handed to him an imperial decree of June 29 which had come by special courier from the board of war in Peking to the treasurer of Chih-li Province and thence to the taotai of Shanghai who had forwarded it to Minister Wu. The decree had been ten days on the way but it proved that there still existed, however circuitous, a channel of communication with Peking, where the Legations had been cut off for a month. It occurred to Hay that by utilizing Wu Ting-fang, it might be possible to communicate again with Peking by the same route over which the decree had passed. The Secretary proposed the experiment to Wu who was eager to be of service. In cipher, therefore, July 11, Hay sent Conger the brief message, "Communicate tidings bearer." The telegram, sent forward by Wu, reached its destination in five days. On the 16th Conger replied, in cipher:

"For one month we have been besieged in British Legation under continued shot and shell from Chinese troops. Quick relief only can prevent general massacre." The Chinese Minister received the mes-

[1] *British Docs.*, II, p. 4; Great Britain Despatches, July 18; Choate to Hay, Dept. of State.

sage at the breakfast table, July 20. Breathless and proud, he delivered it, still in code, to Hay.[1] Adee nervously decoded and pronounced it genuine.

The world was incredulous. Only six days before, the newspapers had carried an apparently authentic report that the foreigners in Peking had been massacred. Plans were already well advanced in London to hold a memorial service in St. Paul's Cathedral. Hay stuck to his belief that the foreigners were alive, and although the other foreign offices were slow to credit the Conger message, the Secretary was within a few days able, in a variety of ways, to prove its authenticity. This was just the sort of diplomatic work for the press to dramatize, and Hay's fame for cleverness went to the ends of the earth.

From the sensational success with the message emerged the third step in American policy, to build up confidence in the local Chinese officials. Again Hay was able partially to carry the other foreign offices with him, although he had to meet a growing popular hysteria in which the Chinese were being portrayed as nothing less than barbarians.

China was not slow to follow up the advantage which Hay had made possible. On the same day that Wu delivered the message from Conger, he received a communication from the Emperor of China for the President. The Chinese Government, now plainly alarmed and even a little repentant, begged the United States to devise measures and take the initiative in bringing about a concert of the Powers for the restoration of order and peace.[2] This appeal gave Hay an opportunity. Through the President he replied, naming three conditions which must first be complied with: public assurance by the Chinese Government that the foreign representatives were still alive; free communication for the ministers with their governments; and co-operation by the Chinese authorities with the relief expedition which had not yet left Tientsin.[3]

The same day the Secretary had instructed Consul General John Goodnow to interview Li Hung Chang, who, as newly appointed viceroy of Chih-li, had recently arrived in Shanghai on his leisurely ap-

[1] *For. Rel.*, 1900, pp. 155–56, 280.
[2] *Ibid.*, p. 294.
[3] The draft of the reply was read over the telephone to the President at Canton. McKinley removed from it a few words which would have conveyed an intimation that the United States might, as an alternative, resort to the use of military force in a large way: "to use all the resources at its command." Olcott, *William McKinley*, II, p. 243.

proach to Tientsin. The Viceroy, when asked to declare his purpose, replied that he hoped to persuade the Throne to send the Ministers to Tientsin, after which he hoped that the military operations of the foreigners would be suspended.[1] It was a highly impertinent suggestion. "Power to deliver at Tientsin presupposes power to protect and to open communications. This is insisted on," replied Hay. Five days later Conger was permitted to telegraph General Chaffee, in command of the American troops at Tientsin, and, August 10, Minister Wu delivered, in cipher, a message from Conger to the Secretary of State. Free communication had, in fact, been granted by imperial decree of August 5.

For the moment Hay's work was done. The ninety-nine degrees, steady, coupled with the strain of carrying forward a policy which at times had seemed almost childish in its assumptions, had worn the Secretary down and induced an acute attack of the disorder which, five years later, caused his death. On the train to New Hampshire, whence he was fleeing, he caught a cold which aggravated the trouble.

"Please do not, for a day or two, send me anything that is not necessary. I am forced to be very quiet for the moment," he scrawled with pencil on a rough sheet to Adee. The Secretary was very ill.

On August 14 the expeditionary forces, unaided by the Chinese, released the foreigners in Peking. In other respects Hay's confidence had not been misplaced; there had been no massacre, von Kettler and a secretary of the Japanese Legation alone having been murdered. It may never be possible to prove that John Hay saved the lives of the imprisoned foreigners. The fact cannot be overlooked, however, that for at least eight weeks the Boxers, led by Prince Tuan, had the Legations at their mercy, and did not overpower, as they so easily could have done, their flimsy defense. Something stayed their savage hands. The use of force at Taku early in June, far from intimidating the Chinese, had stirred them to new frenzy. No doubt the slowly assembling military forces, and the capture of Tientsin, had a sobering influence. But most important appears to have been the temperate, conciliatory policy of McKinley and Hay, which strengthened the moderate party. If the Chinese had at any time resolutely pressed the attack the foreigners could not have saved themselves. The expeditionary force liberated them, but long before that time some one

[1] *Ibid.*, p. 260.

had been the cause of sparing their lives. Many believed that it was John Hay.

Hay's success had two other aspects.

In the United States he had converted what promised to be a liability to his party in the political campaign into an important asset for the administration. The American Government had not been involved in any European entanglement, it had done at least its share to save the lives of the foreigners, and in place of the open-door commercial policy, the motive of which had been essentially selfish, Hay had presented a new slogan, more inclusive, more fundamental, and essentially philanthropic: the integrity of China. With little regard for party lines the American people were accepting the leadership of John Hay; he had reached the pinnacle of his personal success.

In Europe, while Hay's leadership was never acknowledged, the Powers, each still unable to find the opportunity it sought to advance its own ends, substantially adopted the declaration of war aims which Hay had written, because no Power dared to propose any different purpose. The concert of the Powers had thus far been preserved. Only at one point was there immediate danger of divergent aims. The American Government stood consistently for moderation, for placing primarily upon China the responsibility to deal with its own disorders. Europe still clung to the idea that so much trust could not be placed in either Chinese good faith or intelligence. On this point the United States and Germany occupied the extreme opposite positions, the other Powers being ranged between. The ensuing conflict in China centered about this difference of opinion and motive.

JUST as phrases from the Pike County Ballads followed Hay to the end of his life, and quite misrepresented the personality of their author, so was it with the catchword, the "open door," which was not even his. People continued in 1900, and to this day, to assume that the "open door" and American policy in China were equivalent terms. They were not. In place of the "open door" of the notes of September 6, 1899, Hay had, by the circular of July 3, 1900, attempted to substitute "the territorial and administrative entity" of China, and the "principle of equal and impartial trade with all parts of the Empire." The attempt was not crowned with complete success. He had also added the "protection of foreigners," the "establishment of safety and peace," as well as "guarding and protecting all legitimate American interests." These were commonplace phrases but more nearly within the range of attainment. As to method, he had affirmed the intention of his government to act concurrently with the other Powers. Even the method broke down, measurably, within a year. In the thirteen months which remained of the McKinley Administration after the liberation of the foreigners in Peking, Hay, still undiscouraged, set out bravely on the first leg of a long journey, on which, as these lines are being written thirty-two years later, the American Government is still only moderately advanced.

In the summer of 1900, Hay had taken great satisfaction that his circular had operated to unite rather than to divide the Powers. His was a European as well as a Chinese policy. Twice during July he had been quick to prevent the impression that he was working in closer cooperation with one Power than with another. The exigencies of the presidential campaign, the hunger of the Republican Committee for Irish and German votes, as well as the precarious international relations in Europe demanded great caution at this point. For the sake of securing cooperation the American Government relapsed into playing a lone hand. So great, however, was the suspicion of Hay's Anglophilism that the public was slow to believe the facts.

The Democratic *Brooklyn Eagle* commended the July circular, but slyly suggested that, "possibly the British Minister for Foreign Affairs was familiarized with the terms of the document before the other European diplomats had a chance at it." Hay instantly wrote to St. Clair McKelway to correct the misapprehension.[1]

"I must thank you for the leader in yesterday's *Eagle* on the Chinese circular. I am under great obligations to you for your kind opinion and your powerful support in this as in many other matters." Then, after quoting the objectionable surmise, the Secretary added: "I wish to say, purely for your own information and not for any public reference, that no Power whatever was consulted in advance as to the terms of the circular, and that it was delivered by our Ambassadors on the same day to all the Powers. We have been particularly anxious to avoid, and even to do what we could to prevent, a splitting up of the Powers into groups and combinations, and so far successfully. Everybody told us that we would find France, in alliance with Russia, opposed to our views, but this has, fortunately, not been the case. The French Government has been in close and constant accord with us from the beginning. I do not mean to say that the action of Russia has been hostile, but, perhaps on account of the absence of the Ambassador from Washington, there has not been so much communication between us as with some of the other Powers."

In presenting the circular to Lord Salisbury, Choate had made a slip, adding a sentence from which it might have been inferred that the *Eagle's* surmise was correct. In a tactful personal letter the Secretary asked Choate to withdraw his note and substitute another.

"The reason for this will, I imagine, at once occur to you," wrote Hay, July 18. "The note of the 3rd of July was identical in its terms, and, so far as I know, has been so presented to all the Powers. When the correspondence comes to be published, as sooner or later everything gets into print, the note presented by you to England conveys an impression of unity of action with that country differentiating our relations with England from those we hold with other Powers. I think it rather important that such an impression should not obtain currency in this country or elsewhere."

It was inevitable that, to maintain the concert, in due time some concessions would have to be made. Germany presented the first situa-

[1] July 12, 1900.

tion of this sort. The Kaiser desired to send Field Marshal Count von Waldersee to command the international army which the German Emperor evidently expected to play a controlling part in the settlement of China's affairs. Underlying the scheme was an assumption, in direct conflict with the Hay policy, that the main reliance was to be upon military force and intimidation. In a courteous telegram, signed by Adee, the American Government welcomed the services of such a distinguished officer, but there was in the note a qualifying phrase: "for any combined military operations in which the American troops take part after the arrival of that officer in China to attain the purposes declared by this Government in the circular note delivered to the Powers under date of July 3." It was not expected that Waldersee could arrive in China within much less than two months. The relief expedition was already well advanced toward Peking. A new hand was apparent in the drafting of American diplomatic notes. It was that of the Secretary of War, Elihu Root, to whom the invitation, as a military measure, was referred. The American acceptance only looked like a concession to Germany but it probably seemed satisfactory to German-American voters.[1]

"I congratulate you on your management of the Chinese case," wrote Hay to Adee, August 9. "It is nearing its critical stage. I wish I were there to help work with you but I know that you and Root will handle it better than I should."

The next Power to be placed in good humor was Russia.

A Chinese imperial edict, the text of which reached Washington August 12, named Li Hung Chang as Chinese plenipotentiary to negotiate with the Powers.[2] The Legations had not yet been set free, but more than two weeks earlier Hay had anticipated the time when negotiations would replace military operations by sending Rockhill to the Far East to survey the ground. The other Powers were still preoccupied with military plans. They were unprepared to consider negotiation and some of them, especially England, were still less prepared to recognize Li Hung Chang, whose previous relations with Russia were decidedly suspect. Nevertheless the American Govern-

---

[1] The reply to Germany as originally drafted and read over the telephone from Secretary Root's office (Olcott, II, pp. 246 ff.), was less qualified than the note in final form. The President wished to make the reply more cordial than as Root, or Adee, had written it, but eventually still further qualifications were added, notably the reference to the circular of July 3.

[2] *Ibid.*, pp. 285–86.

ment promptly recognized the wily Viceroy as having sufficient powers for the moment. It was not until September 22 that Lord Salisbury could bring himself to give assent to any negotiations with Li Hung Chang and with Prince Ching, who, meanwhile, had been associated with Li.[1] From Lake Sunapee, Hay approved the decision to deal with the Viceroy. He knew that Li was "an unmitigated scoundrel,"— "thoroughly corrupt and treacherous." "But he represents China and we must deal with him; and it is certain that it has been, hitherto, to our advantage to deal with him, with Liu-Kun-Yih, and with Chang-Chi-Tung, as if we trusted them." [2]

Of more significance was the evident desire of Russia, first to prevent the expeditionary force from entering Peking at all, and the subsequent proposal, August 29, that the Powers withdraw both legations and troops from the capital. It was believed that Russia was seeking a private understanding with China and that she would, in due time, put in a substantial claim upon China in return for what looked like an interposition in the latter's behalf. The Russian proposal of the 29th argued with some force that, the Court having fled from Peking on the approach of the expeditionary force, and its return being improbable while the foreign armies were in possession of the city, the date at which negotiations might be initiated was uncertain.[3]

The proposal was timed to coincide with the needs of the McKinley campaign. Stung by the Democratic charges that he was misusing his powers, nervous also about the complications in China which might follow the arrival of Count von Waldersee, the President would have liked nothing better than to have been able to say that, the relief of the Legations having been accomplished, he had ordered the withdrawal of American troops. Upon receipt of the Russian suggestion the Cabinet was summoned to what proved to be a long meeting. Adee was invited to attend. It was reported in the New York *Tribune* the following morning that the Cabinet had spent the entire day drafting the reply to Russia. The draft was finished that afternoon and put on the wires. The next day the newspapers carried the headlines that the American and the Russian troops were to be with-

---

[1] *British and Foreign State Papers*, Vol. 94, p. 1284.
[2] Hay to Adee, Sept. 14, 1900.
[3] *For. Rel.*, 1900, pp. 374; 1901, App., p. 19.

drawn from Peking. A similar report in London and on the Continent.
caused consternation. The reported decision of the American Government appeared to indicate a radical change of policy in several respects. If true, it meant that the United States had decided to break
up the concert, and that it had gone over to the side of Russia, placing
itself in opposition both to Great Britain and to Germany. Waldersee
was on his way to command an army which would have been largely
dispersed before his arrival.

The Cabinet may have given much attention to the note and Adee
is known to have made the first draft, but there was only one man
present who could have put together such a reply as went to Russia.
The circular of July 3 had been as clear and incisive as a cameo; every
time one looks at the note of August 29, it means something different. Several paragraphs were made up of single sentences fifty or
more words long. Each sentence began with a generous agreement with
Russia and dwindled through successive qualifications, to little or
nothing. Actually, the American Government seems to have been inviting the other Powers to agree with it not to withdraw.

"The result of these considerations is," read one of the less complicated paragraphs, "that, unless there is such a general expression
by the Powers in favor of continued occupation as to modify the views
expressed by the Government of Russia and lead to a general agreement for continued occupation, we shall give instructions to the commander of the American forces in China to withdraw our troops from
Peking, after due conference with the other commanders as to the
time and manner of withdrawal."

"How will you swap a murdered Old English Alliance for a nice
new clean Russian article painted yellow?" jovially asked the Secretary of War.[1] "I hope you take the frustration of your hellish designs
with complacency. . . .

"It appears that diplomacy, as viewed from the opposition American
standpoint, has but two phases. If we agree with any Power on any
subject there is a secret alliance; if we disagree there is a conspiracy
to get up a war and foist a soldier on the back of every American
laborer."

There can be no doubt but that Secretary Root had given the Hay
policy an unexpected turn.

[1] Root to Hay, Sunday, September 4; Dennis, p. 231.

"Anxious, therefore, as I am to get away from Pekin," wrote Hay,[1] a little apprehensively, "I cannot help fearing that if we retire with Russia, it will end in these unfortunate consequences: Russia will betray us. China will fall back on her *non possumus*, if we try to make separate terms with her. England and Germany being left in Pekin, Germany by superior brute selfishness will have her way, and we shall be left out in the cold. . . ."

The hungry reporters seized on the apparent change of policy at the beginning of September to publish reports that Hay was sulking in New Hampshire because Root had reversed his policy. The rumor was enlarged upon to make it appear that all through August, Mr. Adee had been letting the Hay policy slip until it had become pro-Russian. The New York *Times*, September 16, carried such a story. Mr. Root clipped and enclosed it to Hay with a scrawl:

> And so from hour to hour
> We ripe and ripe,
> And then from hour to hour
> We rot and rot.

Hay seems to have sensed the situation but he was, none the less, a little disturbed, both because of the injustice to Adee, and because of the possible effect in London. His letters to Adee were full of affection and approval, while to Choate he wrote, September 8:

It seems a hopeless task to try to correct misapprehensions, and I take it for granted that you do not share the errors of European papers & chanceries about our Chinese policy. Our Yellows go so far as to say that I am sulking away from Washington because the President and Root have turned me down &c. I need not say this is stupid lying. We have all been absolutely at one from the beginning and are now. Root writes me "Until this last round we had nothing to do but stick close to the lines you had laid down and there was really nothing to decide. But the approach of the much prepared Waldersee seemed a peril. There was danger that after all the Emperor's windy eloquence he might feel the necessity of kicking up a row to justify the appointment of Waldersee. I was very glad therefore that the Russians gave us an opportunity to say that we wd. stay under definite understanding and not otherwise. It begins to look as if there was some chance for the Open Door after all."

Adee, referring to the story that we have thrown over England and allied ourselves with Russia says: "If you break up a quiet whist party by saying,

'Well, I'm going to bed, are you?' and I have to go, the game being spoiled, does it follow that I go home with you and get into your bed?" "The point is," Adee continues, "that Russia has invited us and the other Powers to no agreement. She does not propose to submit her action to the chances of a vote of the Powers. We, on the contrary, invite an international accord in the opposite sense, in the hope of persuading Russia to recede, but we are careful to avoid inviting them to join us in an anti-Russian League."

I believe that we shall be the gainers in the end. I addressed some weeks ago a serious inquiry to St. Petersburg about New Chwang and have received a reply, most positive and satisfactory, that their occupation was military and temporary and that our commercial interests should not in any case be limited or injured. . . .

I am decidedly better these last days, but I was in bad shape when I arrived here, and even now my Doctor, while he says there is nothing much amiss, says I am not to think of Washington for a while, under penalty of worse things happening. All which is very dull.

The papers were half right. The President desired to extricate the American Government from China as soon as possible. Even back in July he had proposed that Americans in the danger zones outside of North China should be brought down to the coast. Hay had gently argued him out of the idea.[1] It is at least possible that even McKinley had not quite caught the meaning of the note of August 29. At any rate, in the midst of his front-porch campaign, he returned to the subject very soon. "Is there any further reason known to you," he inquired, September 9, in his own handwriting—unusual for him—and with less patience than was his custom, "for keeping our troops in Peking except for [a] guard to [the] Legation. And what would you say to sending Conger to [a] Seaport town, leaving him whatever Guard he wants?" The President enclosed a telegram from General Chaffee which seemed to favor such a course. Two days earlier he had forwarded, without comment, a letter from Senator Morgan strongly advocating it. Morgan argued that to remain in China would involve not only war with the Chinese, but also other grave entanglements: with Russia, which would surely hold what she had and perhaps grab more; and with Germany, which appeared to the Senator to be planning a war with either China or the other Powers. The tone of Morgan's letter was threatening.

Hay sought to quiet the President but the latter was not satisfied and renewed the discussion September 14. "I know of no way to get out but

[1] Hay to McKinley, July 6, 1900.

to come out, . . ." argued McKinley. "I have this general notion that we should get out of Pekin with the least possible delay. Russia is intending to withdraw and we should in accordance with our note, even if there was no other reason, and I think there are many reasons why we should come out. We want to avoid being in Pekin for a long time and it must be a long time if we stay there for diplomatic negotiations, and without our intending it, we may be drawn into currents that would be unfortunate.

"My idea is after Tien Tsin we should take all our troops to the Philippines, have them put in a good camp, keep the force intact and in good condition and be ready for any emergency in China. In the meantime I feel very greatly concerned about American citizens, converts, and others, as to what we should do with them. It is clear to me that when we bring Conger and Chaffee away we ought to bring all with us who desire to accompany us to Tien Tsin, and those who do not wish to accompany the forces ought to be brought to the coast where they can be protected by our ships. The number of ships there can be increased at any time and I am thinking very seriously of having it done. Do you see any objection to this suggestion?"

Hay was, for a few days, in a very tight place, clearly opposed to the President's policy. Fortunately for Hay, telegrams from Conger and Chaffee, received while McKinley's letter to Hay was in the mail, led the President to postpone action in the matter.[1]

"Thus far there have been no mistakes," wrote Hay, with relief, September 24.[2] But American forces, which in September amounted to 5000, were rapidly reduced and by the end of the year less than two-fifths remained.

The chronicle of the daily events and interchanges from the first of October, when Hay resumed active direction of the Department of State, until September 7, 1901, when representatives of eleven governments signed the Boxer Protocol, is, at best, a dull tale. To repeat it here would discourage many and might also obscure the broad issue which was: how much should be conceded, especially in Manchuria, to maintain the semblance of a concert of Powers which had such conflicting ambitions and pretensions?

Throughout the summer of 1900 the Hay policy, while firm, had been

[1] Hay's very firm reply to the President is printed in Dennis, p. 233.
[2] To Adee.

designed to make the fullest possible use of existing Chinese agencies, such as the Southern Viceroys, with a view to building up rather than tearing down the semblance of a Chinese government. The decision of the President—the McKinley policy—to withdraw American troops at the earliest possible moment carried with it the necessity that in settling differences both with the Chinese and with the Powers at Peking, the American Government would abstain from intimidation and threats. The Anglo-German agreement of October 16, 1900, to which extended reference is made below, introduced new factors, diverse, contradictory, and hard to classify; it did not strengthen the concert which had been maintained through the summer, and left the American Government continually tempted to concede in fact what it denied in principle.

Much depended upon hastening the opening of direct negotiations with the Chinese. The longer the Powers delayed, the greater the opportunity for disagreement among themselves; the longer the foreign troops remained, the greater the indemnity to be demanded, and the greater the demoralization of Chinese administrative machinery. The first task was to promote among the Powers an agreement which, in turn, could be presented to China.

The negotiations for a formal protocol, the equivalent of a treaty of peace, began in January, 1901. The American Government was most of all concerned that the total indemnity be fixed at a figure not above China's capacity to pay, and that the method of payment be so arranged that the Chinese Administration would not be thereby crippled in function. The total was at length put at a third of a billion dollars, of which the American share was $25,000,000. But for the United States the total would have been larger.

"It is true that the proposal of the United States to scale down the indemnity," wrote Commissioner Rockhill, who had replaced Conger as American plenipotentiary, May 25, 1901,[1] "has not met with the approval of a single one of the Powers, but our insistence in the cause of moderation has unquestionably been instrumental in forcing them to limit their demands. Had it not been for our endeavors, China would, without a doubt, have been obliged to consent to infinitely harder terms than those which will be probably submitted.

"In numerous other ways have the United States been able to exer-

[1] *For. Rel.*, 1901, App., p. 175.

cise a moderating influence in the councils of the Powers, while still maintaining the concert, which, clumsy as it undoubtedly is, is still, as long as it exists, a tolerable guarantee of the maintenance of Chinese integrity and of equal trade privileges for all the world."

The Protocol conferences in Peking revealed many differences of opinion, large and small, but the real drama was withheld from the public gaze and, at the time, was only vaguely referred to in the published correspondence. The grave problem was Russia which insisted that Manchuria was not a part of China; that questions relating to the northern provinces could not properly be brought before the conference at all; that Russia had, in fact, acquired there, as well as at Tientsin, new privileges "by right of conquest"; and that she was at liberty to make with China a separate treaty which was not reviewable by the other Powers.

When, at the end of the preceding August, Russia was inviting the United States to withdraw from Peking, Count Lamsdorff had declared verbally to H. H. D. Peirce, American chargé, that Russia had no intention whatever of seeking or retaining "a single inch of territory in either China or Manchuria." [1]

"Russia has been more outspoken than before in her adhesion to the Open Door," declared Hay to Choate, a few days later, "and though her vows are false as dicers' oaths when treachery is profitable, yet in this case it is for us to take care that treachery shall not be profitable." Hay wrote this, however, before he had received the President's letters insisting upon the withdrawal of the American troops.

The far-famed policy of the integrity of China had a grave defect. The circular of July 3 had replaced the open-door notes as a definition of American aims, but it had made no impression on the Powers as offering a basis for definite agreement. In sparing the lives of the foreigners in Peking while the Powers were mobilizing their forces at Tientsin, it had been of service, probably of very great service; in helping to preserve the concert until the Legations were relieved, it had been useful; but it was by no means an engagement of the Powers with one another, notwithstanding Hay's repeated assurances that it was substantial. One foreign minister after another had assented in general terms, but none had cared to repeat in writing and sign the pledge about the territorial and administrative entity of China. For

[1] *For. Rel.*, 1900, p. 372.

a few weeks the Powers had been permitting John Hay, as, later, another group of Powers permitted Woodrow Wilson, to speak for them, but while he talked they had their tongues in their cheeks. In the confidential correspondence, which passed between London, Paris, Berlin, and St. Petersburg, now published in England and Germany, the Hay circular was rarely, if ever, even mentioned.

Hay saw a clear coincidence of American and British interests in the Far East, particularly in North China and in Manchuria. The commercial advantages of the two Powers would be best served by the adoption of the principle of equal and impartial trade with all parts of the Chinese Empire. Any restriction of this principle was potentially, if not actually, a threat to the United States as well as to Great Britain. In point of fact in about half of China this freedom was imperilled. Even in the Yangtse Valley the British assertions of special privilege had not been recognized by her competitors. There was suspicion that the German pretensions in Shantung were much larger than had appeared from any published document, that they might include claims to the valley of the Yellow River and reach even to the north bank of the Yangtse. Furthermore, the seizure of Newchwang early in August and the appropriation of the railway line thence to Peking, confirmed the broadest suspicions as to Russian designs. The railway was mortgaged to British bondholders. If the Russians and the Germans were to come to an agreement in North China, if also the Chinese capital were to remain at Peking, argued Francis Bertie of the British Foreign Office, the two Powers, even without the partition of the Empire, would be able to control China to the detriment of England.[1]

Under such circumstances one might have expected Lord Pauncefote to be a frequent visitor at the Department of State in the summer of 1900. Quite to the contrary. This was the time selected for a complete refurbishment of the old embassy building on Connecticut Avenue. Lord Pauncefote moved to Newport in June, and the communications with Washington were neither frequent nor important. At the beginning of the China trouble Hay had found the British Ambassador uncommunicative and, apparently, without instructions. In August, Root was equally puzzled. Perhaps the British Foreign Office, remembering the pits which lay in the path of Sackville-West twelve years before, was

[1] *British Docs.*, II, pp. 1–11.

helping Pauncefote to "pull Hay through," to recall Henry Adams's expression, by avoiding even the appearance of cooperation. Pauncefote did not return to Washington until the presidential election.

On the other hand, it was in North China that American commercial prospects were brightest. Any diminution of commercial privileges in that region would touch what promised to be the best American market in China.

"If it were not for our domestic politics, we could, and should, join with England, whose interests are identical with ours, and make our ideas prevail," Hay wrote Adee on September 14. "But in the present morbid state of the public mind toward England that is not to be thought of—and we must look idly on, and see her making terms with Germany instead of with us." The last clause is significant, for, although the Anglo-German Agreement was not concluded until October 16, and the terms were withheld for another four days, the Secretary was evidently informed that the conversations had already begun.[1] The source of his information is unknown; probably it was Spring Rice, Joseph Chamberlain, or both.

The Anglo-German Agreement purported to be an engagement between the two Powers to uphold the principle of the open door and the policy of maintaining undiminished the territorial condition of the Chinese Empire. The two signatories reserved for themselves to come to an understanding to protect their own interests in case any other Power sought to make use of the existing complications to secure a territorial advantage, and invited the Powers chiefly interested in China to accept the principles thus set forth. There was in the language some faint echos of the July circular, but there were also vague terms and qualifying phrases of which Hay may not have been at first informed.

The American evening papers of the 20th first carried the news of the agreement. Hay read the report on the train returning from Princeton where he had just received an honorary degree. The next day he wrote to his wife that the news, on top of the enthusiasm with which he had been received at Princeton, made "the 20th of October a great day in my little life." [2]

---

[1] *British Docs.*, II, pp. 7–16; *Die Grosse Politik*, XVI, pp. 199 ff.

[2] In his very short address at Princeton Hay had made a brief reference to the position of the United States among the Powers: "We can no longer cling to the isolated position among the nations that we formerly rejoiced in." New York *Evening Post*, October 20, 1900.

"When I got on the train," he wrote,[1] "I saw in the evening papers the news of the Anglo-German agreement to defend the integrity of China and the Open Door. This was the greatest triumph of all. Lord Salisbury proposed this to me, before I left England. I could not accept it, because I knew that unspeakable Senate of ours would not ratify it, and ever since I have been laboring to bring it about without any help, and succeeded as far as was possible for one Power to do it. Now these two great Powers who are not dependent upon Senates, come together & form a compact to confirm and fortify my work. . . ." [2] When Lord Pauncefote communicated to him, October 23, the official text of the agreement, he replied politely two days later: "I have received your letter of the 23rd of October and also the text of the Anglo-German agreement, which you have been so good as to send me. You are right in guessing at the purport of my answer. I note what you so kindly say about my copyright. My friend, Mr. Adams, when asked to take part in the movement for international copyright, some years ago, refused on the ground that the dearest wish of his life was to be pirated. I can heartily express the same sentiment in the present situation."

Perhaps the Secretary had not yet detected the jokers. However, already he must have had suspicions. The next day, October 25, he was able to point out to the President correctly the "true inwardness" of the agreement which in another letter he described as "a horrible practical joke on England," as, in fact, it was.

"I enclose a draft of an answer to the Anglo-German agreement note," he wrote to McKinley. "You will see that the object I have aimed at is, first, to express our gratification at the two great Powers having planted themselves firmly on the ground of the open door and the integrity of the Chinese Empire, second,—to keep ourselves free from any entangling alliances in the matter; and, third, to intimate that we do not suspect any Power of any ulterior intentions outside of the purposes which they have already avowed.

"I inquired of Jackson at Berlin and Choate at London, several days ago, what they could find out in regard to the true inwardness of the

---

[1] The letter itself is undated; in *Letters and Diaries*, (Vol. III, p. 200) the date is incorrectly given as October 31, a fact which has misled many.

[2] For the circumstances under which the first and second Salisbury proposals to the American government had been declined, see pp. 285–86; Hay's memory had played him somewhat false.

agreement. I have heard nothing from Choate, but Jackson wires me that in the course of the negotiations Germany proposed restricting them to the Yangtse Valley. Great Britain wished to take in all of China, including the Amoor District and Manchuria. To this Germany objected as it was thought that it might offend Russia, and 'all Chinese territory as far as they can exercise influence' was adopted as a kind of compromise. In Berlin, Jackson says, the agreement is not considered as directed against Russia. My impression from the beginning has been that the whole scheme started with Germany and was intended to guard herself against being discriminated against in the trade of the Yangtse Valley which England has preempted as her sphere of influence." If Hay had had before him all of the correspondence which is now published to the world he could have added only one other significant fact, namely, that in promoting the agreement the German Emperor had sought also to weaken, in the aging mind of Lord Salisbury, the confidence which the latter had hitherto shown toward the United States.

In the Anglo-German agreement Hay actually lost whatever prospect there had been a few months earlier that he could draw England, Japan, Germany, and the United States together in agreement on the terms of the July circular. In negotiating the treaty, and subsequently in explaining it, Germany took the ground that Manchuria was not a part of China, and Great Britain acquiesced. This novel idea carried with it the repeated assertion in the next few months that Germany regarded the Russian designs in Manchuria as legitimate, although, perhaps, a trifle premature. October 16, 1900, became a very important date in modern history, the significance of which was directly contrary to what Hay had at first supposed. Actually, it marked the defeat of his China policy; from that time onward he was engaged in rear-guard actions, saving only fragments of a thwarted purpose.

For the sake of still maintaining the semblance of accord Hay recommended that the United States adhere to those parts of the Anglo-German agreement which purported to support the open door, and the President agreed. It became, however, every day more clear in Peking that Russia was determined to break away from the concert and undertake separate negotiations with China, probably as soon as the preliminary agreement of the Powers was signed.

On January 8, 1901, Conger telegraphed that, according to reliable information, China had consented to separate negotiations with Russia, and four days later he enclosed a text of a preliminary agreement, the effect of which would have been to place Manchuria as much under the control of Russia as, for example, was Bokhara.

It was to meet such a situation as this that the third article of the Anglo-German agreement had stated that "In case of another Power making use of the complications in China in order to obtain under any form whatever such territorial advantages," the two signatories would come to an understanding as to the steps to be taken to protect their own interests. Japan had adhered to the agreement and sought to discover what England was now prepared to do. Early in February the two Powers warned China not to make with any Power any arrangements affecting her territorial rights. A few days later Germany also issued a warning but quite different in tone. Germany advised China not to conclude a separate treaty before the Powers had agreed on the amount of the Chinese obligations which would result from the Boxer uprising. In other words, China should not dissipate her assets before her creditors were satisfied.[1] This notice, however, was immediately followed by private and then public assurances to Russia that the ultimate fate of Manchuria was a matter of indifference to Germany.

Hay thereupon seized one more opportunity to recall to memory his circular of July 3. In a note to the Chinese Minister, February 17, he stated that it would be "unwise and dangerous in the extreme" for China to make any such arrangements as those reported from Manchuria. He desired to impress China with "the impropriety, inexpediency and even extreme danger to the interests of China" of making such arrangements, at least without the full knowledge and approval of the Powers which were still in conference in Peking. He based his warning on the fact that "the preservation of the territorial integrity of China" had been recognized by all the Powers then engaged in the joint negotiations, and he referred specifically to the July circular.[2]

Hay's note was the strongest, but it was a blank cartridge. Within a month the President decided to withdraw all troops from China, leaving only a Legation Guard. Though Rockhill protested "strenuously," the Secretary was able to telegraph him only that the order could not be reversed; that the best Rockhill could hope for was that

[1] *British Docs.*, II, p. 24; *Die Grosse Politik*, Vol. 16, pp. 312 ff.
[2] *For. Rel.*, 1901, App., pp. 363–64.

the date of complete withdrawal might be postponed again from week to week.[1] Russia, in turn, yielded not to England, Japan, and the United States, but to Germany; she decided to defer, but not to abandon the prosecution of her Manchurian plans.

To some extent time was on Hay's side. It would never be possible to accomplish in China all that Hay had set out to do in 1900, but some of the objects, unobtainable by frontal attack, were in the way of realization through a realignment of the Powers. In due and logical sequence the formation of the Anglo-Japanese Alliance followed the renewal of Russia's demands on China. Its terms were announced early in 1902. Two years later Japan launched her attack on Russia while England, and also the United States, looked on benevolently.

The doctrine of the integrity of China was a noble conception, philanthropic and also in accord with American interest but, pressed to its logical conclusion when the Powers could not agree to the *status quo* in either Europe or Asia, it involved intervention in a region where American interests were actually very small. The best that could be hoped for, the preservation of the undiminished historical relation of Manchuria to the Chinese Empire, promised to the United States no benefit proportionate to the responsibilities which would have had to be assumed.

[1] Rockhill to Hay, March 19, 1901; Dept. of State.

THROUGH many of John Hay's letters during and after his illness in 1900 runs a note of disappointment and frustration. They were, in part, the letters of a sick man.

"This old tabernacle which I have inhabited for sixty years," he explained to Whitelaw Reid, September 1, when exaggerated reports of his illness were current, "is getting quite ramshackle in the furnace, the plumbing and the electrical arrangements." Poisons were backing up into his system, depressing his spirits and causing him to brood. By such letters he should not be judged. On the other hand, having made due allowance for the situation under which the letters were written, they supply important clues for a broad general statement of Hay's ideas of a proper foreign policy for the United States, such as he never ventured to place on paper.

To his old Scottish friend, Sir John Clark, September 18, he wrote:

I was kept in Washington long after the time at which our capital becomes intolerable by various diplomatic complications. When at last I was able to get away, I went to pieces all at once from heat and exhaustion and have had six weeks of disgusting invalidity. I am no longer at the age when repairs are quickly made to the inner economy; and besides if I felt a little better on any day, the evening mail was sure to bring me some annoying news or inquiry which nullified the advantage gained. But I am now, I hope, decidedly better and am counting on going back to my work on the 1st of October.

The worst of it is to have so many "fool friends" in the Press who make a point of standing by the State Department when I am in Washington, and whacking it right and left when I am away, saying "This is not what Hay would have done"—when perhaps it was precisely what I have advised and directed.

Take it all together I shall be glad to finish at the first hour when I can get out with honor and propriety. If my health lasts, I shall stay until next spring, when I shall cease to be *héritier présomptif* to the Presidency. I see no reason as yet to doubt that McKinley will be reëlected. But even in that case, the composition of our Senate, and the original constitutional error which gives a third of that body a power to veto on treaties, render it impossible for me to carry out the policies which I have cherished all my life, and in which I have the loyal support of the President and my colleagues in the Cabinet. So like many another better man before me, I find power and place when it comes late in life, not much more than dust and ashes. I have done some good—all I could do under the circumstances—and the failures I foresee in the wrangle of next winter, though they may discredit me, will leave the results of my work untouched.

Such a letter raises the question as to what policies there were, which he had cherished all his life, policies which the President and Cabinet approved, but which he, now at the height of his influence, was prevented from carrying out. There were many more such letters.

"I did not imagine when I left Washington, how bad it was," he replied to the anxious inquiry of his old friend Nicolay,[1] the man who had known him longest and most intimately. "If I had stayed another day I should not have got away at all. I have had two or three slight complications—the last and most agreeable is a lumbago which makes me walk slantendicular, so I don't walk much."[2] He went on:

In fact, I have lived—and there is not much more to expect. My dreams when I was a little boy at Warsaw and Pittsfield have absolutely and literally been fullfilled. The most important part of my public life came late, but it came in precisely the shape I dreamed when I was a boy. There has been less public speaking than I anticipated, but that is the only difference. I will do myself the justice to say I never thought of the Presidency, but I have been next to it—only one life between—for a year. I should have thought that this close proximity would be an object of care and anxiety, but it has never given me an instant's thought. My work has been easy to do, and not worrying. The thing that has aged me and broken me up has been the attitude of the minority of the Senate which brings to naught all the work a State Department can do. In any proper sense of the word, Diplomacy is impossible to us. No fair arrangement between us and another Power will ever be accepted by the Senate. We must get everything and give nothing. . . .

On the twenty-fifth of September, after the President had so clearly disclosed his intention to withdraw the troops from China, Hay wrote Adams that he had "dawdled up here for two months, most of the time abed. But I am now able to 'sit up and take nourishment,' and to walk two miles up hill. So that I have no excuse for further shirking. I go to Washington the last of this week, if nothing prevents. The papers, which try to be good-natured, say things have gone to the Adversary in my absence and only my presence at the Capital can save the floundering State. But Adee has done nothing I would not have done, and

---

[1] August 21, 1900; *Letters and Diaries*, III, pp. 184–85.
[2] Evidently the original letter, which is not in the Hay Papers, was edited at this point by an omission.

he has more sense than the whole gang of newspaper men and politicians. I shall take pleasure in telling them so. They talk like—what they are—about our duty to boss the job in China, to force the other powers to follow our lead when we have no army, and no central government. . . ." Hay had been disillusioned.

The last sentence reminds one of another in a letter to Adee: [1] "The talk of the papers about 'our preëminent moral position giving us the authority to dictate to the world' is mere flap-doodle."

Hay continued to brood, and the following summer, a month before McKinley's assassination, he wrote to Adams from Newbury: [2]

I am going to Washington again next week. There are a dozen or so jobs to attend to—and then the President wants me to go to Canton to talk things over. I go, I hardly see why. I have no conceit about my usefulness. Anyone else could do all I do—given the Senate and the Major. The things I might do, which would be of some little advantage, I am not allowed to do, even with the free hand the President has always given me. I can not blame him for my sins or my failures. He has no more freedom than I have. If I were in his place I would not do so well as he does—I am clear as to that. I can not even find it in my heart to rail at the Senators. They are as God made them, and they act according to the law of their being. But why I should stay in the State Department knowing the sterility of my best intentions, is more than I can tell you. Perhaps with me also it is in interest, obstinacy, disinclination to let the other fellow down me.[3] To take the best view of it, it may be the dregs of a puritan conscience which makes me stay simply because I don't want to. . . .

If we could know what these things were which Hay would have liked to do it would be possible with more certainty to outline the foreign policy of the McKinley Administration.

From decade to decade, even from generation to generation, American foreign policy shows a continuity in spite of party platforms and the peculiar qualities of succeeding Presidents. The changes in the fundamental geographical, political, and economic facts, which determine the channel through which the policy must flow are glacial, not sudden. Foreign policy represents the collaboration of many minds. Congress, by the control of the purse; the Senate, by its share in the appointing and treaty-making powers; the party managers, upon whom rests the responsibility for the next election; the President's Cabinet,

---

[1] September 14, 1900.
[2] August 9, 1901; *Letters and Diaries*, III, p. 224–25. Original presumably lost.
[3] The sentence appears to have been edited imperfectly in the printed copy.

in which are always several members directly interested in the international relations of the government; all these are such important factors in shaping American relations with other states that while we may, for convenience, speak of the policy of an administration, usually it is deceptive to ascribe it exclusively to a President; even more misleading to credit it to a Secretary of State. It is evident, however, from the letters just quoted, that in the policies Hay would have liked to adopt there was something so peculiar as to set them far apart from those which had to be pursued. "Always doing the thing I know is wrong," Hay had written to Adams, at the beginning of the Boxer trouble, "must be in time ruinous to the Immortal Soul—but that I charge to the American people whose fault it is."

To the clues afforded in Hay's intimate letters Henry Adams supplied another in the word "McKinleyism," which was his summary of the spirit of the new age which followed the panic of 1893. He defined McKinleyism as "the system of combinations, consolidations, trusts, realized at home, and realizable abroad." [1]

This is the broadest, as well as the most suggestive, definition of the purposes of McKinley's foreign policy which has been attempted. Perhaps it is also the the most authentic. A Secretary of State is rarely in a position publicly to defend himself. He cannot often take the public into his confidence and declare to the world his objectives. Chess is not played that way. Neither can a Secretary of State indulge in the glittering general statements which could cost Henry Adams nothing. But in those quiet walks up Sixteenth Street before tea the Secretary of State could tell his friend what he was trying to accomplish, and, without embarrassment to anyone, Adams could record the statement in a book which was not to be published for a long time.

In the repeal of the Silver Act at the special session of Congress in 1893 Henry Adams thought he saw an American revolution. The American people, by the adoption of the single gold standard, had surrendered to capitalism. "He had known for years," Adams wrote,[2] "that he must accept the régime, but he had known a great many disagreeable certainties—like age, senility, and death—against which one made what little resistance one could. The matter was settled at last by the people. For a hundred years, between 1793

[1] *Education*, p. 423.
[2] *Education*, pp. 343–44.

and 1893—the American people had hesitated, vacillated, swayed forward and back, between two forces, one simply industrial, the other capitalistic, centralizing, and mechanical. In 1893, the issue came on the single gold standard, and the majority at last declared itself once for all, in favor of the capitalistic system with all its necessary machinery. All one's friends, all one's best citizens, reformers, churches, colleges, educated classes, had joined the banks to force submission to capitalism; a submission long foreseen by the mere law of mass." Starting with the fact of this revolution, Adams resigned himself to the conviction that a capitalistic system must be run by capital and by capitalistic methods, "for nothing could surpass the nonsensity of trying to run so complex and so concentrated a machine by Southern and Western farmers in grotesque alliance with city day-laborers, as had been tried in 1800 and in 1828, and had failed even under simple conditions."

The inference from Adams's comments is that, having looked with such a benevolent eye upon the merger of railroads and the creation at home of huge industrial combinations, McKinley permitted Hay to see what he could do in the way of bringing the Powers abroad into a grand concert of agreement upon their common world-wide interests. Very many of the facts fit into this generalization, although it must be admitted at once that Hay was less the leader of this international movement than the affectionate references by Adams would indicate. Every Secretary of State, upon assuming office, looks around to see what ragged edges in American foreign relations are most in need of repair, but it is doubtful whether any Secretary prior to 1898, had ever included so much in his purview.

Adams points out that his friend began with England. This we know to be true. "Hay thought England must be brought first into the combine; but at that time Germany, Russia, and France were all combining against England, and the Boer War helped them. For the moment Hay had no ally, abroad or at home, except Pauncefote, and Adams always maintained that Pauncefote alone pulled him through." [1]

Another and far more difficult step was to draw Germany into the circle, while, "at the end of the vista, most unmanageable of all, Russia remained to be satisfied and disarmed. This was the instinct of what might be called McKinleyism. . . . Either Germany must de-

[1] *Ibid.*, p. 374.

stroy England and France to create the next inevitable unification as a system of continent against continent—or she must pool interests. Both schemes in turn were attributed to the Kaiser; one or the other he would have to choose; opinion was balanced doubtfully on their merits; but, granting both to be feasible, Hay's and McKinley's statesmanship turned on the point of persuading the Kaiser to join what might be called the Coal-power combination, rather than to build up the only possible alternative, a Gun-power combination by merging Germany in Russia." Then Adams added, mischievously, "Thus Bebel and Jaurès, McKinley and Hay, were partners." [1]

That the McKinley Administration was consciously engaged in an effort to promote a concert of the Powers is evident from other sources.

Coincident with the settlement of the Samoan affair, and the visit of the German Emperor and his advisers to England in November, 1899, there were renewed discussions for an Anglo-German understanding. Joseph Chamberlain, the Colonial Secretary, was the agitator in England—he who had married Mary Endicott back in the days when Hay had first settled in Washington and the Four of Hearts was in its pristine vigor.[2] Encouraged by von Bülow, Chamberlain made his famous Leicester speech, November 30; it was an effort to popularize in very general terms in England the idea that the best interests of the two nations would be well served if Germany and England could only come to an understanding and adopt a common policy in their international relations. Chamberlain was in a something-ought-to-be-done-about-it state of mind; he was worried about Russian designs all across the Continent from Turkey through Persia to China, but at Leicester he did not to that extent take his audience into his confidence. Instead, he led into his theme by referring to the good understanding between Great Britain and the United States which had resulted from the Spanish-American War, and then brought forward the project that a similar era of good feeling should be inaugurated with Germany.

"I rejoice—," he said, "it is perhaps natural that I should take a personal interest in the matter—in the friendly feeling, which I hope

---

[1] *Ibid.*, pp. 423–24.
[2] Erich Brandenburg, *From Bismarck to the World War*, p. 138; Baron von Eckardstein, *Ten Years at the Court of St. James's, 1895–1905*, p. 130.

is now the persistent feeling, between the two great branches of the Anglo-Saxon race. I have as many friends in the United States of America almost as I have here, and I can conceive of no greater disaster which could befall the two countries, or which could befall mankind, than that they should find themselves at any time in a hostile attitude, the one to the other." After referring to the war with Spain he continued, a little recklessly, "The union—the alliance, if you please—the understanding between these two great nations is indeed a guarantee for the peace of the world."

With this introduction Chamberlain passed to the subject of Germany, with which he thought England had no antagonistic interests. Indeed, he declared "the natural alliance is between ourselves and the great German Empire." Without mentioning Russia by name he continued:

> I can foresee many things in the future which must cause anxiety to the statesmen of Europe, but in which our interests are clearly the same as the interests of Germany, and in which that good understanding of which I have spoken in the case of America might, if extended to Germany, do more perhaps than any combination of arms in order to preserve the peace of the world. . . . If the union between England and America is a powerful factor in the cause of peace, a new Triple Alliance between the Teutonic race and the two great branches of the Anglo-Saxon race will be a still more potent influence in the future of the world.

Chamberlain was using words so loosely that it is impossible to know just what he had in mind. It would appear, however, that if military arrangements with Germany were in the background of his thought, they were at least secondary to his hope that the mere establishment of an agreement would be likely to deter Russia from such further colonial advances as would break the peace. "I have used the word 'alliance' sometimes in the course of what I have said," he explained, "but again I desire to make it clear that to me it seems to matter little whether you have an alliance which is committed to paper or whether you have an understanding which exists in the minds of the statesmen of the respective countries. An understanding, perhaps, is better than an alliance, which may stereotype arrangements which cannot be accepted as permanent in view of the changing circumstances from day to day."

With the storm of disapproval which greeted the speech in Ger-

many, with Chamberlain's consequent resentment over what he regarded as von Bülow's betrayal of him, or, with the not very much
better response from the American newspapers, we are not concerned.
The importance of the speech in the history of American foreign policy
is that both McKinley and Hay approved it, except for the loose use
of the word "alliance."

"Do you ever see Chamberlain?" inquired Hay of Henry White,
December 27, in replying to a Christmas letter. "If so I wish you
would tell him how idiotic are the stories in the English & American
papers about his speech having influenced the President's message to
a tone less cordial to England. The Message was written several weeks
ago, before his speech was made. Neither the President nor I saw
anything but what was right and admirable in the speech—though,
of course, I never use the word 'alliance.' I get profoundly discouraged some times, with the infernal cussedness of the little politicians
who have the power to tip over the best bucket of milk I can fill in
a year's work. Just now it is Cassini who seems likely to spoil all my
'open door' labor, by refusing to agree with the rest of the civilized
world."

Henry Adams's "McKinleyism" was only an American adaptation
of "Chamberlainism."

It is evident that John Hay came back from London in 1898 with
the firm desire to coöperate with Chamberlain and Balfour in stabiliz-
ing the peace of the world. Between England and the United States
there was, and could be, no military alliance, even defensive, but
there was in the minds of the two governments the will to have and
maintain peace between themselves and then to extend the relationship among the Powers. That was the meaning of the secret mission
of Spring Rice to Surrenden just before Hay sailed for home in
September, 1898. The immediately unstable spots in the world were
the Caribbean, the Pacific, South Africa, and Canada. In the Spanish-
American War and in the peace settlement with Spain, England stood
by the United States; in South Africa the American Government was
neutral but benevolent. In Samoa, Germany also had been a willing
member of the "combine," as Adams called it. A technique was beginning to develop. It appeared in the open-door notes as well as in
the Samoan treaty—peace by agreement, a favorite American doctrine. The participation of the United States in the first peace con-

ference at The Hague in 1899 was in harmony with, and a part of, the same policy, although Adams failed to mention it.

Neither McKinley nor Hay was a man of war. Wherever possible all through life, they had evaded conflict, achieving their purposes by compromise and accommodation. Why should not this be the practice among nations? "I detest war," wrote Hay at the outbreak of the conflict with Spain, "and hoped I might never see another one." [1] On another occasion he wrote: "If the press of the world would adopt and persist in the high resolve that war should be no more, the clangor of arms would cease from the rising of the sun to its going down, and we could fancy that at last our ears, no longer stunned by the din of armies, might hear the morning stars singing together and all the sons of God shouting for joy." [2] This sentiment with Hay was no mere lip service to peace which prominent men in those days were so often asked to affect in fancy language for the New Year's edition of the morning paper. As a poet and citizen of the realm of letters he could not feel otherwise.

In so far as international peace was to be achieved by the legally technical methods of arbitration, Hay, who could hardly claim to be a lawyer, had no special interests. The devising of methods he left to the experts. The American Delegation to The Hague in 1899, carried a project for an international court of justice far more substantial in character than emerged from the Conference as the Permanent Court of Arbitration, but Hay did not write the instruction to the commissioners. [3] The subjects actually considered at The Hague were highly technical; Hay merely looked to the Conference to fashion a tool which he could use. Even before the Senate had an opportunity to ratify the Hague Convention, Hay and McKinley joined heartily in the agreement to refer the Samoan claims to the arbitration of the King of Sweden and Norway. Later, both men seized eagerly on the alternative that the amount of the claims to be preferred by the Powers against China in 1900 should be referred to the Hague Court. [4]

To Wayne MacVeagh, one of the American counsel in the Venezuela Arbitration, he wrote June 27, 1903: "The dominant chord for us to

---

[1] *Letters and Diaries*, III, p. 122.
[2] Paul Morton to Hay, January 20, 1905.
[3] David Jayne Hill, *The Problem of a World Court*, p. 1.
[4] *For. Rel.*, 1900, p. xvi; see *For. Rel.*, 1902, App. II, for the Pious Fund case, referred by the United States and Mexico to the new Hague Court.

strike at The Hague is the vindication of the broad principle of the preference to be given to peaceful over hostile means of collecting debts. . . . If this arbitration turns out well, the greatest step ever yet taken to the institution of the 'Parliament of Man' will have been made."

The Boxer affair in 1900 uncovered the only remaining sore spot in which the United States had a direct interest. Hay tried his method again by sending out the circular of July 3. Later he asserted that his circular had been successful, but his evidence was flimsy. The inherent weakness of his scheme was already apparent as it may not have been even to Chamberlain six or seven months before. To be effective such a program required the encirclement of Russia. "Chamberlainism" was weak at still another point, as Lord Salisbury well knew. Russia in the Far East could not be isolated from Russia in the Near East and in the Balkans. The Russian program was intimately bound up also with the fortunes of Austria-Hungary, where it touched the Triple Alliance, French *revanche* for Alsace-Lorraine, and the security of Germany. In a word, the China question was but a phase of European politics, and with the latter the American people would have nothing to do.

"If I could have a free hand, I suppose I should do exactly what you suggest," Hay wrote to John W. Foster on June 23, 1900, adding:

On one side there is a great danger, on the other a great opportunity. I think I see both the danger and the opportunity. It is enough to turn the hair grey not to be allowed to avoid the one and embrace the other. But what can be done in the present diseased state of the public mind? There is such a mad-dog hatred of England prevalent among newspapers and politicians that anything we should now do in China to take care of our imperilled interests would be set down to "subservience to Great Britain." France is Russia's harlot—to her own grievous damage. Germany we could probably get on our side by sufficient concessions, and perhaps with England, Germany and Japan we might manage to save our skins. But such a proceeding would make all our fools throw fits in the market place—and the fools are numerous.

We had great trouble to prevent the Convention from declaring in favor of the Boers, and of the annexation of Canada. Every morning I receive letters cursing me for doing nothing, and others cursing me for being "the tool of England against our good friend Russia." All I have ever done with England is to have wrung great concessions out of her with no compensation, and yet these idiots say I am not an American because I don't say "To hell with the Queen" at every breath.

Cassini has gone to Europe; Cambon was to have sailed last week but has stayed over for a few days; Holleben is absolutely without initiative and in mortal terror of his Kaiser; Pauncefote has apparently no power to act, nor even to talk. And even if he had, every Senator I see says, "For God's sake don't let it appear we have any understanding with England." How can I make bricks without straw? That we should be compelled to refuse the assistance of the greatest Power in the world, *in carrying out our own policy,* because all Irishmen are Democrats and some Germans are fools—is enough to drive a man mad.

Yet we shall do what we can.

Hay did what he could. It was a great help in keeping the Powers together until the Legations had been relieved, but it was not enough to assure England that in an eventuality the American Government would place itself in an attitude of hostility to Russia in North China. The rapid withdrawal of American troops in the autumn of 1900 clearly revealed the determination of the McKinley Administration to escape any responsibility for intervention in what was regarded as a dispute between Russia, on the one side, and England and Japan, on the other. McKinley might approve Hay's policy, the Cabinet might approve, but, as the Secretary remarked, moral leadership, unsupported by at least a moderate display of force, was "mere flap-doodle."

The Anglo-German agreement involved in two respects a repudiation by England of the principle for which "McKinleyism" had come to stand. Germany had thus refused to adhere to Hay's proposal for the territorial and administrative entity of China, as had Russia, and Great Britain had sorely compromised its previous position on that subject. Furthermore, England, previously Hay's only certain support, had at length disclosed its intention of seeking in Europe not merely agreements but understandings which might eventuate in military support.

Hay lived long enough to have the satisfaction of knowing that the American Government could not so easily escape intervention in Asia. The Anglo-Japanese Alliance, and then the Russo-Japanese War, followed the absurd Anglo-German agreement, two and four years later, in inevitable sequence. In the latter McKinley's successor in office did not hesitate to intervene as Hay probably would have liked to do four years before. Roosevelt, in turn, lived long enough to see the United States intervene in Europe itself. The American people drew back in 1900; they would not support John Hay; it is very doubtful whether they would have supported Roosevelt four years later, had they known what he was saying and threatening. But in choosing the one alternative in 1900, the United States only postponed and did not escape another which came in 1917.

Whether the strengthening, rather than the reduction, of American forces in China in 1900 would have diverted the course of events in the Far East and later in Europe is speculative. It is difficult to imagine how, if the Hay policy could have been followed then, the United States would now be more enmeshed in the affairs, alike of Asia and Europe, than at present. At any rate, it is interesting to see how John Hay first travelled the ground which so many Secretaries of State, and Presidents, had later to retraverse.

If we were to attempt a statement of Hay's conclusion at the time, and give it the color of a more modern language, we might put it this way: The idea of world peace by agreement, but without sanctions, is "mere flap-doodle."

One other aspect of "McKinleyism" contained a significant forecast of the development of American foreign policy. Prior to 1899 the United States had been less interested in the *status quo* of European Powers than in the spread of republican principles of government. "McKinleyism" contemplated a stabilization of the existing political order. In this respect, also, it was out of step with the American people of 1900, though less out of harmony with the position which the United States is required to assume a generation later.

"McKinleyism," formulated by Hay, was certainly premature and perhaps not very sound.

BRUISED in body and oppressed in spirit, John Hay entered upon his sixty-third year—his grand climacteric, as he called it—October 12, 1900. Eighteen years before he had published "The Stirrup Cup"— "my short and happy day is done." At the age of fifty he had expected to live not much longer. At sixty-two the Pale Horse was still waiting at the door; the eerie mount would be standing there for almost another five years. The expectant rider returned to Washington after his illness, intending to conclude his responsibilities in the Department of State with the opening of the new Administration the following March. He felt that his work was done.

The overwhelming McKinley victory in November, followed by the affecting request of the President that his old Cabinet continue with him, deeply moved Hay, and so he girded himself for another tour of duty.

The year 1901 was to become the great meridian of his life. His body, never equal to his mind, was breaking down. In this weakened condition he went out to meet adversity, hitherto to him a stranger. One terrible night in June when his family had already gone to New Hampshire a reporter from one of the local papers burst into his bedroom to bring the news that Adelbert had fallen to his death from a window at New Haven while attending the third-year reunion of his class at Yale. In September, President McKinley was stricken down at Buffalo. Theodore Roosevelt became President of the United States. Nicolay died. King burned out in Arizona. For more than sixty-two years John Hay had escaped the kind of personal misfortune which tries man's soul. He had complained much about little troubles, more than he now complained about the real ones, but it was not until 1901 that he had to pass through the fiery furnace.

As father and son, John Hay and Del had not been very well matched. Most of the qualities which had set the father apart in his own family, making him unlike any earlier Hay, had escaped the son. Adelbert had the bone and sinew of the elder John Hay, and a combination of other qualities, the development of which the father had watched with bashful concern. He could not understand and did not know how to guide the boy. Nor did the son understand the father who, out there on the prairie, had been bred to thrift and modest living. Not until Del's notable success as Consul General in South Africa did the boy come on to common ground with the father. Upon the son's return to the United States President McKinley offered him the post of Private Secretary to the President, thus putting the young man on the threshold of a career like his father's. He accepted the position to assume his duties in the fall, and went up to New Haven, the first man in his class to report the achievement of real distinction. Then, just as the father was finding his own boy, came the shocking death, and the last sight of his broken body. Nothing before in John Hay's life had put him to such a test. He cringed under the blow as many a stronger man might have done.

"I wonder if I can write a word to you without going to pieces in the process," he wrote to King.[1] "All my thoughts are with my dead boy. His face is always before me, always smiling and happy—never with the least shadow of pain or resentment against the cruelty of fate."

To the President, who had only two more months of life, Hay wrote on the same day:

I have tested my strength and am convinced I must take a rest. The company of my poor wife—solitude—freedom from other company and other cares are necessary to bring me back to sane thoughts and habits. I keep in mind all the maxims of philosophy and common sense which men have used in ages past as anodynes for sorrow—but every little while the brute grief grips me like a bull dog and I am powerless against it.

There are many consolations, I admit, and I am thankful for them. After a while these will have their influence. Pride, and sweet memories, and the immortality of character, and trust in God—all must in time have power over this sickness of the soul. But the instinct of every wounded animal is to hide. . . . My boy's face is always before me and always smiling.

But I will not weary you any more with my wailings. I am grateful to the heart, for all your goodness to him, as well as to me.

At the time of Del's death, Henry Adams was in Europe with the Lodges. He wrote to Hay, but knowing well how his friend might fall under the load, followed the letter by another to Mrs. Hay,[2] which

[1] July 14, 1901. *Letters and Diaries*, III, p. 217.
[2] Henry Adams to Mrs. Hay, July 25, 1901.

discloses the hidden side of the writer in a manner which the admirers of Adams will be happy to remember:

"Of course, all turns on you. If you break down, John will break down. Even with all your strength, it will be a marvel if you succeed in getting through the next year without much difficulty. . . . Perhaps there is no other way. You may have to carry the whole load alone."

The appeal was unnecessary. Clara Stone had already again become the hero of the story. She carried him through. The Adams letter, however, is so little in the writer's customary vein and reveals so much of the spiritual history of the "Five of Hearts," that it may be appropriately added:

John will have told you why I've not written to you before. Anyone who has been through a shock that crushes one's life, knows that friends count then most for what they feel, rather than for anything they can say; though one is grateful enough for what is said, too, and still more for the sense of companionship in suffering. My deepest regret was, as I telegraphed to John, that I could not be with you; for I remembered the awful horror of solitude, for the hours before friends could reach one, in the first instants of prostration, and I thought that perhaps my knowledge of suffering might make me more useful than another friend could be. For that I was too far away. For writing, I knew that you would be overwhelmed with letters. I knew too that almost anyone would say more than I knew how to do, for I never have learned yet that anything could be said, when silence is all that is left. I was afraid even of doing harm; for the one idea that was uppermost in my mind was that when I was suddenly struck, sixteen years ago, I never did get up again, and never to this moment recovered the energy or interest to return into active life. The object of all others is now to prevent John or you from breaking down that way, and to save what is left, at least until nature has a chance to react. My object in writing now is not so much to express sympathy or feeling or interest,—which you know me well enough to need no expression of,— but to find out if possible, in due time, whether you will want my help, or will care to make me useful. As a matter of medical opinion, I should say that I was not altogether the best sort of help or tonic to persons needing strength and courage. It is so long since I have got the habit of thinking that nothing is worth while! That sort of habit is catching, and I should not like to risk too close contact at a critical moment with a mind disposed to be affected by it.

Notwithstanding the tenderness of the letter, it is for the reason which it states that one inclines to the opinion that the society of the "Five of Hearts" had never been very beneficial. The courage which it had not been able to give John Hay at length found for himself in the solitude of the New Hampshire hills. Then, just as his heart was beginning to heal, came the assassination of President McKinley, and the accession of Theodore Roosevelt.

John Hay belonged to the generation which, regardless of health or of any peculiar conditions, considered men old at fifty, and required that they dress the part. The line between youth and age was then more distinctly drawn than now. Hay was a contemporary of Roosevelt's father and mother. He had known Theodore as a youth and called him by his first name when no title seemed either necessary or appropriate. As Civil Service Commissioner Roosevelt had been much with the Lodges, and thus his orbit overlapped Hay's, but the relationship had always been that of an indulgent older man for a less modulated young one. "We had the Roosevelts and the Lodges to dine once or twice, but I cannot make them gay," wrote Hay to Adams in one of those low moods with which he was much afflicted in the early nineties.[1]

That Roosevelt, on the other hand, looked up to Hay with respect and admiration is apparent from the correspondence. From Albany, after the Senate ratification of the treaty of peace with Spain, the Governor wrote, Feb. 7, 1899: "Just a few lines to congratulate you on bringing to so successful an end so great a work. Ambassador, and Secretary of State, during the most important year that this Republic has seen since Lincoln died—those are positions worth filling, fraught with memories your children's children will recall with eager pride. You have, indeed, led a life eminently worth while, oh writer of books and doer of deeds!—and, in passing, builder of beautiful homes and father of strong sons and fair daughters."

Almost exactly a year later Governor Roosevelt issued his famous statement of opposition to the first canal treaty.[2] In Hay's private letter-book is a copy of a note, Feb. 12, 1900, to "Et Tu." Probably the letter was to the Governor. It clearly revealed the irritation of the older man toward the restless concern of the younger one for matters which Hay seemed to regard as none of Roosevelt's business.

"Cannot you leave a few things to the President and the Senate,

[1] Dec. 12, 1890. *Letters and Diaries,* II, p. 204.
[2] Bishop, I, pp. 144–45. Roosevelt opposed the treaty on two grounds. He believed that if the canal were to be open to warships of the enemy during war it would be a source of military weakness rather than of strength; and, that the provision for a joint guarantee of neutrality violated the Monroe Doctrine.

who are charged with them by the Constitution?

"As to 'Sea Power' and the Monroe Doctrine, we did not act without consulting the best living authorities on those subjects.

"Do you really think the Clayton-Bulwer Treaty preferable to the one now before the Senate? There is no third issue, except dishonor. Elkins and Pettigrew say 'Dishonor be Damned.' I hardly think you will.

"Please do not answer this—but think about it awhile."

As a Presidential possibility, Hay had not regarded Roosevelt seriously. Just before the Republican Convention, June 15, he wrote to Adams:

Teddy has been here: have you heard of it? It was more fun than a goat. He came down, with a somber resolution throned on his strenuous brow, to let McKinley and Hanna know, once for all, that he would not be Vice President, and found to his stupefaction that nobody in Washington, except Platt, had ever dreamed of such a thing. He did not even have a chance to launch his nolo episcopari at the Major. That statesman said that he did not want him on the ticket—that he would be far more valuable in New York—and Root said, with his frank and murderous smile, "Of course not—you are not fit for it." And so he went back, quite eased in mind but considerably bruised in his amour-propre.

The Vice Presidency is, at this date, anybody's persimmon. As you will know all about it before this reaches you I will say nothing, except that the utmost artesian boring has not availed to elicit from the President his choice. I get a little fun out of it. All the statesmen who want it come and offer their state delegation's vote to me.

Nothing—but nothing—would induce me to stay where I am, or take anything else when my term of enlistment has expired.

Whatever may have been Hay's surprise at the outcome of the Philadelphia Convention, he did not fail to offer Roosevelt his prompt congratulations.[1] "You have received the greatest compliment the country could pay you, and although it was not precisely what you and your friends desired, I have no doubt it is all for the best. Nothing can keep you from doing good work wherever you are—nor from getting lots of fun out of it. We Washingtonians of course have our own little point of view. You can't lose us; and we shall be uncommonly glad to see you here again."

In the letters from Hay to Roosevelt, thus far quoted, candor stands

[1] June 21, 1900.

out. Governor Roosevelt could not have had any difficulty in concluding that Hay was sometimes annoyed at him and that he was not
wholly satisfied with his nomination.

Hay did not relish the idea of Roosevelt as Vice President but, as
a loyal Republican, rejoicing at the reelection of McKinley, he extracted some comfort out of the thought that even Roosevelt as Vice
President would be better than Bryan as President. To Adams he
wrote, Nov. 21:

"I thank you from the bottom of a bruised spirit for your letter
of the 7th. We did wallop them proper and I am glad not to live under
Bryan and his gang for the next four years—if I am to survive them.
He is quite too halcyon and vociferous. He would be worse than
Teddy; yes, I tell you, worse. For Teddy will probably want to
occupy his chair a good deal, & so must hold his tongue.

"But oh Lordy! how the Autumn lowers and the Winter looms
before me. Every Senator has promised his dozens of Consulates &
Cabot is already here, yelping for loot like a Christian in China. And
I am as dis-consolate as you are in the abode of gilded sin which men
call Paris."

Adams mischievously reminded Hay that while Roosevelt had been
elected only Vice President, he was already famed for his luck.

The death of Adelbert, Hay's distress of body and mind, his often
reiterated desire to resign, and his lack of confidence in Roosevelt,
would have seemed to be preparing the way for his retirement to
private life at the time of McKinley's death. No previous decision that
he had ever made, unless it was the one three years before at Surrenden, appeared to indicate that John Hay would have the courage
to go on—but he did. His letter to Roosevelt immediately following
McKinley's death carried a hint of resignation, but it was not difficult to read between the lines a wistful desire to continue in office.
It was one of the best letters he ever wrote: [1]

If the Presidency had come to you in any other way, no one could have
congratulated you with better heart than I. My sincere affection and esteem
for you, and my old-time love for your Father—would he could have lived to
see you where you are!—would have been deeply gratified.

And even from the depths of the sorrow where I sit with my grief for the
President mingled and confused with that for my boy, so that I scarcely know

[1] Sept. 15, 1901.

from hour to hour the true source of my tears,—I do still congratulate you, not only on the threshold of an official career which I know will be glorious but on that opportunity for useful work which lies before you. With your youth, your ability, your health and strength and the courage God has given you to do right, there are no bounds to the good you can accomplish for your country and the name you will leave in its annals.

My official life is at an end—my natural life will not be long extended, and so, in the dawn of what I am sure will be a great and splendid future, I venture to give you the heartfelt benediction of the past. God bless You

There was in the letter to Roosevelt a new note. For two months John Hay had been fighting the battle of his life with an opponent whom he had rarely faced before—himself. His letter to Adams in August had carried tidings of the fight. Hay had written that he could no longer find it in his heart to rail even at Senators, while a disinclination to let the other fellow down him and the "dregs of a puritan conscience" had made him determined to try again. The forces which he had summoned to his aid in his sorrow now fortified him to meet still a new test.

As Secretary of State Hay had well begun but had not quite finished the work which was to be associated chiefly with his name. The second canal treaty was in its final form. It even had the approval of Senator Lodge, but it could not be referred to the Senate until December. The negotiations with the isthmian republics were still in the preliminary stages. The Boxer Protocol was signed, but there remained the negotiations for a new commercial treaty, and the Russians were still in Manchuria. A temporary agreement had been reached with Canada but the time was not yet ripe for a final settlement of the boundary question. The establishment of the proposed new Bureau of Insular Affairs in the Department of State was hanging fire. Furthermore, the files of incoming correspondence indicated that many very reputable citizens, alarmed at the prospect of the Rough Rider for President, felt that Hay's services were more than ever indispensable.

A few weeks before every sign would have pointed to the probability of Hay's retirement at McKinley's death. Indeed, it would have been very reasonable to expect Roosevelt to decline to have Hay in his cabinet. The new President did hesitate. There were rumors that Lodge would replace him, than which nothing would have humiliated

Hay more. Over the first canal treaty their old friendship had worn thin if not through.[1]

As a further anodyne for sorrow, Hay needed the invitation to continue in office, and Roosevelt was too good a politician to withhold it. The reappointment of Hay was reassuring to an anxious nation, to more than one nation. Whatever radical policies in foreign relations Hay may have set out with, he had not carried them far. He had the confidence of the country as both skillful and conservative. On the other hand, the tender of office and its acceptance did not change the fundamental fact that the two men, Hay and Roosevelt, were very imperfectly suited to work together. This comes out in another letter to Adams, September 19:

> I have just received your letter from Stockholm, and shuddered at the awful clairvoyance of your last phrase about Theodore's luck.
>
> Well, here he is in the saddle again. That is, he is in Canton, & will have his first Cabinet meeting in the White House today. He came down from Buffalo Monday night—and in the station, without waiting an instant, he told me I must stay with him—that I could not decline nor even consider. I saw, of course, that it was best for him to start off that way, & so said I would stay forever, of course, for it would be worse to say I would stay a while, than it would be to go out at once. I can still go at any time he gets tired of me, or when I collapse.
>
> He has made a splendid impression on public opinion. I have only seen two men who hinted at trouble ahead; Wanamaker and Gage. They talk, separately, just alike; not precisely pessimistic but anxious. Though both of them like Roosevelt & think he is all right. It is a situation that seems to them big with possibilities of change.

In making the transfer from McKinley to Roosevelt, Hay's extraordinary adaptability came to his rescue. He had already revealed the ability to pass from Abraham Lincoln to Horace Greeley, from Blaine to Hayes, from Sherman to Hanna and McKinley. The new adjustment would prove the most difficult of all; it was coming at an age when convictions usually grow hard and inflexible. In Hay, however, there had recently appeared a gentleness of spirit suggestive of the benign Dr. Hay of Warsaw.

John Hay already possessed all the emoluments which the office of Secretary of State could give. His fame was secure. What remained

[1] Nevins' *White,* p. 157.

of his life was his free gift to his party, and to his country.

As the old Secretary and the new President settled down in the new relationship, the former thought less and less of resigning; his letters carried fewer references to ill health. To George W. Smalley he wrote July 9, 1903, "There is no reason in the world why people should talk of my resigning now any more than any time during the last four years. My personal relations with the President are still those of a friendship which he inherited from his father. . . .

After the election he again wrote to Smalley.[1] "As to the announcement of my remaining here the rest of my life—for it amounts to that—it was a very characteristic action of the President. He has always appeared to take it for granted that I was to stay here as long as he did, and has several times somewhat vehemently said so, but he has never formally asked me to remain through his next term, and I have never formally consented to do so. The announcement in the newspapers was a proceeding of his own, dictated by occult motives into which it would be hardly reverent to inquire. There is, perhaps, no reason why I should not stay, except weariness of mind and spirit, but that seems not to be a sufficient reason. But, how long is a question for providence and the doctors to decide."

It was Roosevelt's eager desire without delay to sweep away the difference in age, as well as the customary formalities of the official relationship. Indeed, as early as November 10, 1900, in acknowledging Hay's letter of congratulation on his election as Vice President, he had written:

"In the first place, I wish you would always call me Theodore as you used to do."

Hay, however, could not forget that on October 12, 1901, he would be sixty-three years old; "Theodore" was difficult.

"On that day," he wrote,[2] "I become an old man—without the possibility of denial or evasion, and there is nothing worse in the arsenal of evil that can happen to any man. Brazen it out as we like —when the clock strikes that hour, there is nothing to do but say Habet! What a splendid achievement for you lies between now and Then!" Twenty years and very different philosophies of life lay between them.

[1] November 22, 1904.
[2] Oct. 2, 1901.

To this Roosevelt hastened to reply, with the evident desire of drawing his Secretary of State into his intimate circle. He wrote:[1]

Dear John,

This seems disrespectful, and I only use the address because I am afraid you would not use "Theodore" if I did not. Edith and I have held a solemn conclave on the matter, and we hope this was the right conclusion.

I read her your letter, and pronounced the last sentence, about your age "affectation," whereupon she answered severely "not at all! I know just what he means, and I feel exactly that way myself!" She is forty, and I do not think I deceive myself when I say that she neither looks nor acts or feels as if she was [sic] more than thirty. As for me, on the whole I have continued all my life to have a better time year after year.

This hearty, exuberant, youthful attitude toward sixty-third birthdays was good for Hay, more invigorating than the intimate society to which he was accustomed. At times, in the next three years, Roosevelt carried this attitude to the point where it amounted to the intolerance of good for poor health. He failed to recognize that his Secretary of State was not a well man, but he tried, in his robustious way, to be considerate.

"I have your note of the 15th," wrote Roosevelt,[2] "For Heaven's sake, take a real and thorough rest. Whenever I see you and Root looking under the weather I sympathize deeply with Mr. Winkle's emotion when he besought Mr. Pickwick for his sake not to drown."

It became the custom for the President each Sunday on his way back from church to stop at 800 Sixteenth Street for a chat before lunch. The Secretary of State slowly, and with evident self-consciousness, fell into the familiar "Theodore," except in official correspondence, and the facts seem to warrant the statement that the personal relationship ripened into as much affection as the two men were able to muster for each other.

Hay was deeply touched by Roosevelt's hearty expressions of confidence and continued intimacies. For the President's enthusiasms he had at first apprehension, but, in time, tolerant smiles. Often alone, or with the cooperation of Elihu Root, he sought to anticipate his chief, to protect him from what he feared would be his rashness. When rumor had it that King Edward contemplated conferring upon Roosevelt a military distinction which would have been politically embar-

[1] Oct. 5, 1901.
[2] July 17, 1902.

rassing both at home and abroad, Hay quietly took matters into his own hands and wrote to Choate, September 29, 1902: [1]

I see in several newspapers a story that the King is thinking of making the President Honorary Colonel of one of the Regiments of the British Army. I presume this is mere silly season gossip—but out of excess of caution I am writing this word.

In case Lord Lansdowne should mention the matter to you I wish you would say to him that you think it not desirable that the offer should be made. The President being constitutionally prohibited from accepting such an honor without authorization from Congress, it might give rise to a debate in which things would be said by opposition members which would be unpleasant to read. If Sir Michael Herbert says anything about it to me, I shall give him the same answer without referring it to the President. I think it decidedly advisable that the matter should not come before him, for acceptance or refusal.

In December, 1902, Hay took similar action in a more important matter. When the German Government invited Roosevelt to act as arbitrator in the Venezuelan affair, Hay was alarmed. He feared that the President would accept, but he felt that it would be much better to have the matter referred to the Hague Court, the importance of which he was trying to build up. It is remembered that he came back from the Department one afternoon at tea-time and strode up and down the room, exclaiming: "I have it all arranged, I have it all arranged. If only Teddy will keep his mouth shut until tomorrow noon!" The dispute went to The Hague.[2]

At appropriate places in this narrative other instances will be pointed out where there were differences of opinion in matters of foreign policy. These were a part of the give and take of official life. They resulted in no rift in the personal relations of the two men.

In many matters wholly unrelated to foreign affairs the President sought Hay's advice. On some of these occasions the Secretary of State may have been less helpful than when operating in his field of special and expert knowledge. As might have been expected from Hay's opinions previously expressed in *The Bread-Winners*, he was not stirred, as Roosevelt appeared to be, by the "malefactors of great

[1] There is a pencilled draft of this letter in the Hay Papers.
[2] In recounting the incident thirteen years later to William Roscoe Thayer, August 21, 1916, in the much discussed letter which was included in the second edition of Thayer's *Hay*, and also in Bishop's *Roosevelt* (I, p. 224), Roosevelt did not mention—perhaps he never knew—that Hay was the one who diverted the Venezuela Arbitration to The Hague.

"THESE ARE MY JEWELS"

This cartoon appeared October 6, 1904, during the presidential campaign, in *Life,* by courtesy of which it is reproduced here.

"Whenever I see you and Root looking under the weather I sympathize deeply with Mr. Winkle's emotion when he besought Mr. Pickwick for his sake not to drown." Roosevelt to Hay, July 17, 1902, p. 345.

"In the Department of State his [Hay's] usefulness to me was almost exclusively that of a fine figurehead." Roosevelt to Lodge, January 28, 1909, p. 349.

Ocb. 21. 1903

The newspapers do not seem to get the
rights of the Portland Channel. There
are two entrances to it like this,
with two little islands in it. We
alama

a Canada

Boundary B

agree that the Boundary shall be
by the North channel instead of
the South, which gives them those
two little Islands — worth nothing
to us. That is all poor Canada
gets by the decision, and I do
not wonder they are furious.
But as Will Thomson used to
say "Serves 'em right, if they
can't take a joke".

"That is all poor Canada gets by this decision [of the Alaska Boundary Tribunal], and I do not wonder they are furious. But as Will Thomson used to say 'Serves 'em right, if they can't take a joke.'" Secretary Hay to Mrs. Hay, the day after the decision was handed down.

wealth," although he was quick enough to detect such attempts as were made to use the good offices of the Secretary of State for special privilege. Hay was, consistently, not an under-dog man. Once Roosevelt sent to him a clipping from the New York *Evening Post* which Hay returned with the following comment, October 14, 1903:

I return with this the editorials you gave me. It is a thing I know nothing about, and I shrewdly suspect that Ogden and Bishop know very little more than I do.

We are passing through a moment of pretty general attack upon all men engaged in great affairs, which may have its origin in the instinctive resentment of human nature against what appears undue prosperity. I think if we wait a while we will see that the wicked are not prospering as much as we thought. It is impossible that a country should prosper unless the rewards of great enterprises are large and no means has yet been devised by man to equalize all the results of prosperity. The lambs will have to be satisfied with a less proportion of the spoils than that the bulls will take in, and when the inevitable reaction comes, the bulls will lose their millions where we small investors will lose our hundreds. I am one of those helpless sufferers, but I do not see that there is any kick coming to me.

Thus ends my futile homily

That Hay was often irritated by the President there can be no doubt. "I wonder if it is to be like this all summer," he wrote to Mrs. Hay, July 4, 1903, from Newport, where he was visiting his daughter over the holiday. He had been summoned to Oyster Bay. "And there is no comfort about going to see him anyhow. When McKinley sent for me he gave me all his time till we got through: but I always find T. R. engaged with a dozen other people, and it is an hour's wait and a minute's talk—and a certainty that there was no necessity of my coming at all.

"Destroy this mutinous and disloyal letter as soon as you have read it."

The conference at Oyster Bay turned out much as Hay had expected. "Kearns, Senator from Utah, was in the carriage with us and shortly after we arrived the Hannas and Griscoms (Mr., Mrs., & Pansy) arrived, and Guy W. Carryl, the poet, came. So what I predicted came to pass; the President could not speak to me until all the guests had gone and then he said, 'Will you excuse me till I play a game of tennis with Winty Chanler (who that moment appeared)? I have had no exercise all day.' So I went off for a little stroll and did not see him until after dinner when, at last, we had our long talk, which was very satisfactory." [1]

But less than a week later Hay wrote to the President, July 13, 1903: "I thank you a thousand times for your kind and generous letter of the 11th. It is a comfort to work for a President who, besides being a lot of other things, happened to be born a gentleman."

President McKinley had acknowledged Hay's Christmas gift through his Secretary with a form letter, but, when at Christmas, 1904, Hay sent his token to Roosevelt, the latter replied with a four-page letter in his own handwriting. The last paragraph was: "With a very merry Xmas for you and yours, and with heartiest thanks for what you give, and above all for what you do and what you are,

"ever your friend

"Theodore Roosevelt."

At the inauguration in March, 1905, the President wore, the gift of Hay, a ring in which had been mounted some of Abraham Lincoln's hair. In acknowledging it Roosevelt had written:

Dear John,

Surely no other President, on the eve of his inauguration, has ever received such a gift from such a friend. I am wearing the ring now; I shall think of it and you as I take the oath tomorrow.

I wonder if you have any idea what your strength and wisdom and sympathy, what the guidance you have given me and the mere delight in your companionship, have meant to me in these three and a half years?

With love and gratitude,

Ever yours,

Theodore Roosevelt.

Such letters as these, and there are many more of them, are the contemporaneous evidence of the relations between the two men. To make the friendship what it was no doubt both had to make efforts. In the years which have elapsed since the death of the principals these letters have assumed a new importance, for, after Hay's death, Roosevelt seems to have changed his opinion of his Secretary of State.

Hay would not argue with Roosevelt, the latter complained to John T. Leary, Jr.; [2] he would not fight for his opinions. "He would approve *en bloc* anything I put before him." When the three volumes of letters and diaries, distributed in 1909, were placed in his hand,

---

[1] To Mrs. Hay, July 8, 1903.
[2] *Talks with T. R.*, pp. 217–18.

Roosevelt's *amour propre* seems to have been deeply wounded; there were included in the collection some of the letters from which quotations have just been made. The President was then moved to indite a critical estimate of Hay, which he addressed to Senator Lodge, with a view to leaving another of his footnotes to history.[1] After paying tribute to his literary and social gifts Roosevelt went on to say: "But he was not a great Secretary of State. . . . He had a very ease-loving nature and a moral timidity which made him shrink from all that was rough in life, and therefore from practical affairs. He was at his best at the dinner table or in a drawing room, and in neither place have I ever seen anyone's best that was better than his. But his temptation was to associate as far as possible only with men of refined and cultivated tastes, who lived apart from the world of affairs, and who, if Americans, were wholly lacking in robustness of fibre. . . ."

Then Roosevelt added: "In public life, during the time he was Secretary of State under me he accomplished little. . . . In the Department of State his usefulness to me was almost exclusively the usefulness of a fine figurehead. . . ."

These statements, beside so many of contrary import by the same hand, are more difficult for the biographer of Roosevelt than for one who writes of Hay. That the latter did not always agree with his chief, and that he did not always approve *en bloc,* is abundantly supported by evidence; that he did not argue with the President may be conceded. He did not argue with McKinley, but to both men he stated his views, when he had any, freely and yet with a courtesy and deference which he never failed to show to the office. Perhaps Roosevelt, ready for a rough-and-tumble, failed at times to catch the tones of disapproval. As for the initiation of policy, as we view it now, the new creative period in American foreign relations which followed the War of 1898 closed in 1901. Probably Roosevelt would have been shocked to discover how little foreign policy he himself created. There was left to him little but to follow the paths which McKinley, Root, and chiefly Hay, had thought out and projected. American diplomacy changed in character, as when one turns from chess to six-ounce gloves, but there was nothing new as to objectives; only the method changed, losing a delicate touch.

[1] January 28, 1909; quoted in part in Henry F. Pringle. *Theodore Roosevelt,* p. 243.

Chapter XXIX   *Roosevelt and the Alaska Boundary*

THE actual relations of President Roosevelt and Secretary Hay appear so clearly in the later phases of the Alaska boundary controversy with England and Canada that this chapter may be regarded as illustrative of a general situation as well as descriptive of an important episode.

"One of the problems that Roosevelt inherited from the McKinley Administration," wrote Joseph Bucklin Bishop,[1] "was the Alaska boundary dispute between the United States and Canada. An effort to settle it through a Joint High Commission had failed, and in the last days of the McKinley Administration a proposal was made by the British Government that the matter be submitted to arbitration. This was under discussion when Roosevelt acceded to the Presidency. He at once took control of the question, flatly declined arbitration, and secured in January, 1903, through the British Minister at Washington, the negotiation of a treaty with Great Britain which provided for a mixed tribunal of six members, three Americans, and three representative of Great Britain, to consider the matter." The foregoing quotation is given thus at length because it is generally understood that the first volume of Bishop's *Roosevelt* was approved by its subject before the latter died, and because the summary, therein provided, of the boundary settlement is in accord with other statements which Roosevelt is known to have made.[2]

While verbally incorrect only in minor respects, the above paragraph is so entirely wrong as a statement of fact that one hardly knows where to begin the corrections, for in it hero-worship and megalomania have embraced one another.

From the McKinley Administration Roosevelt had inherited not a dispute but a provisional settlement. The latter had been so satisfactory that it had worked with no trouble in Alaska; in November, 1900, McKinley and Roosevelt had carried every State the interests

[1] *Op. cit.,* I, p. 258.
[2] James Ford Rhodes, in his *McKinley and Roosevelt Administrations, 1897–1909,* p. 256, takes a similar view of the Alaska settlement, basing his account in part upon a conversation with Roosevelt, Nov. 17, 1905.

of which had been directly involved; and it had been sufficiently acceptable to England for the British Cabinet, with the acquiescence of Canada, to consent to the first Hay-Pauncefote convention, and, a year and a half later, to the complete abrogation of the Clayton-Bulwer Treaty. In the last days of the McKinley Administration there were before the American Government for consideration no proposals substantially different from those which had been before the Joint High Commission at its adjournment in 1899. As for immediately taking control of a situation which, by inference, was running wild, the abundant documentary evidence which remains does not read that way. No one ran wild until, about two years after the provisional settlement, Roosevelt became eager, for reasons known best to himself, to make a demonstration. What, by the alleged intervention through the British Ambassador, he secured, was a treaty which his Secretary of State quietly and tactfully had been pressing for four years.

"Let sleeping dogs lie," was the President's parting word to Choate in January, 1902, when the latter called at the Department, and at the White House, for "sailing orders" before returning to his post in London.[1] At the end of June, Choate was startled to have Lord Lansdowne arouse these dogs.

The British Foreign Secretary asked the Ambassador to talk with Sir Wilfrid Laurier and with Lord Minto, who were then in London. Both the British and the Canadians wished to reopen the discussions which had never been officially closed. Without instructions, remembering Roosevelt's parting injunction, Choate reported Lansdowne's request to the Department and asked for orders. Hay was away. Through Dr. Hill, Acting Secretary, the President replied in not very diplomatic language, which was incorporated into the telegram, to the effect that Choate might talk with Laurier and Minto, but that Roosevelt believed the Canadian claim to be without a leg to stand on. The American Government, declared the President, would not compromise.

That was the position which Hay had taken for four years. The most recent exchange in the very leisurely and unofficial conversations between the Secretary and Lord Pauncefote had been on Febru-

---

[1] Choate to Hay, July 5, 1902. Appendix II.

ary 28, 1902.[1] On that date the Ambassador submitted his comments on a draft treaty which Hay had offered him in May, 1901. The Hay draft was substantially what he had several times suggested, a tribunal of jurists, three on a side, decision by majority vote, to interpret the geographical terms of the treaty of 1825 between Russia and England. The significant part of Pauncefote's reply was the evidence it afforded that Canada was becoming conciliatory. The Ambassador hinted that, in case the tribunal should decide that Dyea, Skagway, and, presumably, even Pyramid Harbor, were in Canadian territory, Canada would be satisfied with compensation and would not demand that the ports be turned over to England.

The circumstances surrounding the reopening of the boundary question are completely given in Choate's letter of July 5, to Hay. The somewhat wordy letter so well exhibits the way in which Choate was discharging his duties, that the communication is given in full in Appendix II. The substance is as follows:

In the course of two informal conversations Laurier conceded to Choate that the Canadians would accept Hay's favorite scheme of a tribunal of six and, furthermore, would be satisfied, even if the Canadians won the decision, to accept some form of compensation other than the transfer of Skagway and Dyea to Canada.

A few days before the arrival in Washington of Choate's letter, Hay received one from Henry White on the same subject.[2] White's letter, while not so complete, indicated even more clearly than Choate's that Laurier was looking for an opportunity to "save his face" before his own people. The letter completely exploded, also, the statement made by Lodge to White in a previous letter that the Canadians were really willing to adopt the American view as to a method of settlement but were being prevented by the British Government. Such an assertion was absurd, as White knew, but he was glad to have it confuted by Sir Wilfred himself. Unfortunately, however, the Lodge assertion seems to have been made also to the President, who was revealing, at times, a disposition to draw his opinions on foreign relations from his old friend, rather than from his Secretary of State— a situation always potentially annoying to Hay, and in this instance particularly so.

---

[1] Miscellaneous Letters, Dept. of State, February 28, 1902; Pauncefote to Hay.
[2] June 28, 1902. This letter is printed in Nevins' *White*, pp. 192–93.

It was Hay's loyal practice never to fail to forward to the President any letter from White which would tend to show the latter worthy of promotion. In sending over the one of June 28, Hay added a brief note, July 7, emphasizing that not only Laurier but also Lansdowne appeared to desire a settlement. To this the President replied very impatiently and indecisively, repeating that the Canadian claim had not a leg to stand on.[1]

That the Foreign Office, as well as Laurier, was very much in earnest became clear when Lord Lansdowne, having waited two weeks for some response from Choate, opened the subject again, expressing regret that the Ambassador had thrown cold water on Laurier's overtures. Choate again cabled for definite instructions. Hay did not often betray his resentment at Roosevelt's manner. He appears not to have replied to the President's cavalier comment on White's letter, but the second telegram from Choate compelled him to force his chief to reconsider. The following letter from Hay to the President is written with much restraint and dignity, and yet it reveals some feeling of slight at Roosevelt's indifference to what Hay had always regarded as one of his most important services: [2]

I enclose a copy of a letter dated the 5th of July which I received this morning from Mr. Choate, and also of a telegram which has just arrived.

I regret to bother you with a matter which you seem to have already decided, and yet I feel that I would not be justified in withholding these communications from you. It seems in your letter returning Mr. White's letter that you did not quite understand my point of view, which is precisely the same as yours, in regard to the merits of the case. I do not think they have a leg to stand on, and I think any impartial court of jurists would so decide. At the same time I recognize the danger of submitting such a matter to an ordinary arbitration, the besetting sin of which is to split the difference. My suggestion was a submission of the question of the interpretation of the treaty of 1825 to a tribunal of six, three on a side, a majority to decide.[3]

In this case it is impossible that we should lose, and not at all impossible that a majority should give a verdict in our favor. As to Sir Wilfred's suggestion concerning compensation, it does not mean, as you seem to think, that compensation should be given in case the commission should decide in our

---

[1] Roosevelt to Hay, July 10, 1902.

[2] July 14, 1902.

[3] Hay originally wrote "arbitration of six" and then substituted "tribunal." Roosevelt's misunderstanding of the Hay proposal, and much of the subsequent criticism, arose from confusion in the use of terms. The Alaska Boundary Arbitration, commonly so-called, was an arbitration only in a qualified sense. The word "arbitration" connoted the very method which Hay had for four years been trying to avoid.

favor. His suggestion is that, in the case—which seems to me impossible—of a commission deciding in *their* favor, they still would not insist on the possession of Dyea and Skagway but would then consider the subject of some compensation for our retaining the strip. This is still more clearly brought out in Laurier's conversation with Mr. Choate.

You will observe by Choate's telegram that Lord Lansdowne now wishes to converse with him on the subject. I will be glad to get your instructions as to what I am to say to him. Shall I tell him to drop the matter at once, or talk with Lord Lansdowne and ascertain his wishes?

To this extent did Roosevelt "take control" of the situation, and to this extent also did his Secretary of State fail to defend his opinion and decline to argue with the President. Roosevelt was behaving like one who clung to a "fixed idea," which was shared by Senator Lodge, that Hay could not be trusted to press the just claims of the United States against England.

The negotiations went forward languidly until the arrival, in the fall, of Sir Michael Herbert, Lord Pauncefote's successor. All of the information received during the summer, however, confirmed the impression conveyed by the previous correspondence that Laurier was seeking an opportunity to escape with as little loss of prestige as possible from an awkward situation in which he had placed himself as the champion in Canada of doubtful rights in Alaska. It was equally clear that England was again supporting Canada in an almost perfunctory way, and that Lansdowne himself had as little confidence in the Canadian claim as Lord Pauncefote had often betrayed to Hay. In September Hay learned from Maurice Low that Laurier was even resigned to giving way on the most hotly disputed point, the terms of reference. He would yield to Hay's contention that the tribunal must be limited to passing on the true interpretation of the terms of the treaty of 1825. Roosevelt, nevertheless, continued to nurse his resentment and, as late as July 25, in the following year, wrote to Mr. Justice Holmes: "Nothing but my very earnest desire to get on well with England and my reluctance to come to a break made me consent to this appointment of a Joint Commission in this case; for I regard the attitude of Canada, which England has backed, as having the scantiest possible warrant in justice." [1]

The arrival of Sir Michael Herbert, Lord Pauncefote's successor, in October, gave an impetus to the negotiations and the treaty was

[1] Bishop, I, p. 259.

signed January 24, 1903. The next day Hay wrote to his wife one of those rare letters in which he indulged in some degree of self-satisfaction: [1]

> Yesterday was another memorable day in the family history. At five o'clock in the library of our house I signed with Sir Michael Herbert a treaty for the appointment of a tribunal to determine the Alaska Boundary questions. It is substantially the same treaty which we proposed three years ago and which was rejected by England and Canada, Lord Herschell and Sir Wilfrid Laurier breaking up the Joint High Commission on that issue. Lord Pauncefote thought our proposition reasonable and tried for two years to induce his government to accept it, but was never able to accomplish it; Roosevelt at first was not keen about it, but after a while he came to agree with me, and gradually I got Lodge, Cullom and all the others of the Foreign Relations Committee to see it as I did. Then came Michael Herbert, who wanted to do something to signalize his promotion and I took it up with him. Canada kicked a while but finally consented and last night the work was done. It will go to the Senate Monday morning, with, I think, a fair chance of passing.

The treaty called for "six impartial jurists of repute who shall consider judicially the questions submitted to them"; three to be appointed by the United States, and three by England. The decision was to be by majority vote. Each of the high contracting parties agreed to deliver its evidence to the other within two months from the exchange of ratifications. In two more months each side was required to file its reply. Within the next period of two months the oral arguments were to be made before the commission. The points of reference were limited to the geographical meaning of the vague or disputed terms of the treaty of 1825. The terms of the treaty were still further limited in such a way as to make certain that the decision would be rendered before the November elections in the United States.[2]

Five days after being sent to the Senate the treaty was withdrawn by the President for a significant "correction." In the body of the document the commission of six was uniformly referred to merely as a "tribunal," but in the preamble it was described as an "arbitral tribunal." The adjective was objectionable to some Senators. A new page was engrossed and inserted, no new signatures being required.

---

[1] *Letters and Diaries*, III, pp. 264–65. The printed text appears to have been incorrectly dated; original letter not found in Hay Papers; names, which in printed text were given only as initials, supplied by author.

[2] Text of treaty and subsequent correspondence over the dates is printed in *For. Rel.*, 1903, pp. 488 ff.

Evidently England acquiesced in the deletion of "arbitral." [1] Thus, Great Britain consenting, the treaty was robbed of the last mark which would make the agreement an arbitration.

"The whole machinery of the tribunal," explained Hay to White on April 10, "is got up with the expectation on our part that the British Government would see in it the means of receding from an absolutely untenable position. . . ."

When the Senate was still reluctant to act, Hay wrote Chairman Cullom of the Foreign Relations Committee, February 11, pointing out the political hazard of such a course: "It seems to the President, and I am decidedly of the same mind, that out of all the treaties before the Senate the Alaska boundary one is of the most immediate, pressing importance. If the others should fail of ratification during this session, the President will, of course, call an extraordinary session of the Senate to consider them, but this would be too late for the Alaska treaty. We cannot carry it into effect without a little legislation, and we must have that before the 4th of March or not at all. I have heard some talk about letting it go over until next year, but this would be unfortunate, as the matter being still unsettled, it would be an issue in the Presidential campaign, whereas this being a quiet time in politics, it could be considered on its merits and the whole matter settled before next year."

While Gen. John W. Foster, because of his long familiarity with the controversy, was selected to prepare the case for presentation to the commission, it was the earnest desire both of Roosevelt and Hay that Choate doff his insignia of office as Ambassador and appear as attorney before the tribunal. Choate courteously but firmly declined. Apparently neither the President nor the Secretary realized to what a degree the British Foreign Office had, in confidence, many times revealed to the Ambassador its lack of faith in the Canadian claim, and its disapproval of the manner in which it had been so persistently urged.

"I should not only have enjoyed it very much," explained Choate,[2] "but should have considered it the crowning honor of my long profes-

---

[1] Adee to Hay, Jan. 31, 1903. "The Alaska Tribunal treaty has just been returned to us by a resolution in Executive Session. I have directed Mr. Smith to have the first sheet re-engrossed, with the necessary changes. It will be ready on Monday, when the seals can be broken, the treaty untied, the new sheet substituted, and the blame thing retied ready for re-apposition of the seals, which can be done without re-signing."

[2] March 6, 1903, to Hay.

sional life. So I am sure that you will not regard me, for you cannot justly regard me, as shrinking from a duty. Ever since I came here in March, 1899, I have been in more or less constant communication with the Foreign Office in the discussion of the Alaska Case, in endeavors to settle it, and in the argument of all the questions essential and incidental, involved in it. My first private letter to you of May 19, 1899, shows how fully I was immersed in it from the start, and it was only just before the receipt of your last letter proposing to me this service as counsel that I was trying to get from Lord Lansdowne the report of Col. Cameron in 1886, the inventor of the Canadian claim, and who by the way, I found was a son-in-law of Sir Charles Tupper. All this communication and intercourse was in a way necessarily confidential. It was under the seal of my diplomatic relation, of my office of Ambassador; it brought me into relations first with Lord Salisbury and afterwards with Lord Lansdowne of a very confidential character which they would never have thought of holding with me, if they had supposed that I should afterwards appear in the rôle of counsel for the United States against Great Britain in this very case, and I cannot but think that they would feel justly aggrieved on the part of their government if, after all my dealings with them, I should so appear."

The next major occasion on which the President "took control" of the situation was in the appointment of the three American members of the commission. These were Senator George Turner of Washington, whose term expired with the outgoing Congress; Elihu Root, who was still Secretary of War; and Senator Lodge. The appointment of Lodge was, obviously, the most objectionable. It seemed as though in the entire boundary matter the President was delivered into the possession of his most evil genii. He was not content to leave even the last remnant of conciliation with which his Secretary of State had sought to wrap the disappointment which Laurier well knew he must accept in any form.

Laurier was so shocked that he resorted to the futile expedient of a personal appeal to Hay, February 24. He wrote:

I presume upon the privilege of your personal acquaintance to [lay] aside all formalities to appeal to you directly on a matter which might seriously, if not fatally interfere with the final disposition of the much vexed and long pending difficulty about the delimitation of the boundary line between

Alaska and Canada.

We are informed from Washington that the President has appointed or, to speak more correctly, selected as the American members of the court Messrs. Root, Lodge and Turner.

I appeal to you that these gentlemen under existing circumstances cannot with any fairness be styled "impartial jurists." I do not press the point as to Mr. Root; I learn on good authority that before assuming his duties as a member of the court he will have ceased to be a member of the Administration, & therein lies the sole ground of objection against him as an "impartial jurist."

Unfortunately the case is much more serious as to Messrs. Lodge & Turner, for both in public speeches widely circulated have practically proclaimed that they could not approach the question with an open mind, both having expressed their convictions that one side of the case is so strong as to render almost factious the mere presentation of the other side.

I do not forget the high character of Senator Lodge but in all human affairs concrete cases will always outweigh general considerations. I say this in reference to the effect of the language of Senator Lodge, when the time must come for me to obtain the assent of the Canadian Parliament to the reference of our case to the tribunal of "impartial jurists" as it would be constituted.

You know how difficult it is to move legislative bodies, and you will readily conceive, I am sure, that the hostile attitude of two of the proposed members of the court would make it extremely difficult to obtain & not a little humiliating to grant the legislative assent which we must obtain to carry this vexed question to a conclusion.

Hay, regardless of his personal feelings, publicly stood by the President. However, in the intimacies of his correspondence with Henry White, he revealed to what a degree he shared Laurier's views: [1]

I do not see how anybody could make any objection to Root. He is at the head of the Bar of New York, and it is hardly too much to say that he is the first lawyer in America now that Mr. Choate is out of the country. His being a statesman as well, I should say, does not disqualify him for a place on any tribunal of sufficient importance to claim his services. Of course, the presence of Lodge on the tribunal is, from many points of view, regrettable, and, as if the devil were inspiring him, he took occasion last week to make a speech in Boston, one half of it filled with abuse of the Canadians, and the other half with attacks on the State Department. He is a clever man and a man of a great deal of force in the Senate, but the infirmity of his mind and character is that he never sees but one subject at a time, and just at present it is the acceptability of his son-in-law to the voters of Gloucester. Of course you know his very intimate relations with the President, which make it almost impossible that the President should deny him anything he has to give him, and he insisted upon this appointment on the tribunal.

[1] April 10, 1903; Nevins, *White*, p. 195.

The rough-shod manner of the President was having the worst possible effect on the British Government. As fast as he could Roosevelt was spoiling a perfect case. "I do not disguise my anxiety as to the outcome of the sitting of the tribunal," wrote White.[1] It was recognized that the verdict would lie in the hands of Lord Chief Justice Alverstone, who was the only British member of the commission. A lord chief justice is not accustomed to being brow-beaten.

Having thus publicly flouted Canadian sensibilities, and having made a very poor return for the friendly attitude which the British Foreign Office had uniformly shown toward both Choate and Hay in seeking to compose the difficulty with Canada, as well as over the Clayton-Bulwer Treaty, Roosevelt was still not content to let the affair slip from his clumsy control. It is difficult to resist the conclusion that he had determined to create a Canadian issue for campaign purposes. Passing over, therefore, the details of the negotiations leading up to fixing the date for the meeting of the commission, we turn to Roosevelt's final fling, his attempt to intimidate the commission which he had helped to create.

"I do not think any threats are at this time advisable or needful," firmly replied Hay, July 2, to one of the President's importunities. "We shall be as hard on them as is decent—perhaps rather more so." The entire letter is important:

Dear Theodore

Your letter of the 29th has this moment reached me. We are doing exactly what you suggest—resisting to the utmost bounds of courtesy or of equity every attempt at delay. I do not think they are acting in bad faith. They are availing themselves of every possible pretext the treaty gives them of demanding more time to patch up their deplorably weak case. They see nothing but defeat before them, and they want to make as good a record of their fight as possible.

Choate is conducting the matter admirably in London. Although they said they could not present their counter case on the 3d of July, his last telegram said they would probably do it, though in an incomplete form.

Foster's worst enemy would never accuse him of any tendency to mercy or tenderness to an opponent. The treaty *does* allow for more time in special exigencies—but we are fighting to show they have no right to it now. You remember we crowded them out of two months they wanted, in the negotiation of the treaty.

They are amazed at the strength of our case & the promptness with

[1] Nevins, p. 196.

which it was made ready, and are trying to spar for wind.

I do not think any threats are at this time advisable or needful.

We shall be as hard on them as is decent—perhaps rather more so.

Even such a letter was not sufficient to restrain the President's hand. Already he had written to Lodge that he was contemplating the possibility of declaring the negotiations off, reciting the case to Congress and asking for appropriations to run the boundary as "we " meaning, perhaps, not simply Roosevelt and Lodge, thought best.[1] On the 25th of July he repeated the statement, substantially, in a letter to Mr. Justice Holmes and suggested that he convey the information to Mr. Chamberlain who, as Colonial Secretary, was most immediately concerned with the outcome of the dispute.[2]

The summer of 1903 was a very anxious time in American foreign relations. The Canadians were persisting to the end in dilatory tactics which threatened to postpone the decision of the Alaska Commission until a date too dangerously close to the opening of the new Congress. The Colombians were refusing to ratify the canal treaty, and the Russians over in Manchuria, in defiance of the United States, as well as of Japan and Great Britain, were digging in for what was planned as permanent occupation. Roosevelt fussed about foreign affairs, but on July 11 he burst out enthusiastically to Hay in a note: "When I came in I thought you a great Secretary of State, but now I have had a chance to know far more fully what a really great Secretary of State you are."

Hay, on the other hand, again considered resignation, actually proposing it, July 23. However, at Roosevelt's earnest request he remained in the Cabinet, but his most immediate duty became to keep the President within such reasonable bounds as from day to day seemed possible. Four years before he had to meet the threat that Congress would treat the Clayton-Bulwer Treaty as a scrap of paper. Now he had to deal with a President who seemed spoiling for a wholly unwarranted quarrel with England. A second time he intervened through his friends in London to help protect what he regarded as the honor of his own country. He wrote to Henry White, September 20, "so that it might indiscreetly percolate to Balfour," warning him that the President, in case the tribunal disagreed, would defy the Canadian

---

[1] June 29, 1903; *Roosevelt-Lodge Letters,* II, p. 37.
[2] Bishop, I, p. 259.

claims and hold the disputed territory at all costs. Probably the letter should not have been written, but its spirit was likely to soften the effect of similar letters which the President was writing.[1]

Then Hay made one more effort to keep the President within bounds. On September 25 he gently reminded him that there was nothing further for him to do while the matter was *"sub judice."*

Dear Mr. President:
I had seen this article already and had written to Harry White—so that it might indiscreetly percolate through to Balfour—that it would be a deplorable thing if this Canadian bulldozing succeeded: that I knew, both from Pauncefote and Laurier that they had no belief in their case; that you were brought to consent to this Tribunal purely through your desire for good relations & the settlement of a vexed question honorably to England: that if the Tribunal failed to agree, it would end the matter: that we should hold the property that belongs to us, of our right to which we have never had the shadow of a doubt: that neither you, nor any American President would ever make another attempt to facilitate the escape of Canada from an absolutely untenable position.
Of course the matter is now *sub judice.* You can say nothing about it: I cannot instruct Choate nor can he talk officially to Lansdowne. But I am sure Harry White will leave no doubt of the true state of the case in the mind of the Prime Minister.
And in spite of everything, I cannot help believing that we shall get a verdict. Our written case is impregnable and Foster says Dickinson will make a powerful closing argument.

P. S. And even if they disagree our position is infinitely stronger than it was before.

It would indeed appear as though the President had already done and said enough.

The anxiety and nervous strain were very severe, but gradually Hay's confidence rose. On October 19 he wrote to Mrs. Hay that "Today, if the prospect holds good, we shall get a verdict in the Alaska case. If so, it will be one of the greatest transactions of my life. It will justify a plan which I adopted and carried through against the misgivings of everybody, and the result will prove that I was right in relying on the honor and conscience of an English Judge."

The next day Lord Alverstone gave his decision in favor of substantially all of the American claims.

Three days later Hay added to his wife a summary of the entire

[1] Nevins, p. 198.

story, and mentioned the President's comments in the Cabinet meeting:

The newspapers do not seem to get the rights of the Portland channel. There are two entrances to it like this with two little islands in it [see cut, opposite page].

We agree that the Boundary shall be by the North Channel instead of the South, which gives them those two little Islands—worth nothing to us. That is all poor Canada gets by the decision, and I do not wonder they are furious but as Will Thomson used to say "Serves 'em right, if they can't take a joke." I can hardly believe my eyes and ears when I see how perfectly all my ideas in this great transaction have been carried out. Kasson and I arranged the treaty four years ago. Herschell and Laurier indignantly refused to accept it. Nobody on this side cared much about it. McKinley told me to go ahead. I got Lord Pauncefote enlisted in it—then he died. I began again with Herbert and he went into it cordially & got his Government to accept. I had a hard job to induce the Senate to ratify it, and at one time it seemed to be beaten; but it got through and then came to the naming of the commissioners—which I won't talk about. Since then everybody has worked nobly— especially Foster & Choate and White. Dickinson made a splendid argument—but I think the battle was already won.

The President today had got over all his doubts & fears. He loaded me with compliments today in the Cabinet meeting. "Nobody living could have done the work as I did," &c &c. "It was the biggest success of my life." &c. I think myself that Lord Alverstone is the hero of the hour. No American statesman would have dared to give a decision on his honor and conscience directly against the claim of his own country. The completeness of the victory is something amazing. We have got everything we claimed, including the rich gold fields of Tlehini & Chilkat rivers & the Porcupine, which I feared we might lose and which I would have been willing to lose to secure the heads of the inlets.

Poor little Savage-Landor came in yesterday just back from the Philippines. He admired our Botticelli no end—which is worth regarding for he is a Florentine.

Driving on the Canal one group of darky children cried out "Hello Prest. Roosevelt." A little further on a woman cried "I 'clare! Takes two hosses to ca'y one man." A third group said "Thar goes President Davis!" I must be getting to look like *some* kind of a statesman!

Just as in July, 1900, when Hay had staked his reputation on his confidence that the foreigners in Peking were alive and that most could be gained by conciliating the Southern viceroys, so in 1903 he again stuck to a project in the face of opposition and indifference, and was vindicated. The American case in Alaska must have been good:

otherwise a British judge, in the face of Roosevelt's menaces, would never have dared to support it. The Alaska boundary settlement had been marred only by the rough handling it had from the President; otherwise, it would have been a graceful disposal of a dispute in which the British Government had many times revealed its desire for very friendly relations with the United States. Hay once likened Bryan to an ignorant person who would smash a fine vase without realizing that he was destroying a work of art. Roosevelt acted much that way in the Alaska business.

There is reason to believe that some years later Roosevelt asserted that he had, in the Alaska settlement, rejected every original proposal made by Hay, and that the latter had nothing to do with it in any vital matter.[1]

[1] Confidential source of information.

THEODORE ROOSEVELT, said Henry Adams, had that primitive quality which mediaeval theology assigned to God. He was "pure act." [1]

International relations, however, are no longer primitive as when men first lined up with clubs along their tribal boundaries. Civilization has spun a delicate fabric between states. It has a gossamer quality which John Hay loved to feel and which he was well adapted to weave. When Theodore Roosevelt, with his restless, combative energy, seized one delicate thread while Hay held the other, the relationship between the two men became, as Adams observed, essentially false. The difference was not merely between youth and age; it embraced habits of thought, ways of living, values. Nothing is so likely to disturb the peace and good-will of nations as "pure act." Roosevelt's intervention in the Alaska settlement marred a pattern of foreign affairs which his Secretary of State had designed; the intervention at Panama wrecked another as when a heavy-handed apprentice drives a weary master craftsman from his loom.

Breaking the backbone of a continent, refashioning the surface of a globe now hard and cold, was obviously a Rooseveltian task which the gods might envy. Its accomplishment would be the last achievement of a rich and scientific civilization. The reconciliation of the diverse interests of half a dozen states so that nations could merge their racial pride in a common objective and find glory enough for each in this last gigantic conquest of nature was different. It was a test of whether man in appropriating civilization had, at the same time, become civilized. Throughout the long negotiations which were designed to clear the path for a Goethals and a Gorgas, the answer to this second question was frequently in doubt. At one time it looked as though the Americans would unceremoniously break a solemn promise made in good faith to England half a century before. Then it appeared as if the Canadians might seize the opportunity for the practice of a little blackmail. Skillfully John Hay picked out the threads and untangled them. That part of the work was over before

[1] *Education*, p. 417.

Roosevelt had even a chance to interfere.

The other states concerned were Nicaragua and Costa Rica, which together possessed the sovereignty over the northern—the so-called American—route; Colombia, which controlled the Isthmus at its narrowest point, where de Lesseps began to dig; and France, to whose nationals Colombia had given a concession, and which had already sunk many millions in an abortive enterprise. Indeed, there were still another set of sensibilities to be thought of. The movements of the United States in the Caribbean were being viewed with some suspicion, if not with alarm, by most of those nations of Latin blood which lay in the path of the Yankee advance. Much would depend on how the American Government might conduct itself at the Isthmus.

For a time all went well; Roosevelt let Hay have his way.

It is difficult to pass by in this narrative the fascinating story of how, early in 1902, the American Government, swung over to a choice of the Panama route across the Isthmus, after having for many years dismissed it as impractical. For information on that subject the reader must be referred to Philippe Bunau-Varilla's highly dramatic *Panama,* published in 1913, and to the even more extraordinary *Story of Panama,* published by the Government Printing Office in Washington in the same year, as the hearings before the House Committee on Foreign Affairs on the Rainey Resolution.[1]

In these two documents the former chief engineer of the French canal company is often in conflict with William Nelson Cromwell, the attorney for the company in the United States. Without pausing to attempt to distribute between them the credit, or discredit, it is sufficient to comment that these two publications afford the most complete and authentic record yet available about one of the most remarkable propaganda campaigns ever undertaken in the United States to influence legislation. Some presumptions of a scandalous nature are raised, but not proved. It is a notable episode in American history, but John Hay had no part in it until he was directed to seek from Colombia a project of a treaty which would convey to the American Government the rights which were considered necessary to warrant taking over the

---

[1] The so-called Rainey Resolution (H. Res. 32, 62–1) directed the Foreign Affairs Committee to inquire into the facts relative to Roosevelt's famous statement at the University of California, March 23, 1911: "I took the Canal Zone and let Congress debate, and while the debate goes on the canal does also." The most extended use yet made of these sources is in Pringle's *Roosevelt,* pp. 301–38: two chapters under the captions "Setting for a Melodrama"; and "I Took Panama."

de Lesseps concession and finishing the abortive French enterprise at Panama.

At a time when few thought seriously of any alternative, Hay was a partisan of the Nicaraguan route across the Isthmus. He seems never entirely to have abandoned that conviction, but the growing preference for Panama considerably simplified his diplomatic problem. He was no longer required to negotiate for the purchase of a monopoly.

Although Nicaraguan Canal legislation was already well advanced, the sudden decision of the French company, early in January, 1902, to offer its concession and assets for $40,000,000, influenced Congress, in the next six months, to reverse every vote it had ever taken on the subject by adopting the Spooner Bill, which became a law June 28. It directed the President to seek first from Colombia certain specified rights designed to secure for the United States a perpetual control of the proposed canal. As an alternative it was provided that if such rights were not obtainable within a reasonable time and on reasonable terms, the President should then turn to Nicaragua and Costa Rica. The choice was made also contingent upon the ability of the French company to deliver a clear title but this contingency was soon removed; Attorney General Knox declared the title good. The diplomatic question became solely whether Colombia would meet the conditions laid down in the Spooner Act, or whether the President should turn again to the northern route. The questions of "reasonable terms" and a "reasonable time" were in the law left to the discretion of the President.

It is important, therefore, to remember that the action taken a year and a half later at Panama was one wholly within the discretion of the President. It was not mandatory under the law, and was even contrary to it since the Spooner Act directed him to negotiate with Colombia, Nicaragua, and Costa Rica, not with the new state of Panama. Throughout this narrative it will be observed that the choice was never between a canal or no canal, but rather between the southern and the northern routes. The latter was longer and would be more expensive but the Isthmian Canal Commission had twice reported that it was practical from an engineering point of view. That conclusion has been reaffirmed many times since then and a second canal is now probable at some distant date.

While the hot debate on the Spooner Bill was going forward in the

Senate, Hay sought to maintain an impartial position by trying to secure from each of the three countries concerned protocols of treaties to which they would be willing to agree. The great protagonist of the Nicaraguan route was Senator Morgan. Many times the Senator tried to get the Secretary to help him in his uncompromising fight against Senator Hanna and the Panama crowd. In the letters to Morgan, quoted below, in which Hay explained the difficulties he was meeting, it will be observed that while the Secretary was studiously avoiding partisanship in the debate, his sympathies appeared to incline toward the Morgan side. The first letter is under date of April 22:

It is true that the Panama people have at last made their proposition. I have been trying to induce them to make some changes in it which might render it more acceptable to the Senate and to our people. When it is completed I shall give them a note announcing the readiness of the government of the United States to enter into a Convention respecting the Canal, when the Congress shall have authorized the President to do so, and when the legal officers of the United States shall have been satisfied of the power of the Panama Canal Company to transfer all their rights in the case.

I regret to say that I have not yet been able to get a firm offer from the Government of Nicaragua. I have been striving for this end for some months, and Mr. Corea and I have entirely agreed as to a Convention which we are willing to send to Congress for its information in view of pending legislation. Let me assure you, in strictest confidence, that I was unwilling to send in the Panama proposition until I was able also to send in the Nicaragua proposals. I have been greatly disappointed at the delay of the Nicaraguan Government and have urged upon them in every possible way, the desirability of their coming to a conclusion. The principal difficulty in the case is this; that both in Colombia and in Nicaragua great ignorance exists as to the attitude of the United States. In both countries it is believed that their route is the only one possible or practicable, and that the Government of the United States, in the last resort, will accept any terms they choose to demand. The Ministers here of both powers know perfectly well that this is untrue, and they are doing all they can to convince their people at home that no unreasonable proposition will be considered by the Government of the United States; but it is slow work convincing them.

I should be glad to be informed by you of your own judgment in regard to the present state of affairs. Do you think we had better send in the Panama proposal now, as soon as they get ready, or wait a while to see if we can get the Nicaragua people to listen to reason, and send the two proposals together?

You will understand that in neither case are the proposed conventions exactly what I would have drawn up, nor are they precisely what you would consider the ideal arrangement, but I have thought it was my duty to ascertain the best terms which we could get from both of the Governments, so that the Congress might act with full knowledge of all the circumstances, so far as the Diplomatic Department is concerned.

Evidently Senator Morgan tried to persuade the Secretary to espouse openly the Nicaraguan route, for, the following day, April 23, Hay elaborated still further to Mr. Morgan:

I do not understand you to mean that you think we are estopped from considering any proposition which the Government of Colombia may choose to make to us, nor from agreeing to enter into diplomatic negotiations with that Government as soon as the President is authorized to do so by Congress. This is as far as I think the State Department is justified in going, and it stands in the same attitude in reference to the Governments of Nicaragua and Costa Rica. I conceive my duties to be to try to ascertain the exact purposes and intentions of both Governments, and, when I have done so, to inform your Committee of the results of my investigations, which information they will, doubtless, use wisely in determining the question which route shall be adopted. I do not consider myself justified in advocating either route, as this matter rests within the discretion of Congress. When Congress has spoken, it will then be the duty of the State Department to make the best arrangement possible for whichever route Congress may decide upon.

The Secretary, however, never ceased his efforts to keep the Nicaraguan alternative clearly in view. Mr. Corea, the Nicaraguan Minister, was a difficult diplomat with whom to do business. Hay reported to Morgan, May 12, 1902:

It is impossible for you, as it would be impossible for anyone, to appreciate the exasperating difficulties that have been placed in my way in trying to get a definite proposition from our Central American friends. I have finally sent a note to Mr. Corea, telling him I can wait no longer upon the convenience of his Government; that he must, before Tuesday of this week, let me know what they propose, and that, in case I get no definite proposition from them by that time, I shall submit to Congress the proposition made by the Colombian Government, and also a statement that it has been impossible to get anything definite from the Government of Nicaragua.

Hay added that the President greatly preferred, as had McKinley, that the question of the route should be decided by Congress, but in case it should seem best to Congress to leave to him the decision of the route, he "will not evade that labor and responsibility."

May 14, 1902, Hay wrote to Morgan. "I hope you will not use the

Colombian proposition with your Committee until I am able to send in the document. The Nicaraguan Minister having asked for a delay of only one more day, I feel that I ought not to cut him off without giving him twenty-four hours more grace. If you use the Colombian proposition now it will subject me, and I think justly, to the severe criticism of your colleagues, who have already, as I told you, complained to the President of my giving you information which is not communicated to the rest of them. This, I hope, is the last appeal I shall make to your forbearance."

Nevertheless, the partisans of the Panama route rapidly gained ground. Six weeks before the passage of the Spooner amendment the Secretary was able to transmit to Representative Hepburn, chairman of the House committee on rivers and harbors, a batch of correspondence with the three Central American republics, in which were included projects of treaties with both Colombia and Nicaragua. It was not expected that Costa Rica would make any trouble. The President had given his approval and Hay had formally declared to Señor Concha, the Colombian Minister, that he would be prepared to sign such a treaty as Colombia had proposed, provided the French title proved clear, as soon as Congress gave the necessary authorization.[1] The Nicaraguan draft offered better terms, but evidently Colombia had been influenced in some degree by the competitive bidding which Hay had been able to set up. Nicaragua asked for $6,000,000 and an "annual rent" of $25,000; Colombia desired not less than $7,000,000 and an undetermined "annuity" which would be fixed by arbitration and revisable at the end of each hundred years. A more important difference was that while Nicaragua was willing to lease in perpetuity, Colombia had avoided such explicit words and hedged the proposed "concession" with many reservations in the interest of preserving Colombian sovereignty and retaining a partnership in the administration of the zone. On the other hand, in the first article of the proposed treaty Colombia expressly authorized the transfer of the French rights to the United States and there was nothing in the text to indicate that Colombia would demand of the company additional compensation for consenting to the transfer. The attorney for the canal company had made sure of this point which was to become so important a few months later.

[1] H. Doc. 611, 57–1.

In these preliminary negotiations with Colombia it had been obviously that the strongest influence for securing the treaty was the Panama Canal Company, the assets of which would become worthless if the United States were to choose the northern route. General Concha, formerly minister of war at Bogotá, although sent to Washington expressly to negotiate the protocol, had come with a chip on his shoulder. Throughout the negotiations it was evident that he entertained large ideas as to the share which his country ought to claim in the enterprise, and the precautions which should be taken to safeguard Panama against Yankee absorption. Over money matters he was not disposed to quibble. Upon the arrival of the minister in New York William Nelson Cromwell took the gentleman in charge and, at length, was able to establish such friendly relations that throughout the negotiations Cromwell became in fact, if not in title, the attorney for the Colombian Minister as well as for the company. At least equally potent to influence the Bogotá Government was Bunau-Varilla.[1]

When Concha submitted to Hay his first draft he accompanied it with an exposition by Cromwell, which he expressly approved, and the final draft of April 18 was from the hand of the New York attorney.[2]

The submission to Congress of the Colombian project was quite to the taste of the Senators. Rarely did they have such an opportunity to share in the actual negotiation of a treaty. Hay had been careful to bind Colombia to its offer by accepting it forthwith, but not so the Senators. Having passed the Spooner Bill, Congress adjourned but many of the Senators remained in town to write amendments to the treaty without which they would withhold their approval. From the President, Hay received orders, July 1, to "take personal direction" of the negotiations with Colombia, but on the same day Mr. Cromwell, at the request of Senator Hanna, also placed himself at the Secretary's command, and it was Cromwell who in the next two weeks rushed back and forth from office to office on Capitol Hill, then to Minister Concha, and back to the Department of State. Almost daily he reported to Hay either in person or by letter. The attitude of the Senators afforded the last and most perfect illustration of Hay's often repeated comment that the Senate's idea of negotiation was to take all and give nothing. Hay well knew that there was danger in tampering

[1] Bunau-Varilla, pp. 220 ff.
[2] H. Doc. 611, 57–1, pp. 2–7.

too much with an offer which Colombia had, at length, reluctantly made and which the President had accepted. He urged haste and on July 5 Cromwell was able to submit a redraft. Señor Concha appears to have assumed, for the time, a more cooperative attitude. At the end of two weeks Hay reported to the President: [1]

I have been at work for the last ten days trying to get the Colombian treaty in the shape desired by our friends of the Senate, particularly Spooner and Lodge. I have got at last a draft embodying all the things which are at present possible, and which, if accepted by the other side, will make a very good treaty. As I anticipated, General Concha does not feel strong enough in his instructions or his personal influence, to accept this *en bloc*, without consulting his government. He has sent several long telegrams to Bogotá, and is awaiting an answer. I have no idea that the thing can be done in a moment. It will require a good deal of correspondence between him and Mr. Marroquin to determine how far they will yield on the questions of jurisdiction and other details. I have no doubt that we shall get finally a very good treaty, even if it may be necessary for the Senate to make some slight amendments in it; but, as it looks now, this cannot be accomplished in a few days. I shall, therefore, if nothing further turns up to keep me here, go to my place in New Hampshire the end of next week.

A few days later the Secretary sent to Minister Concha a new draft carrying the amendments desired by Senators, but he was careful to observe in the covering note that, pending the discussion of the proposed changes, the exchange of notes on Concha's earlier draft should "continue in full force." [2] While trying to obtain what others desired, Hay was hoping at least to hold Colombia to what it had already offered. Communication by mail with Bogotá required at least ten weeks. The Senators returned to their homes, Mr. Cromwell to his law practice, and Hay went to New Hampshire, but the situation remained ticklish. Then, in September, just when it was most important to maintain toward Colombia a conciliatory attitude, Commander McLean of the U. S. S. *Cincinnati* landed some marines at Panama during a revolutionary outbreak, to keep the traffic open on the transisthmian railroad. [3]

Such an action was not unusual. It had been taken half a dozen times before under a provision of the treaty of 1846 between the United

[1] July 13, 1902.
[2] *Dip. Cor. of the Panama Canal*, p. 253.
[3] *Moore's Digest*, III, pp. 44–45; *Sen. Docs.* 143, 58–2; 10, 58–*Special Sess.*; Howard C. Hill, *Roosevelt and the Caribbean*, p. 45.

States and Colombia. However, in this instance the naval officers, perhaps a little too eager to come into possession of their heart's desire, did not wait for the formality of securing from Bogotá a request for intervention. This omission was most inopportune, although it does not appear to have greatly offended the Bogotá government. Peace between the government and revolutionary forces was eventually made in the cabin of Admiral Casey's flagship, but, in Washington, General Concha felt that the dignity of his country had been affronted. When the latter was instructed to resume the discussion of the treaty and to conclude the negotiations he observed that his instructions were dated prior to the intervention at Panama. Concha refused to go forward with the negotiations. He was never able to forgive the American Government for having arrogated to itself the authority to decide, without consulting Colombia, when intervention might be necessary. In Washington he appeared as a very stiff-necked old patriot, in poor health. At length Hay, unable to do business with him, complained through the American Minister at Bogotá and Concha was promptly recalled. He disappears from this narrative, clad in a straitjacket, being carried aboard ship in New York. Meanwhile Congress assembled and the treaty remained unsigned. Hay warned that the failure of Colombia to be reasonable might result in the choice of the Nicaraguan route. Such a threat was becoming daily more impotent. The Colombians never considered it very seriously.

Dr. Herran, who took over the negotiations from General Concha, proved conciliatory. The offensive clauses relative to Colombian sovereignty were soon smoothed out, and the discussion passed to the final topic, the size of the indemnity. Hay was willing to move up to $10,-000,000, with an annuity of $100,000. Colombia demanded the annual payment of at least half a million. Cromwell urged that the treaty be drafted so as to leave the amount to be determined by an arbitration commission. Bunau-Varilla shrewdly guessed that the American Government would agree to $250,000 to make sure of the other articles. He was right: the treaty, at that figure, was signed January 22, 1903. Senator Morgan fought it in the Senate and was beaten. Ratification was approved March 17, 1903. There were no amendments.

The testimony brought out in the hearings on the Rainey Resolution raises strong presumptions that Dr. Herran signed the treaty without express authorization from his government.[1] Certain it is that a message was on the way instructing the Chargé to withhold his signature. It is also clear that when the names were affixed to the treaty Cromwell certainly, and probably Hay, as well as the President and many leading Senators, knew that Colombia would renew its demand that the company agree to some further payment to Bogotá.

In Colombia opposition to the treaty gathered rapidly. It was of two kinds. Some felt that the financial terms were much too low; others saw a proposed violation of Colombian sovereignty and an affront to a weak nation by the Colossus of the North.

The first attack on the financial clauses was directed at the article by which Colombia was pledged to acquiesce, without compensation, in the transfer of the rights of the canal company directly to the United States. The company claimed, and, in the subsequent correspondence, Hay supported the contention, that in several ways the Colombian Government had already made an engagement, both with the company and with the United States, not to demand compensation for this permission to transfer the holdings of the old company. The arguments to this effect advanced by Cromwell, Bunau-Varilla, and Hay do not seem convincing. No one was able to show such a contract. On the other hand, in the American Senate the Panama Canal Company, for reasons which still remain obscure, had the very substantial support of such powerful friends as Senator Hanna. The latter had, a year before, at the request of his New York banker, who was also president of the Panama Railroad Company, practically required the Panama Canal Company to reengage Cromwell as its attorney.[2]

In his book Bunau-Varilla refers to the latter somewhat icily as "the lawyer by the name of Cromwell." The Colombian Minister of Finance, nearly a month before the Hay-Herran treaty was signed, had served notice on both the canal company and the railroad, the latter being a separate corporation, that some further negotiations with Colombia would be required before permission to sell would be approved.[3] At Bogotá it was often mentioned that Colombia should require the company to turn over ten of the forty millions as the in-

---

[1] *Story of Panama*, p. 320; Dennis, p. 338, footnote no. 18.
[2] Bunau-Varilla, pp. 214–15.
[3] *For. Rel.*, 1903, pp. 141–42.

demnity for consent to the transfer. Throughout the discussions on this point Hay took the position that the Colombian demand was "wholly inadmissible."

There was also talk in Bogotá of demanding that both the lump-sum payment and the annuity from the United States be increased, perhaps doubled.

In seeking to justify before the American people the action taken in, November, 1903, at Panama, the President and his Secretary of State seem to have given an undue importance to the increased financial demands of Colombia. The political objections were at least equally influential. The Hay-Herran treaty contemplated in the Canal Zone a judicial system of extraterritoriality. It was also proposed that in taking over the shares of the Panama Railroad the United States would come into actual control of the real estate in both Colon and Panama which had been acquired by the railroad. The effect would be to remove the greater part of these two very important Colombian cities from Colombian control. Furthermore, the clause referring to a board of arbitration to settle differences between Colombia and the United States seemed to lack precision.[1]

The substance of the situation appears to have been as follows: Colombia lived a national life remote from the world. Its capital was on an Andean plateau ten days' journey from the coast. Its civilization was agricultural; its political ideas were primitive. Colombians, for the most part, were very imperfectly informed as to how business is transacted in the great outside world, and they were equally indifferent. They realized that in the Isthmus they possessed an extraordinary natural asset. They could not be convinced that the talk of a Nicaraguan alternative was anything but Yankee bluff to be used in bargaining. Sovereignty was a grand idea such as the Latin American mind loves to dwell upon. The political objections to the treaty were genuine. On the other hand, Colombia was a land of revolution where the theoretical processes of representative government were often suspended for long periods. President Marroquin had come into power by a *coup d'état* and had reigned for some years without a legislature. He was, in 1903, about eighty years of age, too old to be firm in his seat or to hold down much longer the counter-revolutionary parties. The treaty

---

[1] A summary and exposition of all of the Colombian objections to the treaty is given in *For. Rel.,* 1903, pp. 172–73.

could not be ratified by constitutional means but, if the United States and the Panama Canal Company had been willing to spend enough money to make it an object, the Colombian leaders, of one party or another, could have arranged another *coup* and could have ratified the treaty. They were, however, unwilling to do this without such substantial remuneration as was represented by the proposed increases in the indemnities.

Throughout 1903 Hay took the position that President Marroquin, by authorizing his representative in Washington to sign the treaty, had assumed an obligation to defend its terms in Bogotá. Hay's case would have been stronger if he could have shown that Herran had actually been so authorized. On the other hand, Marroquin unquestionably had favored the treaty and encouraged the negotiations. In his address, June 20, to the Congress especially assembled to ratify the convention, instead of talking like the dictator he had always been, the President defended the treaty "after the fashion of Pontius Pilate," to use Bunau-Varilla's expression.[1] To this extent there was actual bad faith. The situation at Bogotá was not as it had been in Washington in 1900 when McKinley had presented the first Hay-Pauncefote Treaty to the Senate. In that case the administration kept faith with England by defending the treaty it had made. Marroquin did not.

On August 12, the Colombian Senate, unanimously save for the vote of one delegate from Panama, rejected the treaty. The following day the absent delegate published in the daily paper a solemn warning in which he intimated how great would be the dissatisfaction of the province of Panama, which once had been an independent sovereign state.

"As a matter of fact," reported U. S. Minister Beaupré,[2] "the treaty, as such, has had no active friends or supporters, and if it is ratified at all it will be because of the strong attitude taken by the United States and the earnest repetition of the statement that the friendly understanding between the two countries depended upon it."

For weeks some hope was entertained that Colombia would reconsider. Slowly, however, it dawned on Washington that the Hay-Herran treaty was dead.

For more than six months the Secretary of State had not been at his

---

[1] Bunau-Varilla, p. 269.
[2] *For. Rel.*, 1903, p. 184.

best. In the preceding chapter it has been shown how from an unassailable position as to the Canadian boundary, he had allowed himself to be crowded farther than he should have gone. At the same time he was permitting the very powerful Panama Canal Company lobby to place him in an indefensible position at Bogotá. The facts did not warrant his repeated assertions that the Colombian Senate was in honor bound to ratify the canal treaty without amendment. Hay sent to Bogotá too many telegrams drafted by the canal company's attorney. Eager to please Senator Hanna and not strong enough to resist Cromwell, Hay was slipping more and more into a false position.

Having defeated the treaty, the Bogotá politicians seriously debated one further step and thus confirmed the impression that they were not even as honest as the canal company which they planned to mulct. The French concession would expire in September, 1904. In consideration of the payment of $1,000,000, President Marroquin's government had extended it for six years by legislative decree. In a country where nothing was really very legal it doubtless would have been possible to have the courts declare the extension invalid. Thus Colombia, it was argued, might acquire by forfeiture the property at Panama and then sell it to the United States for the $40,000,000 which would otherwise go to the company.[1] Hay, who entertained very high ideas as to the rights of property, was utterly disgusted. Roosevelt and Hay matched each other in finding suitable epithets for the Colombian politicians. Roosevelt called them "contemptible little creatures," "jack-rabbits," and "foolish and homicidal corruptionists."[2] Hay won; to him they were the "greedy little anthropoids."

To another member of the Cabinet the failure of Colombia to respond to the benevolent intentions of the American Government suggested a limerick. It had been contributed with the inscription: "Lines for the inspiration of the State Department in dealing with Dago Nations." "There was a young lady named Tucker, Who went up to her mother and struck her. Her mother said 'damn! Do you know who I am? You act like you was a mucker!'" The "partnership of beneficence" principle had broken down in the Western Hemisphere.

Never a very ardent fighter for his opinions, Hay had none the less not failed to keep before Roosevelt, as he had before McKinley, his

[1] *For. Rel.*, 1903, p. 205.
[2] Pringle, p. 311.

preferences. He continued to do so, though with decreasing force. There was still the Nicaraguan route, which was obtainable on better terms than those which Colombia had rejected. Twice in the next few weeks Hay brought this alternative to the President's attention.

"You will, before Congress meets, make up your mind which of the two courses you will take," he wrote August 16; [1] "the simple and easy Nicaraguan solution, or the far more difficult and multifurcate scheme, of building the Panama Canal *malgré* Bogotá." The Secretary suggested that nothing be done until the assembling of Congress. Roosevelt agreed that nothing was to be done for the moment.[2] Again, in September, having had a conference with the President at Oyster Bay, and having spent a few days at the Department, Hay outlined the choices once more, not forgetting Nicaragua: [3]

Dear Mr. President:
There is a question whether we ought
1. To save time and to dissipate any uncertainty about our position—say to Colombia that we will not for a moment consider the proposition they are now discussing; or
2. Say nothing and let them go on making fools of themselves until you are ready to act on some other basis.
It is now perfectly clear that in the present state of Colombian politics we cannot now—nor for some time to come—make a satisfactory treaty with Colombia.
It is altogether likely that there will be an insurrection on the Isthmus against the régime of folly and graft that now rules at Bogotá. It is for you to decide whether you will (1) await the result of that movement, or (2) take a hand in rescuing the Isthmus from anarchy, or (3) treat with Nicaragua.
Something we shall be forced to do in the case of a serious insurrectionary movement in Panama, to keep the transit clear. Our intervention should not be at haphazard, nor this time should it be to the profit, as heretofore, of Bogotá. I venture to suggest you let your mind play a little about the subject for two or three weeks, before finally deciding. For my part I think nothing can be lost, and something may be gained, by waiting developments for a while.

We may follow Hay's preference for Nicaragua one step further. There is in the Hay papers a letter from an acquaintance who spent

---

[1] Dennis, p. 342–43.

[2] Pringle represents Hay as having been from July, 1902, merely the mouth-piece of the President in the negotiations with Colombia. It does not appear to the present writer that Roosevelt gave much attention to the matter until September, 1903. In the early part of 1903 it was certain senators, such as Hanna, Spooner, and Lodge, whom Hay was trying to please.

[3] Sept. 13, 1903; Hay to Roosevelt.

an evening with the Secretary some time in November or December. The letter purports to summarize a conversation in which Hay expressed his private opinions on canal matters. A year later this gentleman desired to publish the statement, with a view to clearing the Secretary of the charge, so rife during the presidential campaign of 1904, that Hay had been implicated in the promotion of the revolution at Panama. To have permitted the publication of such a letter would have done Hay much harm and no good, for by that time he had taken his place among the most ardent defenders of the President. On the other hand, as a record of one of the stages through which Hay was dragged in an affair which each week became more noisome, the letter is of some interest.[1]

May I ask your consent to publishing, somewhat in the lines as follows, a summary of the conversation which I had with you last November or December?

I do not think there is much doubt concerning the way in which the Presidential election will go, but I feel all the same that this might, at any rate, turn off some of the abuse directed against yourself by the Anti-Imperialist element. I have not taken the pains to write this out with care, pending your approval, but the general lines of what I mean to say are somewhat as follows:—

In view of the abuse directed especially against the Secretary of State with reference to the Panama Canal question, some knowledge of Mr. Hay's private opinions concerning the canal may be of general interest.

Last fall, after the rejection by Colombia of the treaty offered by the United States, and before negotiations with Panama were taken up, I had the privilege of spending an evening alone with Mr. Hay, in the course of which the conversation turned on the canal question in general. I was surprised to find, first, that personally Mr. Hay was inclined to agree with me that the Nicaraguan route was preferable, and still more so to find that his personal sentiment was against the construction of either canal,[2] and that he would have preferred to have matters remain as they were, though feeling obliged as an officer of the Government to follow out the dictates of the Government in a question which was, after all, a commercial one.

It ought to be evident from this how wide of the mark are those who ascribe Mr. Hay's attitude in this affair to an over-weening desire to meddle with the administration of the Spanish American republics. Probably there are few men in the United States who are more disgusted with the necessity of dipping

[1] N. T. Bacon to Hay, Oct. 6, 1904.
[2] The assertion that Hay did not personally favor any canal is unsupported by other documentary evidence. It is plausible, for Hay's sympathies were generally with the railroads, in which he was an investor.

into the endless turmoils involved by bolstering up the spectres of government in these homes of anarchy.

The value of the Nicaraguan alternative was, in October, 1903, still unimpaired. It could have been utilized in either of two ways. A canal at that point was feasible, notwithstanding Bunau-Varilla's skillful propaganda to the contrary. It might cost more money, but it probably would have cost no ill-will in Latin America. Moreover, if Hay could have held his government firmly to his plan of negotiation, Colombia would have at length faced the fact that it was in danger of losing its only possible customer. Colombia could sell to no other power. If she did not come to terms with the American Government her asset at the Isthmus would be without value.[1] That McKinley, had he lived, would have utilized Hay's plan for all it was worth, there can be little doubt. Under Roosevelt diplomacy had no chance.

As to the choice of routes Roosevelt had at first no very firm convictions, and the interests of the Panama Canal Company probably meant nothing to him; he seems never even to have seen Cromwell until the middle of June. But when Colombia set out to thwart the American Government Roosevelt's combative instincts were aroused: somebody should be chastised. The peaceful settlement of the Alaska boundary deprived him of what seemed a promising opportunity to make a demonstration. Unable to lay that matter before Congress in such a way as to demand militant instructions, the President, in October, planned a somewhat similar move with reference to the canal. He began drafting a message to Congress recommending "that we should at once occupy the Isthmus anyhow, and proceed to dig the canal." [2] With evident regret, Roosevelt would, if Congress so directed, turn to Nicaragua, but he could not forbear to point out "the impropriety from an international point of view of permitting such conduct as that to which Colombia seems to incline." The President sometimes acted, it is true, as though he were only about six years old, but he also, at times, seemed to be yearning to be the man-on-horseback.

By that time Hay had traveled a long way with Roosevelt, and probably he would have followed to the end, but he was unhappy

[1] On November 6, Beaupré telegraphed from Bogotá that General Reyes, who spoke for the Marroquin Government, had offered to approve the treaty by decree, provided the United States would land troops to preserve Colombian sovereignty at the Isthmus. *For. Rel.*, 1903, p. 225.

[2] *Autobiography*, pp. 521, 530–31.

about the prospect. "How on earth a fair-minded man could prefer that the President should have taken possession of the Isthmus with the mailed hand," wrote Hay to Root, Feb. 22, 1904, "rather than the perfectly regular course which the President did follow, passes my comprehension."

It was in such a mood as this that John Hay actually welcomed the Panama Revolution as the less of two evils.

In the last few years so much has been written about the origins of the insurrection at the Isthmus, and the sources of information have been so thoroughly combed, that it seems scarcely necessary even to assert that Hay had no part in the instigation of the revolution. The nearest he came to it was on October 16 when he handed to Bunau-Varilla a copy of Richard Harding Davis's *Captain Macklin* and observed that the story would interest him.[1]

Panama had once been a sovereign state. Bunau-Varilla had for two years been warning Colombia that revolution was inevitable if the Bogotá politicians disregarded Panaman wishes. The completion of the canal was to Panama a matter of life or death. Active propaganda for the revolution appears to have been initiated by Cromwell long before the Colombian Senate rejected the treaty, but probably more as a measure of intimidation against the legislature at Bogotá than with the expectation that an insurrection would actually become necessary. Whatever part Cromwell had to begin with he was forced to drop in September because it endangered the very concession he was trying to save. Furthermore, he had not entirely given up hope of being able to come to terms with Colombia. Deprived of Cromwell's stealthy leadership, the timid revolutionists found a wholly competent successor in Bunau-Varilla. That Hay was fully informed of the progress of the movement after the first of September there is little doubt, but it was not until the middle of October that the revolution on the Isthmus appeared as a substantial alternative. It was perfectly true, as Hay wrote James Ford Rhodes, that the matter came to a head with "amazing celerity." "I had no hesitation," declared Hay, "as to the proper course to take, and have had no doubt of the propriety of it since."[2]

---

[1] Bunau-Varilla, p. 318; Pringle, Chapter VI, "I Took Panama"; Dennis, Chapter XII, "The Panama Canal."
[2] Dec. 8, 1903; *Letters and Diaries,* III, p. 288.

On November 3 and 4 the Panama Junta staged an opera bouffe revolution in the cities of Panama and Colon. Without the presence of the U. S. S. *Nashville* to prevent the landing of Colombian troops it is difficult to see how the insurrection could have been immediately successful. Nor is it likely that without the American naval forces it would have failed. Unsmeared by the subsequent efforts of Roosevelt, Hay, and Root to wrap the episode in sanctions of philanthropy, righteousness, and international law, the policy of the American Government at the time would not have been so open to criticism. The revolution having become an accomplished fact, all the old alternatives disappeared. An actual situation demanded practical measures. "I simply lifted my foot," explained the President in a Cabinet meeting. "Oh, Mr. President," replied Knox, the very useful Attorney General, "do not let so great an achievement suffer from any taint of legality." [1]

The only sufficient statement ever made was by Roosevelt at Berkeley in 1911: "I took the canal zone." [2]

With the least possible delay, November 6, Hay signed his famous telegram, authorizing recognition. The phrasing sounds like that of Adee.[3] "The people of Panama have, by an apparently unanimous movement, dissolved their political connection with the Republic of Colombia and resumed their independence. When you are satisfied that a *de facto* government, republican in form, and without substantial opposition from its own people, has been established in the State of Panama, you will enter into relations with it as the responsible government. . . ."

On the 13th Colonel Bunau-Varilla presented his credentials, such as they were, and amid the creaks and groans of twisted precedents, which would admirably fit the needs of Japan if some day she were to find it profitable to deal with a similarly created Filipino provisional government, and which have already served in the case of Manchukuo, he was received by the President as minister plenipotentiary with power to negotiate a new canal treaty.[4]

The Department of State handed to him two days later a draft treaty which seemed to the new envoy much too timid and modest. There was even some suggestion of dividing the forty millions and giving part of

[1] Lyman Abbott, *Reminiscences*, pp. 139–40.
[2] March 23, 1911, Address at University of California.
[3] *For. Rel.*, 1903, p. 233.
[4] Bunau-Varilla, Chapter XXIX.

it as a sop to Colombia. Bunau-Varilla rewrote the draft in the interests of the United States, of the Panama Canal Company, and of civilization generally. In the Hay library at 800 Sixteenth Street, it was signed November 18, two years to a day after Lord Pauncefote in the same room had affixed his signature to the treaty with England by which the American Government had secured its freedom to make this new one. Bunau-Varilla's credentials and authorization to sign the convention were very sketchy, but the Panaman provisional government by telegram agreed to ratify what it had never seen, and the Senate, after bitter debate, advised ratification February 23, 1904. Many Senators were a little discontented. Notwithstanding all the generous concessions which the erstwhile Panaman envoy had made, they could think of still others which they would have liked to include. During the greater part of the period from the signing of the treaty until its ratification Hay was ill, at times very ill, but he was able to summon enough strength, January 20, just as he was going South for convalescence, to warn Senator Spooner, as he had warned Cullom the day before, that the light-hearted, holiday spirit in which the Panamans had ratified the treaty had passed. It would not be safe to reopen the subject. He wrote:

"I am going away to-day for a little while, and shall not have an opportunity to talk with you about it further, but, even if I had, I cannot flatter myself that I could hold up my own with you in an argument over it. But the facts of the situation seem to me too plain for dispute. As its stands now as soon as the Senate votes we shall have a treaty in the main very satisfactory, vastly advantageous to the United States, and we must confess, with what face we can muster, not so advantageous to Panama."

"With what face we can muster": that seems to have been the way Hay felt about the whole affair. The Secretary of State had for months been merely a chip driven on the waves of a "cosmic tendency." He could have resigned, but resignation would have contributed to nothing but his personal comfort, a consideration which two years before he had resolved to discard.

The saddest aspect of the episode was that it had all been so unnecessary. There had been an alternative, practical and civilized— Nicaragua. Working together, Roosevelt and Hay with Hanna, Spooner, Cullom, and Aldrich, could have chosen it or could have secured the Panaman route honorably. It is doubtful whether Roosevelt and Hay, without the Senators, could have saved the honor of the American Government; the United States never had a Secretary of State who would have been able to do it alone.

IF John Hay was not the most many-sided American of his day then the distinction belongs to Theodore Roosevelt. For this reason, when the two men came together, the relationship was likely to be kaleidoscopic. What was true of one moment might become equally untrue of the next. No list of antonyms is useful to build up the portraiture of this association. Neither could claim possession of any considerable list of distinctive qualities not shared by the other.

Take, for example, the respective attitudes of the two men toward the spectre of the German menace which haunted nearly every diplomatic negotiation of the period.

Both Roosevelt and Hay believed that the German menace was substantial, but they went out to meet it in very different ways. Hay never lost the appearance of being very anti-German, while Roosevelt, who, in opposing Germany went to extremes which must have shocked his Secretary, never drew upon himself the suspicion that he was unfriendly. Equally Roosevelt and Hay agreed upon the importance of the Anglo-American understanding which Hay had done so much to establish. Under Roosevelt this understanding was carried, in the Far East, to an extreme from which Hay would probably have drawn back in dismay, and yet Roosevelt was never regarded as an Anglophile. The art of gesturing, first with one hand and then with the other, which Roosevelt practiced with so great skill in domestic politics, he extended to international relations. Having made a flourish at one Power, he seems to have been eager to find an opportunity to make a similar gesture at another. Thus he could level off the balance. His comments about Germany and England, placed side by side, are at times as amazing as those of the German Emperor, on the one hand, to the Tsar, and, on the other, to Roosevelt and to the Kaiser's Uncle Bertie. John Hay was poor at gestures and, having formed a conviction, or having developed a prejudice, was likely to ride it consistently; he was not so good a politician as his chief.

Menace is, perhaps, too strong a word to characterize German policy toward the United States, but there can be no question but that

German national interest in 1898 and later was so frequently in conflict with the policy of the American Government as to have justly warranted some alarm. In China the seizure of Kiaochow gave a sinister aspect to every subsequent German move in the Far East, and in the Pacific. The behavior of Admiral von Diedrichs at Manila Bay increased the suspicion. There were frequent intimations, now confirmed by the publication of the German diplomatic correspondence as having correctly represented the German Government, that the latter desired, and for a while even expected to secure some coaling stations at American expense, out of the settlement of the war with Spain. From London Hay brought back the impression that the appearance of the United States as a factor in world politics was not welcomed by Germany. The amiable division of Samoa did not suffice to allay the growing suspicion. The frequent letters from Spring Rice, always an alarmist about Germany, seemed to be confirmed by the German interpretation of the Anglo-German agreement, and by the punitive expeditions of Count von Waldersee in North China. The threatening policy of Germany in the Far East lent color to the suspicion that Germany had designs also in the Caribbean, where fear of German aggression became a cardinal assumption of American naval strategists. It seemed very plausible that Germany might desire the Virgin Islands; that, when the American treaty failed at Copenhagen, German intrigue was at work; and, when the Hay-Herran treaty encountered opposition in Colombia, that the Germans again might be at the bottom of it. The suspicions in the three instances last named now appear to have been baseless, but in international relations a state of mind is as formidable a fact as a fortress.

When the probability of Hay's appointment as Secretary of State became known the German Ambassador in Washington was quick to foresee trouble.

"Day's leaving the Department," reported von Holleben to his Foreign Office, August 16, 1898, "means a great loss to us, the more so because his probable successor, Col. John Hay, belongs wholly to the British direction. . . . Hay is the direct opposite of Day, very rich, absolutely *homme du monde,* and withal well educated. Hay is serious and thorough and will certainly perform good services as Secretary of State: I am afraid only that he will do it in a direction unfortunate to us. The French Ambassador, too, is very little edified by the nomination of Mr. Hay. . . . In London Hay had cultivated the English friendship with great warmth, and often in a noisy manner." [1]

The outspoken sympathy of Hay for the British in South Africa tended to confirm von Holleben in his fears. Count Quadt, Chargé in the Ambassador's absence, reported that the Secretary had been attacked strongly and repeatedly on account of his attitude toward the Boers.[2] "As he is of a delicate, soft nature, these attacks have hit him particularly hard and the more so because he had to admit that they were justified. Baron Gevers, the Dutch minister, told me recently that he had come here with a special instruction not to conceal the sympathy which his country felt for the Boers, and he had declared himself therefore, in this sense. Great had been his surprise when he paid a visit to Mr. Hay after the first British success, when Hay greeted him with the words: 'At last we have had a success.' Baron Gevers asked Mr. Hay in which field the United States had scored a success, and Mr. Hay had to admit, somewhat embarrassed, that he had spoken of the British success against the Boers."

When Prince Henry arrived in Washington in March, 1902, on his somewhat vaguely defined mission of good will,[3] the German Ambassador was incensed at what he regarded as Hay's indifference to the importance of the Prince's high mission. The Secretary was alleged to have pleaded that, because he was in personal mourning for his son, he should not be expected to greet the royal visitor at the railway station. "I was astonished by the fact that it became necessary for me to give the Minister of Foreign Affairs a lecture on the importance of such a visit," reported von Holleben, March 7, 1902.[4] "Thereupon Mr. Hay, after having received an express order from the President, appeared at the station." There is nothing in the Hay Papers to support such a statement. Possibly one reason why the Secretary and the Ambassador did not get along well together was that the latter presumed to suppose that he could instruct John Hay in good manners.

On another occasion von Holleben commented on Hay's amateurish command of French, German, and Spanish and contrasted it with the Secretary's greater love of English literature, and life.[5] Hay, he

[1] From a memorandum supplied to the author by Dr. Alfred Vagts.
[2] *Ibid.*, Nov. 9, 1900.
[3] *Die Grosse Politik*, XVII, p. 243.
[4] Vagts, *op. cit.*, March 7, 1902.
[5] *Ibid.*, April 10, 1902.

thought, became more and more a blind protagonist of England. "The English may do what they like, Mr. Hay is with them. He does not make it impossible for them to keep up complete depots of horses in the United States for the South African War; he leaves them alone in Alaska; he is blind to what they do in China."

Such notes would not be worth repeating were it not vividly illustrative of the atmosphere of distrust and jealousy which enveloped German-American relations until the abrupt recall of von Holleben early in January, 1903.

No doubt Hay's well-known dislike of the German Emperor provided a shining target, but neither it nor the British propaganda is sufficient to account for the suspicion of Germany so current in those years. When, following the publication of the terms of the Anglo-German agreement, Hay wrote to Adams,[1] "At least we are spared the infamy of an alliance with Germany. I would rather, I think, be the dupe of China than the chum of the Kaiser," he expressed far more than a personal prejudice.

The German Foreign Office counted much on the accession of Roosevelt to bring about better relations. Baron Richthofen made a minute,[2] probably with satisfaction, of an opinion expressed by Jackson, the American Chargé in Berlin, that under Roosevelt Hay would not be able long to retain his place in the Cabinet. Von Holleben reported, July 1, 1902, that the President had recently expressed to one of his intimates his great dislike of Hay. Roosevelt was alleged to have explained, however, that, if he separated himself from the Secretary, he would be under obligation to take Choate in his place, "and Choate was even worse."

Actually there seems to have been no substantial difference in those years between Hay and Roosevelt on the German question. In one of his first interviews with the President after his arrival in 1903 to replace von Holleben, "Spec" von Sternburg felt obliged to report to von Bülow, February 19:[3] "I felt that the President does not place absolute confidence in Germany's assurance with regard to her respect for the Monroe Doctrine." The new envoy was right. "Both the Dutch and the Danish West Indies in America," observed the President to

[1] November 21, 1900.
[2] September 17, 1901; Vagts, *op. cit.*
[3] Dennis, p. 297.

Hay,[1] "will be a constant temptation to Germany, unless or until we take them. The way to deliver Germany from temptation is to keep on with the upbuilding of our navy."

Roosevelt's researches in the history of the War of 1812 had left no deposit of affection for the English; but it is difficult to believe that he regarded Great Britain in 1902–03 as a menace to American interests, even in Alaska. He viewed "the average Englishman,"[2] to use his own words, as "not a being whom I find congenial or with whom I care to associate. I wish him well, but I wish him well at a distance." Also, it was politically important for Roosevelt always to appear before the American voter in the rôle of a sturdy American, and he often rehearsed the part.

"It is a singular ethnological and political paradox," Hay cautioned the President when he feared that the latter might wish to intervene in China,[3] "that the prime motive of every British subject in America is hostility to every country in the world, including America 'which is not friendly to Germany.' " Hay writhed under the charge that he was an Anglophile, but he did nothing about the matter except to deny it. That was not enough. Roosevelt put up lightning-rods. He mobilized the fleet in the Caribbean in the winter of 1902–03 as a naval demonstration against Germany whom he alleged to have been intent upon breaking down the Monroe Doctrine in Venezuela. Then, as an offset, he threatened to mobilize the troops along the Alaskan border to defend it against the alleged encroachments of England. In both instances he was fighting straw-men, but the gestures served a purpose. They dramatized the President's sturdy Americanism.

Roosevelt's action in the Venezuela imbroglio is important for the light it throws on Roosevelt's character and, indirectly, on the relation of the latter to Hay. The episode is the more noteworthy because in recent years the accuracy of Roosevelt's own assertions as to what he did has been called in question.

The events in the Venezuelan affair have been studied so minutely by competent scholars[4] that it is necessary here only to summarize briefly. Early in 1902 England proposed to Germany that the two Powers undertake joint action against Venezuela to secure the pay-

---

[1] Roosevelt to Hay, Apr. 22, 1903, Library of Congress.
[2] Pringle, p. 281.
[3] Hay to Roosevelt, Apr. 28, 1903.
[4] Rippy, Chapter XI; Dennis, Chapter XI. See also Hill's *Roosevelt and the Caribbean.*

ment of some long-standing claims. The Emperor was not unwilling but wished that action be deferred until after the conclusion of Prince Henry's visit to the United States. In November the two Powers agreed upon a line of procedure involving coöperative coercion of President Castro. On December 7, 1902, the two Powers delivered an ultimatum. The next day they withdrew their legations from Caracas. Four Venezuelan gunboats were seized and three of them were sunk. On the 11th there was instituted a blockade of five ports and of the mouths of the Orinoco. Italy was welcomed into the company of the blockading Powers. On the 13th German and British cruisers bombarded forts at Puerto Cabello, and on that day Venezuela submitted through the American Government a request for arbitration which was forwarded to London and Berlin without comment. Four days later, England and Germany respectively accepted arbitration in principle and in due course requested Roosevelt to act as arbitrator. Pending the settlement of the terms of arbitration the three Powers on December 20 established a formal blockade. In the latter part of January a conference of creditor nations, many of whom had not joined in the coercive measures, was held in Washington. The American Minister at Caracas, Herbert Bowen, was permitted to represent Venezuela in the conference. Meanwhile American public opinion was much excited by the news that Germany had, independently of her allies, bombarded Fort San Carlos in a ruthless fashion. The diplomatic conference in Washington split over the question of whether certain claims of the blockading Powers should receive preferential treatment in determining the terms of reference for the arbitration to which all had agreed in principle. On February 6, the ambassadors in Washington of the allied Powers agreed to submit the disputed point to the arbitration of President Roosevelt. The blockade was raised February 16.

Upon the advice of Hay, Roosevelt had, in December, declined to act as arbitrator because the American Government was among those states having claims which would have to be arbitrated, and Hay persuaded the Powers to elect arbitration before the Hague Court. In January, apparently without reluctance, Roosevelt declined the second request to act as arbitrator and the question of the status of preferential claims was likewise referred to The Hague.

Now, as to the President's part in bringing about the arbitration and as to his veracity:

In a biography of John Hay which was published soon after the outbreak of the World War, under the caption "The German Menace
Looms Up," William Roscoe Thayer somewhat vaguely asserted that
in December, 1902, Roosevelt delivered to Germany an ultimatum that
arbitration must be accepted within a certain number of days. It was
alleged that it was only when the President repeated the demand a few
days later and shortened the time previously specified, that Germany
consented to arbitrate. Thayer's assertions were immediately called in
question. He then disclosed that Roosevelt was his source of information. The latter addressed to Thayer, August 21, 1916, a long letter in
which the assertions were repeated and amplified. This letter was
published first in a second edition of the Thayer biography of Hay
and then, at the request of Roosevelt, was included as a chapter in the
first volume of Joseph Bucklin Bishop's *Theodore Roosevelt and His
Time*.[1]

The disclosure, incidentally, carried with it the inference that in
preparing the Hay biography Thayer had leaned heavily upon Roosevelt for information—a not very trustworthy source, as has been
already pointed out in this narrative.

The substance of the Roosevelt statement, in his own words, is as
follows:

I speedily became convinced that Germany was the leader and the really
formidable party in the transaction. . . . I became convinced that England
would not back Germany in the event of a clash. . . . I also became convinced that Germany intended to seize some Venezuelan harbor and turn
it into a strongly fortified place of arms, on the model of Kiaochau, with
a view to exercising some degree of control over the future Isthmian Canal,
and over South American affairs generally.

. . . I finally decided that no useful purpose would be served by further
delay, and I took action accordingly. I assembled our fleet, under Admiral
Dewey, near Porto Rico, for "maneuvers" . . . I saw the Ambassador, von
Holleben, and explained that in view of the presence of the German
squadron on the Venezuelan coast I could not permit longer delay in an-
swering my request for an arbitration. . . . The Ambassador repeated that
his government would not arbitrate. I then asked him to inform his government that if no notification for arbitration came within a certain number of
days I should be obliged to order Dewey to take his fleet to the Venezuelan
coast and see that the German forces did not take possession of any territory.

[1] Bishop, I, Chapter XX. A somewhat similar statement by Roosevelt regarding his
alleged ultimatum appeared in a long letter which he wrote Henry White on August
14, 1906. Nevins, *White*, 498–500.

. . . I . . . asked him to look at the map, as a glance would show him that there was no spot in the world where Germany in the event of a conflict with the United States would be at a greater disadvantage than in the Caribbean Sea.

A few days later the Ambassador came to see me, talked pleasantly on several subjects, and rose to go. I asked him if he had any answer from his government to my request, and when he said no, I informed him that in such event it was useless to wait as long as I had intended, and that Dewey would be ordered to sail twenty-four hours in advance of the time I set . . . less than twenty-four hours before the time I had appointed for cabling the order to Dewey, the Embassy notified me that his Imperial Majesty, the German Emperor, had directed him to request me to undertake the arbitration myself. . . .

If Theodore Roosevelt were known to be a perfectly trustworthy witness of his deeds of valor this most dramatic of all his gestures would seem plausible, for in his own statement he appears in the rôle which he so often dramatized: "Speak softly and carry a big stick: you will go far." [1] Unhappily, one cannot approach such an account as Roosevelt gave in 1916 in a completely credulous mood. Even a casual comparison of Roosevelt's statements with the known facts of the official record raises questions. For example, the request for arbitration appears to have been initiated not by Roosevelt, but by President Castro. It seems to have been prompted, not by an American ultimatum, but by the allied bombardment of Puerto Cabello. Furthermore, it is quite clear from the published official documents of the American, British, and German foreign offices, that the request for arbitration, once forwarded from Washington, was accepted promptly, in fact, in four days. No evidence has been disclosed that the alleged ultimatum was ever received in Berlin. Indeed, it appears that in December, 1902, the German Government was particularly anxious not to excite the ill-will of the United States. So many presumptions are established of the inaccuracy of the Roosevelt account that it is only reasonable to demand confirmation before incorporating it into the record. Professor J. Fred Rippy, having combed the official record, finds insufficient evidence to conclude that the episode could have taken place in December. Mr. Henry Pringle, having made a second search and having scanned the entire Roosevelt correspondence for the period, concedes that the ac-

[1] This was the theme of his address on the Monroe Doctrine at the University of Chicago, April 2, 1903. Pringle, however, found the quotation in a private letter of Roosevelt's as early as Jan. 26, 1900; *op. cit.,* p. 214.

count is "romantic to the point of absurdity" unless it can be shown that Roosevelt was conducting negotiations independent of the formal diplomatic channels.

There is in the Hay Papers one relevant document in the light of which further confirmation seems necessary before much reliability can be placed upon Roosevelt's assertion that he delivered and then dramatically repeated to Ambassador von Holleben, the alleged ultimatum.

Sometime in the latter part of January, 1903, when the American press had worked itself up to a fever over the continued blockade, Hay drafted with pencil a suggestion for notes, presumably to England, Germany, and Italy, with a view to lifting the blockade. It began with Hay's own narrative of the events in December leading up to the first arbitration proposal. As such it becomes a document of interest to place by the side of Roosevelt's account:

When the differences between the Governments of Germany and of Venezuela first began to take on an aspect of gravity the Government of Germany, through the ambassador in Washington, announced its intention to proceed to measures of coercion and at the same time set forth the principles by which it would be guided in carrying these measures into effect. It spontaneously assured the Government of the United States that it did not contemplate the conquest or the acquisition of any territory whatever; either on the mainland or the islands; and that its sole purpose was the collection of just debts. The President, in acknowledging the courtesy of these assurances, did not enter into the consideration of the justice of the claims referred to, but expressed his confidence that all German officers on duty in Venezuelan waters would be governed by the wishes and the views of His Majesty the German Emperor, thus expressed.

At a later period the Government of Great Britain and still later that of Italy announced their several intentions to take part in measures of coercion against the Government of Venezuela—with a similar purpose and understanding.

The Government of the United States, inspired by sentiments of respect and consideration for all the Powers in interest, took pains to observe an attitude of friendly neutrality through all the painful incidents of the blockade which followed; although our interests suffered severely by it and public opinion in this country was deeply affected by some of the occurrences to which it naturally gave rise. The President embraced the first opportunity wh. presented itself to convey to the blockading powers the desire of the Venezuelan Government for an amicable settlement of the question at issue, and was gratified to receive from all the powers concerned, the assurance of their willingness to accept for that purpose the arbitration of the high Tribunal of The Hague. To facilitate this desirable end, he permitted Mr. Bowen, the American Minister at Caracas, to accept an appointment from President Castro as Minister Plenipotentiary of Venezuela, to proceed to Washington, and to endeavor to arrange a plan of submission to the Hague Tribunal, in case he was unable to settle the pending questions by direct negotiations.

As the President had declined the important and honorable post of arbitrator to which all the Powers had invited him, he has not felt called upon to volunteer his good offices to assist them in coming to an arrangement, however earnestly such a consummation is desired by him and by the people of the United States. We have even forborne to press the claims we hold against the Venezuelan Govt. further than to file notice of their existence and to ask for them the same just and equitable consideration which may be granted to the claims of other countries.

It seems hardly possible that the Secretary of State would have drafted such paragraphs as those just quoted if anything remotely resembling what Roosevelt later described had taken place in December. Nor is it plausible to assume that the latter was at the time acting as his own Secretary of State and carrying on negotiations independent of Hay. Hay betrayed no lack of knowledge of the facts, nor is it likely that they could have been kept from him, even if the President had so desired.

The other explanation advanced by Dr. Rippy, but rejected by Mr. Pringle as invalid from the internal evidence in the contemporary Roosevelt correspondence, is that in 1916 Roosevelt confused the two arbitration proposals, and that the alleged conversations were not with von Holleben, who had been recalled, but with the President's good friend, Spec von Sternburg, who, January 31, came to Washington to replace von Holleben.[1] The remaining paragraphs of the Hay draft offer slight plausibility to Dr. Rippy's conjecture. The paragraphs just quoted were in the nature of a recital which led up to a very sharp request.

"The President sees with profound regret," continued Hay, "that although Mr. Bowen has full powers from the Venezuelan Govt. to arrange for the payment of all the just indebtedness of that Govt., not only to the blockading Powers but to all other nations, and although all the Powers in interest have announced their willingness to submit their differences to the arbitration of The Hague, no substantial prog-

[1] Rippy, p. 195.

ress has been made in either of these directions. A state of unrest and anxiety exists throughout the western hemisphere which, if suffered to increase, might bring about results which would be universally deplored.

"The President in view of these circumstances and actuated only by sentiments of sincere friendship and esteem toward all the Powers engaged in these negotiations, instructs you to bring these considerations before the Minister of Foreign Affairs of the —— Government, and to express his earnest hope that, if it should seem impracticable to come to an amicable settlement by means of the present negotiations, the whole matter may be speedily submitted to that High Tribunal created by the civilized world for precisely such emergencies, and that the blockade—which has already accomplished its purpose of eliciting from Venezuela an assurance of the readiness to pay all just claims—may be declared at an end."

The contemplated notes were never sent; on the other hand, the second arbitration proposal, as outlined in the Hay draft, was actually made and accepted. Quite possibly Roosevelt helped the proposal along by some private talks with Spec, but the fleet had been demobilized at least three weeks before the new German envoy arrived in Washington. That Roosevelt ever declaimed to von Holleben in 1902, or to von Sternburg in 1903, what he dramatized himself in 1916 as having said, is hardly credible.

"We have not interfered," wrote Hay to Henry White, February 16, "except in using what good offices we could dispose of to induce all parties to come to a speedy and an honorable settlement, and in this we have been, I think, eminently successful." No mention of an ultimatum. Hay could think of no reason why the German Government should have taken any offense unless it was because Bowen had said to Sternburg: "Very well, I will pay this money which you demand, because I am not in a position to refuse, but I give you warning that for every thousand dollars you exact in this way, you will lose a million in South American trade."

In the spring of 1903, after the Venezuela incident was closed, the President appears to have been in a mood especially appreciative of Hay's services. "I wonder if you realize," he added in a postscript to a letter, April 16, from the Yellowstone National Park, "how thankful I am to you for having stayed with me. I owe you a great debt, old man."

President Roosevelt's intervention in the direction of American foreign policy, particularly in the Venezuela imbroglio, the Alaska boundary dispute, the Kisheneff massacre affair, and the Panama revolution, created a widespread sentiment which is reflected in this cartoon. Original in the collection of Clarence L. Hay.

When, at the outbreak of the Russo-Japanese War, the German Emperor proposed an international agreement for the neutralization of China during the conflict, Secretary Hay seized the idea but changed the wording of the note in such a way as to include Manchuria which the Kaiser would have been willing to concede to Russia. Original in the collection of Clarence L. Hay.

ONE of the commonest errors in the study of American diplomacy is to neglect the exigencies of domestic politics as factors in the determination of foreign policy. We have observed how, under McKinley in 1900, the political campaign so modified Hay's China policy as to change it into something quite different from what had been designed. Under Roosevelt domestic politics played an increasing influence in foreign affairs, but with a difference. McKinley was quick to modify a policy to placate the voters; Roosevelt was not above making gestures abroad for the sake of winning a nomination. Such practices may be hazardous; few Presidents have dared to resort to them to the extent that Roosevelt did in the earlier years of his administration.

The Alaska boundary and the Venezuela episodes present John Hay as the President's monitor in two such excursions. It was a part which obviously sorely taxed the strength of the Secretary. At times John Hay appears as a rapidly and prematurely aging man who was trying breathlessly to keep up the pace which he did not even approve. Unwilling, as most men are when age creeps upon them, to admit that he was losing his grip, or threatened with a discard, Hay became too willing to please. There follows the narrative of some other already famous incidents, now retold in the light of new sources of information, in which the Secretary continues to appear in rôles to which McKinley would never have assigned him.

The often-cited correspondence in 1902 about the Rumanian Jews turns out, upon reëxamination, to have been not quite what at the time it was reported to be.

The American people saw themselves as having recently twice intervened abroad in the interest of humanity and justice, in Cuba and in China. But the United States, as Henry Adams pointed out, had become a capitalist state. As such, under "McKinleyism," it was committed to the existing political order in all Europe, except, possibly, in Russia. This order rested, in part, on the backs of the oppressed minorities. Among the latter were the Rumanian and Russian Jews.

The case of the Rumanian Jews was pressed upon the attention of the President and the Secretary of State in April, 1902, by Jacob Schiff of Kuhn, Loeb and Company.[1] In the name of humanity some protest seemed to the banker-philanthropist desirable. It was also a cause of domestic concern, for the persecuted Jews flocked to the United States and their distress in the new world was hardly less than in their old homes. They were ill equipped for the new conditions of life and potentially a social menace. It was a delicate problem; the disabilities under which the Jews suffered in Rumania was hardly a proper subject of American diplomatic representation. The President, however, already counting his resources for June and November, 1904, wanted something done. Hay and Adee talked it over. The latter became the craftsman.

By the middle of July, Adee had drafted, under the guise of a discussion of a proposed naturalization treaty with Rumania, a strange document, full of interesting *non sequiturs*.[2] It laid down the principle of selective immigration: "It behooves the State to scrutinize most jealously the character of the immigration from a foreign land." Thence leaping lightly from point to point, Adee came to a statement that "the United States offers asylum to the oppressed of all lands," and finished with the conclusion that "the right of remonstrance against the acts of the Roumanian Government is clearly established." He closed with an appeal to the principles of eternal justice. But Adee was no fool. The essay was not a note to the Rumanian Government; it was only a confidential instruction about a naturalization treaty to the American Chargé. When Rumania learned of its import, she declined forthwith to continue discussion of the treaty. Mr. Schiff, on the other hand, was greatly pleased. It not only said the things he liked to hear, but appeared to be good campaign material. The problem then became how to get the appeal out of its existing form, a confidential instruction, into something which could be published. Adee was equal to that, too. He incorporated the greater part of it into a circular, addressed to the signatories of the Berlin Treaty of 1878, which Rumania was clearly violating.[3] The American Government, not a signatory of the Berlin Treaty, made a futile appeal to Great Britain, Germany, Austria-Hungary, France, Italy, Russia and Turkey—the list becomes slightly

[1] Schiff to Hay, April 6, 1902.
[2] *For. Rel.*, 1902, pp. 910–14.
[3] *Ibid.*, p. 42–45.

ludicrous toward the end—on behalf of this pathetically distressed minority. The circular secured no attention in Europe, but in our own Congressional campaign that fall it helped the Republican party. It was even read in some of the synagogues on the East Side of New York the Saturday before the election.

"The President is greatly pleased with your circular," wrote Hay to Adee,[1] with a "please burn promptly" up in the corner, "and the Hebrews—poor dears! all over the country think we are bully boys, with a glass eye—as the ribald used to say."

The circular sounded so well that Hay thought that they might try another one. The unwillingness of Russia to recognize an American passport if carried by an American Jew seemed to present an opportunity. Those to whom the American Government issued such passports, wrote Hay,[2] "are not agitators, not intending immigrants, not persons who will, in any way, be likely to contravene any of the laws or regulations of the country. They are men of good social standing, men of capital, tourists, students, men engaged in business in this country: in all respects innocent and harmless travelers, of the sort that coming from Russia, receive a friendly and cordial welcome from the U.S. . . .

"Now, you have a genius for taking an idea, letting it soak a while, and bringing it forth in a diplomatic note twice as good as the original idea. Even if Russia does nothing we shall have a good note to print next winter."

While the passport idea was still in soak the Kisheneff massacre at Easter, 1903, presented again to the Department of State the problem of the Jewish minorities. The principles of "McKinleyism," logically applied, would hardly have admitted of an American protest. Hay faced a difficult problem, for domestic politics required that the Administration take some action.

The failure of the Russian authorities to stop what had obviously been a prearranged slaughter of the Jews at Kisheneff shocked the world and aroused world-wide indignation. Ambassador McCormick in St. Petersburg fumbled his opportunity by merely reporting back to Washington that the Foreign Office declared that there was no distress for American philanthropy to relieve.[3] Hay promptly made a

---

[1] August 30, 1902.
[2] August 11, 1902, to Adee.
[3] *For. Rel.*, 1903, pp. 712–15.

personal contribution of $500 to a New York Jewish relief committee which was coöperating with the *Alliance Israelite Universelle;* but it did not seem to him prudent to write a note of protest to Russia. The President was out West.

"In regard to the criticisms to which I have been subjected in the last few days," he wrote, defensively, to Jacob Schiff, May 20, "for not having taken a more aggressive attitude towards the Russian Government in view of the horrible outrages reported from Bessarabia, you can readily see that my position is a most delicate one, especially in the absence of the President from Washington. I cannot go to the newspapers and explain the reasons of the action, or the non-action, of the State Department. I feel precisely as you do in regard to it, but you are free to express your feelings and I am not. Any slight indiscretion of speech on my part might commit this Government to a course of action for which there would be no justification, either in the law or facts of the case. There could be only two motives which could induce this Government to take any positive action in such a case; one is some advantage to itself, and the other is some advantage to the oppressed and persecuted and outraged Jews in Russia. What possible advantage would it be to the United States, and what possible advantage to the Jews of Russia, if we should make a protest against these fiendish cruelties and be told it was none of our business? What would we do if the Government of Russia should protest against mob violence in this country, of which we can hardly open a newspaper without meeting examples? I readily admit that nothing so bad as these Kisheneff horrors has ever taken place in America; but the cases would not be unlike in principle."

Then Hay added, having in mind, no doubt, Adee's Rumanian circular of the year before: "I should have hoped that I would not be required to defend myself against any accusation of neglect of duty in such a matter, but probably I have no reason to complain. I have received unmerited credit so often that I ought not to object occasionally to unmerited blame."

When the President returned there was a conference with some of the Jewish leaders at the White House. The President this time supported his Secretary in the position that an official diplomatic protest was out of the question, but Roosevelt offered to forward to Russia a petition signed by American citizens.

On the first of July, under instructions from his government, Ambassador Cassini in Washington issued to the newspapers a communiqué which only fed the flames of popular indignation. He intimated that the petition would not be received. The Secretary was absent from the city, visiting his daughter at Newport. The President, at Oyster Bay, very angry at the Cassini declaration, wanted to send the petition the next day, but, fortunately, the signatures were not ready. The Secretary of State stepped in with words of caution. He wrote Roosevelt that the Cassini statement seemed to him like the gross outcry of a guilty conscience, but as for sending the petition, after it was known to be unwelcome, he had doubts. "It is a question," he wrote,[1] "for them [the Jewish Committee to which Roosevelt had given his promise] to decide whether, in view of the evident determination of the Russians not to receive the petition, there will not be more advantage in regarding this official publication in Washington and St. Petersburg as a refusal, and then to give the document the utmost publicity in this country and in Europe as having been refused a hearing to the Government of the Tsar. We can then all of us say what we think proper, and Russia can not complain of anything we say among ourselves. We can even print the petition as an American document—in a message to Congress, or in reply to a question from either House, with a statement that the Russian Government in a *communiqué* addressed to the American Press refused in advance to allow it to come to the knowledge of the Emperor."

Two days later, Hay added: "I do not think the matter is as yet serious, and there is no reason why it should become so. They are acting the fool, but we have no interest in precipitating a crisis at this time."

The Secretary sent to Roosevelt a despatch from the American Consul at Odessa, showing that the Russian Government was proceeding with apparent sincerity and severity "against the criminals of Kisheneff." It seemed to Hay evident that the American protests had already become effective. "The less we do and say now, and the sooner we get through with it, the better, in my opinion." [2] The President accepted the suggestion. Having made certain by a telegram to St. Petersburg that Russia would decline to accept the petition, Hay re-

[1] July 1, 1903.
[2] July 11, 1903.

ceived it into the capacious maw of the departmental archives, where it rests today. "What inept asses they are, these Kalmucks! They would have scored by receiving the petition & pigeon-holing it. I think *you* have scored, as it is! You have done the right thing in the right way and Jewry seems really grateful. As to our 'good relations' with Russia —the Russians have more interest in them than we have, and they will soon come around, and lie to us as volubly as ever." [1]

It was Hay who had scored. The President had not been deprived of his demonstration; the petition had served its purpose; and, most important of all, Roosevelt had been steered away from his own rashness. "I am year by year growing more confident," wrote Roosevelt to Hay, just as the petition incident was being closed, "that the country would back me in going to an extreme." [2] He was, at the moment, thinking more especially about the other Russian problem in Manchuria, but the statement was of broader application. All through 1903 Roosevelt was rehearsing the extremes to which he was willing to go.

As for the measures toward Russia for which the President was apparently ready, Hay could not have forgotten the incident of the modest contingent of troops which he had wished to leave in China in 1900. "I am greatly interested in what you say about the country backing you in 'extremes,' " Hay replied July 22. "I have always regarded it as a handicap to us in our negotiations that the country would *not* stand for an extreme policy in that direction. But your judgment of popular currents is better than mine, and if you are right, this would be a trump card to play, in some moment of crisis." This was Hay's polite way of telling Roosevelt that he believed him mistaken.

In July, 1903, just after Hay's most important visit to Oyster Bay, already several times referred to, the Secretary wrote to "My dear Mr. President" [3] a letter containing a paragraph which carried in its last sentence a caution which Roosevelt may have missed. For months the Secretary had been struggling with the President, in regard to Venezuela, the Alaskan boundary, the Kisheneff massacre, and Manchuria, to prevent some rash gesture in the interest of winning the nomination in June, 1904. Hay wrote:

---

[1] July 16, 1903.
[2] Pringle, p. 375.
[3] July 11, 1903.

Of course, the newspapers of the baser sort are utilizing the hot weather season by making all they can of their stupid invention of disagreements in the Cabinet. The "Sun" even nominates Root and me for the Presidency, and to-day the same paper goes further than mere nominating—it appoints Charlie Francis Ambassador to Italy. This is all very silly. They evidently imagine they can sow the seeds of jealousy and distrust in soil which is not propitious to such growths. Root will tell you what we all feel here, that no earthly power can now prevent your unanimous nomination and your triumphant re-election. I know perfectly well that these are considerations which do not enter into your scheme of public duty. You will, of course, do what you think right in any case: but the point I make is that you can, if you like, dismiss the subject of both the nomination and the election from your mind, and do what you think is right without counting your small change.

The "small change" referred to appears, in the light of what we now know, to have been playing the demagogue on an international scale for the sake of winning a presidential nomination. It is a pity that, having thus gently warned Roosevelt, Hay should have lent his cleverness to the support of any more similar gestures.

At the unveiling and consecration of the John Hay Memorial Window at the Temple of the Reform Congregation Keneseth Israel, December 2, 1906, Oscar S. Straus recited:

> Whenever man oppresses man
>   Beneath thy liberal sun,
> O Lord be there; thine arm made bare;
>   Thy righteous will be done.

The speaker thus called back to life the voice of a crusader muted long, long ago. Even into his office in "Mr. Mullett's Masterpiece," Hay's demon had followed him. In "McKinleyism" there was no place for crusading.

The story has often been told, how, while "the lethargic Republican National Convention" was meeting in Chicago, the Secretary of State, by order of the President, stirred it to life by sending to the American Consul General at Tangier the laconic message: "Perdicaris alive or Raisuli dead." Raisuli had swooped down on Perdicaris in the Palace of the Nightingales more than a month before and carried him off for ransom. The captive's release had already been arranged for, but Roosevelt needed an opportunity for another demonstration.

The most absurd aspect of the Perdicaris affair remains to be revealed. More than two weeks before the telegram was sent the Department of State had reason to suspect that Perdicaris was not, in fact, an American citizen and, therefore, not entitled to the protection of the United States. Telegrams of inquiry were sent both to Tangier and to Athens. From the United States Minister, John B. Jackson, the Department learned on June 7 that Perdicaris, although the son of a South Carolinian mother and a naturalized Greek father, had, at the outbreak of the War of Secession, registered himself at Athens as a Greek subject. His motive had been to escape military service with the Confederacy or confiscation of his property. Subsequently Perdicaris had returned to Trenton, N. J., and after a few years established himself at Tangier, where he was commonly known as a Greek. The information in the Department was not complete when the famous telegram was drafted, but Gaillard Hunt, then in charge of the Citizenship Bureau, felt justified in showing the correspondence to the Secretary. Hay requested him to take it across the street and show it to the President. To the latter it was quite unwelcome and Hunt returned with the instruction to send the telegram at once.[1]

---

[1] Personal conversation with the late Gaillard Hunt; Archives of the Dept. of State: A. H. Slocumb, Fayetteville, N. C., to the Dept., May 30, 1904; Secretary of State to Jackson and Gummere, June 4; Jackson to Dept., June 7; June 10; Gummere to the Dept., July 14, enclosing a personal letter of apology and explanation from Perdicaris to Gummere; Hay Papers: Adee to Hay, Sept. 1, 1904. The correspondence was held very confidentially in the Department until Nov. 8, 1905. The Republican campaign managers in the summer of 1904 were much concerned lest it be made public.

ALTHOUGH Roosevelt became President only seven days after the Boxer Protocol was signed he gave relatively little attention to the Far East at least until after the election in November, 1904. Hay remained in control of the China policy.

The policy of the integrity of China, and in some degree the policy of the open door, were policies of intervention in the affairs of another continent. As soon as Hay discovered where such policies were likely to lead he quietly abandoned them to the extent of not pressing them to their logical conclusion. He continued to play with the phrases which had so greatly added to his fame as a statesman, just as his successors in office have done, but the correspondence lost the audacity of Henry Adams and took on the conservatism of William McKinley. When Roosevelt, at length, took hold of the Far Eastern question during the Russo-Japanese War he appears to have started where Hay began in 1899, and with the latter's enthusiasm, but within three or four years he fell back to the position to which Hay had been forced to retire in 1900: the American people simply would not support a policy of intervention in Asia.

From the advanced ground taken in 1900 the Secretary retired to the policy of the open-door notes of 1899. In Manchuria the Russians gave every appearance of preparing to remain indefinitely. Perhaps reluctantly, but none the less definitely, Hay quickly recognized Russia's exceptional position in the province and was careful not to place the American Government in any attitude of apparent hostility. The burden of opposing Russia thus fell where it belonged, upon the Anglo-Japanese Alliance, from which the United States held carefully aloof. At length, in April, 1902, Russia signed with China an evacuation agreement, which, if it had been observed, probably would have averted the otherwise inevitable conflict. The American Government, in company with England and Japan, was satisfied with Russia's proposed program for evacuation.

"What we have been working for two years to accomplish, and what we have at last accomplished, if assurances are to count for anything," explained Hay, May 1, 1902, in an often-quoted letter to the President, who seems not to have been following the situation closely, "is that no matter what happens eventually in North China and Manchuria, the United States shall not be placed in any worse position than while the country was under the unquestioned dominion of China." In other words, the American Government, whatever reservations it made in its correspondence with Russia, recognized that Manchuria no longer was, in fact, under the unquestioned dominion of China. This language in 1902 was very suggestive of the Rockhill memorandum of three years before.

Hay had now taken up a tenable position. Roosevelt, notwithstanding his eagerness for demonstrations in the Western Hemisphere, could not have mustered support in the United States for a gesture in Manchuria where he could only have placed himself, as Hay and McKinley had been placed in 1900, by the side of England and Japan. Much as Hay had been disappointed by McKinley's failure to help him, he did not urge the abandoned policy upon Roosevelt. Indeed, he seems to have been a little alarmed lest the President should adopt such an alternative, in the face of his contrary advice.

In April, 1903, Russia declined to continue the evacuation and demanded, instead, additional concessions from China which would have had the effect of keeping Manchuria, as it had been for three years, practically a Russian province. The new Russian pretensions were a direct challenge to the United States, as well as to Great Britain and Japan.[1] Hay hastened to inform the President, April 25, but did not forget to include a word of caution:

The Russian Secretary, speaking in behalf of Cassini, explained to me that the power aimed at was England and not ourselves, but the first two clauses of the convention are apparently injurious to us, and there is a certain lack of courtesy also in their opposing our demand for free ports and consulates in Manchuria without notice to us, although we had frankly announced to them our intentions more than a month ago.

I am sure you will think it is out of the question that we should adopt any scheme of concerted action with England and Japan. Public opinion in this country would not support such a course, nor do I think it would be to our permanent advantage. . . .

[1] Dennis, pp. 358 ff.; *For. Rel.*, 1903, pp. 53 ff.

There followed an exasperating dispute with Russia over the famous "convention of the seven points." From a variety of sources copies of the Russian demands were placed on Hay's desk and yet the Russian Government continued to deny there was such a proposed convention. "Dealing with a government with whom mendacity is a science," remarked Hay, "is an extremely difficult and delicate matter." [1]

Twice more Hay repeated his advice to the President that intervention would not be feasible. "I take it for granted," he wrote, April 28, "that Russia knows as we do that we will not fight over Manchuria, for the simple reason that we cannot. . . . If our rights and interests in opposition to Russia in the Far East were as clear as noonday, we could never get a treaty through the Senate, the object of which was to check Russian aggression." In the last sentence the Secretary was apparently thinking of the Anglo-Japanese Alliance, to which the United States would have been welcomed with enthusiasm. That same day, in a second letter to the President, he remarked: "The one hopeful symptom is that they [the Russians] are really afraid of Japan. They know perfectly well that there is nothing in the situation which we would consider as justifying us in a resort to arms, but they know that it would require the very least encouragement on the part of the United States or England to induce Japan to seek a violent solution of the question." Cassini, reported Hay, urged the American Government to persuade Japan that her path of safety and honor lay in preserving her insular position. He made, continued Hay, "a rather furtive reference to the triple alliance between us, England, and Japan."

Hay was too good a diplomat to allow such an opportunity to pass. He replied that since the recent trouble had begun in Manchuria the British Government had not discussed such a possibility with him. He added, moreover, that it would be "an infinite source of grief" to the President, and to the people of the United States if they were forced into any other than a friendly attitude toward Russia.

A few weeks later Russia agreed to permit China to open in Manchuria two of the three ports which the United States, as well as England and Japan, had selected. The American Government accepted the compromise, concluded its new commercial treaty with China, and

[1] May 12, 1903, to Roosevelt.

waited for Japan to bring on the war.[1]

In the correspondence between the Secretary and the President the former always appeared as the conservative. In the letter, August 2, 1903, in which Hay replied to Roosevelt's request that he continue in office, he wrote, from Newbury:

I have nothing in particular to say—but it is Sunday and I hate to give up the comfortable habit of a Sunday talk with you.

I think we shall get our treaty with China in good shape in time to lay it before the Senate. I feel almost authorized by what you have said to tell those poor trembling rabbits who even yet hardly dare to do what we ask, for fear of the Bear, that if they keep their engagements with us, we will ourselves see that Russia shall not punish them for doing what Russia has declared she will not object to. I have hitherto vigorously refrained from saying anything of the kind. We have accomplished a good deal in the East, but thus far without the expense of a single commitment or promise.

A month later, Hay, having returned to Washington by way of Oyster Bay to confer chiefly on Panama matters, reported to the President from Washington, September 3:

I have wired Conger that there must be no doubt nor delay about the signature of our treaty on the 8th of October. He has the pessimism about Russia which is almost universal out there. "What's the use? Russia is too big, too crafty, too cruel for us to fight. She will conquer in the end. Why not give up now and be friendly?"

I have had long conversations with Liang and Takahira. Liang is sure his government will keep faith and sign the treaty as agreed, but he fears Russia will somehow punish them for it. I could not promise him any material support, but did tell him what we would do by way of influence, if Russia went back on her solemn pledge to us. Takahira fears the worst from Russian aggression in Korea. But he said, with a tone of quiet resolution, "If she goes any farther we shall have something to say." I thought it proper not to leave him with any illusions, and so told him plainly that we could not take part in any use of force in that region, unless our interests were directly involved.

And it was a hard thing to say.

When, fifteen months later, George Kennan, from Japan, urged that the United States should join the Anglo-Japanese Alliance, Roosevelt

---

[1] For a more detailed account of the events leading up to the Russo-Japanese War, see Dennis, Chaps. XIII, XIV; and Dennett, *Roosevelt and the Russo-Japanese War*.

replied, in language which is reminiscent of Hay, that Kennan was talking academically.[1] "Mind you, I personally entirely agree with you. But if you have followed the difficulty I have had even in getting such obvious things done as those connected with Panama and Santo Domingo you would get some faint idea of the absolute impossibility of carrying out any such policy as you indicate."

It does not lie within the province of a biography of John Hay to make an extended treatment of the Russo-Japanese War. The negotiations, beginning in April, 1905, which eventuated in Roosevelt's personal intervention and the Peace Conference at Portsmouth, were initiated after Hay's last illness began and were carried through after his death. The consummation of the Peace of Portsmouth belongs as much to Theodore Roosevelt as the rescue of the Legations at Peking in 1900 belongs to John Hay. The diplomatic equation which each man had to solve was, however, essentially the same. The unknown quantity in 1900 and again in 1905 was Germany. The problem during the Russo-Japanese War was, as Adams stated it in his exposition of McKinleyism, to separate Germany from Russia and draw the former into a concert of the Powers for the purpose, first, of localizing the conflict, and, second, of restoring peace. While Hay succeeded in holding the Powers together until after the relief of the Legations, his policy eventuated in a failure which was marked by the signing of the Anglo-German Agreement of the following October. Roosevelt was more successful. It must be freely acknowledged that in dealing with Germany he was incomparably superior to either Hay or McKinley. On the other hand, Roosevelt's brilliant success at Portsmouth should not be permitted to eclipse entirely the modest share which rightfully belongs to Hay for some very careful work during the earlier stages of the war in the Far East. Some attention is required at this point because again, unfortunately, we have to deal with instances of what appear to be Roosevelt's treacherous memory.

As the outbreak of hostilities in Manchuria became imminent the Powers looked to the American Government to re-assume the leadership which it had first taken in 1899. The latter responded promptly with a circular, February 10, 1904, proposing that in the war the "neutrality of China and in all practicable ways her administrative

---

[1] Roosevelt to Kennan, May 6, 1905; quoted in *Roosevelt and the Russo-Japanese War*, pp. 115–16.

entity" should be respected by both parties to the conflict.[1] The phrase quoted above was Hay's substitute for "the neutrality of China outside the sphere of military operations," the latter having been suggested by the German Emperor. The effect of the Kaiser's words would have been to exclude from the scope of the circular all of Manchuria, and probably portions of North China, for the military operations must, of necessity, take place in this area. Thus, by changing the phrasing, Hay transformed a proposed pledge from a form which would have expressly permitted Russia liberty of action in these regions into a form which required that she limit more narrowly her belligerent action.

A year later, also at the request of the German Emperor, the American Government sent out a second circular, January 13, 1905, in which it disclaimed any thought of reserved territorial rights or control in the Chinese Empire, and invited the Powers to give expression to their views on the subject.[2] Again, no exception was made as to either North China or Manchuria.

In both instances the circulars met with satisfactory responses.

Shortly after Hay's death in 1905, the President, in a letter to Senator Lodge, parts of which were published in the Lodge-Roosevelt Letters,[3] though without marks to indicate omissions, drew a contrast between his attitude and Hay's toward the German Emperor, and, in citing one or the other of these incidents, appears to have made a complete misstatement of the relevant facts.

Hay "had grown to hate the Kaiser so," declared Roosevelt,[4] "that I could not trust him in dealing with Germany. When, for instance, the Kaiser made the excellent proposition about the integrity of China, Hay wished to refuse and pointed out where the Kaiser's proposition as originally made contained what was inadvisable. I took hold of it myself, accepted the Kaiser's offer, but at the same time blandly changed it so as to wholly remove the objectionable feature (that is, I accepted it as applying to all of China outside of Manchuria, whereas he had proposed in effect that we should allow Russia to work her own sweet will in all northern China), and Hay published it in this form."

[1] The text of the circular is given in *For. Rel.*, 1904, pp. 2–3, 42; see also Dennett, *Roosevelt and the Russo-Japanese War*, p. 69.

[2] *For. Rel.*, 1905, p. 1; Dennett, p. 81.

[3] II, pp. 165–67.

[4] July 11, 1905. Dennett, p. 81.

The circular referred to must be either one or the other of those described above, probably the earlier one. In neither of them did the language used exclude Manchuria, and there is a contemporaneous record that the phrase making the declaration applicable to all China was inserted, not by Roosevelt, but by Hay. When the request from the German Emperor reached Washington, Hay was convalescing from a severe cold in Georgia. Upon his return he called on the President, saw the draft, and that day, February 7, recorded simply in his diary: "I said I thought we ought to eliminate the last clause and include 'the administrative entity of China.' The President agreed."

As for the second circular, if that is the one to which Roosevelt had reference in the letter to Lodge, there is an entry in the Hay diary, January 10, 1905, to the effect that Hay not only approved the text but also drafted it.

In short, as in the Venezuelan incident, we are forced to conclude that Roosevelt's statement of the facts lacks confirmation.

Within a week after Theodore Roosevelt and his party had returned from attending the funeral of his Secretary of State he seems to have fallen into the habit of regarding John Hay as a weak man. Certainly Hay did not grow in strength as he went on with Roosevelt, but one comes to feel that what the President mistook for weakness was, in fact, a kind of strength which Roosevelt could not understand. Hay remained with the Rough Rider because he felt that he had a duty to perform. He must have been stronger than the latter supposed. Otherwise he would have been unable to endure the position assigned to him where the practice of diplomacy was always difficult and, at times, impossible.

The reason why Hay had not long before insisted upon the acceptance of his resignation will become increasingly apparent in the following chapters.

UNCOMFORTABLE as were the official relations of Secretary Hay with President Roosevelt, those of the former with the Senate and with the leaders of the Republican party were even less satisfactory.

Hay's opinions of the Senate have become one of the best-known chapters in American history. Probably this is because of the publication of many scathing paragraphs from the Secretary's private letters. If only Hay could have restrained his too ready pen and equally sharp tongue, or if his editors could have restrained their impulse to publish these very vigorous fragments of English prose, most of the episodes would probably have been long since forgotten. Actually John Hay fared no worse with the Senate than most of his predecessors.

The period from 1898 to 1905 was, in American foreign relations, one of relative innovation. This was reflected, first, in the greatly increased number of treaties negotiated, and, second, in the appearance of some new principles of action. There had been reciprocity treaties before, and there had been many arbitration conventions for the settlement of specific disputes, but never before had there been an effort to give these two principles, reciprocity and arbitration, so general an application. In one other respect the situation was peculiar. Each of these principles was incorporated, not in a single treaty to be submitted to the Senate for its approval as a model for other similar conventions, but in a large number of treaties which were sent to the Senate at approximately the same time.

There was in both instances some warrant for handling these treaties in this precipitate fashion but, on the whole, it may be regarded as having been poor politics. The negotiation of the reciprocity conventions was authorized by the tariff of 1897; the principle had been specifically approved by the Republican platform of 1896. For these reasons President McKinley seems to have felt justified in sending to the Senate in one day no fewer than seven such conventions, and then adding several more before any action had been taken upon those already before the Foreign Relations Committee. Probably he counted upon the force of public opinion to crowd the treaties through. Roosevelt sent five arbitration treaties to the Senate in one day and within a few weeks added six more. The reason in this instance is even more plain. To offer a general arbitration treaty to a single European power in 1904 would have been to make an invidious distinction which would have been much misunderstood abroad. It would have been as highly impolitic as, twenty-four years later, it would have been for Secretary Kellogg to sign the bilateral pact for the prevention of war which was offered by M. Briand. The arbitration treaties were modelled upon the Anglo-French treaty of 1903; the latter was the introductory step to the formation of the Anglo-French Entente. For the United States to have made an arbitration treaty with one but not with another of the Powers would have placed it, in international politics, either with or against the newly formed Entente. On the other hand, although only two principles were involved, when the Senate failed to take action on the reciprocity treaties, and when it later amended the arbitration treaties so that Roosevelt pigeon-holed them, there was actually scored against Hay about forty failed treaties. The count should stand not as forty but as two.

Aside from the two groups of treaties just mentioned Hay suffered from only one major failure, the first canal treaty. Six of the Hay treaties forwarded by McKinley eventually received favorable action from the Senate, as did nine committed by Roosevelt. No other Secretary of State had ever had fifteen treaties pass the Senate.[1]

Nevertheless, Hay's difficulties with the Senate may not thus easily be explained away. The failure of the Republican majority to carry out the party promises as to commercial reciprocity raised with Hay a formidable question of party honesty which offended his moral sense as had the threat to abrogate by unilateral action the objectionable Clayton-Bulwer Treaty. This subject requires more extended treatment and is therefore postponed for a moment. Underlying this specific major dispute were other less defined causes of trouble which may have been even more fundamental.

The rôle which Hay seems to have assigned to himself as Secretary of State appears to have been one for which the Constitution of the

[1] Mr. Hunter Miller has recently compiled two lists from which it is now possible for the first time without very extensive searches to study the record of each Secretary of State as to treaties negotiated and ratified: *List of Certain Unperfected Treaties of the United States;* and, *Subject Index of the Treaty Series and Executive Agreement Series of the United States.* Both were published by the Government Printing Office in 1932. See also, Dangerfield, R. J., *In Defense of the Senate,* 1933.

United States makes no sufficient provision. Modest as he always was as to his personal attainments, Hay stood for the principle of government by experts. His pattern was Salisbury, Lansdowne, or Balfour.

"Your experience of public life in Washington and abroad," he wrote to Bellamy Storer, American Minister at Madrid, January 7, 1901, "gives you the best opportunity of judging the conditions under which we work. It is, as Balfour said the other day in the House of Commons, a thankless and heartbreaking task. The only thing is to stand it as long as we can, and give place to somebody else. The trouble is, of course, constitutional and irreparable. A controlling influence in public affairs is given by the very structure of our Government to men of great energy and force of character, but with no corresponding knowledge of a certain class of affairs. It is impossible for us to deal in diplomatic matters with other countries on a basis of equality. We are so handicapped by the Senate and the House that there is nothing to do but to follow a policy of makeshifts and half measures. I see absolutely no chance of any improvement. The President himself is unable to carry out the measures he thinks best. He is unable even to make the appointments he thinks best, and as for the Secretary of State, he is extremely fortunate if he can bring to pass one tenth of the measures for the public good that the Department has elaborated."

Government by experts is hardly possible under the American Constitution. "If a Secretary of State could work in a vacuum," Hay wrote to a youthful admirer,[1] "and only do the things which would be of advantage to the country, I could imagine no place more delightful than this, but the unconditioned and the absolute are beyond the reach of mortal men, and everything we do must pass the ordeal of a thousand selfish interests and prejudices and spites."

Hay's objections to the constitutional two-thirds rule of the Senate for the ratification of treaties, reiterated so often that they became very tiresome, obscured some of his criticisms which had more point.

The Secretary had great regard for the proprieties of international intercourse. The Senate, as a body, did not. For example, Hay discovered early in his service in the Department that Senators, col-

---

[1] Hay to Spencer Eddy, April 5, 1900. Eddy acted as Hay's private secretary in London and returned with Hay to Washington. Subsequently he entered the diplomatic service. The Secretary revealed in his letters much affection for Eddy.

lectively, could not be trusted to keep secrets. Upon this question of secrecy in the transaction of foreign relations there was, and is, much misunderstanding. Courtesy requires that negotiations and agreements shall not be made public without the consent of both parties. Whatever Americans may think of the practice of a government in withholding information about foreign affairs, it is at least clear that it is unfair, and not conducive to the maintaining of friendly relations, that one party to a negotiation should, without warning to the other side, publish to the world what has been said or agreed to. Publication of such news, to a public unprepared for it, may easily lead to very great popular misunderstandings, even to the downfall of a ministry in a country which has the parliamentary system. Failure to keep confidences may quickly lead to conditions approaching political nonintercourse. Governments have often had to be on their guard in dealing with American diplomats; they could not feel certain that a confidential remark made to an American envoy in the private office of a foreign minister, or at a dinner table, would not eventually find its way into an American newspaper. Such confidences are, in the American system of government, nominally, guarded by the rule of regarding as confidential the proceedings of the Senate Committee on Foreign Relations, and by the practice of discussing treaties in executive session. Leaks, however, are very probable where so many are entrusted with confidential information. Hay, like many another Secretary of State, struggled with the situation but could not control it.

"I can hardly express the mortification I felt that our treaty had been published without previous notice to you," he wrote privately to Lord Pauncefote, February 7, 1900, when the text of the first canal treaty suddenly appeared in the newspapers after a motion in the Senate to make it public had been defeated. "The moment you spoke of the matter, I sent a letter to Senator Davis, requesting him to give me early notice of the intentions of the Committee in regard to the publication of the treaty, but it seems that the treaty was printed confidentially for the use of the Committee, and some one of them must have communicated it to the press. I beg you to believe in my sincere regret and contrition. I ought to have told you to advise your government to act without regard to the Senate."

Hay's desire to magnify the duties of his office, rather than to share them with the Senate, was due, not at all to personal vanity, but to a feeling that otherwise it would be impossible to have both the respect and confidence of foreign governments, without which harmonious foreign relations are impossible.

The rumor was current at the time of the initial debate on the first Hay-Pauncefote Treaty that the Secretary had carried his attitude to a point where it had amounted to an affront to the Foreign Relations Committee. Senator Davis, in a not very convincing letter,[1] denied this, but at the same time betrayed his sense of injury.

"You put the case rather too strongly against the Secretary," he wrote the editor of the *Times*. "I think he would have consulted me if I had been there while the negotiations were being carried on. He has never shown any indisposition to consult. In fact, he has done so freely and frequently. It was merely a happening, I am sure that such consultation was not had in this particular instance. Mr. Hay has shown himself an able Secretary. His 'open door' negotiations will prove of the greatest value to this country."

It seems to have been a fact, however, that Hay not only did not consult Davis, but also failed to take into his confidence his old friend, Senator Lodge. On the other hand, the Secretary appears to have been under the impression that both Davis and Lodge had, to such an extent given their approval to the treaty before it was submitted to the Senate that they were under obligations to defend it when it was attacked.

"Mr. Davis and Mr. Lodge, while they claimed to be friendly to me and to the Treaty," Hay explained to Choate, December 21, 1900, "began to be fearful of its influence in the Presidential canvass. I tried to comfort them by telling them the President had some experience of politics—and a greater stake in the election than anybody else, and that if he was not frightened no one else need be. But they continued to be panicky and finally hit upon the so-called Davis Amendment, which they thought might satisfy the jingoes, without too much danger to the Treaty. Having deformed it with this excrescence, they dropped the whole matter until after election.

"Meanwhile, encouraged by the timidity of our own Senators, the Democrats had joined in attacking the Treaty, and when the Republicans declined to defend it, the opposition hastened to make a political issue of it. The Democratic Convention at Kansas City de-

[1] Minneapolis *Sunday Times*, Dec. 30, 1900.

nounced it as a base surrender to England, and Mr. Bryan, in his letter of acceptance, and afterwards, added his voluble ignorance to the
discussion. . . ."

In a letter two days later to Henry White, Hay did not stop short of
accusing Senator Lodge of bad faith. "The most exasperating thing
about it is that a close analysis of the vote convinces me that the treaty
could have been ratified without any amendment, if our people had had
any pluck, or if Lodge had acted squarely." Nevertheless, Hay did not
take Lodge into his confidence on the second negotiations with Pauncefote in 1901, and it was not until both White and Choate in London
asked permission that Hay allowed Lodge to see the text of the new
treaty.

That Hay actually consulted other Senators very freely is abundantly
revealed by the correspondence, so much of which has been quoted in
previous chapters of this narrative. However, the Secretary somehow
failed to be a "good fellow" with his colleagues on the Hill and even
when he sought to make friends he failed. With Senator Shelby M.
Cullom, who followed Davis as Chairman of the Foreign Relations
Committee, he should have been especially friendly. Cullom was an
old and intimate friend of the Secretary's uncle Milton, and came from
Springfield which was almost Hay's old home. There were many ties
which should have brought and held them together, but they did not.
Hay alienated Cullom. "Secretary Hay was not disposed to cultivate
friendly relations with Senators," declared the Senator,[1] "and certain
remarks he made concerning the Senate as a body were very distasteful
to Senators; and although I had invited him, he seemed very averse to
coming before the Committee on Foreign Relations. I did not press
the point. The result was that important treaties and other matters were
constantly sent in, with which the members of the committee were not
familiar, and we had to grope in the dark, as it were, and inform ourselves concerning them as best we could."

Hay, on the other hand, felt that the Senate was continually seeking
to belittle his office and encroach upon its proper functions. "They
really seem to think," he complained to White,[2] just after Lodge had
issued his communiqué to the newspapers about the Senate's share in
the negotiation of treaties, "the State Department has no function but

[1] *Fifty Years of Public Service*, p. 365.
[2] Dec. 23, 1900.

to provide their friends with offices. Lodge took care to gobble the Italian Embassy for Meyer before the vote on the treaty. Meyer lives in the same district with Gussie Gardner [1] and Lodge has Congressional ambitions for his son-in-law."

The Republican party was as fully committed to a policy of commercial reciprocity as campaign promises in 1896 and 1900 could accomplish it. "Protection and reciprocity are twin measures of Republican policy and go hand in hand," declared the Republican Convention in 1896. "Reciprocity builds up foreign trade and finds an outlet for our surplus." The Dingley tariff act of 1897 provided not only for reciprocity tariff agreements by the Executive, some of which were made, but also for reciprocity treaties, many of which were signed but never ratified.[2] The platform of 1900 was less emphatic but still reaffirmed the promise of reciprocity. Having renewed its faith in the policy of high tariff, the convention delegates added: "We favor the associated policy of reciprocity so directed as to open our markets on favorable terms for what we do not ourselves produce, in return for free foreign markets."

In December, 1899, President McKinley sent to the Senate the first series of reciprocity treaties: one with a European country, France; one with a South American state, Argentina; and five covering British possessions in and around the Caribbean: Barbados, British Guiana, Turks and Caicos Islands, Jamaica, and Bermuda. The following year, although the earlier ones had never even been reported out from the Foreign Relations Committee, the President added four more: Dominican Republic; Ecuador; Nicaragua; and, one with Denmark, covering St. Croix. There seems to be little doubt that McKinley had the definite purpose in his second term to push these treaties through, and probably to add many more, although they were known to be unwelcome to very influential Senators. In his second inaugural address he declared that reciprocal trade arrangements should be cultivated and promoted. On his great western tour in the spring of 1901, on which Hay accompanied him, he returned to the subject. At Memphis the President said: "It is your business as well as mine to see to it that an industrial policy shall be pursued in the United States that shall

---

[1] Augustus Peabody Gardner was elected in 1902 to Congress to fill the vacancy caused by the resignation of William H. Moody to become Attorney-General.

[2] *Reciprocity and Commercial Treaties*, G. P. O., Washington, 1919, pp. 28–30, and *passim.*

open up the widest markets in every part of the world for the products of American soil and American manufactures." [1]

At the Pan-American Exposition in Buffalo, September 5, 1901, McKinley devoted a large part of his address to commercial policy. "Isolation is no longer possible or desirable," he declared. ". . . trade statistics indicate that this country is in a state of unexampled prosperity. The figures are almost appalling. . . . Our capacity to produce has developed so enormously and our products have so multiplied that the problem of more markets requires our urgent and immediate attention. Only a broad and enlightened policy will keep what we have. . . . Reciprocity is the natural outgrowth of our wonderful industrial development under the domestic policy now firmly established. . . . The period of exclusiveness is past. . . . Commercial wars are unprofitable. . . ." [2]

This was McKinley's last message to his party; the following day he was stricken down. Commercial reciprocity was obviously supplementary to the doctrine of "McKinleyism" as we have already pieced it together—the preservation of peace by agreements. [3] Such a program fitted nicely into Hay's policy in Europe, in South America, and especially in the Caribbean, where it seemed so important to bring American interests of all sorts to a paramount position. The Secretary took McKinley's last words seriously. The Republican leaders in the Senate, on the contrary, were not a little troubled over the meaning of this new declaration. [4] Roosevelt's public promise, so quickly given, that he would carry out the McKinley policies, at first added to their anxiety. Then, within a few weeks, came the "gentlemen's agreement" between the new President and the elder statesmen, Aldrich, Allison, Spooner, and Platt of Connecticut, "not Judas Iscariot," as Roosevelt used to say, to distinguish him from Platt of New York. Probably Hanna should be included in the group, for he also was opposed to the threatened breach in the protective wall.

"The more I think of it the better I like the paragraphs of the Message on reciprocity," wrote Lodge to Roosevelt. [5] "I hope you will keep it just as it is. It is a difficult question and you have handled it

---

[1] Edward Stanwood, *History of the Presidency,* 1916 ed., II, p. 84.
[2] The address is printed in full as an appendix to Olcott, II.
[3] See Chapter XXVII.
[4] Nathaniel Wright Stephenson, *Nelson W. Aldrich,* pp. 176 ff.
[5] October 17, 1901; Lodge, I, p. 507.

perfectly." In the message, after a perfunctory reference to it as the "handmaiden of protection," he merely added: "I ask the attention of the Senate to the reciprocity treaties laid before it by my predecessor." [1] As a result of much thought and many conferences Roosevelt had decided to drop commercial reciprocity quietly overboard.

That was the end of one McKinley policy. Two years later Roosevelt called the Senate back into special session to act on the Cuban reciprocity treaty, but that was a special case, where the good faith of the American Government was at stake. Roosevelt was never a substantial help to his Secretary of State in carrying through a policy of commercial reciprocity which, to the latter, was a matter of political wisdom, of honor, and of the redemption of party pledges.

The Senate played hide and seek with the public on the reciprocity treaties. It allowed them to rest quietly in the Committee on Foreign Relations, but there was no intention that they should ever be reported out and voted upon. The party leaders took care that the platform of 1904 should carry the embarrassing promise no longer. The action of his party was to Hay a bitter disappointment.

The depths of Hay's conviction on the subject appear in his memorial address on McKinley, delivered before both houses of Congress, February 27, 1902. There is in the address one impassioned paragraph in which Hay again mounted the pulpit and stopped just short of pointing the finger of shame at the men who had invited him before them. Arguing that McKinley had always been a party man, and a protectionist, Hay recalled the last day that he spent with him at Canton, and intimated the nature of the conversation.[2] The Secretary pictured McKinley as having seen "in the immense evolution of American trade the fulfillment of all his dreams, the reward of all his labors" for protection. "He was—I need not say—an ardent protectionist, never more sincere and devoted than during these last days of his life." As for reciprocity, McKinley looked upon it, not "as a breach, but a fulfillment of the law. The treaties which for four years had been preparing under his personal supervision, he regarded as ancillary to the general scheme. . . . In that mood of high hope, . . . he went to Buffalo, and there, on the threshold of eternity, he delivered that memorable speech, worthy for its loftiness of tone, its blameless

[1] *For. Rel.*, 1901, pp. xxii, xxiii.
[2] *Addresses*, pp. 168 ff.

"We must not repose in fancied security that we can forever sell everything and buy little or nothing. . . . A policy of good will and friendly trade relations will prevent reprisals. . . . Reciprocity treaties are in harmony with the spirit of the times; measures of retaliation are not." President McKinley at Buffalo, September 5, 1901, the day before his assassination.

HENRY CABOT LODGE

"With Hay's personal charm, modesty and magnetism, Lodge would have been a brilliant figure in American history. With Lodge's thoroughness and industry, Hay would have easily ranked above any of his contemporaries," p. 421.

morality, its breadth of view, to be regarded as his testament to the nation. Through all his pride of country and his joy of its success, runs the note of solemn warning, as in Kipling's noble hymn, 'Lest we forget.' " The warning to which Hay referred, and which he proceeded to quote, was the paragraph on reciprocity. . . . "We must not repose in fancied security that we can forever sell everything and buy little or nothing. . . . A policy of good will and friendly trade relations will prevent reprisals. Reciprocity treaties are in harmony with the spirit of the times; measures of retaliation are not."

"His years of apprenticeship had been served," continued Hay, solemnly driving home his point. "He had nothing more to ask of the people. He owed them nothing but truth and faithful service. His mind and heart were purged of the temptations which beset all men engaged in the struggle to survive. . . ." The appeal would have been stronger if he had been holding up the example of a man who had reached this new conviction before, rather than after, his last election. It would have been more persuasive if the speaker had been one of those who had been accustomed each six years to go back home and make peace with restless constituents. Hay seems never to have been aware what a gulf separated him from those in elective office who had to render account for their votes. His appeal to the Senate does not stand very close analysis, but that it was a declaration of his own last political pledge there can be little doubt. Commercial reciprocity was, to the Secretary of State, the great McKinley tradition.

The protest in the memorial address was feeble; no one paid any attention to it. On the one point nearest to Hay's heart all the Republican leaders, including the President, had abandoned him. At the end of another year he was completely disillusioned.

"Root made a very fine speech in Boston," Hay reported to the President, April 5, 1903, after reading the accounts of the Home Markets Club dinner. "I am sorry Lodge did not. It is exasperating that he chooses to take a line so damaging to himself. He ought to be satisfied with killing the reciprocity treaties. Why go on saying he is in favor of them, but opposed to their ratification?" To Eugene G. Hay, not a relative, he wrote on June 1, 1903:

I have received your pamphlet on Reciprocity with Canada, and have read it with very great interest.

You are evidently aware of the serious obstacles in our Senate to any scheme of reciprocity, but I doubt if you appreciate their full power. The experience of four years has left me little hope of any reciprocity treaty with any country passing the Senate. I was told only a few days ago, by one of the leading members of Congress, that he was in favor of reciprocity, but was opposed to any arrangement which would injure any of our industries. I asked him who was to be the judge as to such resulting injuries, and he said, "the industries themselves, of course," which, as you see, gives any one industry in the country a categorical veto on all Government action in the way of reciprocity.

It was a natural result of the pathological conditions under which he did his work in the last few years of his life that he brooded upon his troubles, and also fancied that the antagonism which he encountered in the Senate was even more personal than it actually was. Hay developed a typical "persecution complex." Furthermore, he was evidently again struggling with the old dualism of his own nature: he was both bolter and regular. When the Chairman of the Republican Congressional Committee asked him to make some political speeches in the autumn of 1902, he declined, intimating that if he were to say what he thought, his speeches would not help the party very much. He wrote: [1]

There are now before the Senate a very important series of treaties, which I, at least, ought to do nothing to help defeat. There are already a good many men in the Senate who dislike me, and who vote against anything I am known to be in favor of. I think it highly inexpedient to increase the number of these men, on the Democratic side, by taking so active a part in politics as to still further excite their antagonism. Thirty votes in the Senate will defeat any treaty. If I should make a speech that amounted to anything and attracted any attention at all it would certainly contribute something to this minority of thirty hostile votes. It is in the interests of the public service and Republican policies in general that I shall deprive myself of the pleasure of talking politics much in public.

The only "series of treaties" were those which McKinley had bequeathed to his not wholly sorrowing disciples. What Hay would have said about the treatment they had received at the hands of their party would, for example, not have helped the election of "Gussie" Gardner, who at that moment, under the tutorship of his father-in-law, was running for Congressman for Gloucester, Massachusetts. Indeed, what Hay thought of the Senate had, by that time, come to be personalized in what he thought of Senator Lodge.

[1] Hay to Congressman J. W. Babcock, October 20, 1902.

JOHN HAY and Henry Cabot Lodge ought to have been the best of friends; they appeared to be; but they were not. Members of the same small circle of luminaries for a quarter of a century, neighbors for nearly twenty years, they were exchanging Christmas gifts, birthday greetings, and appreciations of one another's writings as far back as the early nineties. Even then they were, perhaps, excessively polite to each other. Reviewing the relationship in the light of its ending, we may doubt whether they ever genuinely respected each other. Temperamentally they were rivals; each had desirable qualities which the other lacked. With Hay's personal charm, modesty, and magnetism, Lodge would have been a brilliant figure in American history. With Lodge's thoroughness and industry, Hay would have ranked easily above any of his contemporaries. The best abilities and qualities of the two men taken together, less the defects of each, would have made a man of such stature as America in the 19th Century did not produce.

The entrance of Theodore Roosevelt into the White House should have drawn Lodge and Hay together; it probably had the effect of setting them more against each other. Hay, at least, was not a jealous man, but the triangular relationship was trying. Lodge's shadow fell across the White House, darkening every gesture of confidence which Roosevelt and Hay might make to each other. Lodge, also, considered himself an expert in foreign relations, a postgraduate in a harder school than Hay ever had been willing to enter. When John Hay appeared in Washington as Secretary of State he may have seemed to the Senator as one who had entered the kingdom by climbing up some other way. One cannot read the published Lodge-Roosevelt letters of the period, with due attention to Roosevelt's replies to Lodge which the latter chose, in editing, to omit, without sensing that the Senator was at times very critical. It must have been difficult for the Secretary to keep from feeling that the Senator was steadily undercutting him. Lodge rasped on Hay's nerves and the latter wrote some very sharp words, and spoke even sharper ones. He intimated that Lodge was tricky and referred to his "infirmity of mind and character." [1] All his later letters to the

---

[1] Nevins, p. 195.

Senator were characterized by restraint and stiffness.

The final and bitterest falling-out was over the principle of commercial reciprocity.

Between the United States and Newfoundland there was a natural basis for a reciprocal relationship. The Colony was populated by a conservative, almost primitive, people, not inclined to industrial development. Their produce was a little coal, and some fish which they marketed chiefly in Europe. Their commercial opportunity lay in the possession, within their territorial waters, of almost a monopoly of the bait which was required for the Grand Banks, to which the fishermen of many nations, but most of all the Yankees, resorted. Also, from within these territorial waters was obtainable, in the winter months, the "frozen herring" which the Massachusetts fishermen purchased from the Newfoundlanders and entered at their home ports, duty free, as American produce. Closely allied to the economic relationship between the two countries was a political one. Newfoundland cherished its unique position and had steadily resisted all efforts to draw it into the Dominion of Canada. The colony even failed to establish the famous "imperial preference" tariff by which so many of the other British possessions were granting a 33⅓ per cent advantage to Great Britain. On the other hand, Newfoundland had for many years carefully pursued toward the United States a conciliatory, friendly policy. In 1888, following the failure in the Senate of the Bayard-Chamberlain fisheries treaty, the Government of Newfoundland, as a preliminary to the reciprocity treaty which it never ceased to hope for, established a *modus vivendi* whereby Americans were granted from year to year the bait privilege in Newfoundland waters by payment of a small license fee based on the tonnage of the vessels employed. The privilege of taking the "frozen herring" was included.

In 1890 Secretary Blaine negotiated with Sir Robert Bond a reciprocity convention by which it was designed that these privileges of free bait and trade should be confirmed by treaty, in return for the free entry of Newfoundland fish into the United States. The Colony was also prepared to offer a free list of American manufactured goods. The negotiations were well received in the United States. Canada, on the contrary, made a vigorous protest to London, on the ground that Newfoundland ought not, by the concession of privileges which were claimed as the joint property of all the British colonies in North

America, to obtain favors which the American Government refused to grant to the Dominion. When the subject was reopened twelve years later, Adee remembered that one of Mr. Blaine's motives in entering into the negotiations had been to keep up the tension between Newfoundland and the Dominion. "Mr. B. enjoyed setting two dogs by the ears," explained Adee,[1] "as much as any man I ever knew. Besides, he had an idea that a starter in this direction would tend to bring about a movement in Newfoundland for annexation to the United States, in which I think he was oversanguine."

Whether or not one took seriously the question of possible annexation, there were obvious advantages to the American Government, aside from the commercial ones, in meeting Newfoundland in a friendly spirit.

Hay was at Newbury when Sir Robert Bond arrived in the United States in August, 1902, to take the initiative for reviving the old Blaine-Bond project. The Premier from the beginning disclosed a disposition to deal directly with the Department of State, rather than through the British Embassy. Sir Robert immediately received a tactful hint from Adee that the communications would have to be through the Embassy. That question being disposed of, Hay instructed Adee to receive whatever propositions Newfoundland had to make, for submission to the President. Hay actually was embarrassed and doubtful. "It is for *us* to consider whether in the present attitude of the Senate toward *all* reciprocity arrangements, it would not be a waste of time and a sort of discourtesy to a friendly country to make a treaty with them." [2] The President, preoccupied with preparations for a speaking trip through the West, and perhaps not ignorant of the political snares which lay in reciprocity treaties, left the matter entirely to Hay's judgment.[3]

Sir Robert waited somewhat impatiently for the Secretary to resume his duties in the Department, and for the President to return from the West. After conversations with the Premier, and with the President, who approved, the Secretary decided to seek the opinion of Senators Lodge and Frye. To them on October 10, he sent the telegram: "Confidential. Sir Robert Bond is here anxious to renew the Bond-Blaine

[1] Adee to Hay, Sept. 15, 1902.
[2] Hay to Adee, Sept. 25, 1902.
[3] Cortelyou to Hay, Sept. 13, Oct. 16, 1902.

convention with Newfoundland. The President thinks favorably. How does it strike you?"

By the replies the Secretary felt sufficiently encouraged to go forward, and three days later he reported to the President: "Considering the urgency of the case, and Sir Robert's hurry, I have been breaking the sabbath with him and going over the treaty. He has accepted the three small alterations I suggested, and I think it is a good Treaty— better than Blaine's was. So I will have it engrossed and signed as swiftly as possible and say to Sir Robert, 'Vaya ud. con Dios.' "

The proposed treaty was for five years. It provided for the free entry of salted cod, a product of Newfoundland which, while popular in Europe, was unlike the Gloucester product and not in demand in the United States, and for the free entry, also, of the frozen herring.[1]

Senator Lodge soon began so much to qualify his approval as to threaten the outlook for the treaty in the Senate. Hay did not at first take the Senator's warnings very seriously. On the 13th he wrote:

"I have your letter of the 10th of October and also your telegram.[2] I have seen Sir Robert Bond several times and we are trying to agree upon a satisfactory treaty. I think myself the political advantages of such a treaty would be very great—so great as to outweigh, from our point of view, the slight objections which may be raised on the part of some of our citizens interested in fishing and mining, though, of course, the interests of the American fishermen are looked out for, and fresh, uncured codfish are expressly exempted from free entry."

Hay added as a postscript: "I think that with this treaty Massachusetts will handle the whole output of the Fisheries." Lodge replied urging that the signing of the treaty be delayed until after the election. He also warned that it would be a great risk to close the negotiation without first consulting with some Gloucester representative. He suggested that the Secretary invite the Collector of the Port to confer with him.[3]

On October 16 Hay wrote to the President:

Here is a letter from Cabot saying he is in favor of the Treaty but that if we sign it without the consent of Gloucester he will be obliged to oppose it in the Senate.

I do not see how we are to get the consent of Gloucester.

[1] Senate Ex. Doc. E, 57–2, made public Dec. 10, 1902.
[2] Practically all the Lodge letters have been withdrawn from the Hay Papers.
[3] Lodge to Hay, Oct. 16, 1902.

The treaty is very advantageous to us; the other colonies give England 33 p. c. preference: this lets us in on even terms. The political advantage is very great, and I have retained, in spite of Sir Robert Bond's earnest solicitation, the exclusion of fresh codfish, which the Gloucester men make such a point of.

I have no doubt that under this treaty Massachusetts will handle the whole output. But, of course, if we submit the matter absolutely to Gloucester they will think up some further demands which Newfoundland cannot grant.

Of course, equally, I want to oblige Cabot—but what can we do?

Bond has been waiting here six weeks— He is urgently needed at home as acting Governor in the absence of his chief. I cannot decently ask him to wait till after the election in Massachusetts.

Shall I go ahead, or not?

The President still kept clear of the controversy. Hay delayed signing the convention until after the election, but he did not heed Lodge's other warning; he did not send for Collector Jordan, nor did he show the treaty to Lodge or to any representative of the Gloucester interests.

"I think Gloucester is safe for Captain Gardner by a large majority," Hay wrote tartly to the President the next day, at the same time informing Lodge that in deference to his wishes the signing would be postponed.

Uneasy about the correspondence with the Secretary, the Senator took the matter up with the President, October 20.[1] He reaffirmed his interest in the treaty, but renewed his warnings. "I am very anxious to see some arrangement made with Newfoundland. I think in the broadest view it is very important for us to detach Newfoundland from Canada by some such arrangement, and I hope it can be done. I wrote this to Mr. Hay, but I told him at the same time that it would be impossible for us to sustain the treaty unless it was reasonably satisfactory to the Gloucester people." He remarked that the fishing interests of Massachusetts "are very sensitive and very suspicious of any arrangement with Canada and Newfoundland." He felt that they should be conciliated, the more so because "the fishermen are a most important resource in time of war. Gloucester sent more men into the Navy during the Spanish war in proportion to its size than any city in the country. . . . Therefore, we have to stand by the fishermen." He repeated that neither he nor Senator Hoar could sustain a treaty to which there was serious objection from the fishing interests.

[1] Lodge, I, p. 543.

The appeal was directed at the President's liveliest sympathy but Roosevelt was still careful to keep out of the discussion. He turned the Lodge letter over to be answered by Hay.

The issue was well joined. A small parish interest stood in the way of a larger national one. The Senator spoke for his parish, and, as for conciliating Newfoundland with any risk to Republican majorities in Gloucester, Lodge had no concern. There was also a subsidiary issue. Hay felt that Lodge had at first encouraged him to go forward with the negotiations. Of this second point much was made in the Massachusetts election campaign in 1905, when Osborne Howes charged that Lodge had actually promised to support the treaty and then broke his promise.[1] The specific charge appears to have been incorrect, although there seems to be no doubt but that Hay subsequently felt that Lodge had not dealt fairly.

The larger issue, however, was illustrative of the take-and-not-give attitude of Senators about which Hay so often complained.

The Secretary dictated a long letter to Lodge but, before mailing it, sent it over to the President with a note which clearly reveals Hay's sense of injury. It is to be observed, nevertheless, that he did not consider the alternative of meeting Lodge's second condition by reopening the negotiations and calling in the Gloucester fishermen. To the President he wrote, October 21:

Dear Theodore:

I have written this long letter to Cabot, and hope you may have time to read it. We both know him and are fond of him—but you know him best—and can tell me whether such a letter would do more harm than good.

I hate to open the winter with such a misunderstanding—but I see nothing to do but to go on and sign the convention.

I enclose, as you directed last night, a paragraph for the Message.

The letter to Lodge was evidently from a man who felt deeply wounded, a little fearful, and yet quite determined: [2]

Dear Mr. Lodge:—

I have received your letter of the 18th of October enclosing Mr. Jordan's letter of the 16th. I have read them both over several times, with a sincere desire to get your point of view. I am sorry I can not come to the same conclusions at which you and Mr. Jordan have arrived.

[1] Boston *Herald*, Oct. 28, 29; Boston *Transcript*, Nov. 1; Boston *Advertiser*, Oct. 28, 1905.
[2] Hay to Lodge, Oct. 21, 1902.

When I first heard that Sir Robert Bond had gained the consent of the British Government to a revival of the Blaine-Bond Convention, the news caused me nearly as much regret as surprise. I was astonished that Newfoundland had succeeded in getting the consent of Great Britain to overrule the furious Canadian opposition to any treaty between us, and, at the same time, I foresaw serious trouble in making any treaty which would be satisfactory to you. It was on account of considerations like this that an answer to Sir Robert Bond was so long delayed; but when I arrived here and found that he was still here and anxious to see me, I telegraphed you and Mr. Frye, the two New England members of the Committee on Foreign Relations, to ask how it struck you. Mr. Frye answered at once that, while he had forgotten the terms of the Blaine-Bond convention, he favored it when it was negotiated, and that, in his opinion, the conditions had not changed, and that Newfoundland's interests are all with us. You answered that you had written me urging me to see Bond; that you were strongly in favor of making the convention if we could satisfy Gloucester. I could hardly understand that you meant that the suggestion of satisfying Gloucester was to be taken in an absolute sense, because the experience of the past has shown that this is impossible. At the same time I got your letter of October 10 urging me to see Sir Robert, and, if possible, make a treaty, calling to mind the fact, in which, of course, I agree with you, that Newfoundland stands on a very different footing from Canada. I was fortunate enough also to find Mr. Kasson well enough to discuss the matter with me, and received his earnest approval of the convention. Mr. Foster, another member of the Joint High Commission, who has studied the matter deeply, also strongly approves the convention. The fact that Mr. Blaine's action at the time met with general approval in the country was another factor in the question. Taking all these things into consideration, with the approval of the President, I went into the matter with Sir Robert and agreed upon a convention. At this time I received your urgent telegrams asking for a delay in signing, and, although the time for the signature had been agreed upon, I, at the cost of some personal embarrassment, induced Sir Robert to go home and postponed the signing of the treaty until next month.

I need not say with what great regret I learn of your determination to oppose the treaty, knowing as I do the great and legitimate influence which you exert in the Senate. I can only hope that on a further study of the matter you will recognize the great advantages which we shall gain in the treaty. Our fishing vessels gain exactly the same advantages in the waters of Newfoundland in the purchasing of every kind of bait as the Newfoundland vessels themselves. They have the privilege of touching and trading, buying and selling fish and oil, and procuring supplies on terms of complete equality. Unsalted or fresh codfish are expressly excluded from free entry into this country, a matter we have always been led to consider was one of vital importance to Gloucester. In return we get, beside a great mass of details of free or reduced entry for our commodities, an absolute most favored nation clause. In this way we break, so far as Newfoundland is concerned, the whole Imperial system of preference between Great Britain and her other colonies; we establish on the extreme Eastern flank of the Dominion a relation of friendship which will be of incalculable advantage to us in our future dealings with Canada. It is not merely the thirty-three per cent preferential which we escape, but it is a political advantage of the greatest value, which we gain.

I do not go into the detailed examination of Mr. Jordan's letter for this reason. He says at the start, and continues to say, that he is opposed to any treaty whatever; that none can be made which is satisfactory to him; and that if one is made, the Newfoundland people would not be bound by its provisions. He admits the unsatisfactory character of the present state of things, but the only remedy he suggests is that of hostile legislation by Congress. You know how difficult of accomplishment this would be, and, in my opinion, such legislation, if carried through, would not be found workable.

I have said all this without any illusion as to my power in persuading you to change your mind, but simply as a justification of our action here, which I am sorry does not meet your approval.

The letter, so suggestive of McKinley's last address, accomplished nothing. Roosevelt, for reasons which are not clear, sent the treaty to the Senate, December 3, and Lodge immediately opened his fight against it, as did Captain Gardner, now a member of the House. Protests and petitions rolled in and Lodge had them printed as Senate documents.[1] Outside of Gloucester the treaty received much sympathy and support. Even the Boston *Transcript* warned Gloucester not to be too unreasonable, recalling that Newfoundland was in a position to make it very inconvenient for the fishermen.[2] The treaty was buried in the Foreign Relations Committee until January, 1905, when it was reported out with such amendments as Hay foresaw. It had ceased to be reciprocal in character, and Newfoundland declined to ratify it.

At the Home Markets Club dinner, April 2, 1903, to which reference has already been made, Senator Lodge made a brief but emphatic reference to his attitude. "There is, therefore," he said, "only one test to be applied to a convention of this kind, and that is whether, in return for the concessions which we make, we receive a proper equivalent." In his judgment the treaty was open to the one fatal objection that if cured or salted fish were put on the free list the salting and

---

[1] Senate Docs., 50, 78, 87, 94, 57–2.

[2] *Transcript*, Dec. 11, 1902. See also: S. Doc. 65, 57–2, for reprints of articles in the N. Y. *Tribune*, and in the Boston *Herald;* and, the *Atlantic Monthly*, December, 1902, "The Atlantic Fisheries Question," by P. T. McGrath, a Newfoundland journalist.

curing establishments of Massachusetts would be transferred to New-foundland, whither likewise the fishermen would remove themselves.[1]

Hay seems to have resented most of all the unwillingness of Senator Lodge even to report the treaty out of committee for general discussion. It had friends elsewhere in the Senate. The Senator was not disclosing any genuine interest in any kind of a treaty with Newfoundland. The Secretary begged the President not to take the matter up, but after the election in 1904 the latter did write to Lodge. "Where there are good objections to the treaty, amend it; but show a real purpose of trying to get it," he wrote.[2] That was as far as Roosevelt went by way of support. In the following May and June, when Hay was in Europe on his last vain search for health, the correspondence on the Newfound-land matter between Roosevelt and Lodge was very active. At length the President declared, June 3: [3]

"I am to blame for not having discouraged Bond and not having urged Hay to refuse to treat at all. And Hay is to blame for refusing to consult anyone who knew anything of the subject, despite my prayer that he would, and so making a treaty that any fishery man would have told him in a minute was impossible."

A few months later, when Senator Lodge was challenged on his attitude toward the Newfoundland treaty, and charged with bad faith, he publicly replied: [4]

"Mr. Hay was one of the dearest friends I had, a friend of more than twenty-five years. We differed, as men in public life do differ; but no shadow ever came over our personal friendship." Mr. Osborne Howes had been nearer correct when he declared in Brookline the night before: [5] "Mr. Hay was hurried to a premature death in consequence of diplomatic disappointments, and probably there is no man more responsible for those disappointments than Henry Cabot Lodge."

Between the two men the conventional courtesies never ceased. Too civilized to stand up to a "knock-down-drag-out" fight, both struck only furtively, but they had little in common except their love of fine things and fine people. Even the capacious Republican party was hardly inclusive enough to hold them both.

---

[1] *Transcript,* April 3, 1903.
[2] Lodge, II, p. 110.
[3] *Ibid.*, p. 128.
[4] Boston *Herald,* Oct. 29, 1905
[5] Boston *Herald,* Oct. 28, 1905.

Chapter XXXVI

JOHN HAY had a highly developed dramatic sense. He could view situations instantly as they would appear to the public eye. With unfailing good taste, he dramatized the foreign relations of the United States, and dressed them up in a manner which appealed to the popular imagination. The newspaper men of the day, some of whom still live, dwell upon how patiently he received and guided them, how he prepared their minds for the story which would "break" some days hence. Hay always had a good press, probably the best that any Secretary ever had. Perhaps his greatest contribution to American foreign policy was to popularize it. He dragged a mysterious little government bureaucracy out of its obscurity and seemed to hand it over to the people as a mighty agency of idealism in which they could, and did, take great pride. And yet Hay's dramatic sense failed him when the time came for his resignation. Or, shall we say that, having so successfully dramatized his work, he was unwilling, too modest, to dramatize himself?

Public men, unless death intervenes, are likely to insist upon a dramatically unnecessary fourth act when they should have been content to rest quietly off-stage. That this was the case with Theodore Roosevelt is a commonplace observation; it was true, although in lesser degree, of John Hay.

If this essay were a history, it would be important to touch upon many more episodes of the years 1903 and 1904 in which Hay played a part, but even to list them would bring on an anticlimax. The ascending crises in Hay's life came later than with most men. From 1898 to 1901 he went from strength to strength: he found himself. Tragically, the discovery came when his reservoirs of vitality were too much depleted to sustain the effort at the new altitudes. At the end of these three years he found a level at which he could go forward for another eighteen months. Then should have come the curtain; he should have resigned early in 1903. It is of general as well as particular interest to discover why at that time he ignored the dramatic laws which he knew so well and which he was accustomed to respect.

As a matter of fact he did offer his resignation on July 23, 1903, just after he had rescued the President from the Kisheneff petition; just before he was dragged on into the worst phases of the Panama affair; before, also, he had marred an otherwise perfect record in the Alaska boundary settlement. It was a qualified resignation, but genuine; he offered to make way for Elihu Root. On that date he wrote to the President: [1]

I have heard persistent stories of Root's retirement. He must not go if it can possibly be prevented. He is a tower of strength in your administration. He is about the ablest man today in public life; his popularity is very great; he has the confidence of men in politics, in the financial world, and in private life. You are more independent of your Cabinet than most Presidents, but even to you his loss would be hard to make good.

I venture to say these things for a particular reason which I have already hinted both to you and to him. I have thought that though he may feel he has done the two or three great jobs he proposed to do in the War Department and is therefore ready to lay down that portfolio, he might still be willing to remain as Secretary of State. He has won great renown where he is; he could fill out and amplify his page in history in the State Department. I would most gladly give place to him, if you could retain his services in that way.

I beg you to understand that there is no undercurrent of motive in this suggestion. As I have told you before I will stay where I am as long as you want me, unless something breaks, of which I see no immediate danger, but the prospect of rest is always agreeable to a man of my years, and if I could help you more by going out and getting a man like Root in my place, I would be content to emulate Machiavel as he describes himself in his exile from court, laying off the soiled raiment and sordid cares of the day, putting on his richest robe and sitting down for a long evening in his library.

Beside our delightful official relations I have a great affection for you and for Root. I cannot bear to see you separated, if there is any way to keep you together.

Do not answer this in a hurry. Carry it around in your mind for a while and see if you don't think there is something in it.

Yours affectionately.

John Hay was ready for the curtain. He could have thus finished his career, much more secure in the confidence of many of his countrymen than the man under whom he served.

Roosevelt refused to consider a resignation: "As Secretary of State you stand alone. I could not spare you."

"It is singular," Hay wrote modestly to his wife,[2] "what a chorus of

[1] Hay to Roosevelt, July 23, 1903.
[2] July 14, 1903.

puffing I get from every quarter, especially from the papers that have had nothing but abuse of me for four years. I can't understand it. I suppose the object is to embroil me with the President. But this does not seem to have succeeded. What a beautiful send-off they would give me if I *did* leave now."

Why did he stay on to be made use of as a "fine figurehead"? His constructive work was accomplished. His name was not later associated with any new measures which added to his fame. On the contrary, he was being continually carried on toward policies which tended to damage his reputation, or cheapen it. The Perdicaris telegram, for example, was as unworthy of him as it was of Roosevelt. It was the kind of showman's trick that William McKinley would never have stooped to. Why didn't Hay take advantage of the dramatic moment and make his grand exit from public life in the summer of 1903?

It was not because he had fallen into the common pit of believing that he was indispensable. He recognized Elihu Root as having a strength which he lacked, with which, on occasion, to hold in check the seemingly reckless President. Certainly Root could do as well, perhaps better, as Secretary of State. Nor was it love of position which overcame Hay's faltering resolution to resign. The mere thought, after the President's rather serious Pittsfield accident in 1902, that he might possibly be called to act as President put him in a panic. Position meant nothing to John Hay after Del's death in 1901. Nor did personal comfort. As has already appeared, under Theodore Roosevelt Hay's position could hardly have been called comfortable. Nor was he under any personal obligation to the President to remain. As a matter of fact, if we may trust von Sternburg's reports to his Foreign Office, Roosevelt was actually wishing that he might be rid of Hay.

It was, probably, party loyalty which held Hay in office. Never possessed of great influence in the counsels of his party, he became each year more and more a party man until defense of party, of President, of self, were wrought into a single emotion. To have conceded a criticism of one would have carried acknowledgment of deficiencies in the other two. His party loyalty, remarked Henry Adams,[1] came to resemble that of a "highly cultivated churchman for his Church." The difference between being a Republican and being a Democrat was, to Hay, like that of being respectable or not. His was the party of

[1] *Education,* p. 321.

Abraham Lincoln, whose tradition he had done so much to fix. The party, also, of William McKinley of sainted memory, whose tradition was not yet fixed, whose policies were falling by the way. He longed to tell the world of what he regarded as the treachery of some of the party leaders but he could not do it without damage to the only bulwark against Bryanism, than which nothing seemed more terrifying since the days of the French Revolution. Granting the truth of the premises, the logic was sound. The reelection of McKinley had relieved, but did not wholly quiet, the feeling of alarm. The accession of Roosevelt not only introduced new uncertainties, but also left the McKinley tradition to be conserved, if possible. In fact, to the loyal party man there never is an opportune moment to endanger a vote.

That John Hay was regarded as one of the important assets of his party is abundantly proved by the many importunate letters from the campaign managers, begging him for speeches. A public address was an ordeal. As his reluctance to speak increased, the solicitations were more and more often forwarded to him through the President, whose indorsement was hard indeed to ignore. The invitation to the St. Louis Exposition came that way.

"I have already agreed to go to St. Louis and speak on the 19th, . . ." he wrote to "Dear Theodore," April 14, 1904. "I have thus broken the promise made to myself for good and sufficient reasons, which still seem to me good and sufficient. I have also broken the promises made to my wife, who is witness of what such engagements cost. I have no natural appetite or sleep while the horror lasts; and I know perfectly well it is not worth while."

At the semi-centennial celebration of the Republican Party at Jackson, Mich., on July 6 of the same year, who but John Hay should light the beacon for the approaching campaign? His oration that day is an interesting document in the study of party regularity. Roosevelt called it "one of the few speeches which can rightly be called noble"; sure of a permanent place in American oratory; very valuable, also, as a campaign document.[1] Others less partisan thought that he spoke somewhat extravagantly. "The laudation of the Republican Party," commented Thayer, a partisan who knew not the force of party loyalty, "to which Hay attributed almost every beneficent act in fifty years, except possibly the introduction of antiseptic surgery, must have tickled

[1] July 9, 1904.

Hay's sense of humor. . . ." [1]

Norman Hapgood, who no more than Thayer could understand party loyalty, expressed the belief in *Collier's Weekly* that Hay had in the Jackson speech tried to annex too much territory. To the latter Hay wrote: [2] "I do not think we Republicans are selfish and grasping when we enroll Washington and Lincoln among our spiritual ancestors. We do not 'claim everything.' We leave the other side their Jefferson, their Jackson, their Pierce, and their Buchanan. In fact, when we come to think of it, we are like Lord Clive—astonished at our own moderation."

It was a mistake to assume that Hay spoke with his tongue in his cheek; he had come to believe what he said.

At the close of the campaign it was Hay again who was sent to Carnegie Hall to give the big address. The truth of the matter is that he was being made use of. In New York he labored the point, among others, that while the tariff needed revision, the operation could safely be trusted only to those who loved it. He spoke in good faith and it was only after the election that he learned that the President had decided even to omit from his annual message all reference to tariff revision.[3]

In the same speech the passage about the pacific character of the President's foreign policy must also have been a little difficult: "We are told that he is dangerous to the peace of the world, he is a fire eater, a war lord—he wishes to embroil us in a policy of adventure. . . ." [4] Hay got around the difficulty by averaging. "He and his predecessor have done more in the interest of universal peace than any other two Presidents since our Government was formed."

The next day there came over from the White House the following note:

Dear John:
This morning Knox came in and said to me: "What a magnificent address Hay's was last night! I can never sufficiently congratulate myself on the opportunity of having been intimately associated with him in public life for the last few years." To which I add, amen.
Thanking you for your congratulations on my birthday, I am,
Always yours
Theodore Roosevelt.

[1] Thayer, II, p. 381.
[2] August 8, 1904.
[3] *Diary*, December 4, 1904.
[4] Newspapers of October 27, 1904.

"LOAFING AROUND THE THRONE"

While Secretary Hay was at Bad Nauheim in 1905 both he and
the Department of State were besieged with invitations for him to
visit Berlin, Paris, Brussels, and London. King Leopold was particularly insistent, and eventually called on him, May 25. In Paris,
Hay saw M. Delcassé, and lunched with King Edward in London.
Original in the collection of Clarence L. Hay.

John Hay in 1904, a few months before his death.

Those who do not believe in party loyalty, responsibility, regularity, may feel that to his party John Hay gave more than was required. It is a nice question.

John Hay staggered on until after the inauguration in March, 1905, and then fell under his load. The burden had been growing lighter month by month, for, after the election, the President more and more assumed active direction of foreign affairs, but the Secretary's strength failed even more rapidly.

February was a hard month for Hay with the Senators. In the campaign which had closed in November both the President and the Secretary had discussed in public the proposed series of new arbitration treaties. Both men were convinced that the country would support their program. The treaties were very mild projects in which all questions of "vital interests," "independence," and national "honor" had been subtracted from the scope of arbitration, but they were a beginning on a subject which Hay had much at heart. They were an integral part of "McKinleyism." Possibly they would have received the approval of the Senate but for the fact that in Santo Domingo President Roosevelt was aggressively pushing for a "protocol" which involved the appointment of a receivership and the extension to that unhappy island of the principles of the Platt Amendment. The Senators suspected that in the Santo Domingo affair, by negotiating a protocol rather than a treaty, the President was invading the constitutional prerogatives of the Senate. At length Roosevelt, February 15, 1905, transmitted the agreement to the Senate for its approval. The suspicions of the Senate, however, having been aroused, could not be so easily allayed.

First they turned upon the arbitration treaties and amended the text to provide that no arbitration should be undertaken without, in each instance, the express approval by the Senate of the terms of the reference. Thus, the treaties, first emasculated by the weasel reservations above mentioned, were still further weakened. As amended they were only an engagement to present the discussion of the question of arbitration to the Senate whenever the President recommended it. The President withdrew the treaties and the latter in turn declined to advise ratification of the Santo Domingo protocol. Some people thought that these disappointments broke Hay down. The causes were, in fact, both more elemental and more subtle. The President had already made himself directly responsible for American foreign policy; the failure in February was clearly Roosevelt's, not Hay's.

For thirty years John Hay's heart had been barely adequate to sustain its physical responsibilities. For more than four years—since the illness in August and September, 1900—he suffered from an enlarged prostate gland—a disorder of old age for which in those days there was no trusted remedy. Physically, he was the victim of slow poison; and yet even his close associates in public life often seemed to feel that the Secretary was making too much of his ills. Spiritually, also, it was poison which destroyed him. The old emotional conflicts of a divided personality were tearing him apart. "Politics poisoned him," wrote Henry Adams to Mrs. Hay after his death.[1] "The Senate and the diplomats killed him. He would have had to resign at McKinley's death, if he were to save his own life." The diagnosis was doubtless true. John Hay always protested that he was not a "politician." On occasion he tried the art of gesturing first with the one hand and then with the other, even of doing what he knew to be wrong, but always at a tremendous emotional cost. Unhappiest of all was the fact that so often he lacked positive convictions as to what might be right and what might be wrong. Never, even to the end, was he able completely to unify his convictions and think his way through.

Mrs. Hay and Henry Adams watched his physical decline with apprehension. "Walking with Henry Adams the other day," Hay wrote to Sir George Otto Trevelyan, January 14, 1905, "I expressed my regret that by the time I got out of office I should have lost the faculty of enjoyment. As you know Adams, you can understand the dry malice with which he replied: 'Make your mind easy on that score, sonny; you've lost it now.' "

Hay was confined to his home in January, 1905, with a bronchial cold, from attacks of which he had suffered annually for many years. What little business he transacted was from his room. Absence from the Department did not induce the usual improvement. Then Mrs. Hay, with the help of Adams, took matters into her own hands and

---

[1] August 10, 1905.

engaged passage for Europe. Hay made a brave attempt in New York to mount the long flight of steps from the dock to the *Cretic*, March 18, but the effort was too much. Sinking on a bale of merchandise, he rested a few moments, and was carried on board in a wheel-chair.

On the ocean he revived and reached his destination at Bad Manheim easily. The rest and quiet gave nature its last opportunity to repair what the physicians had failed to understand. As he improved, all Europe wanted to see him. The man who forty-seven years before had returned to the banks of the Mississippi a not very promising youth, had become the statesman for whose favors monarchs were striving. King Leopold—"the old coot," Hay called him—wished to see the American Secretary of State. The Kaiser was even more insistent. In England a degree was waiting at Cambridge. Roosevelt in Washington became alarmed lest his Secretary in accepting one invitation and refusing another should provoke the wrath of nations. Through the Department he telegraphed, May 23:

"President asks me to say German Ambassador has called to say that the Emperor hopes to see you. President thinks if you see anyone at all arrangement should be made to see Emperor. In case you do not see him, President thinks it would be well not to see either French Minister for Foreign Affairs, or Sweden and Norway; [or] English Minister for Foreign Affairs."

Hay replied, May 24:

I at once wired you that I could not go to Berlin, but that I would obey your alternative wish: i.e. go through Paris and London without calling on Delcassé or Lansdowne. I stayed two weeks in Italy and did not go to Rome and they were perfectly reasonable about it. I explained the situation to Tower and I do not understand that Bulow or Richthofen took it amiss. Goluchowski was perfectly gentlemanly in the messages I exchanged with him. There is a difference in going several hundred miles out of the way to call on an Emperor, and crossing the street to say howdy to a gentleman in my own line of business. But if "meddlesome Willy" insists, we must humor him. The only way I can see to manage it is to be too ill in Paris and London to leave my hotel.

They have invited me to Cambridge to accept a Degree. But I shall be too ill for that also.

Even if I were well enough—which I am not—and it were convenient to go to Berlin I should not do it. The Emperor would begin at once on the reciprocity question. What could I say to him? I could not foul my own nest by telling the truth about the Senate. Our attitude is indefensible, and it is hard enough to have to stand the racket in Washington without going to Berlin, *sans y être obligé.*

Evidently the reciprocity treaty question weighed heaviest on Hay's mind. "Spencer Eddy came all the way from St. Petersburg," he reported to the President,[1] "to say how anxious the Russians were to make a Convention with us, ready to give us almost anything we want. I had to send them [him] away heart broken, with the reminder of the fact which they [he] had seemed to have forgotten, that we have a Senate; and that no reciprocity treaty can pass the Senate to which any constituent of any Senator can object. It is a sickening situation which nothing but the pinch of serious disaster can remedy. And when our hard times come, and we ask for reciprocity, we shall not be able to get the terms which everybody is now eager to offer us."

In spite of the President's warning Hay did see Delcassé in Paris on May 29. While in London on the way back he saw Lord Lansdowne, and, at the urgent invitation of King Edward, lunched at Buckingham Palace. It was his last fling, unless we count a letter written on shipboard, June 10.

The Senate had declined to pass a resolution permitting Hay to accept from the French Government the Grand Cross of the Legion of Honor. The distinction was offered as an acknowledgment of his services in behalf of world peace. One of Hay's last letters was to Senator Cullom asking that the resolution be withdrawn. He wrote: [2]

I rarely ask a favor personal to myself, but I shall be greatly obliged to you, if you will prevent any further consideration by the Senate of the Resolution you presented last winter permitting me to accept the distinction of Grand Cross of the Legion of Honor conferred upon me by the French Government.

Perhaps you will pardon me in a word of explanation. It has more than once occurred that I have been informed that such tokens of good will were contemplated by foreign governments. But I have always replied with grateful acknowledgments of the honor intended and a request that the offer should not officially be made. On this occasion, however, in view of the statement by the Government of the French Republic that the compliment was tendered in recognition of the work done by the American Government during the last seven years in the interest of the world's peace, it was felt by me and by those whom I consulted that it could not properly be declined; and that it was probable that no objection would be made in any quarter.

[1] Hay to Roosevelt, May 20, 1905.
[2] *Diary,* June 10, 1905.

In this I was mistaken. I was entirely unaware of the feeling existing towards me among some prominent members of my own party. But since it is evident that such a feeling exists, I beg that you will prevent the further consideration of your Resolution which failed of adoption last winter, as it would lead to a discussion which would be without advantage in any way, and would inevitably not be agreeable to the Government of a friendly Republic which was offering us a token of courtesy and good will.

As the *Baltic* came up the Narrows, June 15, Mrs. Hay was handed a letter from the President, assuring her that her husband must have a further respite. "I suppose nothing will keep John away from Washington," the President wrote,[1] "but he must not stay here more than forty-eight hours. Then he must rest for the summer. I shall handle the whole business of the State Department myself this summer, with Penfield as my assistant when Loomis is away."

Hay's sense of duty remained with him to the end. He not only went to Washington but stayed there ten days. The trip to Lake Sunapee was very like that of five years before when he had been forced to turn over the reins to Adee in the midst of the Boxer affair. The Secretary contracted another cold on the train and at Newbury the old symptoms reappeared. Temporary relief seemed to give encouragement, but in the early hours of July 1, his Pale Horse, which had so long waited at the door, bore him away.

John Hay had to die to prove that he was unwell.

On July 5 in Cleveland, in the presence of the President, the Cabinet, members of the Supreme Court, the Secretary of the Japanese Legation in Washington, and many old friends, as well as the members of his family, John Hay's worn-out body was laid at rest by the side of Del's with such pomp and circumstance as all his life he had sought to avoid.

"John was my Father's friend; I dearly loved him," the President had written to Mrs. Hay. "There is no one who with any of us can quite fill the place he held. He was not only my wise and patient adviser in affairs of state; he was the most devoted and at the same time the most charming of friends."

From Europe, where Henry Adams was travelling with the Lodges, came a deeper response: "As for me, it is time to bid good-bye. I am tired. My last hold on life is lost with him. . . . He and I began life together. We will stop together."

[1] Roosevelt to Mrs. Hay, June 12, 1905.

Since January 1, 1904, John Hay had kept a diary. After the funeral Mrs. Hay, still the heroine of this tale, added to the diary, in her own handwriting: "The funeral was arranged for today. The services were held at the Waite Memorial Chapel at Lake View Cemetery. President Roosevelt and all his cabinet but Mr. Taft who was on the way to the Philippines with the gentlemen who had been members of the Cabinet met at the Chamber of Commerce and, escorted by Troop A, went to the cemetery. The services were very simple—conducted by Dr. Haydn and Doctor Meldrum and the Chapel was full of friends. The floral tributes at the grave were very numerous & beautiful. The service there was all very simple and I could not realize that it was he who was being lowered from my sight. All signs of death were concealed and nothing to show that it was the end—was terrible. I cannot yet realize what has happened. I am paralyzed and numb. I suppose I will wake up some day and will know."

This has been the narrative of a man who would have preferred, to use his own words, "to lie in the orchard and eat the sunny side of peaches," but who at last found himself. The discovery came late. Gifted, or shall we say burdened, with an aptitude for many vocations, able easily to adapt himself to changing situations and tasks, bored by routine, and never quite sure what he wanted to do or be, he almost frittered away his life, doing many things well but nothing as well as he might have done it, until suddenly, at the age of sixty, he was lifted up and set down, though unwillingly, in the right place. There he gathered up all his fragments of experience from a varied and wavering life and brought them into play to high purpose and with such notable success that his name will be long remembered far beyond the boundaries of his own country. He was never a representative American for too few of his countrymen were like him. For similar reasons it cannot be claimed that Franklin or Jefferson was a representative American.

The age was many-sided, productive along so many lines that the net accomplishment was considerable. There was no outstanding characteristic. Patriotic orators liked to dwell upon its progressive character—an age of progress. There was some progress, but the orators usually confused it with expansion. It was an expansive age, a road-making, bridge-building, sod-breaking age. With the expansion came diversification, and some anarchy. Who will say that it was more characteristic of the time that it had vigilance committees, or that they were needed? Law, moral as well as legal, lagged behind the outburst of human activity. The nation gave freedom to the slaves, and then itself became the too willing slave to greed. It was an age of organizing, where men were always attempting to sort out, classify, pull together, and unify conflicting forces, and never quite succeeding. Domestic virtues flourished in an era of political corruption. Vulgarity and good taste fought an inconclusive battle; feelings and reason could find no common ground beneath them. It was an age of sentimentality, of piracy, of philanthropy, of freedom, and of conventionality. Critics alleged to have discovered a dead level of mediocrity. They were obviously wrong, for such a generalization left out of account too many magnificent individuals whose virtues, or whose vices, were far from mediocre. The last half of the last century in the United States was lived, not on the plain, but in the foot-hills, where there were many peaks high enough to cast long shadows.

John Hay accepted the age as he found it and showed forth its character. His enthusiasm for democracy fought with his love of birth and breeding; he was a non-conformist who conformed; he might have been a poet if he had been less a man of affairs. He studied respectability, yet he was more heretic than orthodox. He was both indolent and industrious; thrifty and extravagant; an esthete but not an idealist; an artist, veined with sentiments of a small-town Presbyterian. He could keep a cool head in a crisis, as during the siege of Peking, and yet he could express many intemperate judgments of both men and affairs. He was often called a snob, but he could catch the character of Jim Bludso and he could express the homely philosophy of the common, unthinking man. Few personalities are so simple that traits contrary to one another never appear, but surely few men had wrapped up in themselves so many and so great contradictions.

Hay's versatility matched the expansiveness of the period. The age of specialization had not come; men were jacks-of-all-trades, and proud of it. It was the badge of the resourcefulness by which they conquered a continent. Hay was one of those men who could have made at least a moderate success of almost anything. More imitative than inventive, he did, in fact, achieve creditably in at least half a dozen widely variant careers. At the age of twenty-six he was already a secretary to a President of the United States, and on the threshold of a political career in which his association with the great Lincoln might have carried him far in Illinois politics. At thirty-one he was a successful diplomat. Three years later he was the talk of the literary world, his poems all but hawked about the streets, and his Spanish essays running in the *Atlantic*. It seemed as though he might be about to step into the place of Irving, or Holmes, or Lowell. At the age of thirty-seven he had retired from the staff of the New York *Daily Tribune*, an accomplished editorial writer. Next he became a business man. His previous successes had been of such a character as to make both his friends and the public unwilling to believe that John Hay could be a successful man of affairs, and yet such he became. Bred in a home of respectable poverty, where thrift and judgment of things economic were enforced by the necessities of the case, he learned from his father-in-law how to be a good investor, and the fortune entrusted to his care, prospered under his attentions. John Hay had a good business sense.

Few can match such versatility as this, but Hay went far beyond it. He was the most successful novelist of the season, 1883–84. Three years later there began the serial publication of *Abraham Lincoln: A History*," published in 1890 in ten volumes. He had turned from business, from novel-writing, from poetry, from politics, to make a creditable success as biographer and historian. Collaborating with Nicolay, he had fixed the Lincoln tradition in the world. During this period he had been for seventeen months Assistant Secretary of State under Evarts, and he finished his career, at the age of sixty-six, the most popular Secretary of State since the Civil War, and, by popular vote, one of the greatest statesmen of the western world and of the modern age.

Such was the dazzling career of this many-sided American of the Gilded Age. The facets of John Hay's personality caught and threw back most of the qualities which gave character to the period and made in modern history a figure which might have been impossible in any other time and place. To explain him one would have to explain the age, and the latter was too complex and manifold for formulas, or simple statements.

The clue to John Hay's character seems to be its sensitiveness to impressions. He was quick to appropriate his environment. He could dispense with some of the processes of thought which most mortals require and "sense a situation." Here lay both strength and weakness.

His ability to receive impressions exceeded his capacity to unify them. He lived through almost every kind of life that an illogical, antithetical age afforded. Perhaps as a direct result of this, his life lacked unity. His philosophy, if, indeed, it can be claimed that he had any, was wholly pragmatic, and grew more out of feelings than out of convictions. He was a patchwork of his ancestry, and a part of all that he had met.

Of John Hay's works one may write with moderation and yet with some assurance. "Jim Bludso" lives in pristine vigor. The "Open Door" is still a phrase to conjure with. But Hay had more than the gifts of rhymster and phrasemaker. If the Anglo-American entente ever does disappear we may earnestly hope that it will do so only to be replaced by that larger understanding which was the objective of "McKinleyism."

Of Hay himself one may write with more assurance. This has been no hero tale and yet there has appeared a vein of heroism as convincing as it was unostentatious. Indolent by nature, John Hay worked hard, and long after he had a valid reason to quit. An individualist, a better man than his party, he chose to cling to the latter, at the cost of such discomfort as only sensitive souls can appraise. A vagrant in life, he bowed before a sense of duty and yielded to its discipline. Evading most of the rough spots, nevertheless he fell into some—and marched through like a man. In a rather brutal, masterful age, he achieved a better part: he overcame himself.

The End

Bibliography of References

Sources which, in the foregoing pages, have been cited by abbreviated titles.

MANUSCRIPT COLLECTIONS

Clippings on John Hay. N. Y. Public Library, Rare Book Room.
James A. Garfield Papers. Library of Congress.
Benjamin Harrison Papers. Library of Congress.
John Hay Papers.
Louttit Collection on John Hay. Privately owned by William Easton Louttit, Jr. of Providence, R. I.
Richard Olney Papers. Library of Congress.
Theodore Roosevelt Papers. Library of Congress.
Carl Schurz Papers. Library of Congress.
John Sherman Papers. Library of Congress.
Charles Sumner Papers. Widener Library, Harvard University.
U. S. Department of State Archives.
John Russell Young Papers. Library of Congress.

OFFICIAL PUBLICATIONS

Diplomatic History of the Panama Canal, Senate Document 474, 63rd Cong., 2nd Session.
Foreign Relations of the United States, 1895–1905; 1917.
House Doc. 611, 57th Cong., 1st Session.
House Report 2749, 57th Cong., 1st Session.
Reciprocity and Commercial Treaties. G.P.O., 1919.
Senate Document 268, 56th Cong., 1st Session, March 9, 1900.
Senate Report, Ex. M., 57th Cong., 1st Session.
Senate Ex. Document E, 57th Cong., 2nd Session.
Senate Documents 50, 65, 78, 87, 94, 57th Cong., 2nd Session.
Senate Document 143, 58th Cong., 2nd Session.
Senate Document 10, 58th Cong., Special Session.
Subject Index of the Treaty Series and the Executive Agreement Series. G.P.O., July 1, 1931.
The Story of Panama—Hearings on the Rainey Resolution before the Committee on Foreign Affairs of the House of Representatives. G.P.O., 1913.
List of Treaties Submitted to the Senate, 1789–1931, Which Have Not Gone Into Force. G.P.O., October 1, 1932.
Die Grosse Politik der Europäischen Kabinette, 1871–1914. Edited by Johannes Lepsius, Albrecht M. Bartholdy, and Fredrich Thimme.

British Documents on the Origins of the World War. Ed. by G. P. Gooch and Harold Temperley.

BOOKS AND PERIODICALS

Abbott, Lyman. Reminiscences. Boston and N. Y., 1915.

Adams, Charles Francis. An autobiography. Boston and N. Y., 1916.

Adams, Henry. Democracy. N. Y., 1880.

Adams, Henry. Education of Henry Adams. Boston and N. Y., 1918.

[Adams, Henry.] "United States exploration of the fortieth parallel by Clarence King." *North American Review*, July, 1871.

Adams, James Truslow. The Adams family. Boston, 1930.

Angell, James B. Address at the Dedication of the John Hay Library, Providence, 1911.

Bassett, John S. "Later historians." Cambridge History of American Literature, Vol. III. N. Y.

Beard, Charles A. and Mary R. The rise of American civilization. 2 vols., N. Y., 1927.

Benét, William Rose. Poems of youth, an American anthology. N. Y., 1925.

Bigelow, John. Retrospections of an active life. 5 vols., N. Y., 1909–13.

Bishop, Joseph Bucklin. Notes and anecdotes of many years. N. Y., 1925.

Bishop, Joseph Bucklin. Theodore Roosevelt and his time. 2 vols. N. Y., 1920.

Brandenburg, Erich. From Bismarck to the world war. London, 1927.

Bronson, Walter C. The history of Brown University, 1764–1914. Providence, 1914.

Bryce, James. The American commonwealth. 2 vols., London and N. Y., 1913.

Bunau-Varilla, Philippe. Panama. N. Y., 1913.

Carr, Clark E. The Illini, a story of the prairie. Chicago, 1904.

Chapman, A. S. The boyhood of John Hay. *Century*, July, 1909.

Clemens, Samuel L. John Hay and the ballads. *Harper's Weekly*, Oct. 21, 1905.

Cortissoz, Royal. The life of Whitelaw Reid. 2 vols., N. Y., 1921.

Croly, Herbert. Marcus Alonzo Hanna. N. Y., 1923.

Cullom, Shelby M. Fifty years of public service. Chicago, 1911.

Dennett, Tyler. Americans in eastern Asia. N. Y., 1922.

Dennett, Tyler. Roosevelt and the Russo-Japanese War. Garden City, 1925.

Dennis, Alfred L. P. Adventures in American diplomacy, 1896–1906. N. Y., 1928.

Eckardstein, Baron von. Ten Years at the court of St. James's, 1895–1906. London, 1921.

Eckenrode, H. J. Rutherford B. Hayes, statesman of reunion. N. Y., 1930.

Foraker, Joseph B. Notes of a busy life. 2 vols., Cincinnati, 1916.

Ford, Worthington Chauncey [Ed.]. Letters of Henry Adams, 1858–1891. Boston and N. Y., 1930.

Foster, J. W. Diplomatic memoirs. 2 vols., Boston and N. Y., 1909.

Gilder, J. L. & J. B. [Eds.]. Authors at home. N. Y., 1905.

Gouverneur, Marian. As I remember. N. Y., 1911.

Gurowski, Adam. Diary 1863–'64–'65. 3 vols., Washington, 1866.

Gwynn, Stephen [Ed.]. The letters and friendships of Sir Cecil Spring-Rice. 2 vols., London, 1929.

Haley, William D. [Ed.]. Phillip's Washington described. N. Y., 1861.

Hamilton, Gail [Mary Abigail Dodge]. James G. Blaine. Norwich, 1895.

Hay, Clarence L. [Ed.]. The complete poetical works of John Hay, with an introduction by Clarence L. Hay. Boston and N. Y., 1916.

Hay, John. Personal reminiscences of Colonel E. E. Ellsworth. *Atlantic*, July, 1861.

Hay, John. Castilian Days. Boston, 1871.

Hay, John. See also Nicolay.

Hay, John. "Open letters: the Bread-winners." *Century*, November, 1883, and March, 1884.

Hay, John. The Bread-winners. N. Y., 1884.

[Hay, John]. Amasa Stone. Born April 27, 1818. Died May 11, 1883. Privately printed at the DeVinne Press.

[Hay, John]. Dr. Charles Hay. N. Y., 1885. Privately printed at the De-Vinne Press.

Hay, John. "Life in the White House in the time of Lincoln." *Century*, November, 1890.

Hay, John. "A young hero." *McClure's*, March, 1896.

Hay, John. "The pioneers of Ohio." *Magazine of Western History*. Extra Nos. 101–108, Cleveland.

Hay, John. Letters of, and Extracts from Diary. Printed but not published. 3 vols., Washington, 1908.

Hicks, Granville. "The conversion of John Hay." *New Republic*, June 10, 1931.

Hill, David Jayne. The problem of a world court. N. Y., 1927.

Hill, Howard Copeland. Roosevelt and the Caribbean. Chicago, 1927.

Holt, Henry. Garrulities of an octogenarian editor. Boston and N. Y., 1924.

Howe, M. A. DeWolfe. James Ford Rhodes, American historian. N. Y., 1929.

Howells, William Dean. "John Hay in literature." *North American Review*, September, 1905.

Illinois. Biographical Review of Hancock County. Chicago, 1907.

Illinois. Historical Encyclopedia of Illinois and History of Sangamon County. Chicago, 1912.

Johnson, Robert Underwood. Remembered yesterdays. Boston, 1923.

Keenan, Henry F. The money makers, a social parable. N. Y., 1885.

King, Clarence. Mountaineering in the Sierra Nevada. Boston, 1870.

[King, Clarence?]. John Hay. *Scribner's*, April, 1874.

King, Clarence. The Biographers of Lincoln. *Century*, Oct., 1886.

King Memorial Association. Clarence King memoirs. N. Y., 1904.

Latané, John H. A history of American foreign policy. N. Y., 1927.

Leary, John J. Talks with T. R. from the diaries of John J. Leary. Boston and N. Y., 1920.

Leonard, Manning. Memorial: genealogical, historical, and biographical of Solomon Leonard, 1637, of Duxbury and Bridgewater, Massachusetts, and some of his descendants. Southbridge, Mass., 1896.

Lodge, Henry Cabot. Selections from the correspondence of Theodore Roosevelt and Henry Cabot Lodge, 1884–1918. 2 vols., N. Y., 1925.

Lubbock, Percy [Ed.]. The letters of Henry James. 2 vols., N. Y., 1920.

MacNair, Harley F. Modern Chinese history readings. Shanghai, 1927.

McCaleb, Walter F. Theodore Roosevelt. N. Y., 1931.

McGrath, P. T. The Atlantic fisheries question. *Atlantic Monthly,* December, 1902.

Mitchell, Edward P. Memoirs of an editor. N. Y., 1924.

Moore, John Bassett. Digest of international law. 7 vols., Washington, 1906.

Mowat, R. B. The life of Lord Pauncefote, first ambassador to the United States. London, 1929.

Nevins, Allan. Henry White: thirty years of American diplomacy. N. Y., 1930.

Nicolay, Helen. Our capital on the Potomac. N. Y. and London, 1924.

Nicolay, John G. The outbreak of rebellion. N. Y., 1881.

Nicolay, John G., and Hay, John. Abraham Lincoln: a history. 10 vols., N. Y., 1890.

Nicolay, John G., and Hay, John. Abraham Lincoln: complete works. 2 vols., N. Y., 1894.

Ohio Bureau of Labor Statistics, Annual Report. 1879.
     "   "   "   "   "   "   1884.

Olcott, Charles Summers. The life of William McKinley. 2 vols., Boston and N. Y., 1916.

Parrington, Vernon Louis. The beginnings of critical realism in America, 1860–1920. N. Y., 1927.

Peet, Rev. Stephen D. The Ashtabula disaster. Chicago, 1877.

Pringle, Henry F. Theodore Roosevelt. N. Y., 1931.

Rhodes, James Ford. Historical essays. N. Y., 1909.

Rhodes, James Ford. The McKinley and Roosevelt administrations, 1897–1909. N. Y., 1927.

Ridgely, Anna. A girl in the sixties. Excerpts from the journal of Anna Ridgely. Journal of Illinois State Historical Society. October, 1929.

Rippy, J. Fred. Latin America in world politics. N. Y., 1928.

Roosevelt, Theodore. Autobiography. N. Y., 1926.

Sears, Lorenzo. John Hay, author and statesman. N. Y., 1914.

Seitz, Don C. Horace Greeley. Indianapolis, 1926.

Seward, Frederick W. Seward in Washington as Senator and Secretary of State. N. Y., 1891.

Sherman, John. Recollections of forty years in the House, Senate and Cabinet. Chicago, 1895.

Shippee, L. B. Germany and the Spanish-American War. *American Historical Review,* July, 1925.

Smith, H. Augustine [Ed.]. Hymns for the living age. N. Y., 1929.

Smith, Theodore Clarke. The life and letters of James Abram Garfield. 2 vols., New Haven, 1925.

Stanton, Theodore. "John Hay and the Bread-winners." *Nation,* August 10, 1916.

Stanwood, Edward. History of the presidency. 2 vols., Boston and N. Y., 1916.

Stephenson, Nathaniel Wright. Nelson W. Aldrich. N. Y., 1930.

Tansill, Charles Callan. Purchase of the Danish West Indies. Baltimore, 1932.

Tarbell, Ida M. The history of the Standard Oil Company. 2 vols., N. Y., 1904.

Thayer, William Roscoe. The life and letters of John Hay. 2 vols., Boston and N. Y., 1915.

Ticknor, Caroline [Ed.]. A poet in exile; early letters of John Hay. Boston and N. Y., 1910.

Ticknor, Caroline. Poe's Helen. N. Y., 1916.

Twain, Mark. See Clemens.

Ward, Sister Saint Ignatius. The poetry of John Hay. Washington, 1930.

Watterson, Henry. Marse Henry. 2 vols., N. Y., 1919.

Webb, Alexander S. The Peninsula: McClellan's campaign of 1862. N. Y., 1881.

Williams, Talcott. John Hay. *Book News,* Aug., 1905.

By William Easton Louttit, Jr.

PERIODICAL PUBLICATIONS

Sa! Sa! Verse. The Brown Paper. Providence, R. I., Nov., 1857.
Personal reminiscences of Colonel E. E. Ellsworth. Atlantic. July, 1861.
Between spring and summer. Verse. Atlantic. July, 1861.
Colonel Baker. Harper's. Dec., 1861.
Northward. Verse. Harper's. June, 1864.
When the boys come home. Verse. Harper's Weekly. June 18, 1864.
The monks of Basle. Verse. Harper's. Nov., 1865.
Shelby Cabell. Harper's. Oct., 1866.
The foster-brothers. Harper's. Sept., 1869.
The Mormon prophet's tragedy. Atlantic. Dec., 1869.
Down the Danube. Putnam's. June, 1870.
Castilian days, I–V. Atlantic. Jan.–Feb., April–May, July, 1871.
The prayer of the Romans. Verse. Harper's Weekly. Feb. 4, 1871.
The blood seedling. Lippincott's. Mar., 1871. Reprinted, Oct., 1905.
Banty Tim. Verse. Harper's Weekly. April 15, 1871.
On the bluff. Verse. Every Saturday. April 22, 1871.
Jim Bludso, of the Prairie Belle; Little Breeches. Verse. Every Saturday.
    May 13, 1871.
Little Breeches. Verse. Harper's Weekly. May 20, 1871.
A woman's love. Verse. Harper's Weekly. May 20, 1871.
The mystery of Gilgal. Verse. Harper's Weekly. May 20, 1871.
The advance-guard. Verse. Harper's Weekly. July 29, 1871.
My castle in Spain. Verse. Harper's. Aug., 1871.
Christine. Verse. Similibus (published by the managers of the Fair for . . .
    the Homeopathic Surgical Hospital). N. Y., April 17, 1872.
A triumph of order. Verse. Atlantic. Aug., 1872.
No playing tricks with love. Verse. Galaxy. Sept., 1872.
Ernst of Edelsheim. Verse. Scribner's. Oct., 1872.
Ye gambolier. Verse. Nast's Illustrated Almanac. N. Y., 1872.
The law of death. Verse. Scribner's. Aug., 1873.
Boudoir prophecies. Verse. Scribner's. Jan., 1874.
The pledge at Spunky Point. Verse. Harper's Weekly (Supplement). March 7,
    1874.
Look ahead. Verse. St. Nicholas. June, 1874.

Mount Tabor. Verse. Scribner's. Jan., 1875.

Religion and doctrine. Verse. Harper's. May, 1875.

The fortunes of the Bonapartes. Harper's. Dec., 1879.

The stirrup-cup. Verse. Scribner's. May, 1881.

The bread-winners. Century. Aug., 1883–Jan., 1884.

Reply to comment on "The bread-winners." Century. Nov., 1883.

Letter from the author of "The bread-winners." Century. March, 1884.

Amasa Stone. Magazine of Western History. Cleveland, Dec., 1885.

Abraham Lincoln: a history. By Nicolay and Hay. Century. Nov., 1886–
    Feb., 1890.

Israel. Verse. Century. May, 1887.

A haunted room. Verse. Scribner's. Feb., 1890.

Distichs. Verse. Scribner's. May, 1890.

Love's dawn. Verse. Century. Sept., 1890.

Life in the White House in the time of Lincoln. Century. Nov., 1890.

Two on the terrace. Verse. Scribner's. July, 1891.

Thy will be done. Verse. Harper's. Oct., 1891.

Night in Venice. Verse. Harper's. Feb., 1892.

Compensation. Verse. Century. Dec., 1892.

My dream. Verse. Shield (published by Theta Delta Chi). Elmira, N. Y.,
    June, 1893.

When Phyllis laughs. Verse. Harper's. Sept., 1893.

A prayer in Thessaly. Verse. Century. Nov., 1893.

Love and music. Verse. Harper's. Nov., 1893.

Accidents. Verse. Century. Feb., 1895.

Sorrento. Verse. Scribner's. June, 1895.

Paestum. Verse. Harper's. Feb., 1896.

A young hero. McClure's. March, 1896.

Twilight on Sandusky marsh. Verse. Harper's. Aug., 1896.

Sir Walter Scott in Westminster. Critic. May 29, 1897.

Ambassador Hay's Easter speech. Critic. May 28, 1898.

The Hon. John Hay on Omar Khayýam. Critic. Dec., 1898.

Speech at the 52d annual convention of Theta Delta Chi. Shield. Ithaca,
    N. Y., March, 1900.

Extract from "Erato." Verse. Brown Alumni Monthly. Providence, R. I.,
    March, 1901.

Speech at a dinner . . . of the Ohio Society of New York. Ohio Society of
    New York, Annual publications. N. Y., 1902–1903.

The sewers of Paris and their origin. The Hesperian Tree: An annual of the
    Ohio Valley. Columbus, Ohio, 1903.

Thanatos athanatos. Verse. Century. June, 1904.

Tom Taggart of Pike county.[1] Verse. Harper's Weekly. N. Y., Sept., 24, 1904.

----

[1] This poem is "The Mystery of Gilgal" (Harper's Weekly, May 20, 1871) with a
new title.

John Hay speaks for the nation: Two addresses. National Magazine. Boston, Nov., 1904.

Extract from "Erato." [1] Verse. Brown Alumni Monthly. Providence, R. I., July, 1905.

Liberty; The stirrup cup; Selections from "Distichs." Verse. Current Literature. Aug., 1905.

Franklin in France. Century. Jan., 1906.

[Centennial ode:] A hundred times the bells of Brown. (In: Celebration of the 100th anniversary of the founding of Brown University. Rider, Providence, R. I., 1865.)

Chicago; New Orleans; Edmund Clarence Stedman. Putnam's. Oct., 1906.

Lincoln at the helm. Century. Feb., 1909.

David Augustus Leonard . . . by his grandson. Brown Alumni Monthly. Providence, R. I., Feb., 1910.

To Theodore Roosevelt. Verse. Atlantic. June, 1916.

Dying young; Thanatos athanatos. Verse. Outlook. Sept. 18, 1918.

The pioneers of Ohio. (Reprint.) Magazine of history with notes and queries. Extra number, 103. Tarrytown-on-Hudson, N. Y., 1924.

TRANSLATIONS

The Republican movement in Europe. By Emilio Castelar. [Translated by John Hay.] Harper's. June, 1872–Oct., 1875.

BOOKS

Castilian days. Osgood, Boston, 1871. Houghton, Boston, 1882.
  Same. Houghton, Boston, 1890, 1899. Rev. ed.
  Same. Lane, London, 1897.
  Same. Houghton, Boston, 1903, 1907. Ill. by Joseph Pennell.
  Same. Heinemann, London, 1903. Ill. by Joseph Pennell.
Pike county ballads and other pieces. Osgood, Boston, 1871, 1873, 1876. Hotten, London, 1871 (under title: Little Breeches, and other pièces humourous, descriptive and pathetic.) Houghton, Boston, 1880, 1882.
  Same. Routledge, London, 1891, 1897. (Contains also six poems by Sir Walter Scott.)
Amasa Stone. [DeVinne, N. Y., 1883.]
The bread-winners. Warne, London, 1883. Harper, N. Y., [c1883,] 1884, 1893, 1905, [1916 (c1911)]. Tauchnitz, Leipzig, 1884.
  Same. Harper, N. Y., 1899. Biographical edition.
Bien (le) d'autrui, étude de moeurs américaines. Roman traduit de l'anglais par Hephell. Paris, Hachette, 1886.

---

[1] "Erato" was Hay's class poem. Pamphlet publication, Providence, 1858.

454 JOHN HAY

Doctor Charles Hay. Priv. print., N. Y., [1884.]

[Articles on] Abraham Lincoln, Whitelaw Reid, and Amasa Stone. (In: Wilson, James G., and Fiske, John, eds. Appleton's Cyclopedia of American biography. Appleton, N. Y., 1887, 1888, vols. 3 and 5.)

Abraham Lincoln: A history. By John G. Nicolay and John Hay. 10 vols. Century, N. Y., 1890.

Poems. Houghton, Boston, 1890, 1892, 1897, [c1899,] 1899, [c1913.]

Euthanasia. (In: Liber scriptorum. Authors club, N. Y., 1893).

Abraham Lincoln, complete works. Edited by John G. Nicolay and John Hay. 2 vols. Century, N. Y., 1894, 1902, 1920.

 Same. 12 vols. Lamb, N. Y., [c1905.] Tandy, N. Y., [c1905.]

Abraham Lincoln. (In: Wilson, James G., ed. Presidents of the United States. Appleton, N. Y., 1894. This is a reprint of the article on Lincoln in Appleton's Cyclopedia as noted above.)

David Augustus Leonard. (In: Leonard, Manning. Memorial . . . of Solomon Leonard 1637. [Knapp, Peck and Thompson press, Auburn, N. Y., 1896.])

In praise of Omar. Mosher, Portland, Me., 1898, 1899, 1905, 1913, 1920.

 Same. (In: Rubaiyat, FitzGerald, priv. print. for Col. Fane Sewell for presentation only.)

 Same. Rosemary press, Needham, Mass., 1914.

 (*Note:* This address has also been reprinted many times in various editions of the FitzGerald translation of the Rubaiyat of Omar Khayyám, and in the Book of the Omar Khayyam club, 1910.)

Opening of the door. (In: Boyd, James P., ed. Men and issues of 1900. n. p., [c1900.])

Clarence King. (In: Clarence King memoirs. Putnam, N. Y., 1904.)

The Pike County ballads. Houghton, Boston, [1912.]

America's love of peace. (In: Bowman, J. C., et al., eds. Essays for college English. 2d series. Heath, Boston, [1918.])

PAMPHLETS

Erato (In: Oration and poem delivered in the chapel of Brown University in 1858.)

Little Breeches: A Pike county view of special providence. Redfield, N. Y., 1871. 4p.

Jim Bludso of the Prairie Belle, and Little Breeches. Verse. Osgood, Boston, 1871.

The pioneers of Ohio. An address. Leader print. co., Cleveland, O., 1879. 20p.

The balance sheet of the two parties. A speech. Leader print. co., Cleveland, O., 1880. 38p.

Robert Burns. [Basel, 1888.] 33p.

The enchanted shirt. Revell, N. Y., 1889. 16p.

The platform of anarchy. An address. [Cleveland, 1896.] 27p.

Speech . . . at the unveiling of the bust of Sir Walter Scott. Harper, N. Y., [1897.] 12p.

Same. Lane, London, 1897. 14p.

Remarks . . . at a dinner of the N. Y. chamber of commerce. [N. Y., 1901.] 11p.

Speech . . . at a dinner . . . Board of directors of the Pan-American exposition to the National editorial association, Buffalo, June 13, 1901. Washington, 1901. 4p.

William McKinley; memorial address. Crowell, N. Y. [c1902.]

Memorial address on the life and character of William McKinley. Transylvania Press. [Lexington, Ky., 1902.] 20p.

Same. Govt. print. off., Washington, 1903. 70p.

Remarks . . . 36th national encampment, G. A. R. White Lot, Washington, 1902. 4p.

Address . . . at the opening of the press parliament of the world at St. Louis on May 19, 1904. 13p.

Fifty years of the Republican party. An address delivered at Jackson, Mich., July 6, 1904. 29p.

Thirteenth international peace congress. An address. [Oct. 3, 1904.] 12p.

Speech . . . delivered at Carnegie hall, N. Y. [Oct. 26, 1904.] 19p.

Banty Tim. Boston, [Robinson press,] n.d. 4p.

Extracts from Hay. n.p., n.d. (15 copies printed. Listed in American Book Prices Current, v. 25, p. 370. 1919.)

LYRICS AND HYMNS

Fill up your blushing goblets. (In: Theta Delta Chi fraternity. Songs of the Theta Delta Chi. Welch, Bigelow, Cambridge, 1869.)

Zeta shouts her chorus. (In: Songs of the Theta Delta Chi.)

On the bluff. Music by J. R. Thomas. Pond, N. Y., 1874, [c1902.]

Student's song: Love and song and wine. Music by Edward B. Birge. (In: Barbour, John B., et al., eds. Songs of Brown University. Silver Burdette, Boston, 1891. New edition published by Brown University, 1921.)

Invocation hymn: Lord, from far-severed climes we come. Written for the fifteenth international Christian Endeavor convention, 1896. Tune, Federal Street.

Through the long days. Music by Francis Korbay. Pond, N. Y., n.d.

Same. Music by Arthur Foote. Schmidt, Boston. [c1898.]

Defend us, O Lord. Music by John W. Metcalf. Schmidt, Boston, [c1906.]

I sent my love two roses. Music by H. F. Simson, Boosey, N. Y., [c1907.]

Expectation. Music by Alexander Russell. John Church, Cincinnati, [c1911.]

When the boys come home. Music by Oley Speaks. Schirmer, N. Y., [c1917.]

Same. Music by W. T. Porter. Willis, Cincinnati, [c1918.]

Thy will be done. (In: Smith, H. Augustine, ed. Hymns for the living age. New York, 1929.)

COLLECTED WORKS

Addresses. Century, N. Y., 1906.
　　Same. Century, N. Y., 1907.
Letters . . . and extracts from diary. 3 vols. Printed but not published, Washington, 1908. (Approx. 200 copies.)
A poet in exile: early letters. Ed. by Caroline Ticknor. Houghton, Boston, 1910.
The complete poetical works. Houghton, Boston, 1916, 1917.

Lord Lansdowne pressed me very strongly the other day to give Sir Wilfrid Laurier and Lord Minto, who are now here for the Coronation, an opportunity to talk over with me the Alaska Boundary Question. I expressed some reluctance and told him that the time was not very opportune for taking up such a question now while an important election was approaching which would probably involve much more pressing and important questions. I thought everything relating to the question was quiet and would probably remain so, but he insisted and said that Sir Wilfrid and Lord M. represented that in case of the discovery of gold in the disputed territory, there was serious danger of a conflict at any time, which might lead to serious consequences. I told him that I could not judge whether a talk such as he proposed would be of any use, unless I knew before hand what their present views were as I had heard hardly anything of the matter since my long note to Lord Salisbury of Jany 22nd, 1900, which had never been answered. Well, he said, the views which the Canadians wished to press were well set forth in the memorandum which Lord Pauncefote sent to you in February last. As I had not heard of this before, he very kindly offered to send me a copy. A few days afterwards, on June 23d, he sent me a print of Lord Pauncefote's paper, and of the Draft Arbitration Treaty proposed by you in May, 1901, and which Lord Pauncefote's paper discusses as "communicated to him unofficially in May last." On reading these papers it naturally occurred to me that you might not wish to follow the matter up at present at all, or might prefer to take it up yourself with Lord Pauncefote's successor.

I accordingly sent you on the 29th a cypher cable of which the translation is, "Confidential. Lord Lansdowne urges me to have interview with Lord Minto and Sir Wilfrid Laurier on Alaska Boundary matter before they return to Canada shortly. He has furnished me a print of Lord Pauncefote's memorandum of last February upon your previous draft convention. They wish especially to explain urgency of situation as requiring early action or at least provisional agreement along entire boundary line to prevent possible conflicts."

On the 1st of July I received from Dr. Hill doubtless in your absence, the following reply in cypher. "Confidential. The President directs me to say to have interview with Lord Minto and Sir Wilfrid but thinks the Canadian claim has not a leg to stand on and that compromise is impossible."

I was at the same time endeavoring to get an interview with Sir Wilfrid about the murderer Rice about whose case you had asked me to consult with him, but some days elapsed before he was able to see me, because of his various pressing engagements. We met however on Wednesday and had a long talk. I

of course took my tone from the President's latest instruction, and insisted
substantially as I had in my unanswered letter to Lord Salisbury that there
really was no question, that neither the Canadian Government nor the Imperial Government had raised any until the instructions to the British Commissioners in 1898, that complete acquiescence in the Russian and American
claim had been shown by both—that the discussions which culminated in the
Treaty of 1825 showed that the imperative insistence of Russia was to keep
the British back at least ten marine leagues from tidewater, and that the
British after trying their best to overcome this barrier and get to the coast,
finally yielded the point and signed the Treaty as it was, and the maps made
then and ever since showed exactly what the Treaty meant and what all
parties knew it meant, etc., etc. You can well imagine his positions denying
everything, asserting that it was clear from the language of the Treaty of
1825 that it was a compromise Treaty splitting the difference between the
rival contentions of Russia and Great Britain, that the maps amounted to
nothing—that it was impossible for surveyors to take up the Treaty and, without further instructions, draw a boundary line. He relied to some extent on
the positions taken by Lord Pauncefote in his memorandum, and insisted from
first to last our Government's position that there was no claim, and nothing
to arbitrate, of course, made any settlement of the question impossible, and
was very unfortunate. I reminded him that the mere fact of your Draft Treaty
of May, 1901, tendered to Lord Pauncefote showed an actual desire for a settlement of the matter. He said that your draft started with the idea that the
line must be drawn on our theory. But I called his attention to the alternative,
viz., "If not, how should said line of demarcation be traced to conform to the
conditions of said treaty?"

The conversation thus far was rather a rehash of old contentions. But he
did confidentially yield on one or two points which are worth noting. In speaking of your proposed court of six he renewed Lord Pauncefote's objections to
it as preventing probably a conclusive determination, but he gave me to understand, strictly confidentially, that if the question to be arbitrated could be
satisfactorily arranged he would not be disposed to hold out against your way
of constituting the court, that it was so important to get the matter settled
that, other things being satisfactory, they would not stand out on that. Another
point was that they could agree to an arbitration which should provide that
if the Court found Skagway & Dyea to be in British territory, they should
remain American—they didn't want them. They are American towns, full of
American people, and would be troublesome to govern—and the arbitration
might give in that case any kind of compensation.

In the course of the conversation I had urged that the mere making of an
unfounded claim, and insisting upon it, could not justly be made the basis of
a demand for an arbitration, and had supposed the case of their claiming Buffalo or a strip of land on the East side of the Niagara River after 120 years of
acquiescence in a settled boundary, but he thought that was not a parallel
case, that he honestly believed they had a just claim, that if the case was as

clear as we believed it was, the arbitrators would so decide and thus settle the matter and they would submit with a good face.

He constantly pressed the necessity of some arrangement and the danger of hostilities among a rough population of miners of various nationalities in the not improbable case of a discovery of gold in the disputed territory. I probed him as closely as I could on this, with the result that he admitted everything was fortunately quiet up to date, and I reminded him of what Lord Salisbury once said to me, when we were discussing a provisional boundary some years ago about this time of year, that, "Winter, our mutual friend, will soon set in in those regions, and relieve us of the question for the time being."

After a very long and friendly conversation he left me saying that he was very disappointed, that he should try again, but he was not at all hopeful.

Last night at the Indian Reception I saw him again and he again renewed the conversation saying that he had thought a great deal about our talk of Wednesday, and was exceedingly disappointed. I told him that he had let drop one or two points confidentially that were new, and which, if he would let me transmit them in the same way to you, might, on receipt of your reply (for he expects to be here a month) be the basis for further talk between us, referring to the constitution of the court of six judges, and their no longer wanting Skagway or Dyea. I said, "You did not exactly say so the other day, but reading between the lines, I understood you to mean that you would not in the impossible event of a decision in your favor claim, or insist upon any port at all but would be content with *pecuniary* damages." He said, "Yes, that is what I mean, or any kind of compensation." He again reiterated that our position that their claim was without foundation made it impossible to settle at all, and left a dangerous question open, but I reminded him of our repeated efforts to come to an agreement and how near we came to it when Lord Pauncefote was here two years ago, but the plan proved futile.

He constantly recognized the difficulty of the President satisfying either Senate or people, if he gave up anything which was clearly American territory, but he insisted that he too had constituents who would endanger his position if he gave up anything which they believed was Canadian territory.

I have given you the skeleton of what was quite a protracted conversation, and which left on my mind the impression that the Canadians are more anxious than heretofore to settle, and will yield more in the arrangement of the terms of arbitration than they have been willing to contemplate before. If I can be of service further in this matter you will of course advise me, and in any case you will I think see the importance of my being kept advised up to date of anything that transpires between you and the British Embassy in Washington bearing on the question. I do think it highly desirable to adjust a matter fraught with such possible dangers, if any practicable way can be found to do it.

Index

Abbey, Edwin A., 173
Abbott, *Reminiscences,* 381 (note)
Aberdeen, Lord and Lady, 148
Abolition—*see* slavery
Abraham Lincoln: A History, Nicolay and Hay, 16, 21, 25, 43, 45, 47, 50, 98, 107, 131, 133-42
Acker, W. Bertrand, 35 (note)
Adair, Mrs., 149
Adams, Charles Francis, the elder, 120, 157, 164, 182, 207
Adams, Charles Francis, 61, 136, 157, 401
  An Autobiography, 157 (note)
Adams, Henry, 21, 46 (note), 94, 98, 107 (note), 108, 110, 117, 129, 133, 142, 143, 144, 147, 150, 151, 153, 154 (note), 156; friendship with Hay, 157-67; 174, 178, 181, 183, 186, 188, 193, 195, 237, 264, 277, 278, 289, 290, 301, 320; on capitalism, 327-28; on "McKinleyism," 328-29; 337-38, 364, 387, 395, 403, 407, 432, 436, 439
  Democracy, 110, 165
  Education of Henry Adams, 179, 237, and notes on 98, 158, 165, 327, 328, 364, 432
Adams, Mrs. Henry (Marian Hooper). 156, 157, 162, 163
Adams, Herbert Baxter, 136
Adams, John, 116
Adams, John Quincy, 51, 196, 205, 266
Adee, Alvey A., 63 (note), 197; association with Hay, 199 f.; literary gift, 199-200; functions, 200-02; 262, 269, 291, 305, 310, 313, 314, 319, 325, 326, 356 (note), 381, 396, 397, 398, 423
Adventures in American Diplomacy, Dennis (all refs. in notes), 219, 241, 265, 297, 313, 315, 380, 387, 388, 404, 406
Advertiser, Boston, 426 (note)
Alaska, 210, 212, 213, 224-25
  — purchase of, 67, 214, 224, 266
  — boundary question, 207, 217, 224-39; affected by increased commercial value of Alaska, 225; by party politics in Canada and U. S., 225; Joint High Commission, 225 f., 351; proposed settlements, 225-26; position of U. S., 228-29; provisional draft treaty, 228-29, 352; Canadian proposal, 230; places claimed by Canada, 232; Pyramid Harbor conceded, 233; situation made a campaign issue, 233-34; Hay's proposal to lease railroad area to Canada, 235-37

later status under Roosevelt, 350-63; incorrect version of Hay's part in settlement, 350 f.; first Hay-Pauncefote convention, 250, 351; T. R.'s position same as Hay's, 351-52; further negotiations, 353-54; treaty signed, 355; its provisions, 355-56; U. S. tribunal members, 357; their fitness, 357-58; decision rendered for U. S., 361; defined, 362; 364; Choate letter, 457-58
Alaska Commercial Co., 184
Albemarle, Lord and Lady, 149
Albert Edward, Prince of Wales, 198. *See also* Edward VII
Alcasta, Lord and Lady, 149
Aldrich, Nelson W., 258, 382, 417
Allen, Charles H., 204
Alverstone, Lord Chief Justice, 359, 361, 362
Amasa Stone, etc., Hay, 99 (note), 102
American Commonwealth, The, Bryce, 145 (note)
American Foreign Policy, Latané, 271 (note)
American Legation, London, 157
Americans in Eastern Asia, Dennett, 285 (note)
Amnesty offered to loyal Southerners, 43
Angell, James B., 20, 22, 47, 49
Anglo-American relations, 181-96, 214-23, 224-39, 253, 261; Chamberlain on, 329-30
  See also Alaska boundary; Boer War; Panama Canal; Samoa; Open Door policy
Anglo-French Entente, 411
Anglo-French treaty of 1903, 411
Anglo-German agreement about China, 316, 319-21, 334, 385, 407
Anglo-German understanding, 329-30
Anglo-Japanese Alliance, 212, 323, 334, 403, 405, 406
Anti-Imperialist League, 277
Apia bombardment, 281, 332
Appomattox, 57, 101
Arbitration, 206
  — in Venezuela dispute, 176, 181, 389
  — in fur seals controversy, 184-85
  — proposed in Alaska boundary dispute, 226, 235-36, 353
  — in claims arising from Samoa disturbances, 282
Arbitration treaties, 411, 435-36
As I Remember, Gouverneur, 53
Ashtabula disaster, 101, 102

461